PELICAN BOOKS

A249

THE CONCERTO

EDITED BY RALPH HILL

The Concerto

EDITED BY RALPH HILL

PENGUIN BOOKS

Penguin Books Ltd, Harmondsworth, Middlesex
U.S.A.: Penguin Books Inc., 3300 Clipper Mill Road, Baltimore 11, Md
CANADA: Penguin Books (Canada) Ltd, 178 Norseman Street,
Toronto 18, Ontario
AUSTRALIA: Penguin Books Pty Ltd, 762 Whitehorse Road,
Mitcham, Victoria
SOUTH AFRICA: Penguin Books (S.A.) Pty Ltd, Gibraltar House,
Regent Road, Sea Point, Cape Town
—
First published 1952
Reprinted 1954, 1956

NOTE

At the time of Mr Ralph Hill's death,
all the contributions for this book
had been written, with one exception:
his own article on Brahms. At the
publishers' request, Mr Hubert Foss
consented to fill the gap. In all other
respects the book is issued exactly as
its editor – who, alas! was never to
see its proofs – had planned it.

Made and printed in Great Britain
by Hazell Watson and Viney Ltd
Aylesbury and London

CONTENTS

I

The Concerto and Its Development

J. RAYMOND TOBIN

IN recent days a vast army of music-lovers has discovered the Concerto. The discovery is robbed of none of its thrill by the fact that the first concerto happens to have been composed centuries ago, or that, for example, it is nearly one hundred and fifty years since Beethoven put the final touches to his Op. 73, the so-called *Emperor Concerto*. Each generation has to make its own discoveries; and discovery is ever-new though the art-form or the music may be old. This awakening to the power and possibilities of a design is an inevitable feature in the development of the appreciation of music. Every art in spreading its influence must, in the main, follow two courses: knowledge, understanding, appreciation, discrimination, intellectual or emotional response – call it what you will – may be deepened in the individual, or it may spread itself to reach a new and wider public. Fortunately a desire to deepen knowledge almost inescapably follows in the tracks of the widening process. Those whose imagination has been captured by the concerto seek to know more about a form of music which has appeal; and they realize that, in spite of the vast differences in sound and style, there is a kinship, an area of common ground in concertos written by Tchaikovsky, Grieg, Mendelssohn, Schumann, Rachmaninov, and other composers. That we can and do speak of 'the concerto' means that there is a basic design for concertos or, at least, fixed principles which are applied with frequency and flexibility by all composers. So the question 'What is a concerto?' is posed. Put it to the music-lover and the answer may be that a concerto spells dazzle, display, delight, dexterity, that it is a spot-lighting of a performer and his instrument, an impressive example of mental concentration and physical endurance, an exciting contest between a solitary artist and a

full orchestra, with victory on the side of the soloist, even
though the performer be but a slip of a girl. All this is true;
and, despite the apparent emphasis on externals, it is possibly as good a general description as may be achieved,
except that the effort of the soloist and orchestra is not a com-
bat but a carefully-planned co-operation which has, as its
objective, the provision of contrast in tone-amount and tone-
colour. In sober terms, a concerto is a musical composition
which is intended to display the capacities of a musical
instrument, through the skill and artistry of a performer.
That is the objective. The transcendental technique, the
tone-contrasts, the variety of theme, texture and treatment
are the means to that end; they reveal the range, the sonority, the brilliance, the delicacy of nuance, the power and
poetry of which an instrument is capable in the hands of a
well-equipped artist; they proclaim the advance in the constructional design of a musical instrument and the ability of
the creative mind to employ the constructional gains in the
extension of the expressive power of music.

The question 'What is a concerto?' may seem to be a
simple and a sane one. Actually, it is no more reasonable
than if one were to ask 'What is a house?' The story of the
house stretches from the meanness of the mud hut to the
magnificence of the mansion, while the most recent chapter,
the pre-fab of to-day, is a reminder that, while progress is
not always on the onward and upward line, even austerity
does not rule out some advance and advantage. The answer
to 'What is a house?' depends upon factors such as period,
purpose, peoples and place. Often most depends upon the
quality and stature of the architect or architect-builder. And
so it is with the concerto: it means different things in different ages and at different stages of development. The view of
a concerto as a kind of symphony composed for an Eileen
Joyce, a Heifetz or a Menuhin aided and abetted by an
orchestra is, of course, a limited one. The early concertos
were mostly written for a group of soloists. Bach's *Italian
Concerto* was written for a single instrument – a double-
decker harpsichord. Schumann did not always regard the
orchestra as indispensable: his Sonata for Pianoforte, Op. 14,

was originally titled *Concerto sans Orchestre*. Chausson composed a Concerto for Pianoforte, Violin and String Quartet; Arthur Bliss wrote one for Pianoforte, Tenor voice, Xylophone and Strings, but, later, revised it for two pianos and orchestra. Alan Rawsthorne has written a concerto for String Quartet; and so great is the advance in orchestral technique that in 1944 Bela Bartók produced a *Concerto for Orchestra*.

Conveniently, however, concertos may be classified as (a) The Concerto Grosso (late seventeenth and early eighteenth century); (b) the Classical Concerto, which reached its peak with Mozart; (c) the Modern Concerto; and, while the shape, content and style of these varieties of concertos vary enormously, it is possible to recognize and relish certain characteristics which persist from one end of the story to the other. The recognition will be all the more ready if we remember that while the use and application of music's basic or raw material is illimitable, the material itself is curiously limited. A composer has at his command only two things – sound and silence; his score is made up of notes and rests, though a wide range of symbols may be employed to modify the sound or silence, particularly the sound. Sound and silence provide the element of contrast. Again, during the long stretch of time between the overthrow of the ancient Greek modes and the assault on diatonicism in the twentieth century, a composer had a choice of composing his music only in a major key or in a minor key. Yet here again the contrast is vivid. And when one contemplates the number of fine tunes composed since the dawn of history, it is surprising to recall that in the making of a melody a sound can be succeeded only by a sound that is either higher or lower; but, here too, we have the diametric.contrast of up and down movement. In the texture of music too, the composer has, at base, only harmony (or chords) as an alternative to the single notes of melody. Yet the contrast between the one and the other can be magical. By now, the importance of the element of contrast will be obvious; and it is also clear that the sole alternative to contrast is repetition. In music, speech or other means of communicating ideas we may say the same thing again or we may say something new. The content and the design of music depend, ultimately, on the use of *contrast* and *repetition*, each serving its turn and each used in fair proportion. Repetition can stress, underline or drive home an idea, but, if used to excess, becomes boredom. Contrast (or variety) can grip and hold the interest of ear and mind of young and old; but only the untutored mind demands or can endure continual change. Contrast, indeed, depends for its force upon alternation with repetition. Here we have the very core of every design in music. Together with display, contrast provides the twin pillars which support the concerto form.

In the concerto grosso, which reached full flower in the wonderful *Brandenburg Concertos* by Bach, the element of contrast is provided by the use of a group of solo players in conjunction with a full orchestra; the variety in tone-amount and tone-colour aided the composer in holding the interest of the listener.* The solo orchestra was called *concertino ;* the full orchestra *ripieno.* To-day we use the terms *solo* (one) and *tutti* (all). The *ripieno* section consisted, in the main, of the stringed instruments supported possibly by a keyboard instrument; and the *concertino* often included the more colourful wood-wind. The two sections were used, sometimes independently and sometimes in combination, to secure the utmost contrast. The shape of the concerto grosso was decided largely by the then popular overture and the suite. There was a diminishing emphasis on the dance, though in the *Brandenburgs* we have examples of the minuet, polacca and courante. Slow movements alternated with allegros and the richness and invention of the contrapuntal and fugal devices employed further tended to obscure the dance rhythms. The number of movements in the concerto grosso varies – two, three, four or more – but there is early evidence of an inclination to stabilize on the three-movement plan which is almost invariably employed by the modern composer and which provides the contrast of a slow movement separating a First movement and a quick finale.

* The same device was employed in the Minuet and Trio: the minuet was played by the full orchestra and a second minuet was played by three instruments only: hence the name *trio*.

It may be said that the element of display is lacking in the *concerto grosso* and that nowhere is it less obvious than in the finest examples of the form by Bach. It is important, however, to remember that the concertino section often included instruments now obsolete and that, in consequence, the music has had to be adapted to suit the instruments of to-day. Bach in the first Brandenburg wrote for a *Violino piccolo concertato*. This was an instrument smaller than the violin of to-day but somewhat larger than the pocket-sized fiddle which, at that date, was part of the kit of the dancing master. This little violin or quart-geige would seem to have been a transposing instrument. Its small size and the closeness of its strings made possible not only double-stopping but also chords of three and four notes which, on the ordinary instrument, would have defeated even a Paganini. The concerto grosso belonged to an age which prevailed before the solo artist and public concert-giving had secured a hold. It was conditioned by the artistic and social background of its period. Broadly it was concerted music of a co-equal, polyphonic kind and cast in a shape approximating to the classical suite: a step along the road to the symphony.

When the instrumental suite gave place to the sonata or symphony plan, the concerto grosso was supplanted by the classical concerto. The sonata design was hammered out and perfected by that mighty trio – Haydn, Mozart and Beethoven; but, while the minuet and trio (later transformed to the scherzo) was carried over from suite to symphony, it found no favour in the concerto. It may be, indeed, that the dance suggested a communal rather than an individual effort, or that adherence to its rhythmic outline prevented the elaboration necessary for display.* Whatever the cause, the concerto quickly settled into the three-movement plan, while symphonists remained constant to the four movements. The regular plan of the classical concerto was:

* Brahms introduced a scherzo into his *Concerto for Pianoforte in B flat* and so did Litolff in *Concerto Symphonique in E flat;* and curiously enough this Litolff movement leapt to popularity recently – possibly the sole survivor of this composer's huge output. *Concerto for Orchestra* (Bartók), referred to earlier, creates a record with its five movements, the second of which (*Giuco delle coppie*) is, in effect, a scherzo.

I First Movement
II Slow Movement
III Finale

This is often called the Quick-Slow-Quick plan, but I is characterized by strength rather than speed, II is lyrical rather than slow, and III, light and gay-hearted. The music of the first movement is traditionally but not by any means invariably built in the sonata (or 'first movement') form. This is a movement which falls into three sections. In the first section there are two main themes – the first theme is in the key of the concerto, the second in some other key. In the early classical concerto this second key is closely related to the first key, a next-door-neighbour key which has one sharp more or one flat less in its make-up. This change of tonality or pitch-level provides an element of variety. To-day composers are said to be more adventurous, but the truth is that Bach, Beethoven and Schubert paved the way for this freedom of the keys and that all later composers reaped the benefit of their courage and initiative. The two themes which constitute the first section are contrasted in matter, mood and meaning as well as in key; and they provide the material for the middle section.

The middle section is descriptively called the Development or Working-out, because in this part of the movement the composer toys with, develops, and works out one or both of the main themes as one might elaborate a text or subject matter. (The themes are technically known as *subjects*.) The third portion of a first-movement plan consists of a repetition of the opening section, with such modifications, extensions, and curtailments as artistry or the listening ear may require. In this section, for instance, it is requisite that the second theme shall be presented in the main key of the concerto.

In the early classical concertos the orchestra played the main themes before the entry of the solo part; but it soon became apparent that this procedure robbed the form of force, because it not only made the soloist echo the sentiments of others but, by keeping him cooling his heels during a lengthy tutti, robbed his entry of spectacle and drama.

Mozart, whose architectural sense in music was supreme, was quick to see that the *tutti* must be curtailed; and, while it was necessary for him to respect tradition, his *Concerto for Pianoforte in E flat* (*K. 271*) brings in the soloist at the second bar and enables him to share in the initial statement of the main theme. Mozart here threw out a hint which others were quick to seize upon, so that to-day the opening orchestral tutti is a thing of the past. The repeated use of tutti and solo before and between and after the soloist's presentation to the thematic material was a carry-over from the concerto grosso.

Only slowly did the soloist secure the complete dominance he enjoys in the modern concerto. Formerly, the cadenza, which is still the highlight for the performer, was a main and closely-concentrated period of display. It was customary towards the end of the opening movement for a composer to introduce a pause chord known as a 'six-four of the dominant'. This simple chord, which once ranked as a near-discord, created an air of suspense or non-completion. At this point, the soloist was at liberty to improvise a cadenza, an elaborate solo passage in which he could display his technical prowess. This ended, he would play a prolonged shake (or alternation of adjacent sounds) during which the orchestra would enter with a short and final tutti. The orchestra having remained silent during the cadenza, the soloist returned the compliment by remaining silent during the final bars of the movement. In some of his later concertos, Mozart made the soloist join in the final rally; and Beethoven followed his example. Thus the element of display was increasingly recognized. The practice of permitting the soloist to improvise his own cadenzas quickly revealed weaknesses. It has been said that if the frenzy of inspiration could be trusted to come at the right moment, impromptu cadenzas would be the most effective; but the creative and interpretative fields in music demand different qualities. A spacious and all-sufficient instrumental technique, even when accompanied by sound musicianship, is no fit match for creative genius; and, in spite of all the finger fireworks, the improvised cadenza became an excrescence instead of an ornament. And when performers were guilty of the crime of introducing one stock cadenza in different concertos by different composers, the clamorous clatter of the keys became the death-rattle of the improvised cadenza. Mozart's fertile mind and disciplined, eloquent fingers must have put together hundreds of cadenzas. Of these, thirty-six remain. As these were for his own use as a soloist, the practice by composers of supplying the cadenza in full may be said to have begun with Beethoven's E Flat Concerto. Beethoven also composed cadenzas for Mozart concertos; and great executants such as Moscheles, Bülow, Joachim, Vieuxtemps, Dohnányi and Busoni composed and published cadenzas for concertos in the standard repertoire.

The Slow movement of a concerto was usually written in song form, but, while the pace of the music was slow, the soloist's part often contained rapid, elaborate ornamentation and even short cadenzas.

The Finale was formerly a simple rondo; a dance-like movement with a gay, lilting theme. Compared with the first movement its construction and character were almost naïve. Gradually, however, the rondo took on something of the structural strength of the Sonata plan, but the light-hearted gaiety of the early dance persisted. To increase the climactic effect, Beethoven restricted, on occasions, the use of the cadenza to the finale. This over-all design of the classical concerto still retains its authority and usefulness. Its three movements, with at least one of them based on the sonata plan, remains the master pattern. In the term 'concerto form' we embrace the shape and structural characteristics of all the successful concertos that have ever been written or played; it is a pattern in time as well as in space. It is a living, growing thing; and, as with the leaves or other parts of a plant, its shape, texture, size, colour, proportions and details undergo a gradual but ceaseless change during growth.

The great instrumental performers, particularly those born at the end of the eighteenth century, did much to establish the popularity of the concerto. The pianoforte was then a comparatively new instrument (invented Cristofori,

1710), and first heard in this country at Covent Garden in 1767. These players knew the exact extent of their own and the instrument's capacities and it was they who, at any given moment, defined the limits of technique attainable. They naturally wished to display their mastery, and in the music which they composed – primarily for their own use – each was careful to include any new trick of technique of which he alone – or very few – held the secret, and this sometimes led to an ostentation that was opposed to artistry. As individual mastery advanced, general technique expanded. In the case of the pianoforte, for example, Dussek (1760–1812), Hummel (1778–1837), Kalkbrenner (1798–1849), Czerny (1791–1857), Moscheles (1794–1870), Thalberg (1812–71) were among those who gained a new command over the hands and the keyboard. The performer-composer concertos were, in their day, highly acceptable; and, although they are almost all forgotten now, they served to place an extended technical resource at the disposal of later composers, some of whom employed the devices to finer purpose. The truly great composers were often indifferent performers, but their greater musical-artistic vision – aided, sometimes, by their limited keyboard technique – led to the writing of passages which served as an incentive to those who specialized upon performance and who were not content until their fingers had successfully met the challenge. Whenever skill in composition, in performance or in instrument construction jumped ahead, one or the other, musicians or instrument makers made special efforts to secure alignment. Thus, the work of a considerable number of brilliant players whose compositions are now regarded as second-rate combined with the inventive, mechanical genius of great craftsmen such as Stein, Broadwood, Stodart, Erard, Chickering and Bösendorfer gave a creative-executant impulse to the concerto – and made possible the transition from its classical to its romantic phase.

The Modern concerto is rooted in the Classical concerto. It differs from those composed during the classical and romantic periods in its spirit and musical content; it follows the trend of all creative music in that it seeks not only to reflect moods and emotions but to express thoughts and philosophy. Of fundamental changes there are few. Modifications generally tend to exalt and glorify the soloist so that display trespasses upon the domain of contrast. Artistry seeks to make technique a means rather than an end and vulgar showmanship is eliminated or reduced. The music of the solo part has a difficulty which places the performer under greater pressure for longer periods; and, as a consequence, the determination to put instrument and player to full stretch has been known to result in cadenzas remarkable more for their difficulty than for their musical effect. To-day, the soloist jumps into the front of the picture at the outset. He is there at the final climax, with many peak points on the way and with only enough rest (or *tacit*) bars to afford essential relief to the ear of the listener and the fingers of the player. The work of the solo instrument and the orchestra is more closely knit and artistically purposed. The orchestra is a partner rather than a servile accompanist. Composers strive to increase the cohesion of the concerto as a whole and seek to prevent the sense of anti-climax in the finale after the vigour and force of the opening movement. A like problem exists with the symphony, in which Beethoven linked successive movements and used in his Finale some of the thematic matter of the opening movement. César Franck, the greatest near-genius, pursued this line of thought. Liszt evolved a plan which made the three movements into three sections of one expanded movement. Delius wrote a piano concerto in a single movement with *tempi* contrasts which conform to the three-movement plan although the music is continuous. The single movement would seem to offer the most satisfactory solution but, in practice, it falls down. It may be that it does not place the soloist under an endurance test long enough to thrill the listener; or it may be that the effort to secure homogeneity reduces too far the element of contrast and variety. It may even be that the hand of tradition, of the old suite, lies too heavily on us all. That the design of the classical concerto as a container for modern thought in music is not outworn is evident from the magnificent work of Elgar, while some contemporary composers, e.g., Vaughan Williams in his *Concerto Accademico* and Walton's use of the title *Sinfonia Concertante* suggest a harking back to early ideals. It is interesting to note that the first known use of the word *concerti* was when it served to describe collections of motets for voices and organ or strings which were published as early as the sixteenth century. The latest use of the term is its application to works such as Manuel de Falla's *Nights in the Garden of Spain* or even Gershwin's *Rhapsody in Blue*. So we may be led to qualify our definition of a concerto: it is not only a vehicle of display for instrument and performer but it must be cast in a mould approximating to that fixed by the originator of the virtuoso concerto, the man who composed more than fifty concertos for various instruments and who foreshadowed almost every improvement in its design since his time – Mozart.

2

Johann Sebastian Bach (*1685–1750*)

FRANK HOWES

INTRODUCTION

ANY concerto is the contrivance of an equilibrium of un-equal forces. The idea of contest, opposition, antithesis is implicit in the word from its derivation from the Latin *certare*, to contest, but equally strong is the implication of another word, whose root differs from it by only one con-sonant, *concentus*, a singing together. Bach's concertos show different degrees of emphasis upon these two opposed notions. The Brandenburg concertos are essentially *concerti grossi*, in which the antithetical forces are a *concertante* of several solo instruments and a tutti in which the *ripieno*, or accompanying strings of the orchestra, join and swamp the soloists, who may (or may not) be playing with them. The contest is between mass and skill, bludgeon and rapier. But the disequilibrium which a soloist in the concertos of Mozart's time and onwards has to overcome is more ex-treme – the orchestral bludgeon is weighted, if not with lead, at any rate with brass, and the soloist, if he is a violinist playing Beethoven or Brahms, wields a rapier of high temper but of extraordinary tenuity. There are solo concertos com-posed by Bach – a dissection of four of them follows – in which the idea of contest is beginning to emerge though the handicapping is nothing like as drastic – there is still more of *concentus* than of *certamen* about them, for the violin plays the main theme in the tutti with the other strings, and the keyboard when not playing solos is busy providing the con-tinuo part for the orchestra. Another trend for co-operation (as opposed to the assertion of individuality) is provided by the foundation of the whole upon what is basically one thematic subject, which is enunciated in the ritornello.

The ritornello is a musical paragraph which, as its name implies, is always returning. It is in fact like a rondo, but it differs from a rondo in appearing in different keys. The rondo came later – it was in fact only stabilized by Beethoven into the two forms of short rondo and sonata rondo – and by then the evolution of sonata form had determined that the episodes between the recurrences of the rondo should be in contrasted keys (second subjects virtually), so that the rondo always reasserted the tonic key. In Bach's time the first stages of constructing movements round related but contrasted keys had begun, as the subsequent analyses will show, but the soloists' material, although contrasted in weight and elaboration with the ritornello, was not thematically contrasted with it, nor did it make a point of being in a different key. In fact Bach's concerted movements were neither ternary like the developed sonata form of Mozart, nor binary like the dances composing the suite, but unitary like fugue and variation. Ritornello form is mono-thematic form and the solo material is more or less closely derived from the ritornello.

Schweitzer, greatest of Bach's commentators and a philosophical theologian, gives a rather metaphysical account of Bach's instrumental form, which needs correction only in that it exaggerates the difference of ritornello and solo material. He says: 'The concerto is really the evolution and vicissitudes of the theme. We really seem to see before us what the philosophy of all ages conceives as the fundamental mystery of things – that self-unfolding of the idea in which it creates its own opposite in order to overcome it, creates another, which again it overcomes and so on until it finally returns to itself, having meanwhile traversed the whole of existence. We have the same impression of incomprehensible necessity and mysterious contentment when we pursue the theme of one of these concertos, from its entry in the tutti, through its enigmatic struggle with its opposite, to the moment when it enters into possession of itself again in the final tutti.'

'Opposite' may seem a little strong – as compared with

the knowledge and ignorance, good and evil, motion and rest, of the 'fundamental mystery of things' – to apply to the soloists' material, which is usually less strongly contrasted with its source and origin, the ritornello, than is the second subject from the first in the later sonata form. All the same, the solo material is an assertion *against* the ripieno even if it employs very similar language, and the manoeuvres through different tonalities form a musical equivalent of the same idea, creating and overcoming another opposite on new ground. Certainly any listener is aware of the feeling of mysterious necessity and some instinctive kind of contentment that comes from following the evolution and vicissitudes of the theme embodied in the ritornello.

Most of Bach's instrumental works are assigned to the seven years (1717–23) which he spent in the service of the Prince of Anhalt-Cöthen, at whose Calvinistic court he was free from ecclesiastical duties and had an establishment of seventeen musicians to direct. The violin concertos belong to this period, but the clavier concertos were the product of Bach's association with the Telemann Musical Society, the Leipzig University Collegium Musicum, in the seventeen-thirties. His boys were growing up and he taught them to play the clavier – the concertos for two, three and four claviers, transcriptions some of them of Vivaldi, were arranged for Bach to play with his sons at home or with his pupils at these weekly gatherings. Indeed the harpsichord concerto seems to have been Bach's personal innovation, as the organ concerto was Handel's. Corelli had been the starting-point for the concerto grosso and the solo concerto for violin; Bach took over (and as always with him, transformed) the form evolved by the Italian violin school. Needing music for the Collegium Musicum he transcribed his own and other men's violin concertos for keyboard and thereby initiated a new form of musical art.

The keyboard versions are usually a tone lower than the originals – Bach had no fewer than four standard pitches to cope with, two for organs which were high and two for chamber music which were lower, and the differences between church and chamber were as much as a minor third. It may be that the transpositions were determined by differences in Cöthen and Leipzig tunings. Bach was an inveterate borrower from himself and even used a number of these concerto movements in cantatas. As the canon now stands there are some seven clavier concertos of which the claims to originality of No. 1 in D minor are discussed below; No. 2 in E had its movements requisitioned for two church cantatas; No. 3 in D is a transposition of the violin concerto in E; No. 4 in A and No. 5 in F minor are probably transcriptions of violin concertos; No. 6 is identical with the fourth Brandenburg Concerto, and No. 7 in G minor is a transcription of the A minor violin concerto. Of the three concertos for two claviers, No. 3 in C minor is identical with the double violin concerto in D minor, No. 2 in C major is an original work for keyboards and No. 1 in C minor is regarded as a transcription of a lost original for violin and oboe. There are two concertos for three claviers, in D minor and C major (a glorious work), and one for four claviers in A minor, which is a transcription of a concerto for four violins by Vivaldi. Of the lost violin concertos three have survived, as detailed above, in the form of clavier transcriptions. Bach's lack of consideration for posterity in thus confronting his posthumous students with editorial tangles is comparable to that of Dvořák in the numbering of his symphonies and of Moussorgsky in the confusions of *Boris Godunov*. But we may be thankful to have the music, in which the quick movements present us with a different Bach from the Bach we know as organist and church composer, a robust, cheerful and charming personality, while the slow movements take us behind his religion to the mind of the man himself. Religion meant much to Bach, craftsmanship was another big element in his make-up, his irritability is well attested, and all have to be accommodated into our view of his personality, but without the concertos, both the Brandenburg and the solo concertos, we should have an incomplete idea of what he was like both as man and musician.

CONCERTO NO. 1 IN D MINOR FOR CLAVIER
AND STRINGS

THE violin concerto from which this clavier concerto, whether Bach's own or another's, is thought to have been derived, is lost. The figuration of the soloist's second solo is sometimes cited as evidence of a violinistic origin,

but the D minor Toccata for organ shows that such a figure suits the genius of a keyboard instrument with two manuals. In any case the work now belongs indefeasibly to the modern piano, even though it has not the harpsichord's two manuals. Tovey forthrightly says of it that the only composer who could have planned it is Johann Sebastian Bach. Parry assigns it to Bach's Cöthen period. The first movement was afterwards used (by Bach himself) as an organ prelude and the slow movement as the first chorus of the Church Cantata No. 146, *Wir müssen durch viel Trübsal*.

The ritornello which supplies the material for the first movement is a vigorous unison theme of six bars' length

of which the initial phase *a* is much used for purposes of propulsion later on. The expanding leaps in the middle and the emphatic quavers at the end contribute much to the sturdy character of the theme. The soloist's *concertante* material is all derived from it but monotony is avoided by its peregrinations through the neighbouring keys, which may now be traced in detail.

The solo, having of course played at being the continuo of the exposition of Ex. 2, at once breaks off upon its independent career with a change of figuration. The first port of call is the dominant minor (A minor) where the soloist continues this new figuration but soon adds a toccata-like figure in the manner of Ex. 1. This brings him to the relative major (F), where portions, but not the whole, of Ex. 2 are put in counterpoint against a new theme on the first violins. At the next statement of the ritornello (in A minor) it is given in full. The soloist now takes up Ex. 1 and the accompaniment gradually falls away to a mere pedal point on the violas. This is treated as a dominant and ushers in the ritornello (the loose, not the strict form) in C major. The next appearance of the ritornello is entrusted to the strings, with the soloist reduced to playing a counterpoint. He immediately reasserts himself in a swift cadenza, and we now have what in the classical concerto would be called a development, in which figure *a* is hustled in sequence by descending steps which take the movement as far as B flat major. The soloist forcibly thrusts it back into the tonic over a long pedal point hammered away chop-stick fashion in the manner of Ex. 1. A more florid cadenza supervenes and the ritornello returns first in a free form and finally in its most precise unison form. Could anything be more compact yet give so spacious a sense of ordered progression?

The slow movement is also in a minor mode (G), an exceptional feature in Bach's concertos and sonatas in minor keys in which a major key is customary for the slow movement. This movement gains further in solemnity and spaciousness by being constructed on a basso ostinato (like the two violin concertos). It cannot, however, be called a chaconne, because the 'ground' of twelve bars' length

modulates after its first two appearances, and there is a suggestion of binary structure, in that half-way through there is a cadence in the relative major key of B flat. On either side of it the repetitions of the modulating ground bass are respectively in G minor to C minor in the first half and in C minor to G minor in the second half. The symmetry of the movement is further emphasized by the fact that the final appearance of the main theme, against which the soloist has been engaged in weaving arabesques of melody of increasingly florid character, is in unison, as it was upon its first enunciation. The basso ostinato is thus also the ritornello, and the movement is a singularly cogent example of an unusual, though clear and logical, structure.

The construction of the finale is very similar to that of the first movement. It is built on a ritornello of twelve bars, which begins thus:

The soloist again has a toccata-like figure for his first main solo

and before the final statement of the ritornello, Ex. 4, he has a short but substantial cadenza, which is an additional point of resemblance to the first movement. It will be observed that in Ex. 4 the bass and treble sometimes change places, which is to say that they are in double counterpoint.

CONCERTO FOR CLAVIER AND STRING ORCHESTRA
NO. 5 IN F MINOR

COMPARED with the majestic Concerto in D minor (No. 1), a work on which Bach lavished sufficient care to produce three versions and two transcriptions, the Concerto in F minor is a light-weight. It is confidently believed to be itself a transcription of a violin concerto like its brethren, and scholars have been busy trying to assign the authorship of them all to Vivaldi or lesser and unknown Germans. There is no need to do ány such thing. There is nothing inconsistent in this concerto with Bach's personal idiom and the slow movement is an example of his more elaborate but still characteristic arabesque-like melodies.

The first movement is founded on a ritornello, in which within the space of four bars (out of fourteen) there are sufficient features of marked character to supply all the material.

Ex.6

The firm bass figure (b) is much used; the triplet figure (c) is the germ of all the writing for the solo keyboard; the decisive figure (a) ensures that the movement never gets very far from its main idea. The solo episodes are all securely held to the ritornello by the pretty prompt appearance of Ex. 6b in the bass. The form is not unlike the Beethovenian sonata-rondo though less fully developed, the order of events being: exposition of ritornello (fourteen bars) tutti; exposition by the soloist of his triplet material lightly accompanied; counter-exposition of ritornello in A flat; episode or middle section in, of all keys, the tonic, which begins with a rolling figure for the solo instrument over a tonic pedal in order to work up a little momentum which is after eight bars reinforced by a reference to Ex. 6 in the accompaniment, but settles down again to triplet figures for the soloist (twenty-four bars in all); Ex. 6 reappears in B flat minor going to its relative D flat major and is the equivalent of a recapitulation of the first tutti, since it is followed by the equivalent of the soloist's recapitulation of his first triplet material; final appearance of Ex. 6 compressed to eight bars.

The antithesis is thus not one of key or of contrasted second subjects or episodes but one of a sturdy square figure representing the orchestra and a stream of triplets representing the soloist.

The slow movement in A flat major is a lengthy (twenty-one bars) arabesque very lightly accompanied by regular quaver figures on the strings which serve to keep the rhythm under this florid rhapsody dead steady. The ornaments on the melody are so thickly encrusted that for once in a way one can understand why German scholars call Bach baroque, and thus apply an architectural term to a musical style. A single bar taken from the middle shows the sort of thing it is and the sort of thing the pulsing accompaniment is:

Ex.7

The finale is another vigorous allegro movement in F minor but more flowing, being in triple time, than the first, yet reproducing one feature of that movement, to wit, the echo of the cadence figure by way of punctuation. This trick is isolated and made much of at two points in the finale – thus:

Ex.8

The ritornello is an extended but highly wrought paragraph of twenty-four bars, of which the first eight show its character:

Ex.9

Strings

The alternation between treble and bass of the constituent figures gives way in the second part of the theme to running scale passages in similar and contrary motion which culminate in a very strong cadence. What follows, as in the first movement, is a development by the soloist, though here he has no distinctive material of his own, only a loosening out of what we have already heard. The ritornello **Ex. 9** next appears in A flat major. An episode based on a curious little figure

Ex.10

leads up to the crashing chords of Ex. 8 and the whole section come to an emphatic cadence in C, in which key the soloist recapitulates his first main solo. No wholehearted restatement of the ritornello occurs until the final one, but it makes its presence felt in the section just before that in which Ex. 10 is mentioned again. In its final statement the chords of Ex. 8 reappear.

CONCERTO IN C FOR TWO CLAVIERS AND STRINGS

THE concertos for clavier which Bach and his sons used to perform in the family circle and at the concerts of the Telemann Music Society at Leipzig are most of them re-arrangements of concertos which he had originally written for violin at Cöthen. This concerto for two claviers is, however, an exception and unlike the two other concertos for two claviers is an original work, in which the solo parts are more, and the orchestral accompaniment less, elaborate than in the concertos for string instruments, which naturally require from the accompaniment harmonic support which the piano is capable of supplying for itself.

The first movement is largely based on two pithy phrases:

The two pianos conduct a dialogue on these and relevant topics punctuated by occasional assent from the strings, which always enter to put the conclusion of each section of the discussion beyond doubt. But it is wrong to talk of discussion and doubt in music of this kind. Each instrument says the same thing in the same tone of voice. Why then are there two to say one thing? The answer to that question goes straight to the root of musical form. In music a plain statement does not make sense: there must be antithesis. One primitive and satisfying form of antithesis is antiphony, as is shown to perfection in the Psalms. Bach is here employing the method of Hebrew poetry, and, like the Psalmist, produces by the method of parallel phrases a force and beauty of expression to be obtained in no other way.

The slow movement (*Adagio ovvero Largo* in A minor) is given to the soloists alone and is constructed on the same principle upon the single theme:

One subtle complication of rhythm renders this undulating tune still more flexible – the regular sequences of four bars overlap each other at intervals of three bars. One simple complication of harmony – the use of suspensions – binds the antiphony into an even tighter union.

The finale is a fugue, in which the subject, counter-subject and episodes are announced by one or other of the claviers. The subject is a fluid theme running to four bars:

The counter-subject contains, besides a similar mixture of quaver and semiquaver figures, a useful leaping figure of wide intervals.

The middle section begins with some episodic material by which modulation is made in the first place to D minor. Middle entries of the subject (Ex. 13) continue the process to A minor, F major and finally C minor. On arrival at these points the strings make it their business to enter and clamp down the cadences. Their brief contrapuntal entry at the end completes an exhilarating polyphony in six parts.

CONCERTO IN A MINOR FOR VIOLIN AND ORCHESTRA

SCHWEITZER says of the two surviving violin concertos that it is useless to employ the method of analysis upon them. And it is certainly true that the texture is almost seamless, that in the slow movements the arabesque winds itself endlessly on over a recurrent bass and that there is some organic principle, rather than architectural formality, about the way the allegro movements develop. Yet the basic principle which gives them their strength and cogency is that of the ritornello.

In the case of the first movement of the A minor concerto the ritornello of twenty-four bars dominates the whole movement not only by the vigour of its opening phrase, which gives the movement its character, but because the solo music is all derived from it and has little real independence:

The complete statement of this ritornello forms a paragraph which ends with a firm dominant cadence. The first solo returns firmly to A minor and takes up the idea of the tied-over quaver, but soon drops it in favour of straightforward quaver runs, the orchestra meanwhile contributing no more than short figures derived from various places in the ritornello. The actual thematic interest is reduced and the function of the solo is to show how its impetus runs on. It shortly arrives at C major where the orchestra butts in firmly with the ritornello, slightly shortened and loosened, which gradually draws the solo into itself. The next solo entry is in E minor, which begins as a transposition of the first solo but soon picks up the idea contained in bars 5 and 6 of Ex. 15 and develops it at length, going as far to the flat side of the key as D minor. After a time the orchestra asserts A minor tonality and the claims of the ritornello in the first four bars of Ex. 15. This has the effect of driving the solo from a high to a low part of its range. Sequences, however, soon raise it again and a little demisemiquaver flourish that had modestly obtruded itself in the first solo

reappears with greater insistence. It is the soloist's last flicker of a not very strong independence. The ritornello returns in the orchestra and soon absorbs the solo by means of some resolute sequences, though it takes a few extra bars (twenty-nine in all) to secure complete unanimity.

The slow movement, here as in so many of Bach's concertos, seems to be a distillation of the essence of his thought. The quick movements are extraverted and show, as it were, his mind dealing with the world about him; the slow movements draw a curtain to reveal the same mind turned in on itself in meditation.

Structurally the movement consists of a basso ostinato, one bar in length, repeated at different pitches with gaps between the repetitions, beneath an arabesque, also intermittent, for the solo instrument. At first basso ostinato and solo arabesque alternate but before long they do partially overlap, and of course end together. The key is C major.

The basso ostinato conforms to this unvarying shape:

The first phrase of the solo arabesque shows the kind of thing it is – the triplets are the predominant feature:

The ritornello of the finale is an accompanied fughetta on the subject:

The exposition runs to twenty-four bars. The soloist then over a very light accompaniment expatiates on the main idea of this subject but introduces variety of rhythm. After twenty bars it says the same thing again a fifth higher but rather more briefly, making some thirty-five bars in all for the soloist. The orchestra now joins in with twelve bars of ritornello. In its second solo the violin develops some cross-the-strings writing and then comes to an emphatic pause on the dominant some eighteen bars later. Four bars of ritornello (containing a point of imitation to remind us that it was once a fully fledged fugal exposition) reassert the tonic key and allow the soloist a recapitulation of his first solo – or part of it, for during the last twelve bars of it he goes in for some even more essentially violinistic figuration of repeated notes across the strings. The final statement of the ritornello in full is played by solo and orchestra in a vigorous tutti similar to the opening statement of it.

After the practical-minded vigour of the first movement and the quiet reflexion of the second, the finale is a relaxation. One cannot say that it is careless or thoughtless, but it is care-free and nimble-witted – the thought is effortless. This clear juxtaposition of different kinds of mental activity somehow related to a common subject is one of the things that music is uniquely capable of displaying. The three movements plainly belong together, though formally they are linked only by a key relationship, yet they seem to represent different points of view. Their unity and their diversity are equally apparent. This is the aesthetic principle which symphonic music most characteristically illustrates. This concerto, which also shows a similar antithesis of identity and difference in its use of ritornello and solo, illustrates these aesthetic laws as cogently and concisely as anything in the whole realm of music.

CONCERTO NO. 2 IN E FOR VIOLIN AND STRING ORCHESTRA

Not all of Bach's concertos for violin have survived; those that passed on his death to his son Friedmann are lost, three that went to Philipp Emanuel have survived, but the one in G major is more familiar as the fourth Brandenburg concerto. We have therefore two only as pure violin concertos – No. 1 in A minor and No. 2 in E major. Of these Schweitzer remarked, as already observed, that it is useless to analyse them and they must be put into the category, 'of which Forkel (Bach's first biographer) briefly and eloquently observes: "One can never say enough of their beauty" '. Of the E major concerto he goes on to say that it is 'full of an unconquerable joy of life, that sings its song of triumph in the first and last movements'. With this all commentators will concur. They too will feel that analysis is akin to vivisection. They may, however, allow themselves to observe with what economy of material Bach creates such exuberance of riches. It all comes from this:

except that the solo violin is fond of this little embellishment:

That is to say, Bach has in his main theme four constituent ideas – *a, b, c, d*. In the middle section (C sharp minor) the solo violin achieves a limited independence but one or other of the four figures is never very far away.

In the slow movement (Adagio, C sharp minor) the solo violin glides to and fro over a basso ostinato of this shape:

The little demisemiquaver figure (Ex. 21) persists in its original and in an inverted form. In all the movements of the melody there is something very bird-like: it enters high up and motionless, swoops gently up and down, now with a minute thrust of its wing it climbs, only to drop down a scale passage below the other strings of the orchestra. Yet the general feeling of the movement with its persistent bass is solemn. Of these Bach slow movements one feels less with

Forkel that 'one can never say enough' than with Shaw's
Eve in *Back to Methuselah* that when these lovely patterns of
sound in the air are woven together they 'raise the soul to
things for which I have no words'.

The third movement, *Allegro assai*, begins

Ex. 23

The little slurred two-note figure of the second bar is the
principal feature of all tutti passages; it is found also in the
cadences of the first movement and it plays an important
part in the middle of the slow movement. The demisemiquaver figure (Ex. 21) also occurs in the solo part of this as
of the other two movements. Thus does Bach relate his
thematic material and so enhance the feeling of unity behind
so much diversity of melody and rhythm and mood. Or it
would probably be truer from a psychological point of view
to say that the unity of Bach's conception betrays itself in
these melodic turns of phrase, for they are not a conscious
contrivance but a spontaneous expression of three aspects of
a single idea.

CONCERTO FOR TWO VIOLINS AND STRING
ORCHESTRA IN D MINOR

THIS concerto for two violins also exists in a version for two
claviers in C minor, a transcription no doubt made by Bach
himself for use at the concerts of the Telemann Musical
Society. Its chief beauty is in the flow of the parts: both the
ripieno violins of the orchestra and the two soloists indulge
in imitation and overlapping. Tutti alternates with concertino so that there are three main solo sections, the middle
one quite short, the other two substantial. This gives a rondo
form in which episodes have a greater independence, as far
as material is concerned, than in some other of Bach's concertos, where it all seems to derive pretty directly from the
ritornello. The cycle of keys traversed is very narrow – the
first episode being in F, the relative major, the second in A
minor and the third in G minor.

The ritornello, in which the soloists join, is announced by the second violins and taken up by the first violins a fifth higher as in a fugal exposition, but the lower strings play an independent part:

Ex.24

This exposition extends for twenty-one bars and closes in D minor. The soloists' first solo entry is made by the first violin playing

Ex.25

The second violin follows at the same pitch. During this concertino section the accompaniment consists sometimes of chords for the harpsichord, sometimes of scraps of Ex. 24. It ends with a restatement of Ex. 25 a fourth lower by the second violin, which is followed four bars later by the first violin playing it again at the same pitch. The middle entries of tutti and solo are both short, four bars long each, the tutti playing the ritornello (Ex. 24) and the soloists a version of Ex. 25. Another four bars of tutti in which the ritornello appears in the bass leads to the third episode, which occupies the remainder of the movement except for the final statement of the ritornello. This solo consists first of passages of semiquavers for one violin and quavers for the other, each bandying them to the other in turn, and then of the reappearance of Ex. 25, again imitated at four bars' distance at the same pitch. The solo material is thus differentiated from the ritornello quite decisively, but the total effect is one of the most harmonious flow of an apparently endless arabesque. The artifice of the movement, a huge canon, is thus concealed by art.

The slow movement might be a translation into musical
terms of Sir Philip Sidney's poem:

> My true love hath my heart, and I have his
> By just exchange the one to the other given,
> . . . .
> He loves my heart, for once it was his own,
> I cherish his because in me it bides.

For the ritornello theme

enshrines the heart of the violin and by just exchange it is
passed to and fro, from one to the other; so too is the second
theme, which they begin together in sixths:

and so also is the third theme appended thereunto, which is
in the nature of an invertible counterpoint to the long
arabesque played by the other partner.

The movement, in F major, opens with the enunciation
by the second violin of Ex. 26 which is followed at two bars'
distance by the entry of the first violin with the theme in the
dominant, while the second violin continues as a counter-
subject the sequential sextuplets which constitute the arabesque just mentioned. A counter-subject to the sextuplets
themselves when they in turn are finishing off the second
subject is a widely spaced rocking octave:

This is a reinforcement of the gentle motion which the
orchestra maintains in pastoral rhythm. Beyond this and
defining the progression of keys the orchestra takes no part
in the serene dialogue. The second subject duly proceeds to
the dominant, i.e. from F to C and thence to A minor,
where the main subject, Ex. 26, is announced, again by the

second violin with the first violin following suit a fifth higher, where it turns aside for a moment into B flat. A recapitulation, ten bars in length, repeats Ex. 26 in the tonic with its concomitant a fifth higher and alludes also to the parallel sixths of Ex. 27. Each soloist thus participates in all the material but always in canonic order and in invertible counterpoint. The parallel sixths of Ex. 27 provide brief moments of homophony, which is immediately abandoned after making its point of contrasted movement.

'There never was a better bargain driven.'

In the brisk finale there is more variety of movement, in which the orchestra participates, constantly ejaculating figure *a* of Ex. 29 in whole or in part so as to push the

Ex.29

business on. The main subject begins canonically, freely in its first phase, Ex. 29, and strictly in its second. There is, however, homophonic movement both in the orchestral and in the solo parts, which clinch the cadence into the dominant minor with actual chords, emphatically reiterated on up and down bows. The material is all closely related to the ritornello but two more motifs besides Ex. 29 are taken up and developed after the full ritornello of twenty bars has been brought to a strong cadence. These occupy all the middle of the movement. The recapitulation occurs in the wrong key (G minor) and without the formality of an introductory cadence. Ex. 29 is presented in its own key an octave higher as if to protest at being treated so casually, but its treatment is still casual, for it is far from a literal statement, and the two other themes, including the chordal passage, are more prominent to the end than the main ritornello, though the orchestra remains faithful to figure *a*. Ex. 29 itself, when it occurs, is intensified with a triplet figure which had first made its appearance in the exposition. Thus the form, though still in principle unitary with episodes derived from the main ritornello, is not strict, but begins to show some resemblance to sonata form.

3

Joseph Haydn (1732–1809)

A. HYATT KING

INTRODUCTION

THE great re-valuation of Haydn, which has been gradually taking place during the last fifty years, has centred
principally on his symphonies and string quartets, the two
forms for whose perfecting he, more than any other, was
responsible. If, meanwhile, his concertos have been neglected, this has been due not so much to lack of interest as
to the paucity of printed material available for study. Even
now it is impossible to say exactly how many concertos
Haydn composed. The complete edition of his works begun
by Breitkopf in 1909 petered out in the late 1930's after
producing, out of a projected eighty volumes, fewer than
fifteen, among which not a single concerto occurs. It appears, however, that he wrote upwards of forty, though of
those many are of doubtful authenticity, and barely a dozen
have been printed in score. Yet it seems unlikely that the
ultimate publication of all Haydn's concertos, in the great
complete edition projected in 1949 by the Austro-American
Haydn Society, will make many people change their opinion
that in this field he falls far short of the stature he attained
in his symphonies and quartets.

The primary reason for this lies in the fact that neither
by training nor by temperament had Haydn much of the
virtuoso in him. Though a competent and quite inspiring
conductor, he seldom performed publicly on any instrument. Partly through lack of dramatic instinct, he did not
realize the possibilities inherent in the concerto principle,
combined with thematic expansion on the scale of his symphonies, but did his best work along the lines of contrast
in timbre and volume. Within these limits he produced

some charming and delightful music, finely wrought for entertainment in the elegant eighteenth-century tradition.

Although only a few concertos can be dated definitely, there is not much doubt about their broad chronological sequence. It is noteworthy that Haydn wrote considerably more of them before 1785 than after it. Earliest of all is a work of 1756 for organ and orchestra, the first of about fifteen concertos for keyboard which are mostly unpublished and were written before 1770. (In this class it is hard to distinguish between concertos proper, and the twenty-two divertimenti which include a fairly prominent part for harpsichord.) Next, in 1765 came a double concerto for harpsichord and violin. A harpsichord work in F was composed sometime before 1771, one in G in about 1770 and the well-known one in D before 1784. All three were printed in Haydn's lifetime.

During his first two decades in the court at Esterhazy (1761–80) he wrote various concertos for members of the orchestra there: eight for violin (some doubtful) four for violoncello (two doubtful, one lost), one for double bass (lost), two for baryton and one for two barytons (all lost). (The baryton was a large member of the viol family, on which Prince Nicolas Esterhazy was proficient: it usually had six or seven strings, with ten to fifteen additional ones of metal, set under the bridge for the player's thumb to pluck.) Haydn also wrote one concerto for flute (lost), and one for oboe (very doubtful). Of three works for horn, one is lost, one is doubtful, and the third, of 1762, is a fine piece of considerable difficulty. A concerto for two horns has disappeared. In 1786 Haydn composed five concertos for two *lire organizzate*, to the commission of King Ferdinand of Naples, whose favourite instrument this was for solo playing in company with his instructor. It belonged to the hurdy-gurdy (or vielle) type, and incorporated a small pipe-organ, to which air was supplied from tiny bellows worked by the wheel which at the turn of a handle acted from beneath on the strings as a bow. The trumpet concerto of 1796 well deserves its recent revival, as does also the *sinfonia concertante* of 1792.

VIOLONCELLO CONCERTO IN D

THERE is no reason to doubt that this concerto is of Haydn's own composition. It appears in the thematic catalogue of his works which his copyist Johann Elssler compiled under his supervision in 1805, and the score in his autograph bearing the date 1783 was in existence in the mid nineteenth century (though it has, unfortunately, disappeared since then). These two salient facts were apparently unknown to Tovey when, in vol. 3 of his *Essays in Musical Analysis* (third impression, p. ix), he plumped for Anton Kraft as the rightful author. It was the publication of an inadequately documented miniature score which led Tovey to strengthen his earlier misgivings, based on hazardous grounds of style, and to reject Haydn in favour of Kraft.

The claim of this musician, a violoncellist in the Esterhazy court orchestra, for whom Haydn composed the concerto, had been advanced as early as 1837 (in vol. 4 of Schilling's *Encyklopädie der Tonkunst*) in an article on Kraft based, most probably, on information from his son. But in view of the two facts I have mentioned, it is reasonable to limit Kraft's share in the concerto to practical advice on the lay-out of *bravura* passages for the solo instrument. (This has been a common practice for nearly two hundred years: one famous instance was the reliance which Brahms placed on Joachim in composing for the violin). The result is a delightful if not profound concerto, conceived as a unity, fluently written and lightly scored for oboes, horns and strings. The ponderous version, with a much larger orchestra, in which it is too frequently heard, is due to the tasteless re-scoring and editing done by F. A. Gevaert in 1890.

First movement: *Allegro moderato*. Throughout the short orchestral prelude, as indeed in all the other tuttis, the solo violoncello joins the orchestra to strengthen harmony and rhythm. The first subject

Ex.1

proceeds with genial smoothness on the violins. It is repeated with reinforcement from oboes and horns, and then ex-

panded into a bridge passage in the dominant for the second
subject,

Ex.2

stated by oboes and violins. In the closing bars of this tutti
a short figure

Ex.3

becomes prominent. The last two bars re-introduce Ex. 1 on
oboes and horns, prior to its re-statement and enlargement
by the soloist, in a passage of flowing felicity, perfectly calculated to set off all his range and nimbleness. Apart from a
brief episode in B minor, the procedure of development and
recapitulation is reasonably regular, in both form and tonal
structure. Consequently, the interest lies mainly in the
beautifully varied rhythms and *fioriture* of the solo part,
which soars up, just after the cadenza, to A in alt. The coda
is formed of reiterations of Ex. 3, followed by a final word
from Ex. 1 on horns and oboes.

Second movement. *Adagio*. The soloist introduces the
principal melody

Ex.4

supported by a prominent part for viola, and enlarges on
the second section of this after a short tutti. Recapitulation
of Ex. 4 in the treble register is followed by another tutti,
whence arises a subsidiary theme in C major

Ex.5

Such is the material of this charming *arioso* structure, a
model of tasteful brevity.

Third Movement. *Rondo*, *allegro*. In the rollicking good

humour of 6/8 time, this rondo is dominated by the lilting tune stated by the soloist

Ex.6

and repeated by the tutti. A second, contrasting, theme follows:

Ex.7

After discussion of this material, with new figures of lesser weight, an arresting episode in D minor opens with Ex. 6, in that key, and proceeds with a new, wholly charming melody:

Ex.8

(Its style reminds one of Sullivan's affinity with the eighteenth century). This occupies most of the remainder of the minor section. With the return to the tonic major, for the coda, Ex. 6 dominates the scene. It is twice heard on unsupported horns and oboes with a degree of prominence which is made all the more effective by their generally discreet and sparing use elsewhere, outside the tuttis.

PIANOFORTE CONCERTO IN D MAJOR

HAYDN's keyboard concertos, about a dozen in number, are mostly early or middle period works, the first dating from the 1760's. Only three of them appear to have been printed (in parts not in score) during his lifetime; one in F, one in G, and one in D, which is the subject of this analysis. While not strikingly adventurous in form it is a most attractive and lively concerto, composed some time before 1784 and scored for oboes, horns and strings. While it draws its effect principally from inexhaustible springs of rhythmical energy, it also reveals some unexpectedly sombre depths. The title-page of the first edition (1784) describes it as 'per il clavicembalo o il forte piano', but the repetitive treatment of much of the thematic material calls for a varied range of tone-colour scarcely obtainable on a pianoforte. How effectively registration on the harpsichord can be used in this concerto is shown in the admirable records of it made by Wanda Landowska. The solo part was intended to join the tutti passages, in order to strengthen the harmony.

First Movement. *Vivace*. The vigorous, square-cut opening theme

is typical of Haydn in his most sportive vein, with regular accents, and faithful adherence to tonic and dominant. The contrasting second subject

still in D major, is uttered by violin and oboes. There follows a short transition passage based on fanciful expansion of Ex. 9a, which is broken by syncopation before the resounding emphasis of

bursts in to wind up the introduction. The soloist then enters and repeats Ex. 9 and Ex. 10 with slight modifications, and proceeds, via a neat figure based on an inversion of Ex. 9a, to a striking terminal passage,

which begins in A minor and modulates to A major for the restatement of Ex. 9 in that key, reinforced with octaves. But Ex. 10 does not re-appear, as one might have expected. Instead, Haydn modulates sharply to B minor for a further expansion of Ex. 9, in which the figure marked 'b' is very prominent in the strings and keyboard bass. Thereafter comes the full recapitulation, making further play with Ex. 9*b*, and the inversion of Ex. 9*a*. Ex. 12 is heard again, in D minor, as clever foil to the final statement of Ex. 9, in the tonic major, with the figure 'b' in octave imitation. After the cadenza (Haydn's own), the coda consists solely of Ex. 11 with brisk and characteristic alternations of *piano* and *forte*.

Second Movement. *Un poco adagio*. In sheer beauty of sustained melodic line, this movement (in A major) ranks with the great adagios of the Op. 76 quartets and of the last three pianoforte sonatas, even though it lacks the emotional depth of those noble inspirations. The simple theme

Ex.13

based on the common chord, gradually blossoms into a truly poetic wealth of embellishment, graceful arabesques, and chromatic *pointillisme*. As a contrast, Haydn devised a triplet figure of austere simplicity

Ex.14

which takes on an unimagined loveliness in a dialogue between soloist and strings. It springs to new life in the graceful coda, for which Haydn reserves a long pedal point for the horns, and some expressive phrases on the oboes.

Third Movement. *Rondo all' Ungherese*. The sparkling rhythms and flexible tonality of this delightful piece exemplify a vein thoroughly suited to Haydn's temperament. (There is a later instance of it in the so-called 'gypsy

rondo' of the pianoforte trio in G major.) Here the mainspring of the whole is the opening theme

played by the soloist, whose second entry, in the remoteness
of E minor, alters the shape of the second bar (see Ex. 15*b*
above). With these two varieties, Ex. 15 evolves into a Protean force which clarifies the structure through its incessant
repetition, and imparts a wild, dance-like flavour to the
music. An episode in D minor introduces a consistently
darker tone with

whose smoothness is accentuated by another outburst from
Ex. 15, which is then repeated in the tonic major as a
transition to a new subject in B minor. In the following
recapitulation, Haydn adds a piquant touch by inverting
the phrase Ex. 15*b*, and concludes with a re-statement of
Ex. 15 in its original shape, and an antiphonal fanfare between soloist and orchestra, based on a figure derived from
Ex. 15*a*.

SINFONIA CONCERTANTE FOR OBOE, BASSOON, VIOLIN AND VIOLONCELLO IN B FLAT

WHEN Haydn paid his first visit to London in 1791–2 he
composed, in addition to the six symphonies commissioned
by J. P. Salomon, a number of other works, among which
this sinfonia concertante is outstanding. It was first performed on 9 March 1792, with great success, and was
repeated several times that season. Although the music in
Haydn's most genial vein is attractive and delightful, it
has been unwarrantably neglected in modern times. This
may be attributed partly to the costly luxury of four
soloists, and partly to the overwhelming popularity of the

Salomon symphonies, but there is also some cause in the nature of the work.

By reverting here to the archaic *concerto grosso* style, Haydn denied himself an opportunity of overcoming his chronic disinclination to exploit the dramatic possibilities of the concerto form. A further chance came in 1796 with the composition of the trumpet concerto, but both this and the Sinfonia Concertante are generally lacking in the dynamic impetus, the tension, the emotional depth, and bold, comprehensive planning of the Salomon symphonies. Indeed, both these two concertos have an air as of relaxation after the strain which Haydn incurred while composing and conducting symphonies during his two visits to London.

The Sinfonia Concertante contains some engaging and witty surprises, contrived with a simplicity of style so disarming as to belie its wealth of harmonic and melodic resource. The chief interest throughout lies in the treatment of the four soloists in varied and contrasting groups, and in their blending with, rather than in their opposition to, the orchestra, which comprises flute, oboes, bassoons, horns, trumpets, drums and strings.

First Movement. *Allegro*. Violins, reinforced by the flute, announce the first subject

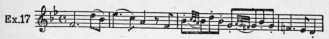

which is expanded by the full orchestra, with a brisk figure

of some subsequent interest. A second theme

is akin to the first in style. It commences on the dominant and passes back to the tonic and then scarcely is this complete when the solo group, led by the oboe, interrupt with the same melody, only to be cut short by the tutti with Ex. 18 and other emphatic phrases. Only then does the solo group proceed normally with Ex. 17, either singly or in pairs. The interplay of soloists and tutti in the following development is of some complexity, and eludes brief analysis. It is especially notable for clever antiphonal effects, for some masterly modulations and for some deft changes of rhythm, with the prominent use of a figure in minims as a pivotal change from the generally even flow of semiquavers. One of the finest passages opens with the restatement of Ex. 17 in D flat major, and its transformation 'into something rich and strange' by excursions into remote keys with some glorious part-writing, which breaks up the melody into its rhythmical components. In the short cadenza the felicitous interplay of the parts and the interlocking of contrasted rhythms are masterly. Quietly, but emphatically, the peculiar character of each instrument is restated here, just before the coda, based on Ex. 18 and its train of bustling figures.

Second Movement. *Andante.* The change to F major in 6/8 time brings a reflective mood, characterized by the beauty of the tranquil opening melody

played first by the solo bassoon and violin, and then by oboe and violoncello. A transition passage, based on Ex. 20a, leads to a second, squarer tune, allotted to violoncello against Alberti figures on the violin. The tutti repeats Ex. 20, the violin expands the section 'a'; the second tune reappears, this time on the violin, with the violoncello reverting to its more proper study in Alberti bass. After the four soloists have restated Ex. 20, with slight but effective changes of rhythm and harmony, the movement closes quietly with chords from the full orchestra, the horns being given unexpected prominence.

Third Movement. *Allegro con spirito*. After fifteen bars of a turbulent tutti, the solo violin breaks in with six bars of pleading recitative, in a style not uncommon in Haydn's very early symphonies. Another outburst from the tutti is succeeded by more recitative, and only then does the violin continue with the full main subject

of which the phrase 'a' had formed the chief burden of the tuttis. Such other thematic material as Haydn introduces in this spacious rondo is unimportant compared to Ex. 21 in its numerous guises and derivatives. Besides the wealth of statement and answer between soloists and tutti, the development contains many surprises, in both modulation and form, such as an episode based on a bold expansion of Ex. 21a. Just before the final tutti, the recitative of the opening bars is heard again, still on the solo violin.

4

Wolfgang Amadeus Mozart (1756–1791)

A. HYATT KING

INTRODUCTION

In 1765, during his ninth year, Mozart arranged three sonata movements by J. C. Bach for harpsichord and orchestra (K. 107): this was his first work in concerto form. The last was the clarinet concerto of 1791, composed two months before his death. In the twenty-six intervening years he wrote over forty concertos. It was to Mozart more than to any other composer that this form owed its growth to a stature comparable with that of the symphony. Of all the instruments then in general use, only the violoncello and trombone did not receive some contribution from him, as the following brief summary will show.

Besides twenty-three works for keyboard, Mozart wrote for the violin five concertos (1775), and two rondos (1776, 81); one concertone for two violins (1773); one sinfonia concertante for violin and viola (1779); one concerto for bassoon (1774), one for flute (K. 314, 1778); one for oboe (K. 313, 1778)* four concertos and one rondo for French horn (1781–86); one concerto for flute and harp (1778), and one for clarinet (1791). Mozart's earliest original concerto was one for the trumpet (1768), which has unfortunately disappeared. Several other important works he left unfinished: we have a long fragment of a magnificent concerto for harpsichord and violin (1778), another of a work for violin, viola and violoncello (1779), and another of a second concerto for oboe (1783).

Mozart was the prince of concerto writers. No other composer has ever combined such variety and quantity with

* Only in 1949 was it published in its true form: until then it had always been printed in an arrangement for flute.

such a generally high range of quality. One common characteristic of all these works is the remarkable understanding they display of the true nature of each and every solo instrument, even when it was not an especial favourite, or one which he played himself. The tale of Mozart's concertos might have been very different had he not enjoyed the friendship of many professional musicians – such as Leutgeb and Stadler, outstanding virtuosos on horn and clarinet respectively – and of noble patrons of ability and taste such as Baron Dürnitz, a lover of the bassoon, and the Duc de Guines, a flautist of distinction. But nearly all the keyboard concertos were written by Mozart for himself, partly to display his very fine technique, and partly to secure himself a livelihood. These masterly creations, spread over his whole lifetime, form the most important single group in all his prodigious output, and constitute his most original contribution to musical evolution. Limitation of space precludes analysis of all twenty-three within the present chapter, but we may briefly review them as a chronological series, before passing to matters of principle and style.

Mozart's first six original concertos were all composed at Salzburg between 1773 and 1779 – the D major (K. 175), the B flat major (K. 238), the F major, for three harpsichords (K. 242), the C major (K. 246), the E flat major (K. 271) and another (K. 365) in the same key, for two harpsichords. While K. 175 is the best of the first four, with its effective contrapuntal finale, there is nothing in any of them to foreshadow the astonishing genius revealed in K. 271. As subsequent analysis will show, it is hardly an exaggeration to claim that this work forms a landmark in the history of the concerto comparable to the *Eroica* in that of the symphony.

The qualities of the first three concertos which Mozart composed in Vienna, all in 1782 – the F major (K. 413), the A major (K. 414), and the C major (K. 415) – are if less startling than those of K. 271, certainly more subtle. This trilogy leads logically to the phenomenal series of really great works which Mozart produced throughout 1784 in an effort to establish himself in his adopted city. From February to December in this *annus mirabilis*, he composed six concertos, as follows: E flat major (K. 449), B flat major (K. 450), D major (K. 451), G major (K. 453), B flat major (K. 456), F major (K. 459). Next year, 1785, came three more: D minor (K. 466), C major (K. 467), E flat major (K. 482). 1786, the year of *Figaro*, brought another three, the finest so far: A major (K. 488), C minor (K. 491), C major (K. 503). But as one hope after another failed him, his urge for self-exploitation as a performer grew less, and only two more pianoforte concertos came from his pen, the D major (K. 537, 1788) and the B flat major (K. 595, 1791). He also wrote, during 1782, two separate rondos for pianoforte and orchestra, one in D major (K. 382) most probably for his own use as an alternative to the finale of K. 175, and one in A major (K. 386), which seems to have served as the original version of the finale of K. 414.

The prodigious creative effort underlying the twelve masterpieces of 1784–6 is all the more remarkable if we remember that simultaneously Mozart was composing a continual stream of chamber works, songs and operas.

From this main series of concertos, it is not easy to select the five mature works which must be omitted from the analyses that follow. Of the three composed in 1782, K. 413 and K. 415 are less highly organized than K. 414, which demands inclusion as the most Mozartian of the set. The concerto K. 449, the very first composition which Mozart entered in his own thematic catalogue, is an important and beautiful work, but must regretfully be excluded because it is scarcely ever performed. The D major, K. 451, is also very little known, but is relatively superficial, being mostly cast in Mozart's *bravura* style. It has, however, a poetic and dreamy andante, built on an unusual chromatic theme. This, and the last D major, K. 537, must both be omitted. The latter is brilliant, at times almost superficial, so that it seems as if the composer is parodying himself. Its popularity has lasted from the nineteenth century to the present day, but it does not mark any technical or emotional advance in Mozart's progress as a concerto writer. Moreover, the autograph of the solo part is a mere sketch. A large part of the printed version in general use is a late eighteenth-century reconstruction of his probable intention.

Up till the end of 1786, he used a steadily-growing range of orchestral volume and colour, but the transformation which he brought about lay principally in the structural expansion of the first movements, of which no two are exactly alike. Their variety defies analysis on 'textbook principles' exactly as do the fugues of Bach's '48' or the first movements of Beethoven's sonatas.

Mozart's achievement can be briefly summed up by saying that he combined a totally new conception of the concerto principle – fundamentally still one of contrast in timbre and volume – with the maximum of tonal and structural flexibility. He did not wholly jettison the older idea of two principal subjects in related keys, stated, developed, recapitulated, and rounded off. He expanded his thematic material so that each 'subject' might include a group of two or more themes, sometimes making six or seven in all. Almost any two of them might be woven into kaleidoscopic patterns by the orchestra and soloist in combination and opposition. Mozart often went still further and allotted the soloist one or more wholly new melodies, whose entry gains in dramatic power through not having been stated in the orchestral exposition.

These movements are, in fact, voiceless dramas, full of tension, nobility and pathos. Their melodies are just as alive and individual as Mozart's operatic characters. It is just this sense of dramatic values, re-created in instrumental terms, which enhances the revolutionary power of many of these concertos, as the expression of profound personal emotion. From K. 271 onwards, Mozart gradually turned his back on the older conception of the pianoforte concerto as entertainment music designed for social occasions. And herein lay, partly, the reason why this noble series failed to bring him security and a well-paid position – the fashionable public wanted to be entertained, not moved.

The subtlety of these creations makes verbal analysis an unsatisfactory substitute for knowledge of the actual scores, which the lover of concertos will find an inexhaustible treasure. Without the scores, the modern listener may often find himself in agreement with Mozart's friend and contemporary, Dittersdorf, who wrote, 'I have never yet met with a composer who had such an amazing wealth of ideas: I could almost wish he were not so lavish in using them. He leaves his hearer out of breath; for hardly has he grasped one beautiful thought when one of greater fascination dispels the first, and this goes on throughout, so that in the end it is impossible to retain any of these beautiful melodies.'

But even if analysis cannot explore all the complex by-paths of Mozart's first movements, it can indicate the broad pattern of his thought. While still a marked advance on any earlier concertos, the other movements are relatively simpler, the second chiefly consisting either of a simple sonata or *arioso* structure, or of theme and variations, and the third being either an elaborate rondo or, again, variations. Many of these second and third movements are embellished with long and important passages in which wood-wind and horns play with little or no support from the strings. It is hardly fanciful to see in these the natural successors of the serenades and divertimenti on which Mozart lavished loving care during his years at Salzburg.

To pass from the pianoforte concertos to those for violin, is rather like a descent from a great range of mountains to the lower slopes along their foothills. But here the air is just as fresh as on the majestic peaks, and the surroundings gain not a little by being more intimate. It is, emphatically, transition – not anticlimax, for the violin concertos contain better music than the harpsichord concertos (except K. 271) of nearly the same period. Indeed, Mozart, being a good enough violinist to appear as soloist in public, and fully competent to take the viola in quartet playing, could write his concertos with an expert hand, and though not always as difficult as the first violin parts in some of his divertimenti, they do not fall far short of the highest standards of that day.

The five concertos composed between April and December 1775 (K. 207, 211, 216, 218, 219), were probably all intended for Mozart's own performance in court service at Salzburg. Though the scoring is light and the keys all major ones, the whole group is serious and dignified in tone, and varied in structure. In addition, there are three other violin concertos which often appear in concert programmes under Mozart's name – the so-called *Adélaide Concerto*, a work in D (K. 271a), and another in E flat (K. 268). The first is of doubtful authenticity; the second probably consists of an early nineteenth-century elaboration of a Mozartian draft; the third is definitely known to be an arrangement, made by a contemporary Munich violinist named Eck, of yet another set of sketches. But by far the finest of Mozart's concertos for strings is the *Sinfonia Concertante* in E flat (K. 364) for violin and viola. We do not know either the occasion or the players for which he wrote it. We can only surmise that its passionate feeling, discernible in other Salzburg works of the same year, 1779, was born of his discontent with the trials and frustrations of life in the Archbishop's court.

In his continual striving after perfection, Mozart wrote alternative movements for two of his concertos, a rondo in B flat (K. 269) for K. 207, and an exquisite adagio in E major (K. 261), for K. 219. There is also a charming unrelated rondo in C (K. 373). Except perhaps for K. 364, all these works for violin bear eloquent testimony to the cosmopolitan nature of his style at this period. In the first and second movements the smooth cantilena shows strong influence of the northern Italian composers such as Sammartini. Most of the finales are headed 'rondeau', a spelling which fully accords with the French style in which, broadly, these delightful movements are written. Where an element of seriousness breaks in, it is in that finely-drawn Germanic mood which lends such an intimate, personal quality to many of Mozart's works at this time.

CONCERTO NO. 9, K. 271, IN E FLAT MAJOR

DURING January 1777, when a French virtuoso named Mlle. Jeunehomme was visiting Salzburg, Mozart wrote for her this masterly concerto. Unfortunately, nothing whatever is known of this lady, but she must have been a fine player, for this work demands both power of interpretation and brilliant technique. Excepting K. 242, all Mozart's earlier and rather superficial concertos had been composed for his personal performance. It was quite characteristic of his creative detachment to express some profound feeling in this piece, which was in his most serious key, and was destined, at least in the first instance, for other hands than his own. The autograph bears the words 'per il clavicembalo', which can only mean 'for the harpsichord', and it is clear that in several places effects are intended which could be obtained far more naturally on that instrument, with its two keyboards and the wide range of tonal colour effected by registration, than on the pianoforte. The orchestra comprises only strings, oboes and horns.

First Movement. *Allegro.* Mozart was not by nature an innovator, but here we have one of his boldest experiments in form. He uses six or seven contrasting themes with ease and fluency, welding them by bold strokes into perfect unity. There is no precedent for the prominence given to the soloist in bars 2 to 7, in the building up of the opening statement. To the emphatic tutti:

the soloist replies with Ex. 1*b*, these phrases being repeated before the violins expand the thematic group of Ex. 1*c*. A vigorous tutti leads to a new lyrical and contrasting melody, statement and answer

of great beauty, partly due to the shift in the salient beat.

After two contrasted closing themes, of which the first

Ex.3

is important, the soloist enters again with a long trill on a high B flat, but it is a kind of false entry, with a new theme (heard nowhere else), and is cut short by a repetition of the opening tutti, and only after this delay does the solo re-appear with the proper intention of developing Ex. 1a and Ex. 2a in succession, the latter to a triplet accompaniment. An allusion to Ex. 2b by the orchestra terminates in a rising scale, with octave *acciaccature*, for the solo to introduce another secondary theme, in the relative minor.

A restatement of Ex. 3 shifts the tonal centre to B flat, and the soloist briefly enlarges on Ex. 1c, only to be inter-rupted by another tutti. But he reasserts his importance in a striking passage (with the right hand swooping down into the bass) for the development, by extension and inver-sion, of Ex. 1a through many keys, accompanied – most unusually and effectively – by long-held chords on the oboes. A further discussion of Ex. 1c leads to some brilliant passage work heralding an orchestral climax, after which Ex. 3 reappears as a prelude to the repeated tutti of Ex. 1, which dissolves into Mozart's own superb cadenza. The final bars of this athletic and spacious movement reassert the tonic of E flat in a sequence of resounding arpeggios and common chords heard in the first tutti.

Second Movement. *Andantino*. This sorrowful and deeply felt piece in C minor opens by a statement of the lengthy main theme

Ex.4

in canon, on violins, which, with the violas and violoncellos, play muted throughout until six bars from the end. The form is a blend of binary and aria. When the soloist enters, it is to provide a free but gravely woven descant over a repetition of Ex. 4. The richness of the figuration increases as the secondary theme progresses (in E flat major) to the accompaniment of crossed rhythms on the keyboard, leading to the recapitulation. Gradually, the emotional interest passes to the solo part, rising to a new pitch of anguish at the cadenza. The mutes are removed as the descant breaks into recitative preceding the strong final chords.

Third Movement. *Rondo : Presto*. This is one of Mozart's bravest and most vigorous adventures in rondo form. In the headlong rush of the first thirty-five bars the soloist, unaccompanied, announces two of the principal themes,

Ex. 5

in octaves in the bass, and

Ex. 6

Ex. 5 is simplified in outline by the orchestra, so that it seems strangely akin to Monostatos's air 'Alles fühlt' in *The Magic Flute*. With other subsidiary material these are brought into several unpredictable and happy conjunctions separated by episodes of scintillating passage work, until there comes a dramatic cadenza, in sections marked *Presto – Andantino – Presto – Andante – Presto*. After this the recapitulation and development of Ex. 5 and 6, with a new, rather menacing theme

Ex. 7

dramatically interpolated, leads, after several modulations in minor key, to a stately and melodious minuet! It was a stroke of genius to provide contrast in this way, for this lovely interlude – a theme with four elaborate variations – is enriched by some of Mozart's most poetic touches, such as the sustained chords on horns and oboes over modulating arpeggios on the keyboard. A second cadenza leads to a further repetition of Ex. 5, 6 and 7, the latter in an expanded form. The whole texture fairly quivers with excitement until Ex. 5 and 6 reassert themselves quietly in a smoother continuum before the end. Despite the bustle of this rondo, the tone of the whole work is heroic, with the soloist in command throughout.

CONCERTO NO. 10, K. 365, IN E FLAT MAJOR
(*For two pianofortes*)

To put the word 'pianoforte' in the above heading is really to beg a large question, for it seems much more probable, from internal evidence, that it was with two harpsichords in mind that Mozart wrote this border-line concerto early in 1779, for himself and his sister Nannerl. He has been reproached by certain critics with having rather superfluously employed two keyboards when there is only enough music for one. It would, however, need a very athletic player to cope with all the elaborate figuration so compressed, and in any case it is more reasonable to give Mozart credit for knowing his own intentions, which, if the work is played on two harpsichords, become crystal clear. The large number of passages containing statement and answer, sound and echo, divided between the two players become alive and vital if played with the sharply contrasted range of colour so simply attained on harpsichords, but almost impossible for the more uniform timbre of pianofortes. It is perhaps significant that the duet sonata K. 448 of November 1781 has fewer passages of this kind, and was therefore probably for pianofortes.

As a whole, K. 365 is unpretentious in mood and structure, but worth studying as the sole concerto of Mozart's in this particular medium. The only addition to the orchestra of K. 271 is two bassoons, skilfully used. We cannot expect Mozart to be wholly serious all the time, and when he is in the mood to produce perfect entertainment music of this kind, with the minimum of tension and contrast, we should accept the fact, and be grateful for his impeccable craftsmanship. Instead of the interplay of orchestra and soloists, he centres the interest in that of the soloists themselves, and there is comparatively little *bravura* or free writing. The scheme is easily grasped at first hearing, and needs no elaborate analysis.

First Movement. *Allegro*. The tutti opens with a resounding octave leap on the tonic chord, shifting to the dominant,

Two more melodies are quickly brought forward for discussion, of which the second

is the more important, given to violins and violas. Before the entry of the soloists, a fourth subject is heard on the oboes moving in thirds

The soloists enter together with an expanded version of Ex. 8, which they break up and elaborate in turn. When the tutti reasserts itself, it is not with either of the main themes, but with Ex. 10. A further piece of exposition is given to the soloists who make great play with

and after the third short tutti, they are sent off in pursuit of

Ex. 12

derived from the secondary material of the orchestral prelude. The full recapitulation makes great play with Ex. 8, which modulates into darker keys, working back to the tonic in which Ex. 11 is expanded. After an allusion by the soloists to Ex. 8*b*, some brilliant passage work leads to the cadenza

(Mozart's own), and the movement ends on the inexhaustible Ex. 10.

Second Movement. *Andante*. The principal melody is announced by the violins in thirds joined in bar 3 by oboes:

This is by far the most important factor in the 105 bars of this charming piece, for which Mozart chose the related and complementary key of B flat major, the favourite for love-duets in his operas. There are two or three subsidiary melodies, but they hardly merit quotation, as the main interest centres on the delicate patterns into which Mozart dissolves Ex. 13, with elaborate figuration given to one or other of the soloists. His skill and resource in devising ornamentation, not for its own sake, but as part of a structural plan, however simple, is seen in this *andante* at its very best. His use of the woodwind is especially effective through its restraint. Note the piquant touch in the last bar but one, when the bassoon by itself fills out the harmony of the close on the strings.

Third Movement. *Rondo : Allegro*. This, one of the longest of all Mozart's finales, runs to 504 bars. Yet so bright is the flame of the melodic invention, and so swift and varied are the contrasts, that even this great length seems all too short. No fewer than fourteen times does Mozart reiterate the principal theme

announced by the orchestra. The first soloist then makes a gesture of independence with a tune of quite different character

with a triplet accompaniment foreshadowing marvels to come of the same kind. The flexibility and brilliant chrom-

aticism of this and later triplet passages offsets the squareness and syncopated emphasis of Ex. 14. Only after two
more subjects, of which the second

Ex.16

must be quoted, have been treated by the soloists, are they
allowed to take up Ex. 14, over one-third of the way through
the movement. A transitional theme, in G minor

Ex.17

cast in the same shape as one of Papageno's frightened cries
in Act 2 of *The Magic Flute* appears briefly in the solo parts,
which then settle down to a modulating discussion of Ex. 14,
cleverly varied by cross rhythms and antiphonal treatment
of Ex. 16. The cadenza, by Mozart himself, follows, and
the coda consists of Ex. 14, restated in valedictory octaves
by the first soloist, with a triumphant flood of triplets for
the second.

CONCERTO NO. 15, K. 414, IN A MAJOR

THIS is, in many ways, the most Mozartian of the three
concertos composed at Salzburg during 1782. It contains
music of great elegance, cast in such a deceptively simple
mould that its underlying strength is apt to go unnoticed,
though it repays many hearings. The key is one which
Mozart used with a high degree of consistency. Comparison
of K. 414 with such A major works as the symphony,
K. 201, the clarinet quintet and concerto, the string quartet
(K. 464) and the later pianoforte concerto (K. 488) reveals
certain definite characteristics which all six have in common,
a fresh, vernal quality, a preference for smooth, cantabile
melodies, and a general lack of obviously strenuous counterpoint. Here in K. 414, the strings are supported only by
horns and oboes; it is one of the most homogeneous of all,

with a strong likeness, probably intentional, between some of the melodies.

First movement. *Allegro*. The first violins announce the gracefully curving first subject

and also, after a short transitional passage of contrast, the second theme:

In this the violas share, at the points marked*. The violas also add a piquant touch in a third shapely melody

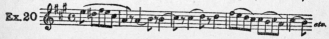

which immediately precedes the strong concluding cadences of the first tutti. At its first entry, the pianoforte quotes Ex. 18 almost verbatim, enlarges skilfully on the subsidiary material, and then springs a surprise by developing a delightful idea

which is evolved from the cadential phrase of the first tutti. After the orchestra has begun to restate Ex. 20, the solo breaks in, the right hand swooping down into the bass to point the rhythm. A fine passage of *bravura*, with more hand-crossing, leads to the restatement of the cadential phrase by the orchestra, to which the soloist replies with a wholly new tune, bolder in style:

Soloist and orchestra share in a development section in this same spirit, rising to a climax from a striking passage, which modulates to C sharp minor. In the following recapitulation, the pianoforte makes great play with Ex. 20, giving it the deserved prominence which it did not receive at its first appearance. The cadential figure from the first tutti rounds off the movement. These unpretentious, effortless surprises are at the root of the endless pleasure to be won from Mozart's concerto style.

Second Movement. *Andante*. Though in D major, usually one of Mozart's more brilliant keys, this movement is cast in a pensive, almost solemn, mood to which its broad binary form is well matched. The principal theme

is given out by the strings, and is succeeded almost at once by another very important tune

which, from its strong resemblance to Ex. 18, is clearly designed to link the two movements closely. Noteworthy, too, is the sonority of the chords with which the soloist's entry transmutes Ex. 23 into a more imposing vein. Another feature of this *andante* is the intricate beauty and shifting accents in the broken figuration with which each of the principal subjects is treated by soloist and orchestra, successively and in combination.

Third Movement. *Allegretto*. Not, be it noted, *allegro* as this affable little rondo is all too often taken, to its detriment. For too quick a pace spoils the effect of the many trills, and of the later demisemiquaver runs. It must surely have been by malice aforethought that Mozart introduces the movement with a gay and self-important trilling theme

followed by

This latter, in its disingenuous smoothness, might be deemed of secondary importance, but it turns out to be the mainspring of the whole movement, chiefly because its sinuosity makes it so easily susceptible of piquant modulations and much rhythmical variation. It is also true that the pianoforte's first entry with an unaccompanied passage of seventeen bars brings forward yet another theme

Ex. 27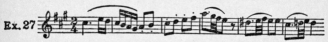

but it is solely the resources of Ex. 26 which enrich the first section of development. The tutti recapitulates Ex. 25: Ex. 26 follows, and modulates through E minor to D major, in which key Mozart allots a further melody

Ex. 28

to the soloist. This is expanded by pianoforte and orchestra, but the irrepressible Ex. 26 re-enters on the strings, is split up among oboes and first violins, with violas and violoncellos following in imitation. This leads at once to the cadenza, after which ensues a short, amusing dialogue based on Ex. 27, punctuated by two mock-heroic pauses. Mozart then lets Ex. 25 have the last word.

CONCERTO NO. 15, K.450 IN B FLAT MAJOR

ON 24th May 1784 Mozart wrote to his father: 'I cannot decide between those two concertos in B flat (K. 450) and D (K. 451). I think both are concertos which make one sweat: but the one in B flat surpasses the one in D for difficulty'. K. 450 is, indeed, one of the most difficult of the whole series, and gives quite exceptional prominence to the soloist, in long sections of *bravura* which are calculated as part of the organic growth, and not inserted as mere display. In many passages of quickly changing rhythms the pianoforte conflicts with the steady beat of the modest orchestra, comprising strings, oboes, bassoons and horns, with one flute in the finale. This is a cheerful, intimate concerto, not without seriousness, in very much the same mood as the contemporary B flat *Hunt* Quartet (K. 458).

First Movement. *Allegro*. Here in the first sixty bars, we find five themes of varying importance. The first

moves compactly in thirds, and is given, most unusually, to oboes and bassoons. The second section of this subject comprises an arpeggio figure on the violins, after which the first is repeated by the woodwind with identical notes, but with a clever shift of the accent. Then, as a strong contrast to Ex. 29, the violins, well reinforced, give out, *forte*, a leaping, rakish tune

which subsides before a shapely melody of singular beauty,

This passes from octave unison on the strings to the woodwind, with a flowing counterpoint on the violins. Another change of mood brings two more subjects, first

compact again, like Ex. 29, and then

a skittish affair, which might come out of an *opera buffa*. Impatiently, the soloist breaks in with a brilliant toccatalike prelude before settling down to the urbanity of Ex. 29, suitably expanded into triplet figures, which introduce an entirely new tune, in G minor. This has, however, no structural significance, although another new melody in the dominant,

is important. But this solo part is an impulsive creature. Without more ado it dashes off into coruscating passages of broken chords and scales, which demand the cleanest of playing, and subsides with a trill on the dominant in the face of an imperious repetition of Ex. 30 by the orchestra, in a brief tutti that ends with Ex. 33.

So impetuous is this solo-part that there is hardly any proper development, but in its place we have a procession of themes, lightly accompanied by the wind and strings in successive groupings. Ex. 29 and Ex. 30 are restated with interruptions from the pianoforte, which is allotted yet another lesser subject, in C minor, before it hastens off on its own once more and soon modulates back to the tonic for the restatement of Ex. 34. Perhaps the most wonderfully poetic touch in the whole movement comes in the recapitulation of Ex. 31 on the strings, taken up in octaves by the solo, which then accompanies its repetition on the woodwind with flowing scales. The tutti reintroduces Ex. 32 both before and after the cadenza, and the end comes with the appearance of Ex. 33, treated in whimsical dialogue by woodwind and first violins. Hardly any two of the first movements of these concertos end in the same way: their closing bars repay study as fully as do their openings.

Second Movement. *Andante*. In Mozart's characteristically grave mood of E flat, the strings announce the symmetrical theme which falls into two eight-bar sections, of which the first is

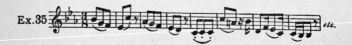

The solo answers with an expanded version; the strings give out the second section which the solo repeats with slight elaboration, and then joins forces with the strings to open the first of the two long variations. The broad alternation of solo and tutti makes the structure admirably clear. This movement is a fine instance of Mozart's infinite resource in devising figuration and harmony to adorn a melody, which remains basically unchanged, even when deepened into a sonorous chordal fabric. The short coda is delicately scored, rising up in broken sentences for the soloist to say his final word, expressed in a *gruppetto* on E flat in alt.

Third Movement. *Allegro.* For this rondo, in 6/8 time, Mozart uses almost as many themes as for his first movement, but only four of them need be quoted here. The others will fall into place easily once the main outlines are grasped. The most delectable and important is the opening

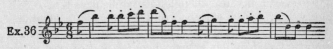

stated by the pianoforte in its brief first entry, and taken up by the tutti, but abandoned in favour of a piece of bubbling merriment worthy of Leporello,

Mozart's love of contrast caused him to space out the next melody,

more widely, rather in the manner of Ex. 30. But when the solo re-enters, it is with an entirely new, cantabile theme

and not with any of the material from the prelude. Such are

the principal ingredients of this delicious piece of comedy, in which the successive reappearances of the protagonist, Ex. 36, are prepared and devised with exquisite wit and imagination. Note especially the cross rhythms of much of the passage work and the art of the second reprise, heralded by a page of inimitable dialogue between woodwind and pianoforte, modulating through remote keys. In the coda the hero, Ex. 36, is bowed politely but briskly off the stage by the buffo character, Ex. 37, who runs riotously through solo, horns, woodwind and strings, and asserts his superiority right up to the last bar.

CONCERTO NO. 17, K. 453 IN G MAJOR

In April, 1784 Mozart completed this concerto for one of his favourite Viennese pupils, Barbara Ployer, presumably a gifted player, because, though not as difficult as K. 450, it is not an easy work to play well. Still less easy is it to determine the spirit of the music, because, as in the string quartet of the same key and similar temper, here we find Mozart at his most ambiguous. Despite the cheerful turn at the end of the finale, the mood is generally serious, but beyond that little definite can be said. The sensitive listener will discover that the music has iridescent, unfathomable depths which can be interpreted as variously as his own mood may vary. Even in this third Viennese concerto there are still no drums, trumpets or clarinets. But the scoring is a marvel of resource.

First Movement. *Allegro*. Once more Mozart packs the seventy-five bars of the orchestral prelude with six glorious themes, which grow out of one another and yet are amply contrasted. Very quietly the violins play

Ex.40

over a long-held tonic octave chord on the horns, with flute and oboes hovering airily above – a magical touch. **After** the tutti has stated a bold subject of a more conventional type, a stealthy rising figure on the bassoons

quickly doubled by the flute, ushers in what approximates to the second subject

Brief discussion of this restrained, but very lovely tune, is broken off by an electrifying modulation, veering from D major to E flat for a new theme

rooted in the clash of A flat and B flat, which produces a distinctly menacing quality. For the closing group of the tutti, Mozart returns to the tonic, giving point to the penultimate theme

by a sharpened octave, and ending with the quiet humour of

accompanied by staccato mockery on the bassoons.

Orthodoxy governs the entry of the solo until Ex. 40 and its sequel are disposed of, and a series of arpeggios modulates from A major to D major for an entirely new subject, Ex. 44, elaborated at some length, until the irrepressible bassoon of Ex. 41*a* rises again, from the depths of A major, and the solo re-enters with Ex. 41*b*. For the brief first *reprise*

Mozart uses unquoted material from the prelude, but quickly passes, with almost Schubertian suddenness, to B flat major, for the beginning of a plethora of running triplets, from which the pianoforte diverges to a contrasting and rather autumnal episode, which modulates freely in minor keys, and then comes back to the final recapitulation. From this

Ex. 45

re-emerges with great show of compulsive semiquavers, until the now familiar bassoon figure brings back Ex. 41*b* in emphatic octaves. A startling reappearance of Ex. 42 leads to the cadenza, for which Mozart himself provided two excellent alternative versions. Thereafter, Ex. 44 is heard again, but the last word is given to the bassoon's motif Ex. 41*a*, which is taken up by the whole orchestra. The whole movement perfectly illustrates Edward Fitzgerald's remark: 'Mozart is so beautiful that people cannot recognize that he is powerful'.

Second Movement. *Andante*. Lack of space precludes a detailed analysis of this dramatic, profound and remarkable movement. Endowed with five clearly distinguishable themes, it is cast in a kind of sonata form, and moves into remote keys with a mysterious intensity of feeling. The strong resemblance between the opening melody

Ex. 46

and Ex. 41*b* above can scarcely be accidental. Following its statement on the strings alone, the woodwind introduces new material, tinged with melancholy, and treated in close imitation on a rising arpeggio tune

Ex. 47

which gives way to a more positive mood, only to sink down
into

for the end of the exposition. The solo repeats Ex. 46,
pauses, and then plunges into a new, powerful theme in
G minor. Ex. 47 reappears on the woodwind in A major,
passes to the pianoforte, and the tutti restates first Ex. 48
and then Ex. 46 which shifts to the woodwind, solo, and dies
away still in D major. Another pause. The soloist is then
given a new, chromatic theme, and the development follows, very sadly, with incessant shifting of key. In spite of a
repeat of Ex. 46 in G major, followed by a fresh, almost
heroic, gesture in E flat major

the mood of passionate melancholy remains undispelled at
the end, after Mozart's own truly elegiac cadenza.

Third Movement. *Allegretto.* This delightful finale, consisting of theme, variations and coda, is rich in 'the chosen
coin of fancy', and is structurally easy to follow. But it is
important to notice that Mozart does not confine himself to
mere alteration of the outline and rhythm of the tune

by elaborate figuration. This chirping melody, derived in
part from the song of Mozart's pet starling, is broken up and
broadened very cleverly, especially in the minor variation,
for which it is rewoven into a marvellous web of chromatic

counterpoint. The tempo changes to presto for the finale section and a new tune appears

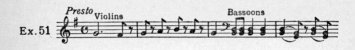

Ex. 51

followed by a hesitant phrase over shifting minims

Ex. 52

which twice holds up momentarily the riotous return of Ex. 50.

CONCERTO NO. 18, K. 456 IN B FLAT MAJOR

IT is reasonably certain that Mozart composed this concerto in September 1784 for Maria Theresia Paradis, a blind girl who enjoyed European fame as a virtuoso. Nearly every book on Mozart has stated that she actually performed it in Paris in this same year, but recent investigation* has shown that this is a baseless assumption, which opens up a complicated little chapter in musical history. However, it is a delectable concerto, a masterpiece in miniature. But it is miniature only in the same degree as are the poems of Villon or Burns, for it has hidden depths of passion and is endowed with a strange ambiguity of mood and character that make it enduringly attractive. It is also notable for the subtle kinship of its compact themes, which seem to grow out of each other with inevitable smoothness. The scoring is for strings, flute, oboes, bassoons and horns, handled with resource and economy.

* Hermann Ullrich: 'Maria Theresia Paradis and Mozart' in *Music and Letters*, Vol. 27, No. 4.

First Movement. *Allegro vivace*. The strings announce the first theme

(identical in rhythm with the openings of K. 453 and K. 459); the wind repeats it; a transitional melody leads to a bolder subject for full orchestra

which passes into a passage of broken arpeggios, embellished with *gruppetti*. Between this first melodic group and the second come the ten bars

contrasted in pace and dark with modulations. This is one of the pivots of the structure. Of the three remaining tunes,

and

are cheerful in an operatic vein, separated by

more serious in mood.

With the soloist's entry Ex. 53 and 54 are treated normally, but after some rather bare scale passages, the pianoforte plunges into an entirely new and brilliant melody,

which gives rise to some enchanting passage-work in continually changing colours, with sustained harmonies on wind and strings. The sparkling procession of the development brings back first Ex. 56, which leads in a sequence of triplets to Ex. 57, and finally to a tutti, with a powerful restatement of Ex. 54. But the solo part remains obstinately individual, for after a reappearance of Ex. 58 in the dominant, the pianoforte is given yet a further melody

which opens in that key. The rhythm of Ex. 58 persists in the woodwind over some finely poised scale-passages leading, ultimately, to the recapitulation. Ex. 59 is heard again, strengthened by bold modulations, passing through a restatement of Ex. 56, 57 and 58, into the cadenza. In the coda, Ex. 58 has the last word. The whole movement is a masterly essay in the unexpected, built from what are, considered separately, commonplace tunes, and from an uncanny variety of rhythmical device.

Second Movement. *Andante un poco sostenuto*. For this, one of his very few sets of slow variations in G minor, Mozart chose a theme

not unlike that pathetic little tune sung in Act 4 of *Figaro* by Barbarina as she searches for her pin. For sheer poignancy, these wonderful pages rank with all the other deeply moving works that Mozart wrote in G minor, the two symphonies, the string quintet, and Pamina's 'Ach, ich fühl's'. The figuration in the pianoforte part is rich and poetical: the soloist is used with great skill both as partner in a dialogue, and as an integral part of the ensemble. A radiant transition to the tonic major for a brief interlude lifts the shadows, but they soon thicken again as a return to the minor brings rapping sequences of broken octaves, which lead to a final statement of the theme, likewise in octaves, answered cynically by the deepest notes of the oboe.

Third Movement. *Allegro vivace.* This movement is no exception to the rule that no rondo of Mozart's contains less than six good tunes, but it was with characteristic and almost certainly intentional irony that he modelled his opening melody

on the theme of the preceding variations. Save in one section all the melodies are designed to transport the hearer to the world of *opera buffa*, with a troop of gnomes thrown in for good measure to speed the swift action of plot and counterplot. At its first entry the pianoforte will dance to none of the four tunes given in the exposition, but romps away with its own private joke

supported by chuckles from the woodwind, who are in the secret as usual. Its second personal excursion begins with a leaping figure in the dominant

Throughout the succeeding development, the woodwind keeps up a commentary, in short rhythmical phrases. Then flute, oboes and bassoons take complete command of the transition, through a beautiful passage played over long chromatic sighings on the strings, back to the restatement of Ex. 62 by the soloist. Another chromatic miracle leads to one of the most dramatic episodes in all these concertos, a further new theme for the pianoforte

Ex. 65
etc.

in the remote key of B minor. Soloist and woodwind move in 2/4 time, against the 6/8 of the strings. But this shadow, which conjures up the mood of the andante, quickly disperses, and the remainder of this delectable rondo steers its flashing course as near to the rocks of normality as can reasonably be expected of Mozart in 1784.

CONCERTO NO. 19, K. 459 IN F MAJOR

OF all Mozart's concertos this, the last of the six composed in 1784, is the most uniformly cheerful. It is also notable for the extraordinary character of the first movement, for the virile strength of the whole structure, and for being the longest of the whole series. With 1,075 bars it comfortably exceeds its nearest rival K. 482, but the tempi are so quick that its playing time is shorter. It is one of the least operatic in conception, tending rather towards true symphonic thinking, for which the orchestra still consists of flute, oboes, bassoons, horns and strings. When, however, Mozart himself revived this concerto at Frankfurt in 1790, he augmented its first and last movements with trumpets and drums, which could, with judicious scoring, be regularly included to enhance its festal spirit.

First Movement. *Allegro.* When a piece of music has a prodigal allowance of eight themes, as in this wonderful *allegro*, it might seem absurd to call it monothematic. Yet the opening subject

Ex.66

dominates the structure so completely that it appears in substance or in its distinctive military rhythm in over one third of the total number of bars. (Other instances of this unusual, but effective, scheme occur in the first movements of the *Haffner Symphony* (K. 385) and of the clarinet trio (K. 498).) Only two of the other six tunes contained in the orchestral prelude of seventy-one bars play much part in the several stages of the development.

Ex.67

is also worth quoting as a sample of finely drawn line, and

Ex.68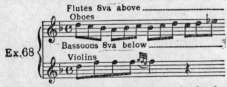

is based on effectively opposed rhythms. But two new themes of much consequence are both allotted to the soloist. Such is the infinite variety of Mozart's structural invention, on the principle that, for the exposition, 'Heard melodies are sweet, but those unheard are sweeter'.

It is important to note that, when the soloist enters and discusses Ex. 66, a triplet accompaniment is given to the left hand. This flowing rhythm, used previously in Ex. 68, furnishes an ubiquitous counterpoise to the jerky persistence of Ex. 66. A restatement of Ex. 67 leads to the first of the soloist's new themes

Ex.69

in C major. A few bars later, Ex. 66 returns on the wood-wind alone in free imitation, a delightful touch. Tutti and soloist enlarge on their now familiar rhythm, expanding its framework with bold upward leaps and a spate of modulation, from which emerges the soloist's second personal subject which is taken up from the violins and woodwind.

Ex.70

A further restatement of Ex. 66, with some fresh material, leads to a vigorous section in which the predominant rhythm is heard on the woodwind over and between modulating triplets for the keyboard. In the full recapitulation Ex. 66 and 67 are followed by a reappearance of Ex. 69 and by way of rhythmical contrast Mozart adds a piquant touch with the reintroduction of Ex. 68. The approach to the cadenza is made exciting by a last, almost frenzied statement of Ex. 66 on the full orchestra. After the cadenza – one of Mozart's best – the coda brings back two strands of melody previously heard only at the end of the orchestral prelude.

Second Movement. *Allegretto*. The use of 6/8 rhythm in slow or medium tempo usually means something special in Mozart. This delightful piece, in C major, is no exception. Cast in a modified type of sonata form, it shows his genius for the subtle varying of repeats, and for deft craftsmanship in welding together overlapping themes. The first subject

Ex.71

falls into two sections, 'a' stated by the full orchestra, moving together, with a short answer on violins alone, and 'b' by the tutti again, but heightened by contrary motion in both wind and strings. In the middle section, a new melody is confined to woodwind and first violins; the exposition closes with an expanded version of 71a. The soloist states Ex. 71 with the addition of an inserted *gruppetto* : supported by the woodwind, expands it down into the bass with the counterbalance of an upward semiquaver scale. From this

episode, in G major, a sudden modulation to G minor
brings the second subject:

Ex. 72

on the oboes. The remainder of the movement is built up
from this material, with some neat overlapping of the low
semiquaver scale between woodwind and soloist before the
latter's parting whisper of Ex. 71*a*. Are these bars not the
very image of the postlude to Susanna's 'Deh vieni non
tardar' in *Figaro*?

Third Movement. *Allegro assai*. In a brief analysis it is
impossible to do justice to the complex structure and content of this magnificent finale to which the first two movements logically lead up. The whimsical opening theme

Ex. 73

stated and expanded by soloist and woodwind alternately,
provides a brilliant foil to the striding counterpoint of the
second theme

Ex. 74

announced by bassoon, violoncellos and basses in unison.
This vein of allusive, fugal writing, not long sustained, but
used episodically for contrast with homophony, shows
Mozart's hard-won contrapuntal gifts at their happiest, and,
seemingly, most effortless. Just before the soloist's entry
there occurs a hilarious figure

Ex. 75

(derived from bars 3–5 of Ex. 73) of the familiar *opera buffa*
type, which is found in the codas of K. 453 and K. 466.

Of the glittering procession of secondary themes from which, with Ex. 73 and 74, this spacious rondo is built, these two must be quoted

Ex.76

Ex.77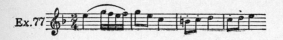

Ex. 77 plays an important part in the development. In the coda Ex. 73 has to give way before the unexpected onset of Ex. 75, tossed between soloist and orchestra like a shuttle-cock.

CONCERTO NO. 20, K. 466 IN D MINOR

WITH the completion of this work in February, 1785, Mozart cut the few remaining links that bound him to the traditional conception of the keyboard concerto. Formally, he had broken away in 1777 with K. 271. In the slow movement of that work, and of K. 456, he had contrived to combine the expression of passionate sorrow with the concerto principle. But now, in K. 466, by adopting his demonic key of D minor for both the first and last movements, he put aside all pretence of writing entertainment music, at least until the last ninety bars or so. In the tumultuous and, at times, sinister power of this great work, there is something of the unearthly qualities both of the closing scene of *Don Giovanni* and of the arias of the Queen of the Night. For the first time in this series, trumpets and drums reinforce the strings, horns and woodwind: clarinets, however, are still to seek. Mozart left no cadenzas for this work.

First Movement. *Allegro*. In the orchestral prelude to this movement – which begins, and ends, with a shudder, as Mr Blom has so aptly said – the scoring is superb. Over the syncopations of violins and violas with the rising theme in the basses and violoncellos

Ex. 78

Mozart brings in the woodwind and horns one after the other, with the effect of lightning flickering over the ominous horizon. After unleashing the full power of the orchestra up to the climax on the dominant seventh, Mozart makes a transition to the major for the second theme, of which the effect is bewitching:

Ex. 79

With Ex. 78 this is by far the most important of the melodies in the whole majestic prelude. Finally there supervenes a calmer atmosphere for the soloist's personal entry with

Ex. 80

But it lasts only for a dozen bars or so before this too is caught up in the renewed tumult of Ex. 78. After sharing in a restatement of Ex. 79, the pianoforte introduces the now customary second personal theme

Ex. 81

in F major. Some scintillating passage-work leads to an interim recapitulation in which Ex. 78 and Ex. 80 are linked in succession, and thrice repeated by tutti and solo. The full recapitulation quickly follows, culminating in a shattering broadside from Ex. 78 which, after the cadenza, dies away to a distant rumbling for the end of the movement.

Second Movement. *Romanze.* The German word is significant, and will remind many hearers of the similar use in *Eine kleine Nachtmusik.* The general tone of this piece, especially in contrast with its surroundings, was representative of one, rather limited, aspect of Mozart for the nineteenth-century audiences, with whom this D minor concerto was long popular, to the exclusion of most of the others. The ternary form demands the repetition of the limpid opening melody

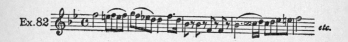

no fewer than fourteen times which, even with Mozart's ingenious ornamentation, is excessive. The second subject

though more widely spaced than Ex. 82, affords but little variety of mood. When the stormy G minor episode begins as a contrast to the pervasive sweetness of B flat major, it strikes a slightly artificial note, although it is effective enough *per se* with the rising and falling of broken triplets and with the dramatic swooping of the right hand down into the bass. There is no doubt that as a whole this is one of the least successful slow movements in all Mozart's concertos.

Third Movement. *Rondo : allegro assai.* Though the key of D minor is vigorously re-established, the mood differs from that of the opening movement, the ominous, sinister tone of which is here replaced by a turbulent grimness. The change is brought about partly by freer modulation but more by the different method in scoring, for the unusual symphonic style of the first movement is discarded in favour of the lighter technique suitable to the concerto form. In this intricate rondo there are four principal themes, a comparatively modest number. The pianoforte, unaccompanied, enters with the arrowy vigour of

Ex. 84

which is repeated with forceful elaboration by the tutti. This is linked to a subsidiary theme preceding the second entry of the soloist with

Ex. 85

followed immediately by a repetition of Ex. 84, with the orchestra, modulating to C major. A plunge into F minor introduces

Ex. 86

A further development section, in C major, ushers in

Ex. 87

which is to serve as the lever of the whole transformation scene in the coda. From this material, Mozart builds up a kaleidoscopic series of episodes, of which the two most arresting present Ex. 85 successively in A minor and A major. A highly original touch comes after the cadenza, when from a brief allusion to Ex. 84, Mozart quietly passes to Ex. 87 – played in D major on oboes, bassoons and horns.

The grimness vanishes utterly, an upward twist of Ex. 87 introduces a *buffo* motive

Ex. 88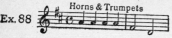

(remarkably like Ex. 77 in K. 459), and the coda ends in a riot of disarming 'Gemütlichkeit'.

CONCERTO NO. 21, K. 467 IN C MAJOR

BOTH this concerto and K. 466 are scored for exactly the same orchestra, yet they are diametrically opposed in mood and character. The fact that barely a month separates their respective entries (10th February and 9th March, 1785) in Mozart's own thematic catalogue, strongly suggests that he must have been working on both simultaneously, and provides a notable instance of his ingrained habit of producing contrasted pieces in pairs. (The string quintets in C major and G minor, of 19 April and 16 May 1787, furnish another instance.) K. 467 is Mozart's third pianoforte concerto in C, this choice of a neutral key here serving as a basis for exhilarating freedom of modulation which, for Mozart, was far less compatible with such key signatures – admittedly infrequent – as F minor or E major. Mozart left no cadenzas to this concerto.

First Movement. *Allegro maestoso.* The sombre epithet is curiously at variance with the generally resplendent and forthright tone of fully three-quarters of this allegro which, as in the first movement of K. 459, is dominated by a pervasive march rhythm with its answering phrase on woodwind, brass and drums:

Ex. 89

This section marked 'a' is heard nearly a dozen times in the seventy bars of the orchestral prelude, which is full of virile

counterpoint and bold scoring. Of several other striking
themes one of the most important is

which leads to a restatement of Ex. 89, out of which springs
a singularly haunting melody on the violins

The soloist enters with broken phrases in the dominant,
rises on flowing semiquavers to a pause, and restarts on a
long shake on G, over Ex. 89a in the strings, passing via
Ex. 89b, into a new melody

After a short *bravura* passage, the tutti returns with a vigorous
rising scale of G, whence the solo passes to G minor, with a
phrase (heard only here) which is an interesting anticipation of the opening of the G minor symphony. But the Key
of G major quickly returns with a lovely cantabile subject
for the pianoforte

which it repeats with antiphonal wood wind. More *bravura*
and a shortened repetition of the first tutti lead to a pause on

the chord of B major, from which the pianoforte turns to a new theme in E minor:

Ex. 94

In the recapitulation, the tutti is followed by a short discussion of Ex. 89a, by solo, flute and oboes, which leads to Ex. 93 in the tonic. But it is the rhythm of Ex. 89a which continues to rule both as a transition to Ex. 90 (in which the solo now takes part) and the tutti preceding the cadenza and the coda.

Second Movement. *Andante*. Here it is less important to analyse in detail the broad binary form, in which the melodies stand out clearly, than to realize the factors which render this movement unique in all Mozart's concertos. The orchestration is amazingly resourceful. For the first thirty-six bars the violins and violas play muted, the first violins in 4/4, supported by violoncellos and basses, against continuous triplets in the other strings. The first theme

Ex. 95

is followed by

Ex. 96

over which the wind weaves a fabric of shifting harmonies, scarcely to be adequately shown in compressed score. When the soloist enters in triplets, with Ex. 95, the strings revert to 4/4, and so in alternation throughout. Apart from the expressive opposing rhythms and hovering beauty of the modulations, it is the rhapsodic, dreamlike quality of this music that makes it one of the earliest blooms of romanticism. Such an episode as the statement of Ex. 95, beginning in A flat, first over *pizzicato* strings, and then under held semibreves on oboes and bassoons, conveys profound emotion, with an enchanting effect that is belied by the baldness of cold print.

Third Movement. *Allegro vivace assai.* The opening tune of this scintillating rondo

is cunningly contrived within the span of a sixth. Announced by the orchestra and repeated by the pianoforte, this germinal theme gives way to the more spacious coruscations of

but recurs in a series of chromatic enlargements, until the woodwind breaks in with

jaunty and cheerful in the manner of Mozart's youthful serenades. Its headlong development is interrupted by the soloist with a new and slightly more reposeful tune:

Such are the pieces from which this glittering mosaic is built up, around the predominant idea of Ex. 97, especially of its first six notes. In the development this figure, stated in octaves, forms a passage of emphatic dialogue between the bass of the pianoforte and the woodwind. It also serves as the core of a series of excursions into remote keys, with desolate twists and pauses. By way of final contrast, Ex. 100, transferred to the woodwind, falls soothingly on the ear just before the cadenza.

CONCERTO NO. 22, K. 482 IN E FLAT MAJOR

By common consent, this ranks as the most queenly of all Mozart's pianoforte concertos, combining affability with dignity – 'vera incessu patuit dea'. Warmth of colouring comes partly from the omission of oboes and the use of clarinets for the first time in this keyboard series. Trumpets and drums are retained. In the first and last movements Mozart relies for contrast more on changes in the shape and rhythm of his themes than on tonal fluidity. It might be thought that this broadly urbane character, coming after the rather forceful asperities of K. 466 and K. 467, denoted a return to the earlier conception of concertos as 'entertainment music', were this not belied by the personal intensity of the *andante*. But it was this movement which had to be repeated at the first performance, given, admittedly, before a select, private audience. There are, indeed, some strong parallels between this work and Mozart's earliest E flat concerto, K. 271, but for K. 482, unfortunately, he left no cadenzas.

First Movement. *Allegro*. From the sonorous procession of eight themes in the prelude, four must be quoted for the sake of clarity. The first is a lengthy, unhurried affair. Its unison opening

is of exactly the type used by Mozart in his early symphony in E flat (K. 184), and in his *Sinfonia concertante* (K. 364, cf. p. 54. Its continuation on the bassoon Ex. 100 emphasizes the mocking, satirical use of this instrument, as in the *adagio* of the 'Linz' symphony. An immediate repeat is extended with an important little phrase on the flute,

Ex. 101

which is bandied about through the transitional passage leading to:

Ex.102

Horns, flutes and violins then breathe dulcet persuasion with

Ex.103

supported by a delightful counterpoint on clarinet and bassoon. Of the two terminal themes

Ex.104

is the more important. The solo enters with the first of its three personal themes

Ex.105

passing to a brief episode, with some two-octave, operatic skips before two repeats of Ex. 100*a* and Ex. 100*b*. Some *bravura* leads to the second theme of the soloist, in B flat minor and soon after, from a free passage working back to the dominant, comes the third:

Ex.106

a smoothly rising scale. As the development proceeds, the pianoforte picks up Ex. 104 from the orchestra, and dashes off into some fine passage-work over a series of modulating arpeggio figures on the strings. After an allusion by the soloist to an expanded form of Ex. 105, the opening tutti is heard again. The soloist, alternating with the orchestra, makes great play with Ex. 100, until a further tutti re-emphasizes Ex. 102, as a prelude to an unexpected elaboration of Ex. 103 followed by Ex. 106. A vigorous transition to some strong rhythms derived from the first tutti leads to the cadenza and to a sturdy closure with Ex. 104.

Second Movement. *Andante*. This consists of four variations in C minor (broken by two interludes, in E flat major and C major) on a two-section theme, of which the first is

Ex.107

This opening is similar to those of the slow movements of K. 271 and K. 364. The strings play muted throughout, emphasizing the sombre pathos. The marvellous *fioriture* of the pianoforte are matched by the glorious, soaring arabesques of the part-writing for the woodwind, here enhanced by divided clarinets and bassoons. It is the blend of the varied timbres of the serenade with the intricate figuration of the solo part which makes this movement unique.

Third Movement. *Allegro*. Return of cheerfulness does not necessarily mean a lowering of standards, for the tunes of this delightful rondo have an aristocratic air about them, and it excels in the dexterous and varied orchestration of their several returns. The opening melody:

Ex.108

stated by the pianoforte and repeated by orchestra and again by soloist, is cast in a familiar 6/8 mould. A second

tutti introduces a lilting melody on the first clarinet, and the
soloist passes to

Ex.109

and, after some free *bravura*, to

Ex.110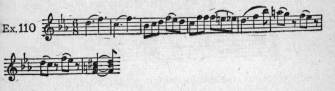

which is taken up by clarinet and bassoon. Then Mozart
diverges unexpectedly, as in K. 271, to a forty-five-bar
episode, *andantino – cantabile*, in 3/4; this, with its blend of
smooth woodwind writing and deft syncopations, puts one
in mind of parts of *Cosi fan tutte*. The *reprise* brings elaborations of Ex. 108 and Ex. 110, before the cadenza. The unusually lengthy coda is embellished by the weaving of still
more patterns around Ex. 108, until a few bars from the end,
when Mozart springs his last surprise, in the shape of a new
melody, akin to Ex. 109, played softly by the pianoforte,
under sustained chords on woodwind and horns.

CONCERTO NO. 23, K. 488 IN A MAJOR

THIS is the most lyrical of all Mozart's pianoforte concertos.
Here, as in K. 482, he favours clarinets in preference to
oboes, but drops drums and trumpets, and the mood and
style of K. 414 are developed to a further stage in his logical
progress towards the clarinet quintet and clarinet concerto.
The first movements of all four are informed by the same
gracious, conversational quality. But nowhere does Mozart
sacrifice constructive originality or intellectual power in
order to attain this almost divine limpidity of expression.

First Movement. *Allegro*. In the orchestral introduction

there are four outstanding themes, of alternating contrast.
Of these

announced by strings and repeated by woodwind, sets the
serene tone of this movement. The tutti propounds

more vigorous in rhythm, which is succeeded by

on the violins: this, which must be quoted in full, is incon-
testably the longest and loveliest melody ever devised by
Mozart, of a type which he was wont to lavish on E major
and A major. It utterly refutes those critics who maintain
that his melodic invention consists of little more than sub-
limated clichés. To this 'linkèd sweetness, long drawn out',
a jerky contrast arises in the bolder outlines of the closing
subject, amplified by the full orchestra.

The entry of the soloist proceeds normally with the discussion of Ex. 111, 112 and 113, but with the first *reprise* the
repetition of Ex. 112 introduces an entirely new subject of
deep and haunting beauty in E major:

This dominates the whole development to a far greater extent than any personal subject allotted to the soloist in any
previous concerto. With this brilliant stroke of invention
Mozart startles the listener by deflecting the course of the

movement from the channel of prospective normality. The discussion, expansion and dissection of Ex. 114 reveals many new facets of its beauty. Its treatment is of astonishing diversity: it is presented in inversion, and provides some fine, richly modulating contrapuntal touches, which are interspersed in the recapitulation and lend freshness to the euphonious sequence of Ex. 111, 112 and 113. Thereafter, Ex. 114 reappears, and is heard once more, again prefaced by Ex. 112, just before the sparkling cadenza, provided by Mozart himself.

Second Movement. *Adagio.* The first theme:

Ex. 115

is played by the pianoforte unaccompanied. This and its counterstatement make clear that the serene spirit presiding over the first movement has been overtaken by the sorrows of Niobe. The use of the key of F sharp minor for a whole movement is unparalleled in Mozart. Clarinet and first violin intensify the elegiac mood with the second theme:

Ex. 116

which is treated in *imitation* on the bassoon. This the soloist enlarges upon in a delicately chromatic version. A contrasting episode in A major brings some relief, but the prevailing mood lasts right through into the coda in which sorrow is intensified into bleakness by the effect of eight bars of bare, single-note leaps (as also at * in bar 2 of Ex. 115) for the pianoforte over *pizzicato* violins. Meanwhile, the other strings play smooth quavers and the wind sustains the harmony. Three bars from the end the woodwind play Ex. 116 in unison, as the soloist puts the final touch of desolation with a sequence of the high C sharp repeated ten times.

Third Movement. *Presto.* The striding theme:

Ex. 117

announced in the opening bars by the soloist, re-establishes

the radiance of A major. This is but the first of the pageant
of nearly a dozen melodies, which wind in and out of th
524 bars of this vast rondo. The material of the succeeding
tutti is of less importance structurally than several of th
splendid tunes allotted to the second entry of the soloist
First comes:

Ex. 118

followed almost at once by another upward-leaping figure
springing from a *gruppetto*. Modulating to the minor from
the pianoforte's trill on the dominant, the orchestra utters

Ex. 119

which the solo takes up at once, diverting it to major chan-
nels. A brilliant passage made conspicuous by a downward-
plunging octave theme in the bass of the keyboard leads to

Ex. 120

which Mozart had already used allusively in the first movement of K. 456. The elaboration of this in the dominant
brings back Ex. 117 and the first tutti, which gives way to a
sprawling episode in F sharp minor, followed by another in
D major with an eminently quotable melody:

Ex. 120b

From these materials Mozart builds up the remainder of the
movement, making wonderful play in the development with
Ex. 119 in a series of shimmering modulations shared by

soloist and orchestra. Especially noteworthy is the way the soloist with Ex. 120 takes command in the tonic just before the final *reprise* and again in the rippling merriment of the coda, where the key shifts to the subdominant.

CONCERTO NO. 24, K. 491 IN C MINOR

WHEN Mozart entered this work in his catalogue on 24 March 1786, he completed a creative effort scarcely surpassed by that of his three last symphonies of 1788. For only twenty-two days before, on 2nd March, he had entered K. 488, and during that same month the opera *Figaro* was making heavy demands on his time. This C minor concerto is not only the most sublime of the whole series but also one of the greatest pianoforte concertos ever composed. In its sustained imaginative power, in unity of conception and in the amazing structure of its first movement, devised to contain and resolve stark and tragic passions within formal bounds, it reaches heights of Sophoclean grandeur. Here Mozart included in his orchestra both oboes and clarinets, as well as trumpets and drums, the largest force used in any of these concertos. Study of the autograph* is most rewarding, for it reveals a great number of corrections, including two and even three drafts of certain passages. Here, as often, the perfecting of details assuredly cost Mozart much trouble.

First Movement. *Allegro.* Of the four chief themes in the orchestral prelude, the first is by far the most important,

Announced by strings and bassoons, it is composed of two distinct sections, marked 'a' and 'b'. The rhythm of 'b'

---

* In the Royal College of Music collection, which is deposited on permanent loan in the British Museum.

makes itself heard and felt throughout the whole movement, with many variations in pitch and in the upward leap at the end. It governs the short transition passage on the woodwind to the second theme

which strikes a calmer note, and leads at once into

Ex. 121 intervenes before the concluding melody

is heard. This prelude actually occupies 100 bars out of the total of 524. It is most interesting that in these concertos Mozart drew on the orchestral prelude to a progressively more limited degree, for the main elements of the first movement. Here he lavishes three new themes on the next 160 bars, allotting two of them to the soloist.

The pianoforte's first entry with

heralds the immediate return of Ex. 121a, and a short

bravura passage (of the kind for which this highly organized movement has little room) introduces

When this has been elaborated by soloist and orchestra, the oboe utters

in the relative major, and this lovely melody floats downward through clarinet and bassoon before the pianoforte takes it up with augmentations. In the following transition passage, the flute reiterates Ex. 121, in the ironical tone of E flat minor, above rippling arpeggios on the keyboard. When the tutti reappears it is with Ex. 121*b*, and Ex. 121*a* is not heard until the soloist has briefly interposed with a modulating sequence of Ex. 125, thus making the unison *reprise* all the more effective. The orchestra utters thrice a fluttering secondary theme, which gives way to some *bravura* incorporating Ex. 121*b*, before Ex. 121 is heard again, complete. The startling sequel to this consists of Ex. 127 and Ex. 125, in that order, working up to the tremendous unleashing of Ex. 121 in unison, by the full orchestra. After the cadenza, Ex. 124 is heard again, and, with the soloist giving out broken arpeggios, this storm of passion dies quietly away, matching exactly the conclusion of Mozart's C minor pianoforte sonata.

Second Movement. *Larghetto*. Though not so labelled, this

is a 'romanza' of the type found in K. 466, but more robust in temper, appropriate to E flat major. The opening theme

Ex.128

recurs five times, alternating with two subsidiary melodies. In this calm, lucid structure, the interest lies principally in the varied scoring for woodwind, which is enriched with much rhythmical ingenuity, in Mozart's happiest vein, reminiscent of Salzburg or Mannheim.

Third Movement. *Allegretto.* Writing on 'Variations' in *Grove*, Parry remarked: 'He [Mozart] was not naturally a man of deep feeling or intellectuality, and the result is that his variation-building is neither impressive nor genuinely interesting.' The implication of this is simply that Parry had either never heard any Mozart variations beyond those for pianoforte solo, or had never bothered to examine the concertos for instances of Mozart's marvellous creations in this form. Three of these have already been studied in the analyses of K. 450, 453 and 456. The finale of K. 491 is unquestionably his finest set of all, and forms a worthy conclusion to this sublime concerto. There is no cheerful major ending as in K. 466, or as in the variations of the C minor serenade K. 388. On the contrary, the tragic import of the dynamic theme

Ex.129

gains in intensity right up to the final episode. This tune, a thing of 'fearful symmetry' in two eight-bar sections, is plainly devised to allow the greatest possible diversity of rhythm and figuration in each of the eight variations.

For contrast, Mozart relies partly on the solid block of unaccompanied woodwind, as in the second variation, partly on tonal contrast, as in the one in A flat major which recalls the spirit of the preceding *larghetto.* He also inserts a calmer episode in C major, of profoundly moving simplicity. After the cadenza, Mozart heightens the tension by plunging into 6/8 time

Ex.130

dissolving the theme into impetuous chromaticism. He creates an overwhelming effect by the reiteration of a pathetic phrase

Ex.131

before the movement storms to the last defiant assertion of the chord of C minor.

CONCERTO NO. 25, K. 503 IN C MAJOR

COMPLETED by 4 December 1786, this work reverts to the rather earlier type in which Mozart concentrated the principal interest in the first movement. Despite the sparkle of the finale, the whole has a certain statuesque quality and an unimpassioned aloofness which have prevented it from winning wide popularity. Clarinets are lacking, but the scoring is bold and powerful, and the apparent reserve masks a magnificence of conception which only repeated hearings or a study of the score can fully reveal. From its position, almost midway between *Figaro* and *Don Giovanni*, K. 503 forms an epilogue to the eleven concertos written in the preceding two and a quarter years. No original cadenzas for it are extant.

First Movement. *Allegro maestoso.* The adjective is significant, for despite the major key signature, there are frequent digressions to minor modes. In support of a spacious scheme Mozart devised stately, symmetrical themes, cast mostly within a narrow compass and devoid of operatic skips, so that the whole moves with a measured, relentless tread, attaining grandeur in the manner of Milton's *Samson Agonistes* or of a landscape by Poussin. The introductory

fanfares, opening on the descending notes of the tonic chord,
move to the dominant, die away, and shift again to C minor.
Upon the first violins there steals in mysteriously the theme

Ex.132

which contains the pervasive rhythm (marked *a*) that imparts such strong character to the movement. After expansion in a wonderful piece of writing in six parts, Ex. 132*a* is
combined with new figures based on rising scales, culminating in its emphatic repetition on the dominant G. But this
assertive pause proves to be only a pivot for an immediate
return to the tonic minor, in which the second theme

Ex.133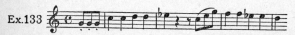

is announced. Modulation to the major, with some lovely
scoring for woodwind, leads to fanfares in which trumpets
answer the rest of the orchestra, and this noble prelude
closes with further allusions to Ex. 132*a*.

Unobtrusively, the solo enters, alternating with trills on
the strings, and a short passage of *bravura* brings a return to
the fanfares of the opening tutti. There follow repetition of
Ex. 132*a* on the violins as the undercurrent to some surging
scale-passages and broken arpeggios for the keyboard. The
full orchestra, after a thrice-repeated Ex. 132*a*, pauses on G,
but the pianoforte moves, as if in quiet defiance, to E flat for
a haunting transition theme

Ex.134

and after a spacious modulation to G announces

Ex.135

which may be taken as the 'second subject'. A further transition passage, dominated by Ex. 132*a*, leads to another powerful unison outburst of this rhythm on G. It is repeated by the soloist on B taken as the dominant of E, to serve as a modulating point to E minor, for the restatement of Ex. 133, which is developed at length through various keys, with a section of sublime polyphony in eight parts. In the following recapitulation, Ex. 134 is heard again on the pianoforte, passing as before into Ex. 135. Further allusion to Ex. 133, here shared by the solo, leads to the cadenza, after which the orchestra closes the movement with bold phrases from the end of the opening tutti.

Second Movement. *Andante*. This is in full sonata form built mainly on two melodies

given in the orchestral introduction. While the structure is plain, the chief interest lies in the quiet but wonderful colouring for woodwind, which is treated here – with great felicity – as part of the whole canvas. It is blended with both solo and strings, and not welded, as in some earlier concertos, into an integral, separate block, in the manner of a serenade. The closing bars based on

which was heard in the prelude, epitomize both the quiet strength of this rather reserved movement and Mozart's incomparable delicacy in the selective mingling of wind with string tone by light figuration on the keyboard.

Third Movement. *Allegretto*. The opening theme, played by the violins

Ex.139

is not unlike the gavotte from the ballet-music to *Idomeneo*, a resemblance of style as well as melody which suggests a moderate pace. Otherwise, the later demisemiquavers and the contrasting triplet passages in which, most unusually, the movement abounds, decline into a scurrying blur. Noteworthy, too, is the sparing but effective use of drums and trumpets. The answering subject to Ex. 139 is given to the wind:

Ex.140

A brief extension of this in C minor leads to the loose-limbed freedom of

Ex.141

curiously archaistic in style. The soloist enters with

Ex.142

and after a short transition passage, introduces another theme

Ex.143

Heralded by modulations over a very long dominant pedal,

comes the recapitulation of Ex. 139 and 140 by the tutti,
succeeded at once by

Ex.144

A sharp modulation to F major brings

Ex.145

which is developed by pianoforte, woodwind and basses, at
greater length than any preceding melody. Such is the noble
train of themes from which this rondo is built up, with
incessant emphasis on the contrast between duple and triple
time.

CONCERTO NO. 27, K. 595 IN B FLAT

MOZART completed this, his last pianoforte concerto and
his fourth in B flat, in January 1791, nearly three years after
the *Coronation Concerto* in D (K. 537, not studied here). If any
one adjective can be applied to the beauty of K. 595 it is
'autumnal', for, like other compositions of this year, it
breathes an air of valedictory resignation. Much of the
music has a restless, foreboding quality, enhanced by the use
of incessant modulation and a strongly chromatic style. So
fluid is the tonality that there is the minimum of sharp contrasts of key. Even the gaiety of the finale is tinged, as is no
other rondo in all these concertos, with a vague sense of
desolation. In this work Mozart omitted clarinets, trumpets
and drums, reverting to the more conventional orchestra of
1785. He left a full set of cadenzas in his sprightliest vein.

First Movement. *Allegro*. The orchestral prelude has the
usual wealth of themes, but they are mostly figures and
phrases, rather than melodies as created in K. 488. The one
exception is the opening subject

Ex.146

announced by first violins after an exceptional prefatory bar
played by second violins and violas. It is followed at once by
a sharply pointed figure Ex. 146a on the wind, which is
ideally shaped to serve as an important transitional pivot.
The strings proceed with a vigorous phrase

(repeated from the finale of the *Jupiter Symphony*), before
passing to a smoother melody

This merges at once into

still on the violins. More explosive material comes with the
re-entry of the full orchestra:

after which a flowing and very lovely transition passage
ushers in the closing figures of which one

must be quoted. The soloist enters with an elaboration of
Ex. 146, punctuated by Ex. 146a, on the strings, and passes
at once to Ex. 147, and then, after introducing a new phrase
in a darker key:

to Ex. 148 and Ex. 149. There then comes a transition of

ethereal beauty, with six bars of long-drawn chords on the
woodwind, leading to the first tutti, which introduces a new
strongly chromatic subject:

Ex.152

A short series of tutti modulations to the minor through
Ex. 150 brings back Ex. 146 in B minor, which is developed
in alteration with Ex. 146*a*, through C major, through E
flat major and E minor and several other sombre keys, to a
radiant recapitulation in the tonic major. The other themes
follow in comparatively normal sequence, up to the tutti
preceding the cadenza, but after it Mozart springs a mild
surprise in the reappearance of Ex. 152, which he links with
Ex. 150*a* to end the movement. The construction is unusual
in that the two themes, Ex. 151 and 152, not stated in the
prelude, have proved to be of such comparatively small
importance, compared with the Protean virtues of Ex. 146
and 146*a*.

Second Movement. *Larghetto*. It would be pleasant to
record that for his last concerto Mozart had composed a
really worthy slow movement, but it is not so. The principal
subject of this *romanza*:

Ex.153

is strongly akin in shape and rhythm to Ex. 150*a*. It is twice
repeated with a chromatic link derived from Ex. 152. The
eightfold reiteration of this over-simplified and distinctly
mediocre tune leads to a certain monotony which the other
themes do little to relieve, in spite of some pretty scoring for
woodwind and a passing allusion to Ex. 146.

Third Movement. *Allegro*. For this lilting rondo (which
may be profitably studied side by side with the finale of the

string trio K. 563), Mozart confined himself to four melodies,
of which the opening one:

is the most important and is played by the solo pianoforte.
After its repetition by the orchestra comes

leading at once to a repeat of Ex. 154, which also concludes
the succeeding tutti.

follows, likewise in B flat, and after some delicious *bravura*,
with remote, modulating allusions to the rhythm of Ex. 154,
we have a change to the dominant, F major, for Ex. 157,

More *bravura* leads to a pause for a cadenza. Ex. 154 recurs
and is developed by the orchestra with some scintillating
broken arpeggios for the soloist, bringing a pause on the
dominant seventh. The solo then plays Ex. 154 in E flat, a
refinement of tonality which makes the tune sound quite
fresh, and prepares the ear for a brilliant series of modulations based on its last two bars. Its rhythmical opening
figure dominates a transition to the return of Ex. 157 in the
tonic major, just before the second cadenza. The coda consists of Ex. 154 and 155 set off with new figuration, and

tinged, in the wind accompaniment, by shadowy modulations. The melodic line of this rondo is a thing of imperishable grace and strength. It soars and dips with the sureness of a bird in flight. Whether or not Mozart had a foreboding that he was composing this concerto in the evening of his life, the modern listener will marvel at its vesperal beauty. Here was truly an 'evening full of the linnet's wings'.

CONCERTO FOR VIOLIN, K. 216 IN G MAJOR

COMBINING, to a degree unusual for 1775, a spacious style and bold planning with whimsical and graceful touches, this concerto well repays study, for its many subtleties defy brief analysis. The orchestra is far from being merely a supporting body: throughout, the scoring ingeniously exploits limited resources, at times achieving an almost symphonic depth.

First Movement. *Allegro.* The strongly rhythmical opening theme:

Ex.158

is given to the first violins, and after a few bars of counter-statement they share with the oboes the second preludial subject:

Ex.159

A transitional passage on horn and oboes over Alberti figures on the violins leads to a chirpy melody:

Ex.160

and the prelude is rounded off by an emphatic melody in

thirds for the oboes. The soloist after stating and expanding
Ex. 158, quickly introduces a new melody

Ex. 161

which sweeps along in a bold dignified style for nearly a
dozen bars. But to be 'always wholly serious' (as Sir Max
Beerbohm put it) was utterly alien to Mozart, and so he
veers away into the delightfully impish tune

Ex. 162

following it up with a *reprise* of Ex. 160. This is discussed by
soloist and tutti before the latter return to Ex. 159, and in
the subsequent working-out some new material is introduced. The oboes, playing in thirds, as before, lead back to
Ex. 158 and the full recapitulation follows. The short coda
is wholly devoted to Ex. 159.

Second Movement. *Adagio*. This ranks very high among
all the slow movements of Mozart's adolescence. Flutes take
the place of oboes and the violins play muted throughout,
mostly in triplets or broken triplets, which rhythm also in-
vades the lower strings intermittently. For this sustained
outpouring of quiet ecstasy Mozart devised an exquisitely
poised theme

Ex 163

which is treated at length, almost in the style of an aria by
J. C. Bach. But the persistent rhythmical contrast, 4/4
against triplets, and the subtle shifts of accent and harmony
are Mozartian gems of the finest water. There is an allusion
to a subsidiary theme in A major, but it is not developed at
length.

Third Movement. *Rondo : allegro*. In the first section of this sparkling comedy there occur numerous melodies of which the principal ones are

Ex.164

announced by the violins; a sly figure

Ex.165

heard just before the soloist's first entry with

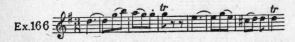

Ex.166

and

Ex.167

in E minor, which bursts in after a short *reprise* of Ex. 164. From these strands Mozart weaves a pattern of exits and entrances which proceeds smoothly enough until suddenly he plunges into G minor for a short pavane-like episode, commencing with

Ex.168

Here the spacing and overlapping of the inner parts played *pizzicato* is a marvel of adroitness. It is followed by a return to the major for another new, but complementary, section marked *allegretto*, in which the oboes take over the melodic rôle usually assigned to the first violins. A last return to Ex. 164 is prepared with skill and humorous suspense. In this whimsical vein, with a last, almost apologetic intrusion of

Ex. 165 the movement bows itself off the stage, to the ironic laughter of horns and oboes, unaccompanied.

CONCERTO FOR VIOLIN, K. 218 IN D MAJOR

FIRST Movement. *Allegro*. The orchestral prelude, occupying the first forty bars, has an unusual wealth of melodic phrases, but only two of them are of much structural weight. The military rhythm of the opening tutti

Ex.169

with its more delicately treading counter-statement (marked 'a') is linked by a piquant transition passage to the compact second subject

Ex.170

contrasted, characteristically, within a narrower compass. The closing phrase of this tutti must also be quoted:

Ex.171

The soloist enters with Ex. 169, played two octaves higher, and quickly passes, not to Ex. 170, but to a new, personal subject:

Ex.172

Only after some nimble passage work does the soloist arrive at Ex. 170, and plays it in the lowest register, with telling effect. Among several themes discussed in the development, Ex. 171 attains to surprising importance in the key of A major; and after the cadenza appears again to round off the movement. Throughout it is remarkable what varied effects Mozart contrives by the sparing use of horns and oboes, both to point and provide contrast in rhythm and to help in balancing the soloist against the other strings.

Second Movement. *Andante cantabile.* From the festal brilliance of D major, the key shifts to the dominant, A major, but in a rather unusually solemn vein, heightened by the absence of any marked tutti interruptions and of a true development. The long opening phrase

Ex. 173

of the short introduction is taken up by the soloist who announces in the second period an inimitable little tune

Ex. 174

which blossoms forth in the dominant, with echoes from the oboes. Later the soloist repeats it, in the tonic, on the top octave, with enchanting effect. After the cadenza the phrase marked 'a' in Ex. 173 brings the quiet close.

Third Movement. *Rondeau: andante grazioso.* The indication of tempo refers, of course, only to the first section of fourteen bars, with its witty, sinuous theme

Ex. 175

for it is succeeded by *allegro ma non troppo* 6/8, opening with

Ex. 176

and expanding its range with

Ex. 177

A repeat of these sections leads to another *andante grazioso* in 4/4 time

Ex.178

in G major. Here occurs a further change of rhythm, and style, and a striking subsidiary theme over a long tonic pedal on the oboes also sustained on the violin. Two further repeats of the two opening sections (with Ex. 176 omitted in the first repeat) round off the whole with a symmetry as satisfying as the subtly varied rhythms with which Mozart enlivens the several transformations of this chameleon-like 'rondeau'. It has all the sparkling freshness of youth, almost unclouded by the transient melancholy that intrudes even among the works of 1775 and 1776.

CONCERTO FOR VIOLIN, K. 219 IN A MAJOR

IN wit and rhythmical variety, in elegance and imaginative power, this work not only excels Mozart's four other concertos for violin, but has no rival throughout the second half of the eighteenth century. Even if he had returned to this form during the years of his Viennese maturity it is doubtful if he could have surpassed the freshness and gracious beauty of this crowning masterpiece of 1775.

First Movement. *Allegro aperto.* The implication of the rarely used term 'aperto' is readily seen in the spacious themes and the clear, pointed scoring. The first 'subject'

Ex.179

consists of a bare harmonic skeleton; the second

Ex.180

has an air of courtly grace. Apart from the closing bars, none of the other melodic elements in the orchestral prelude proves of much significance in the working-out. It was a stroke of genius to bring the soloist in with six bars of a recitative-like adagio with a tranquil, undulating accompaniment, and then to proceed with neither Ex. 179 or 180, but with a far bolder, sweeping period

Ex.181

superimposed above Ex. 179 on the orchestra! Repetition of the closing phrase of the opening tutti gives rise to a piquant, springing figure

Ex.182

treated in imitation, as the second subject in E major. In the course of the development one or two new melodies (the second in C sharp minor) are introduced, but both the main outlines, filled in from the themes quoted above, and the general procedure, are regular enough. In the coda, however, Mozart springs a last surprise by bringing the movement to a close with the solo's rising arpeggio from Ex. 182, as if on an unanswered question.

Second Movement. *Adagio.* In the sensuous sweetness of E major, Mozart pours forth a stream of melody which he concentrates into a marvellously articulated piece of pure lyricism. The opening tutti of twenty-four bars contains the two subjects, the first

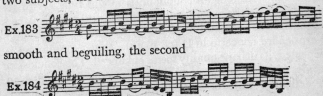

Ex.183

smooth and beguiling, the second

Ex.184

rather less pensive, but equally beautiful. After restating Ex. 183, the solo violin introduces a new melody in B major

Ex.185

bolder in style, while sustaining the lyrical tone. But by means of adroitly timed syncopations and suspensions in the inner parts, and by resourceful variety in preparing the successive return of each theme, Mozart avoids the faintest semblance of monotony.

Third Movement. *Tempo di menuetto.* This is actually an elaborate rondo, beginning with a graceful minuet

Ex.186

which is introduced by the soloist, of a conventional type from which arises a bolder melody. It ends with two figures of some structural import

Ex.187

A secondary theme is treated in alternation with Ex. 186, and the third reiteration of Ex. 187 leads to a more turbulent section which opens with a new melody in F sharp minor. These shadows are dispelled, however, with the soothing strains of Ex. 186 and 187, only to give way to an extraordinary affair in A minor, which serves as the trio. Over 100 bars long, this episode is in 2/4 time. With its angular tunes, sharp contrasts of solo and tutti and displaced accents, it has something of the gypsy flavour of Haydn's harpsichord concerto in D (cf. p. 47). When the minuet is repeated, its urbane quality seems enhanced. The conclusion comes with Ex. 187, leaving this movement, like the first, in a delightful state of suspension, on the arpeggio figure similar to Ex. 182. The whole concerto is an object lesson in the construction of melodies from the notes of the tonic chord.

'SINFONIA CONCERTANTE', FOR VIOLIN AND VIOLA, K. 364 IN E FLAT MAJOR

THIS masterpiece was completed at Salzburg, in the summer or autumn of 1779. Formally, technically, and in sustained dignity and depth of feeling, it is by far Mozart's finest instrumental work up till that date, yet we know nothing of the occasion or performers for whom it was composed. It is scored for strings supported only by oboes and horns, and in sonorous variety of string tone is unparalleled in Mozart's music, and indeed is scarcely surpassed by any other work of the eighteenth century. Violas play divided throughout, often supporting, unaccompanied, the solo viola; violoncellos and double-basses likewise have extensive separate parts. The orchestra plays a rôle of much greater structural importance than in the concerto for two pianofortes, also of 1779. The first movement contains fine samples of the famous 'Mannheim crescendo' which had so amazed Burney a few years before. The soloists join the orchestra in all the tuttis. When playing together in the concertante sections, they move in unison, thirds or sixths; when separately, they favour a style of echo or imitation, well calculated to set off the different timbres of their several registers. Mozart wrote three cadenzas for the first movement, and one for the second. Those generally played foreshadow the masterly technique of his two duets for violin and viola of 1783.

First Movement. *Allegro maestoso.* For sheer thematic wealth this movement hardly falls short of the mature pianoforte concertos of 1784 onwards. The tutti opens with a bold figure

Ex.188

in one of Mozart's favourite rhythms and passes, through

several subsidiary figures, all firmly rooted in the tonic of E flat, to a striking call on the horns

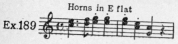

answered by the oboes. There follow sixteen bars of violin trills rising to an exciting crescendo over shifting harmonies for oboes, horns and violas and an insistent series of E flats in the lower strings. Even before the tutti dies away, the soloists enter with the piercing sweetness of

Horns and strings interrupt with a rhythm like Ex. 88 and the violin continues with Ex. 190 which is taken up by the viola. A vigorous sequence of tonic and dominant chords leads to a new melody

on solo violin, in the relative minor, again repeated by the viola. In the subsequent dialogue the tonality slips to the dominant, in which yet another new subject

is heard. Further dialogue introduces fresh subsidiary material, which gives way to an exhilarating tutti, rising on a series of trills to G minor, in which key the violin plays

the third new theme proper to the soloists. This sobbing

utterance is smothered by a new series of sombre trills, from
which it rises again on the viola, and there follows a very
lovely dialogue in darkly modulating keys, leading to the
recapitulation of Ex. 188 and of 190 in full. Then follow Ex.
191 and 192 both in the tonic major, the latter interrupted,
most unexpectedly, by Ex. 189 again on the horns and
oboes. Some attractively echoing *bravura* surges up into the
full power of the orchestra; the cadenza follows, and after
a final flourish of climactic trills, the movement ends with
the inexhaustible reassertion of tonic chords.

Second Movement. *Andante*. This terse and poignant
utterance in C minor stands comparison with the very greatest of Mozart's works in this his tragic key. Its construction
is simple, based largely on two themes

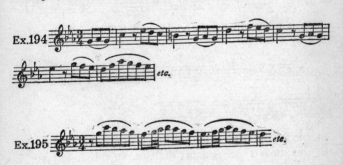

each stated by the tutti, and expanded first by each soloist
in succession, and then discussed in earnest, at times
rhapsodic, dialogue. Especially moving is the transition to
E flat major for Ex. 195, which is woven into a lovely contrapuntal fabric by the strings, and then amplified in grave,
but simple triplets by the soloists. Noteworthy too is the
beautiful reshaping of Ex. 194 at its recapitulation, and the
contrast between the accents of passionate despair (expressed in falling sevenths) which precede the cadenza, and
the calmer, more resigned, grief of the coda.

Third Movement. *Presto*. This exhilarating and powerful
rondo is notable for its splendid cavalcade of themes and for
the absence of contrast from any section in a minor key,

apart from some *bravura* dialogue for the soloists. In answer
to the opening on the violins

comes a brisk tune on the oboes which is repeated by the
violins. A short transition leads to

on the horns, repeated by the oboes, before the fanfares,
which end the tutti. The solo violin then enters with

which is taken up by the viola, and is followed almost at
once by a variant

notable for the triplet rhythm that is so prominent throughout this movement. A short dialogue in this style leads to

(which is first cousin to Ex. 196) played in close imitation.
The soloists restate Ex. 196 together; the viola usurps the
oboe's *motif*, and Ex. 198 follows, in the warmer tones of
A flat major. A third restatement of Ex. 196 ushers in some
new material, which is succeeded by an effective re-appearance of Ex. 197, shortly before the surely calculated climax
of the final tutti.

5

Ludwig van Beethoven (1770–1827)

SCOTT GODDARD

INTRODUCTION

THE concertos of Beethoven were written within the space of fourteen years: from 1795 when he was 25 to 1809, when he was 39 and far beyond half-way through his life.

1795. Pianoforte Concerto in B flat, revised in 1798 and issued as No. 2.

1797. Pianoforte Concerto in C, issued as No. 1.

1800. Pianoforte Concerto in C minor, No. 3.

1805. The Triple Concerto.

1805. Pianoforte Concerto in G, No. 4.

1806. The Violin Concerto.

1809. Pianoforte Concerto in E flat, No. 5.

These fourteen years saw great changes in Beethoven's condition as a man and so as a composer; changes in his state of being, his state of mind, in his outlook on life, his approach to music, in his whole spiritual development. What had happened before the first of these works was the end of a hard boyhood in Bonn and the beginning of a fresh existence in Vienna, with the news from Bonn of the death of his pitiful father making the definitive break in an already tenuous link with his past. Freedom must have seemed enchanting then, and he met it with the ardour of a man impetuously sure of his powers. He was still having lessons from Albrechsberger and had hardly ceased to study under Haydn when the B flat Concerto first appeared. For the first time he was a successful musician, much sought after as a pianist in Vienna, a brilliant executant and a remarkable improvisor. It is to this period of young mastery that the First and Second Concertos belong.

The Third Concerto appeared in the same year as the

First Symphony, the Op. 18 String Quartets, the Septet and the *Prometheus* ballet. It is the time of Beethoven's first maturity. He had learned all his teachers could give him. In this year 1800 he was expressing with absolute clarity and often with astonishing force and cogency a unique individuality. He was to discover many more moves in this manœuvre. For the moment he remembered Mozart's C minor Pianoforte Concerto and thereupon wrote his own in that key, with his own personality strongly imposed on whatever his mind held of Mozart's masterly manipulation of the type. Beethoven then was still the successful concert musician. If his career was momentarily checked it was only by love affairs, disappointing physically and perhaps socially, but not disenchanting artistically nor spiritually hurtful. Health seemed secure.

Within the five years between the Third and Fourth Concertos all had changed. Two years after the C minor he sent the Heiligenstadt Testament to his brothers and within a few weeks noted down the opening theme of the *Eroica Symphony*. The tale has often been told, much discussed, and need not be rehearsed here. To an ardent young nature such as his – for it must be remembered that he was a mere 32 when he became incurably deaf – the turn of events must have seemed hideously capricious. Everything that came after was conditioned by it. And the works near to his discovery of his evil destiny reflect it clearly. They reflect his escape from a crippling introspection, which might have overtaken a man of lesser mental stature, into a state in which Beethoven gazed with a vision directed with equal intensity upon his close bitterness and his distant gaiety; the expression of a personal tragedy which he shared with a minority of cripples and that of a remembered happiness entertained by the heedless majority of his fellows. He had become himself possessed of the insight of a dramatist. He was now the poet who does not need to experience in order to express. He was ready for the creation of *Fidelio*.

The last concerto appeared in the year following the Fifth and Sixth Symphonies. In that year (1808) Beethoven played his Fourth Pianoforte Concerto in public. The Fifth was performed for the first time two years after it was finished (1812), but not by Beethoven. Already he was too stricken to continue his career as a virtuoso. He was fast becoming enclosed within a narrow way of existence, its bounds traced by the decreasing range of hearing. It is improbable that his mind would have been less fecund had his physical powers been less impaired. But this specific form of physical disability and suffering drove him relentlessly back into the country of the mind, and it is astonishing that he could hold such a delicate equilibrium between his failing body and his aspiring mind.

With the Fifth Concerto he said his final word in that type of composition. The display element, that heady delight in finger agility, had not yet begun to threaten the intelligent life of the Concerto. Beethoven, like Mozart, had allowed for it but kept it within strict limits. In the Fifth those limits are reduced still further, so that player and listener alike misconceive the music when they deal with it as *bravura* of the fingers. Beethoven was still to have recourse to the pianoforte, forcing it sometimes beyond its powers of mere brute percussion to express his vision. But either because his hearing would no longer allow him to play in public as a concerto soloist, or because he no longer found the artifice of pitting a solo instrument against an orchestra sufficiently rich in opportunities of expression, he turned to other matters. Thereafter he used the pianoforte for the cooler purposes of chamber music, such as the Op. 97 Trio (1811), and for such solitudes of the solo pianist's domain as the last sonatas and the Diabelli Variations.

PIANO CONCERTO NO. I, IN C

FIRST Movement. *Allegro con brio.* The upstanding vigour of the opening phrase given out by the orchestra suggests such self-assurance as has always been considered the hall-mark and perquisite of young genius.

Beethoven, then a man in the prime flush of creative inspiration and enjoying life as never before, with his early successes in Vienna, writes with youthful eagerness. This is all straightforward, direct, free from oppressive thought. The model for this type of phrase was close to him. The theme exists in the same atmosphere as that of Mozart's pianoforte concertos in the *galant* style and has a similar clarity and grace. Mozart is the presiding deity of the whole first movement. The very look of the score brings the last movement of the *Jupiter Symphony* to mind; and there are other matters of phraseology and scoring which strengthen the resemblance.

The orchestra, having dealt with this forthright affirmation in an appropriately forceful manner, proceeds by way of a strong change of key to a preliminary hint of a new theme. This begins with all the impulse of a real second subject but is broken in upon after its first phrase and is in fact not to be heard complete until, much further on in the movement, the solo instrument at length gives it in full. Its first appearance here is as follows.

The clear tonic-dominant tonalities of the first tune are now to be enriched as the second theme is taken through more distant keys. The orchestral tutti eventually returns to its first utterance, settles on the tonic C major and so leaves the way free for the solo instrument. This makes its entry with a new theme.

The music soon reaches the important point at which the pianoforte begins the subject which the orchestra did not continue, Ex. 2, and makes of it a complete melody that has now the significance of a true second subject. This withholding of an important melody is a dramatic touch of great effectiveness. It brings the solo part to the fore, doing this by the simplest, most unobtrusive means. Not until this particularly gentle melody has been completed does one realize

that the solo has taken the centre of the stage, effecting that
manœuvre not by force but by subtlety, by using not the
compelling first theme but the insinuating second. Thereupon the discussion between solo and orchestra proceeds
with many touches of witty and graceful comment until the
recapitulation of the main material. And here we find we
were right in considering Ex. 2 to be the true second subject;
it returns now invested with the proper symphonic authority
of the tonic key. The pianoforte cadenza then ensues and
the movement ends with the C major octaves of its first
bar.

Second Movement. *Largo.* The tension is now released,
drama is relinquished in favour of a more gentle style of expressiveness and all the pianoforte's lyrical qualities are
brought into play.

Only in the first two bars is the pianoforte accompanied and
then only by strings playing very softly; for the rest of the
melody it plays solo. And throughout the movement it sets
the emotional tone. The orchestra may show signs of restive-
ness but has to give in. The kind of conversation that goes
on between them is shown in this start of the second subject,
where the expressive outline of the solo music is answered by
chords on wind instruments.

And there are other matters, one of them being a grand
melody for the, by now, tamed orchestra, another the
splendid rich coda.

Third Movement. *Allegro scherzando,* a rondo that has this
tune of rich promise for its first theme.

The promise lies in the many possibilities this theme suggests for development, possibilities which we are to see exquisitely fulfilled as the movement proceeds. Between each return of this rondo theme there are episodes of contrasting music, of which this is the first.

Ex.7

Other episodes insert themselves between the statements of the rondo theme and the argument is thrashed out with great vigour until the pianoforte insists on a cadenza; after which the work ends swiftly.

PIANO CONCERTO NO. 2, IN B FLAT

FIRST Movement. *Allegro con brio.* An immediate contrast is established between a feeling of vivacity and a mood of contemplation.

Ex.8

Few opening paragraphs in concertos of this period (1795, that is to say four years after the death of Mozart) have placed the whole contention and aim of the work so directly and patently before the listener. Outward semblance – the instantaneous gesture that betrays the quality of an individual – and inward image, a sign of the questing mind; the one (perhaps) a matter of knowledge, the other of intuition. Those two elements placed in bare opposition are to dominate the whole concerto. And it will be long debated which is the more remarkable aspect of this opening music; its potential dramatic power or its superficial appearance of artlessness. One wonders still at the ease with which these scraps of music are manipulated by a young genius and put to great artistic uses; and wonder increases the more one realizes how easily these two minute statements might have degenerated into pure banality under less poetic manipulation. When the pianoforte enters it brings with it a fresh theme, the first of any appreciable length.

Ex. 9

This sounds new enough to be a true second subject. But more significant material is introduced, again by the solo instrument.

Ex. 10

It is this theme that fulfils the function of the main second subject, complete with its own key on its first appearance and having its conventional position in the recapitulation, where according to custom it is drawn into the orbit of the first subject (that is, the opening music, Ex. 8) and appears in the tonic key of that music.

Second Movement. *Adagio*. This slow, rich and plangent style of expression is now, though it was not then, familiar as the expected style of a slow movement in one of Beethoven's earlier piano sonatas. Instances are the slow movements of the first and third of the Op. 2 group and that of Op. 7; all of them sonatas of this period, though slightly later in date. Here in the Concerto there is that same breadth of phrase, the same tendency to interrupt the melody by rests, as though the underlying passion were too strong for the music to support. And there is the same affectation of drooping cadences and feminine endings. It is music that does, in fact, expend itself generously in exploring the particular mystery hidden in the melody that starts the movement.

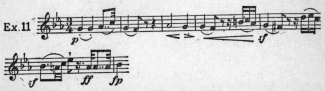

Ex. 11

This, having been announced by the strings, is taken over

by the pianoforte, to which it is equally well suited. Later the solo instrument begins to decorate this theme and is reminded by the orchestra that the original version must not be for ever overlaid with ornament. And at the end there is a diverting episode where the pianoforte tries a last attempt to get the main theme to itself but has to give in to the orchestra which then ends the movement in the style of that dignified calm with which it began. Throughout there has been much effective give and take between solo and tutti with interpolations such as this:

Ex.12

calling forth answering comments and keeping the discussion lively and intense.

Third Movement. *Molto allegro.* Sentiment is now replaced by action. This is a rondo; its chief theme starting thus, and appearing first on the pianoforte.

Ex.13

As soon as the orchestra has dealt with this it proceeds to the first of those fresh ideas that are to come between the various appearances of the rondo theme. This first idea is peculiarly pertinent, for it is a return to the first movement, a deliberate quotation of the extrovert outline (the gesture betraying the individual) which begins Ex. 8. Of the various interpolations this is one of the most important.

Ex.14

The pianoforte announces this new theme which has the significance of something more than a mere episode in a rondo; it will reappear but in the key of the tonic and this fact will give the finale the character not only of rondo but of something nearer to that of a symphonic first movement.

PIANO CONCERTO NO. 3, IN C MINOR

FIRST Movement. *Allegro con brio*. The opening phrase contains those elements on which the music of the first movement is to develop; an arpeggio (*a*), a scale (*b*), and the figuration of drum tap (*c*).

It is a compelling phrase, an inherently energetic and forceful opening to a concerto. Beethoven must have been aware of the sense of expectancy that would be caused by this first appearance of the theme, when played *piano* on the strings. To deny evident possibilities and withhold potentialities is, for a poet of vision and a masterly craftsman, to have the clue to the whole construction. The only difficulty will be to discover a means by which, after so much has been suggested in the orchestral introduction, sufficient significance can be given to the solo music. Beethoven manages this by the simplest means, the most effective as well as the least expected. Obviously one way to do this would be to give the solo instrument the first loud announcement of the large theme. This, however, has already happened in the opening tutti, in a major tonality. What then is left? To give the pianoforte on its first entry a new theme? That was an acknowledged gambit. Beethoven ignores it. The pianoforte enters and for the first time the great opening theme is displayed in full strength in its own minor tonic. In the meanwhile the orchestra has introduced the second main theme, a melody which in contrast to the first flows where the other leaped back and forth and is calm where the other hardly seemed able to restrain its energy.

Now that the solo instrument has been assured of its position by that masterly stroke it has no need to assert itself and the movement can proceed to discuss urbanely those matters suggested by the two subjects quoted above. The essence of that courteous converse between equals is in the coda that follows the solo cadenza and brings the movement to a close; the drum taps (really on drums now) against very soft held string chords and the pianoforte interpolating series of still softer, more distant arpeggio forms, in falling cascades of semiquavers. Then a strong affirmation of the C minor chord and so the end.

Second Movement. *Largo.* As in the preceding concerto this movement belongs to that class of noble slow movements which give the earlier pianoforte sonatas their memorable quality of emotional expression. And by the time this concerto appeared Beethoven had added to those slow movements such things as the *Adagio con molt' espressione* of Op. 22, wherein the vision seems much widened in scope and the emotional tension correspondingly heightened. The C minor concerto begins with one of Beethoven's most splendid melodies and, as will be heard in the outcome, one of his most fecund inventions. It opens in the following manner a solo for the pianoforte.

Ex. 17

From the descending figure here marked (*x*) there develops a rich succession of antiphonal exchanges between bassoon and flute against a background of pianoforte arabesques. It has the effect of moving the music through new tonalities before the great melody returns, at first on the pianoforte as before but soon taken over by the orchestra while the solo instrument wanders off into ornamentations. Far-ranging scale passages, a wide sweep of arpeggios, a short but florid solo cadenza are displayed by the pianoforte. The orchestra allows this to play itself tired and then clinches the argument; a simple reference to the first bar of the chief melody which the pianoforte duly repeats; and that is the end.

Third Movement. *Allegro*. A rondo of ample proportions with this as its first theme:

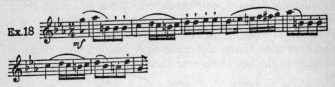

and this as its second:

Both are heard at first from the solo instrument and between them there appears a dramatic pronouncement which makes a wonderfully effective point of contrast, strong C minor chords on wind and percussion answered by rapid rising pianoforte arpeggios. There is a remarkable coda, with a change of speed (*Presto*) and key (the major tonic) while both the main themes appear in part and curiously transformed.

TRIPLE CONCERTO FOR PIANOFORTE, VIOLIN AND VIOLONCELLO

First Movement. *Allegro*. In a work which of necessity has to be of large proportions, since not one but three solo instruments must have their say and make their individual contribution, this movement is no more extended than should be expected. Bass strings alone begin the work with one of Beethoven's most individual touches, this quiet, diffident announcement of the first subject.

That said, and the theme having reached its first complete

form, a few bars return the music from dominant back to tonic and a crescendo sets in. This great passage should be noted, for it suggests that the attendant spirit of Cherubini hovers over the opening of this concerto. It shows too that Beethoven, thinking of Cherubini as in *Weihe des Hauses* he thought of Handel, can break loose from no matter what influence. And that he does here, when after nine bars of a Cherubini crescendo he breaks away into F major and within another nine brings the music to A major before taking it finally to the key of his next theme:

Ex.21

On these themes the opening tutti is founded. The first solo instrument to be heard is the violoncello which enters with the great main theme, Ex. 20, and is joined by the violin and eventually by the piano, both following the violoncello's lead. Later the orchestra has a loud C major theme which at first seems new but in reality is an offshoot of the second subject, Ex. 21, and this in turn, when taken over by the violoncello, leads to the following extension, as important in the construction of the movement as it is impressive.

Ex.22

The trio of solo instruments now becomes the medium for all the more subtle and intimate development of the movement. In the main it is the string solo parts that initiate these matters, the pianoforte being treated with reserve. By that means the balance within the trio is held evenly between the natural exuberance of the keyboard and the dynamic refinements of the fingerboard. One of the great enjoyments of this movement is in the dialogue between the instruments of the solo trio, such a passage as that which comes between the end of the recapitulation and the coda. It is the place where ordinarily a cadenza might intrude. But this trio passage, backed by soft, short chords from the orchestra, has enough of the display quality to take the place of a cadenza

and after it is over a short coda is all that is needed to end
the movement satisfactorily.

Second Movement. *Largo.* Muted strings, playing distantly, start the chief melody and half-way through the
fourth bar the solo violoncello enters and completes the
first strophe.

Ex.23

Again in this movement the music of the pianoforte is delicately balanced with that of the solo strings. With the most
discreet imaginable arabesques the pianoforte takes over
from the violoncello and not until that instrument and the
violin are safely floated in their higher registers does the
pianoforte delve into its lower, heavier register and become
an intense, compelling partner to them. It leads them from
the lyric towards the dramatic. So that at length the orchestra can begin profoundly to disturb the calm, a disturbance
which, though it lasts only a few bars, clears the way for a
final solo dialogue in which there is now a sense of expectancy. Far from the key (A flat) in which the movement began, the music has been shifted during the recent orchestral
disturbance on to G major. The violoncello emphasizes the
expectancy by rapid repeated notes, all of them the tonic of
the new key; and so without interruption the music goes
over into the finale, the violoncello's repeated notes being
the lever from the dominant on to the new tonic G major.

Third Movement. *Rondo alla Polacca.* The high register of
the violoncello gives an ecstatic quality to the main rondo
theme, very strange when really softly played.

Ex.24

A second, shorter tune is dealt with by the orchestra, a formal affair having the character of a piece of military band
music. On this subject the solo instruments at once get
busy and deflate its pomposity before swinging into a repeat
of the rondo theme. The whole atmosphere of the finale is

vivacious and sparkling. There are telling episodes between the reappearances of the rondo theme. The first of these episodes has more of the usual *panache* of a polonaise than the main theme.

The second episode is a double contrast; a minor tonality (it will be noticed that the first episode, Ex. 25, reaches the major) and a falling as against a climbing phrase.

All of this material goes through transitions and transformations. In the coda there is a final and most expressive change in the rhythmic pattern of the rondo theme; that which originally was a sprightly but not ungentle three-in-a-bar is now a boisterous duple time. Then, as in the first movement, brilliant dialogue for the solo instruments instead of a cadenza. After which the original triple time is resumed and the work comes brilliantly to a close.

PIANO CONCERTO NO. 4, IN G

First Movement. *Allegro moderato.*

That is the first thing to be said about this work and the remark belongs by right to the music. Of all the 'speaking parts' ever given to an instrument of music this is one of the most eloquent; so much so that for an illusory moment one is almost persuaded that music is in fact a language. It is indeed a most speaking likeness; but of what?

It is as well to note that Beethoven's G major Concerto has Ex. 27 for its first subject and that this subject is given out by the solo instrument which, most unexpectedly, starts the work, leaving the orchestra to enter with a *pianissimo* key-change at bar 6, and thence to continue as a properly educated tutti should on its own. To it belongs the next theme, which may be called the first second subject.

When at length the pianoforte solo reappears it has less need to assert its authority than is the case in concertos of normal style where this would be its first appearance. Having at the outset said the most significant thing in the movement it now contents itself with some gentle, questioning figures turning into passages of trills and rapid scales to which the orchestra has nothing to add beyond some quiet supporting chords. This continues with increasing ornamentation and brilliance in the solo part until the other main theme, what may be called the companion second subject, is heard.

In the recapitulation both of these appear, each drawn into the orbit of the first subject in key, but their order reversed; that is, the later companion theme has precedence over the other. But before this happens there has been one of Beethoven's finest, most supple development sections in which variants and derivatives of the main themes appear, matter not quoted here that is of great expressiveness, and, since manifestly it belongs in the first place to the pianoforte, gives the solo music an easy ascendancy. It is indeed this sense of ease that most impresses us in listening to this movement. From the moment that the pianoforte solo asserts its presence when starting the work alone it has won the game. All it need do now is to play it out on its own discreet and witty terms.

Second Movement. *Andante con moto*. The slow movement has a significance altogether out of proportion to its length (it is a mere seventy-two bars of music and looks in the score more like an interlude than a reputable slow movement). The simplicity of its construction, its architecture, would seem to imply, did we not know by experience that things were otherwise, a corresponding simplicity of approach. But the implications are deeper and the music has a powerful poetic content, so powerful indeed as to have caused people to attach tales to it. These, even Liszt's, we may safely ignore. The movement is a dialogue between solo and orchestra. It is the orchestra that begins; at the *molto cantabile* the pianoforte gives the first answer.

Part discussion, part contest, the dialogue continues as it began; the orchestra still uttering its urgent rhythmic phrases, the pianoforte still holding to its personal idiom of broader, smoother phrases. Its idiom eventually tells over that of the orchestra and the solo part breaks out into resolute but gentle ornamental phrases, then enters a short cadenza which is slightly stormy. But this too calms down and the orchestra, now accepting the situation and playing in the pianoforte's idiom, settles at last on to a grave E minor above which the pianoforte utters its final, most lovely phrase.

Third Movement. *Vivace*. It is an astonishing thing about this rondo that after so moving an episode as that just ended it should become so inevitably right. It does this by masterly understatement. It opens, for instance, very softly.

Ex.31

Still softly the orchestra, after the pianoforte has lightly ornamented its version of the above, goes on as follows.

Ex.32

The pianoforte solo, having in the preceding movement taken the bite out of the orchestra, now begins perversely to urge the orchestra to a more lively style and pace; and having embarked upon this new phase it thereupon alters its method and proceeds to this serene clime.

Ex.33

But evidently the fundamental intention is a return to gaiety and it is that spirit which increasingly holds the attention of both solo and orchestra. It is hard to describe in words the subtleties of this change, which must be heard to be appreciated, let alone understood. As the end approaches they can perhaps be described as a descending scale followed by a musical-box tune, that in turn followed by fanfares from the first bar of the movement, as in Ex. 31. And that is all, as far as words can tell.

VIOLIN CONCERTO IN D

First Movement. *Allegro ma non troppo*. Of the many remarkable technical facts about the craftsmanship of this work, one of the most masterly, effective and astonishing is in the first two bars.

In the previous year, 1805, Beethoven, as we have seen, produced an effect of extraordinary poetic power by precisely such direct and simple means when he started the Fourth Pianoforte Concerto with a full, soft chord of G major on the solo instrument, which then proceeded to announce the chief theme of the movement. Here it is four drum taps that open the concerto, followed by a melody played with the smooth, gentle tones of oboes, clarinets and bassoons. In the space of these few bars the dramatic and the lyric potentialities of the concerto-form are immediately displayed; and as regards this particular work the contrast between the dry drum monotone and the warm woodwind melody suggests that this is to be a work of profound poetic insight. The example quoted gives the wind melody and shows how the strings then have their version of the drum taps before completing with elegance and strength what the wind began. Upon which the wind start their next phrase, a rising scale from which will come the next great melody, the second subject.

Ex.35

The chief material of the tutti having now been displayed, the orchestra attains a big climax; then suddenly dies down. The withdrawal of tone at this moment is a dramatic gesture that never loses its astonishing effectiveness. And at once the solo violin is heard for the first time entering upon a steep ascent of majestic octaves (majestic, that is, in the hands of a good player) to the security of a high held G, from which it descends in florid outlines to its lowest G, only to rise again still higher; then the drum taps and the solo violin is ready to its own version of the first subject, Ex. 34. The variants that the violin brings to the two main subjects in its personal versions of them are always of great delicacy; the original outlines are ornamented but never obliterated in extraneous embellishments. This is a display concerto, certainly, but it is no pyrotechnic display. One is rather reminded of a fountain intermittently taken by the wind; its outline swayed and its peak broken into feathers of light, while the next moment it plays in its first perfect symmetry. So it is as the violin solo, which always wins by persuasion, breaks into elegant variations of the great themes the orchestra has put at its disposal; then reaches a cadenza which (again in the hands of a musicianly player) should continue this refined artistry; and so leaves the orchestra free for a pregnant moment to remind us of the noble outline of Ex. 35 before the violin enters for its final word.

Second Movement. *Larghetto*. From two large, melodious main themes and one far-flung ornamental theme subsidiary to them a number of variations are created. There is a dreamlike quality about the music. It is caused primarily by the static harmonic plan; for the music moves through a confined key-space, never going far from its tonic, to which it returns after very short absences with what almost seems to be a feeling of relief. Beethoven makes superb play with this static quality of the slow movement when at the end tonality is shifted brusquely into a new sphere. The first theme is orchestral; muted strings.

From (x) arise certain of the ornamental figures for the solo violin. It is that instrument which announces the second main theme.

The rhythm of the first bar, now set for horns, accompanies the solo instrument when it reaches the ornamental subsidiary theme and connects this theme, which itself is nearly related to previous episodes, with the main theme. Finally there is the brusque change of key already mentioned. This leads to a cadenza which carries the music with pause over into the finale.

Third Movement. *Rondo : allegro.* The violin whose cadenza has formed the link with the preceding movement at once takes hold on the rondo theme.

When the orchestra at last gets this to itself it takes it to a climax and adds its own special robust and gay ending; then quietens in time for the violin to announce the first episodic theme to horn accompaniment.

Of the various themes that alternate with the three appearances of the rondo music, this minor episode is notable.

Ex. 40

After the third appearance of the rondo music the discourse between violin and orchestra increases in pungency and high spirits. There is an enchanting dialogue between oboe and solo violin after the latter's cadenza. The end thereupon comes quickly and the last sound is the opening of the rondo theme which the oboe had just failed to persuade the violin to treat earnestly and which now the violin, in its own time, turns to for the close of the concerto.

PIANO CONCERTO NO. 5, IN E FLAT

'FROM the history of the *Eroica* we know how Beethoven would have appreciated the vulgar title by which this concerto is known in the British Isles. So we will say no more about it but attend to the music,' writes Tovey. Nevertheless, we may be permitted to remark that the vulgarity is still a box-office consideration that will not disappear until concert-giving individuals and organizations risk dispensing with these trappings of imperial grandeur and are content with a plain E flat; which, incidentally, Beethoven has shown in his first chord to be something of immense and quite sufficient grandeur.

First Movement. *Allegro.* The orchestra having by its great E flat chord affirmed the key and proclaimed that the concerto is to be a work of nobility and power, the pianoforte solo breaks the chord into arpeggio figures with a florid, improvisatory clause (as near to a true cadenza as it will get in this concerto). These tactics it repeats as alternative orchestral chords are placed in its way, the last being the dominant which eventually brings the introduction to a close and the music to the tonic and to the first subject.

Ex 41

This opening section (an orchestral tutti of particularly spacious design) displays the themes from which the movement is constructed. They are numerous and all significant as well as clearly differentiated and therefore easily apprehended as they progress in the magnificent array of this exposition. The leading theme of the group of second subjects is this.

Ex.42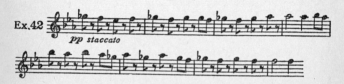

And there is the following transition theme which apart from the uses to which it will be put provides the ear with a clue:

Ex.43

announcing that the exposition is about to cease and the solo instrument to take charge. This it does with a full but fairly soft version of the first subject before breaking into more energetic, forcible and decorative figures. By then the forces are joined and the movement, passing through a second exposition with the solo music now added, reaches its rich development section and eventually the recapitulation of the orchestra's opening period. The expected moment is reached when the orchestra has played the accustomed heralding chord and there is a pause. But the expected cadenza does not materialize. Instead there follows a large coda made up of references to the main first and second subjects (the latter giving rise to intimate conversational exchanges between the solo instrument and the orchestra).

The first subject eventually becomes prominent as the exchanges increase in force and speed. There is a passing mention of the short figure in the second subject group, Ex. 43, before the movement ends in a blaze, not of imperial splendour, but of E flat.

Second Movement. *Adagio un poco mosso*. The tonality changes to B major, a key remote from that of the first movement though it has appeared there very impressively in a passage of ornamentation in the solo part soon after the pianoforte's full entry. There are in this slow movement two main constituents. One is a melody, the other a series of slowly descending curves for the solo pianoforte, interspersed with fragments of the melody repeated by the orchestra. The melody is played at the opening of the movement on strings with the violins muted and the basses *pizzicato*.

Ex.44

At length the solo instrument ceases its ornamentations and comes to rest with a simply adorned version of the melody which is then taken over, again quite simply, clearly and directly, by the orchestra while the pianoforte embellishes this with delicate, tactful comments that keep high above the melody until they follow the orchestra's descending course and stay held on a bass B natural. This note the bassoons in octaves now take from pianoforte and strings, holding it until the octave sinks a semitone and horns take the new bass, a B flat which brings the music within the orbit of the original tonality of the concerto. Upon that the pianoforte starts on an upward course that foreshadows a new idea.

Ex.45

Third Movement. *Allegro*. A sonata-form rondo with three formal appearances of the theme:

the first appearance as exposition, the second beginning the development (which has a fugato formed out of the theme's final bars, as well as three notable entries of the theme in foreign keys). The third starts the recapitulation with the orchestra murmuring the broken, hesitant entries while the pianoforte, which has done it all before and knows every move in that particular game, hovers above in a long octave trill and at last takes the rondo theme once more to itself. The theme is shown above as far as its first half. Of the episodic themes this has special power

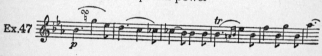

because it appears again in the recapitulation where it is discovered to have the standing of a second subject that somehow has missed appearing in its own key. It is, in fact, the only episodic material of any individuality, the movement being essentially centred upon various elements drawn from the rondo theme. Two years previously Beethoven finished the C minor Symphony. Of that fact we are reminded when studying the music that links the two last movements of this concerto. At the end of the concerto there is another reminder of the Fifth Symphony, the point in that same linking passage where the drum beats out the rhythm of the scherzo. In this concerto Beethoven seems to be recalling his past, when at the close of the final coda the drum beats out the rhythm first heard at the end of the first orchestral tutti in this movement while the solo pianoforte begins a mysterious communing with itself that leads downward to a level from which it gathers itself for the last rising scales that bring in the orchestra and end the work.

6

The Virtuoso Violin Concerto

HUBERT FOSS

INTRODUCTION

THE problem is often debated, and will be until music ceases to be heard – which has had the greater influence, the makers of instruments on the composers, or the composers on the makers of instruments? Similar insoluble questions arise for discussion in other subjects – the relations in war between armament invention and generalship, for example, and even the priority in time of the hen and the egg. In the art of music, we need suffer no shame or vexation because a conclusive answer cannot be given. Instead we can enjoy the fascinating task of following in musical history those avenues that lie between the artists and the mechanicians, the paths which are shadowed alternately but without any formal regularity by the trees of the composer on the one side and those of the inventor-craftsman on the other.

The little section of musical history occupied by the virtuoso violin concerto stretches roughly from Beethoven's masterpiece of 1806 to Brahms's of 1879. It would seem from the very name of the *genre* that in these concertos the instrument was the main source of inspiration to the composer. This is in some sort true; but a sweeping generalization is as unwise here as in all other discussions. For the works themselves, from whatever spring they flow, continue their stream of life to-day only because of the vitality of their purely musical force. Creative ideas in art come from man, not from an inanimate instrument; if we are seeking sources, therefore, we should look rather to the players than to the makers of the violin, and to the conditions during the times in which the players lived.

The violin as a complete and integral instrument entered into the history of music round about the years 1520–30. Long before the close of the sixteenth century the violin had attained under the hands of Andrea Amati and others a perfection of form rare among early instruments. That form remains to this day a model for violin makers, and to all intents and purposes we may say that the form has not essentially changed. There have, of course, been modifications, but they are of so delicate a kind or of such small dimensions as to be of concern only to experts. A new height of perfection was indeed reached by the Stradivari family of craftsmen, but the fundamental form remained, and still remains. In the passage of time the violin has suffered no violent revolutions like those which Boehm, for example, wrought on the flute with his finger-action, or Wagner brought about with the brass instruments.

The art of violin playing, on the other hand, underwent a process of long and lively development all through the eighteenth century. The classic age of the violin begins with Arcangelo Corelli (1653–1713) and Antonio Vivaldi (c.1678–1741), who both as teachers and as composers established the violin on a new, decisive, and steady level of musical importance, equal to that earlier created for the keyboard instruments by the organists and *clavecinistes*. From Italy there rose up many great players and writers, Vitali (c.1675–c.1745), Geminiani (1687–1762), Locatelli (1695–1764), Tartini (1692–1770), Nardini (1722–93), among others. Considerable contributions to the technique and the literature (both academic and creative) of the violin were being made in countries other than Italy – by J. S. Bach himself, for instance, by Stamitz (1717–57), and by Leopold Mozart (1719–87), whose influence reached, through his son, a far wider area than he could have conceived. The Paris School as well, under Leclair (1697–1764) and others, attained a position of great importance, such indeed that the Piedmontese master Viotti (1753–1824) is usually accounted as belonging to Paris. Among his many illustrious pupils were Rode (1774–1830) and Kreutzer (1766–1831), names closely associated in musical history with that of Beethoven.

Ready to hand, then, for Beethoven, when he turned to the violin for expression in his sonatas and quartets, and especially in the monumental concerto, was a proficiency of the highest order in instrumental technique and musical understanding of this long-built-up accomplishment. Beethoven, as we know, made the highest and most original use of it in his Violin Concerto. But Beethoven lived at a time of vast and swift changes; and it is no denigration of his originality to realize that he was the spokesman in music for the changing civilization around him.

The descent from a great peak like the Beethoven Violin Concerto can be rapid, indeed undignified. The fiddlers themselves were quite capable of carrying on the violin concerto without any spark of genius, in a manner which would at that time have contented the public. That the form as a means of musical expression did not suffer this degradation is due largely to the genius of Louis Spohr (1784–1859).

As a composer Spohr had until fairly recent times a faithful and wide following among English choirs and choral societies, for his cantata *The Last Judgement*. The taste for that particular form of Victorian chromaticism has almost died out, and Spohr's works are hardly remembered to-day. Like most composers up to about the middle of the nineteenth century (Beethoven was an exception and a leader into new paths, as usual) Spohr may best be described as 'a provider of music'. He was a celebrated violinist, and to him may be attributed the beginnings of the modern conductor's career; he was the man who substituted the stick for the first violinist's bow. Most of his music was written with a view to immediate performance, as Bach's was. Yet Spohr rose above the mere virtuoso player in his ideals and ambitions. Contemporary accounts show that his style of violin playing was characterized rather by its purity and its classicism than by its chromatic or other more cloying qualities.

Historically Spohr's violin concertos have importance, for they raised the mere display-piece into a high category of art. Musically, though they would not hold a concert-audience's attention to-day, they are full of interest. Spohr's expansive mind sought to extend the expressive range of the concerto; once, we are told, he decided to attract an audience by writing a concerto in the style of an operatic *scena*, a novel idea that had roots in the past (for the concerto sprang from the aria) and far-reaching effects on the future. But for all his extraneous and sometimes irrelevant additions, Spohr had a remarkable sense of formal balance. His works hover a little uncertainly between the old forms and the new Romantic ideas, and are thus well described by Donald Tovey as belonging to a 'pseudo-classical period'.

A more scintillating figure was that of Nicolo Paganini (1784–1840), perhaps the greatest string-virtuoso who ever lived. His astounding career of public success as a player, first in Italy and after 1828 all over Europe, need not be enlarged on here; he became a kind of legendary figure of demoniac power in music, and exercised an astonishing influence far beyond the adoring public – on composers* and pianists as well as on violinists; an influence the more to be wondered at since he refused to allow most of his works to be printed during his playing career, for obvious commercial reasons. His *Twenty-four Caprices*†, however, appeared and were much taken up; two posthumous concertos are also still played. As a composer Paganini had two outstanding gifts – a knack of writing memorable (if not very distinguished) tunes, like the 'second subject' of the E flat Concerto and the opening subject of the *Rondo à la clochette* in the B minor; and a positive genius for exploiting the violin to its utmost technical limits of endurance. It is too easy to dismiss his fantastic ornamentations as mere fireworks; rather, the violin parts of his works have a kind of creative virtuosity, by which finger-tricks take on an artistic value of their own.

Of virtuoso violin concertos taken as a whole it is impossible to generalize in more than the vaguest terms, for the point in which they are most closely akin is precisely the individuality of each specimen. Each is a law unto itself,

* e.g. with the tune of the A minor Caprice which Brahms and Rachmaninov used for variations.

† Several of which were transcribed for piano solo by Schumann and Liszt.

developing its own form from its spiritual and technical ideas. Romantic in spirit and rhapsodic in style, the virtuoso violin concerto nevertheless retains a genuine place among other concertos in musical history, and if often one finds that this or that example is not really big in conception, those examples that survive are of proper concerto dimensions. It is to be expected that the soloist should have the dominating interest, but seldom does this domination become an ill-based tyranny, and the cadenza makes itself more and more into an integral part of the form of the whole movement or work.

The composers of the three concertos briefly analysed below differed almost as much as their works do. Henri Vieuxtemps (1820–81) was, in fact, a Belgian, though having studied with de Bériot, who was a pupil of Viotti, he is usually classed as of the Paris School. There was music in his home, for his father was an instrument-maker and piano-tuner; his career began when he was a prodigy of 7, and for many years he toured incessantly as a soloist, though occupying himself a great deal with composition. His A minor concerto was first given in Paris in 1858. Also associated by long years with Paris, Édouard Lalo (1823–92) was born in Lille and came of Spanish blood. He was a professional, but not a virtuoso string-player, especially of viola in chamber music. Neglect of his early works made him an intermittent composer until with his violin concerto of 1874 and *Symphonie Espagnole* of 1875 (both played first by the great Sarasate) he scored a wide and lasting success. By then he had attained middle age. His stage works include the opera *Le Roi d'Ys* and the ballet *Namouna*. Among numerous other works one observes a liking for the picturesque, in his *Rhapsodie Norvégienne* and *Concerto Russe* for 'cello.

Max Bruch (1838–1920) on the other hand was born in Cologne and except for three years with the Liverpool Philharmonic Society was associated all his life with Germany; moreover he was known principally for his choral music and choir direction, then as a conductor, and later as professor of composition at the Berlin *Hochschule*, where a number of distinguished pupils passed through his hands. Of his three violin concertos, the first in G minor is the most frequently played.

VIEUXTEMPS: VIOLIN CONCERTO NO. 5
IN A MINOR

THE work consists of one movement only: *Allegro non troppo – Adagio – Allegro con fuoco*. The structure of it is as personal as its style and musical content. The thematic ideas are in the main short, simple, and direct in their appeal; nor are either their variants or developments complicated, with the result that the hearer feels the work as a well-designed emotional outpouring. The opening tutti states a plain idea:

and leads it to a climax, after which an extension of it appears in the bass:

This in turn leads to a short forceful phrase, which completes the main thematic material.

The violin enters with some meditative arpeggios, and proceeds to make use of and to play with the material stated. After much passage-work, the soloist states the second subject complete:

The development may be said to begin with the orchestral treatment (soloist decorating) of parts of Ex. 4 and to consist of inventive commentary by both parties on the subjects in hand. There is a short central tutti, after which the violin leads us on to a not exact restatement of Ex. 4, in G major. Some more development brings us to the cadenza; the composer prints two versions, of which the first is perhaps more showy but the second more concerned with the central design of the work. The short adagio section following is as effective as it is unexpected. Its opening bars are thematically akin to Ex. 1 and 2, and its central matter a variant and extension of Ex. 4. After a climax of some tensity, an effective quick coda closes the concerto.

MAX BRUCH: VIOLIN CONCERTO NO. I
IN G MINOR

In formal layout, the Bruch concerto is as individual as the Vieuxtemps. It is ostensibly broken into three movements. The first, *Allegro moderato*, however, is not complete in itself, but is a kind of large-scale, ruminating prelude to what is to come, comparable in many ways to the *Vorspiel* of a Romantic opera. Like many operatic preludes, it has a structural significance, to be discovered when the rest of the music is heard. The linked slow movement comes to a full close; the finale is self-contained in its own pattern.

A short and quiet introduction on the wood-wind

Ex.5

acts as a motto for the prelude. The soloist makes his appearance with two assertive recitatives. The rhythm in the bass

Ex.6

is important in the design. The first main subject has some grandeur

A second more romantic subject completes the material

The discussion is close and fairly equally divided, and partly for this reason no disappointment is felt by the absence of a formal *reprise*. The themes seem to coalesce and melt into the violin's final cadenza. The orchestra then breaks out in E flat (*allegro moderato*), and so leads into the *adagio*, which is a full sonata-form movement. The peaceful but intense main subject

has an important continuing phrase, and there is a separate 'second subject' which I do not quote, first to be heard in the bass under the soloist's passage-work. An interesting point is the version in G flat major; the later recapitulation is not precise, but the effective coda is allusive. An energetic orchestral introduction leads from E flat to G major, which the solo violin establishes with a strong *bravura* main theme

A good deal is made of this in various guises; then after a bridge subject comes the broad second main theme

The development is clear to follow; there is a tutti climax, before an important coda, again allusive.

LALO: 'SYMPHONIE ESPAGNOLE'
FOR VIOLIN AND ORCHESTRA

H. C. COLLES has rightly said (*Oxford History of Music*, Vol. VII) that Lalo's work combines 'the characteristics of the symphony, the concerto, and the suite'. It is a piece of great charm and brilliance, perhaps showing traces of the influence of Schumann, for whose music Lalo had a special affection, and yet very personal. Orchestrally, it could hardly be less like Schumann, for it is delicately scored by a master of deftly sketched-in touches, and as luminous as a sunny water-colour. To the reading eye, indeed, the score is somewhat unrevealing, for the *Symphonie Espagnole* is one of the none-too-common works that are far more effective in performance than in study; its specially Spanish flavour eludes analysis – indeed the whole does to such an extent that to quote mere themes seems unsatisfactory, since nothing less than the entire work gives their proper meaning.

First Movement. *Allegro non troppo*. A fragmentary fifth from Ex. 12 starts the music on its course, with a kind of prophetic phrase on the solo violin. After some orchestral play, the soloist settles down to the main theme

which has an important companion section. After some

charming music, with a new idea hinted at, there comes the second subject, of which I quote but one phrase

The rest of the movement only Lalo and his players can describe, though it may be mentioned that the recapitulation is both regular and imaginative.

Second Movement. *Scherzando : Allegro.* Again words seem to blow away the thistledown qualities of the music; the principal theme can be cited

but not the figurations. We find here Lalo's power of quickly changing his emotions from grave to gay; three bars of touching *poco lento* are followed by tempo primo, in several alternations. The movement dies away in a breath.

Third Movement. *Intermezzo : Allegretto non troppo.* This is more direct in its use of Spanish idioms. Thus a vigorous figure of 3+2 on the strings gives the orchestra some discussion, until the soloist solves the argument with a tune

This allows itself to become in due course a much gayer affair in the key of D major and leads us on a delightful and wayward path to a return of Ex. 15.

Fourth Movement. *Andante.* The music opens solemnly on the lower wind and strings, to preface the violin's entry with another characteristically Spanish melody

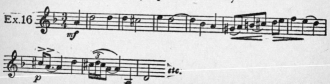

When after adventures it reappears, it has a drum beating below it. Again, the movement fades away as we hear it.

Fifth Movement. *Rondo : Allegro* is lively in both ideas and construction. The orchestra opens with a little figure

which is worked up to some importance: and then comes the soloist with a tune of infectious laughter

These two tunes make the main building of the rondo; but around it flutter all kinds of butterfly ideas that escape the hunter's but not the listener's net, including a variant, *poco piu lento* and very touching, in A major; after which the players fly away to bring this inimitable concerto to a sparkling finish.

7

Felix Mendelssohn (1809–1847)

JOHN WATERHOUSE

INTRODUCTION

MORE than twenty years separate Mendelssohn's G Minor Pianoforte Concerto (1831) from Beethoven's *Emperor* (1809). A great many concertos were composed, played and printed during that period, but not one of them holds a place in the 'standard repertory' of to-day. On the whole this is not surprising. There are, it is true, concertos of the 'teens and twenties' – piano concertos, for instance, by Hummel, Moscheles, Field, even 'Glorious John' Cramer – which are quite good enough to make a refreshing occasional change from our present dismally narrow routine. Yet although those were wonderful years for music in general, the concerto in particular quite undeniably struck a bad patch.

This was not only because the splash virtuosity of the second and third generations of pianist-composers, and the fireworks of fiddlers emulating the demoniac showmanship of Paganini, often made of the concerto a mere ephemeral showpiece with an also-ran accompanying orchestra. Some essential dramatic secret of the great first-movement style of Mozart seemed to have been lost, so that few even of the best of those post-classical concertos can give abiding satisfaction as formal wholes.

The problem relates in the first place to the orchestra's opening exposition, tutti or ritornello. It need not be examined in detail here, for it is repeatedly discussed in the writings of Tovey: see especially his analysis of Beethoven's C Minor Concerto. Tovey maintained that it was this work which became the dangerous model for those many later concertos (not Beethoven's own) wherein the first tutti is treated as though it were an ordinary symphony exposition, with the second subject already planted in the contrasted key. Certainly, by 1831, the 'dramatic expectancy' characteristic of Mozart's openings had largely given place to mere waiting – often impatient waiting – for the entry of the soloist. There are some notable exceptions among those forgotten concertos. But in most cases the orchestral opening sounds as though it had been hastily and mechanically scored after the composition of the soloist-orchestra exposition, and stuck on in front as a matter of routine.

Mendelssohn scrapped this orchestral preamble altogether, and his three published concertos are all 'single exposition' works, with soloist and orchestra sharing the business from the beginning. It is not true that he 'killed the classical concerto'. The classical concerto was just about dead already, and he either did not choose or did not know how to revive it.

His three published concertos (he wrote many more in early days, including two for two pianos) may be placed in order of merit without much fear of contradiction: the Violin Concerto in E minor, 1844; the Piano Concerto in G minor, 1831; the Piano Concerto in D minor (which the editor has not asked me to write about), 1837. It may seem a little odd that the last should be first, in face of the common generalization that Mendelssohn's genius faded as he grew older. Yet that is not really a sound generalization: for there can be no doubt that a 'second wind' of inspiration, a renewal of the fresh genius of his early days, came to Mendelssohn in the last phase of his short life, worn out though his body and nerves were by the intervening years of hectic overwork. Also, the Violin Concerto was the product of long and loving care; whereas the G minor for Piano (as he declared in a letter to his father) was 'a thing quickly thrown off.'

PIANO CONCERTO NO. I IN G MINOR, OP. 25

MENDELSSOHN played this concerto at Munich on 17 October 1831. He was 22, and en route from Italy to

Paris. His wealthy parents, loving and loved but disastrously dominant, had packed him off on a long, leisurely and carefully planned grand tour, because they were determined he should occupy some big and active public position in European music, and wanted him to choose the most suitable field of operations. It was the prelude to the years of overwork and sagging vitality. Already he was hopelessly in the toils, and saddled with a morbidly developed sense of his duty to his kind parents and the polite public. Still, he was thoroughly enjoying himself, and this light-shod concerto is a product of his enjoyment.

First Movement. *Molto Allegro con fuoco. Molto Allegro* indeed, and plenty of *fuoco*. Full orchestra provides six and three-quarter bars of concentrated 'dramatic expectancy', crescendo *pp* to *ff*, and the piano makes a *bravura* entry with a clattering theme in double octaves:

Ex.1

Incited by strings and drums, it announces the main theme of the first subject

Ex.2

which the orchestra soon seizes for a transition passage, while the piano protests at its temporary subjugation with leonine roars in the bass.

It quickly breaks free again and begins the second subject in the relative major over a tapping dominant. This does not sound very interesting

Ex.3

It tries the minor instead, hesitates (a unique occasion in this movement) and moves up into D flat major, which richer key encourages it to become more freely melodious.

There is no grand classical tutti to herald the development section. That also has been scrapped, and development (mainly of Ex. 3) is under way before we notice it. A recurrence of the initial 'dramatic expectancy', however, makes certain the arrival of a recapitulation – one of the shortest on record. Orchestra has just time to mention Ex. 2, piano Ex. 3 (with rude threats of Ex. 1 from orchestra) when a coda begins, on lines very similar to those of the development; and soon the orchestra seems to promise a conclusion and a pause to breathe. But instead, the rhythm of what might have been the final bars of the movement is taken up by a brisk tucket of horns and trumpets, on B natural

Ex.4

This quietens down, and the piano meditatively indicates B major as the dominant of E.

Here, at once, is the Second Movement. *Andante*. Trim and effective though it was, there was nothing particularly remarkable about the orchestration of that first movement. The second has a lovely little score. Oboes, clarinets, trumpets and drums are silent throughout, so also second bassoon and second horn. Violins do not enter until near the end, where they merely shimmer in four parts; and flutes have very little to do. First 'cellos (the 'cellos are divided) are the orchestra's principal singers, with violas usually below them. The fabric is most delicately woven.

The melody itself

Ex.5

and its harmonies, may seem to-day just a little too sweetly restful. Here might be one of the gentler *Songs without Words*, of which Mendelssohn was then assembling his first set. The manner came rather too easily to him in his later years, and was readily aped by our Victorian composers and hymn-tuners. But when this concerto was written there was fresh-ness in it, and with willing ears we may still succumb.

Third Movement. *Presto : Molto Allegro e vivace.* Again there is no pause. Horns and trumpets sound once more their tucket, Ex. 4, now on E. If you are fond of 'motto themes' you are at liberty to call this an early and embryonic example.

With cadencing to A minor, and a mood of much agita-tion, it sounds as though some formidable drama were afoot. But the way is quickly prepared for the soloist to enter brightly in G major. He whisks us a number of diminished-seventh arpeggios (there are hordes of chords of the dimin-ished seventh in this concerto) and when the movement proper begins it is pure fun, if only surface fun (for the under-lying harmonic motion is decidedly sluggish).

Ex.6

The music scurries on, without bothering to develop any real formal scheme; but near the end there are unexpected reappearances of Ex. 1 (orchestra) and Ex. 3 (piano) from the first movement. This 'cyclic' device is a simple and in-significant affair as compared with the elaborate and im-pressive thematic organization of Mendelssohn's remarkable string quartet in A (1827) – the most 'cyclic' work before César Franck. But, like the tucket of horns and trumpets, it helps to bind together this dashingly original little concerto; which is not one of Mendelssohn's greater works, but which most brightly deserves its recent renewal of popularity.

VIOLIN CONCERTO IN E MINOR, OP. 64

THIS lovely and most worthily popular concerto was very far indeed from being 'a thing quickly thrown off'. How far, may be gathered from Mendelssohn's correspondence with the friend for whom it was written, the violinist, Ferdinand

David. A translated extract from one of these letters may be found on pp. 339–40 of J. Selden Goth's admirable selection (Paul Elek, 1946). Mendelssohn had completed the score on 16 September 1844, at Frankfurt. But still, three months later, he was desperately anxious to discuss all manner of tiny details before committing it irrevocably to the hands of Breitkopf and Härtel, the publishers. 'Thank God that the fellow is through with his concerto!' you will say. 'Excuse my bothering you, but what can I do? . . ' The first performance took place at the Leipzig Gewandhaus on 13th March, with David as soloist and the Danish composer Niels W. Gade conducting.

First Movement. *Allegro molto appassionato.* The form of this movement, indeed, of the whole concerto, is crystal-clear. Multitudinous performances have draped it with so many analytical programme-notes that one could not hope to say anything fresh about it. Fortunately, the work itself stays fresh: more so, some may feel, than many another hackneyed masterpiece of more formidable mien.

Again there is no opening orchestral exposition: not even any 'dramatic expectancy'. Just a bar-and-a-half of nicely scored 'till ready', with *pizzicato* bass and quiet drum-taps; and the soloist sings aloft the first subject, barely alighting on the treble stave in the course of twenty bars and more:

Ex.7

There follows a transition theme:

Ex.8

And then comes the second subject:

Ex.9

The scoring of the second subject is of singular beauty and originality, with clarinets above flutes, and the soloist providing a pedal-bass by sustaining his open G string – until he takes over the subject and second clarinet catches the G, being mercifully allowed to break it into repeated notes before his breath runs out.

Unlike the development section in the first piano concerto, this one does not take us unawares. It is heralded by a series of orchestral trillings. It is mainly concerned with the transition-theme and with the opening figure of the first subject. At the end of it comes this concerto's most wholly original feature: a cadenza, far-strayed from its old classical perch of a six-four chord in the coda.

Not nearly so many composers have followed Mendelssohn here as in his rejection of the opening tutti. There is really no right nor wrong to the matter. Ever since cadenza-points were deprived of their original function, as safety-valves for extemporization (ostensible, at least) on the part of the soloist, they have been dubious customers. This, at least, is a very beautiful cadenza: a brief, essentially violinistic meditation with a genuine *extempore* air about it. The high ascents from dotted crotchets, in its middle part, are the only hints of relationship to the main thematic material of the movement (compare, e.g. bars 213 and 217). It is as though the soloist were on the point of adding some 'development' of his own, but changed his mind.

Second Movement. *Andante.* The famous 'link'

which joins the second to the first movement is very different from the corresponding feature in the G minor piano concerto. That tucket of horns and trumpets was abruptly dramatic, preventing all danger of intervenient applause.

Also, the passage served to effect transition to an alien key: from G minor to E major. Here, C major is a near neighbour of E minor, but a simple yet mysterious sequence of harmonies makes it sound like a radiant stranger; and a single, quiet bassoon carrying on the fifth (B) of a loud final chord could hardly hope to hush applause. Mendelssohn, indeed, was here running a risk, in an age when the hearty practice of encoring separate movements had hardly begun to give place to our modern quasi-religious attitude towards symphonies and concertos.

The movement is in ABA form, with the *reprise* shortened, varied and enriched. Section A is reposeful:

Ex. 11

Section B is agitated:

Ex. 12

These two moods are very common in Mendelssohn's later music. But here the one is not saccharine, nor the other merely febrile.

Third Movement. *Allegretto non troppo : Allegro molto vivace.* The soloist, supported by strings only, prefaces the Finale with a wistful little meditation of fourteen bars. Heard in isolation, it might seem no more than a pretty thing of small account. Set in its context, it is of searching eloquence – perhaps the most magical passage in the whole concerto. The main movement has all the ebullience of the finale in the G minor piano concerto, while being at once far more shapely and far more variously inventive. The principal subject:

Ex. 13

dancing in gay company of flutes and oboes, joyously reconquers the authentic fairyland of Mendelssohn's earlier years.

c–6

8

Frederick Chopin (1810–1849)

GEORGE DANNATT

INTRODUCTION

FREDERICK CHOPIN, the son of a French father and a
Polish mother, was born near Warsaw in February, 1810, and
died an emigré in Paris at the early age of thirty-nine, a
traditionally French yet immortally Polish personality.
His stature as a composer for the pianoforte, as an experi-
menter in the comparatively small forms to which, after the
age of twenty, he decided to restrict himself, and as an harmonic innovator, has increased with the years. From our
point of vantage a century later we can see that he was in
the forefront of his contemporaries for the boldness of his
harmonic thought, even though these composers temporarily
captured the field with their hyperbolic symphonic poems
and intoxicating music-dramas.

The two pianoforte concertos (No. 2 in F minor, Op.
21–1829, and the later composed but earlier numbered
E minor, Op. 11–1830) together with the four other large
scale works for piano and orchestra*, were a necessary stage
in Chopin's development, both as a creative artist and as
a performing musician with his mark to make. The concertos do not contribute to the form as such, but rather
represent an uneasy effort to confine a new and revolutionary technique within the limits of the classical mould.
Chopin was not happy in attempting large-scale compositions, or in their orchestration. These six works were all
written during his first, evolutionary, period – 1822–31 –
and thereafter (with the exception of the *Allegro de Concert*,
Op. 46, never scored) he made no effort to unite piano

---

* The Op. 2 Variations (1827), Op. 13 Fantasia (1828), Op. 14 'Krak-
owiak' Concert Rondo (1828) and Op. 22 Grand Polonaise (1830-1).

and orchestra again. From that time the piano as a solo instrument was his chosen medium, and his decision to keep to it was absolutely justified.

Rearrangement of another artist's work is, like everything else, a question of taste. Attempts have been made to cut and patch, to re-orchestrate, and to 'arrange' Chopin's pianoforte writing to suit the new orchestrations – notably by Carl Tausig of the E minor concerto and Carl Klindworth of the F minor concerto. Their arrangements do not warrant the liberties taken, particularly those of Tausig: the very nature of Chopin's pianoforte writing may defy adequate orchestration of the accompaniments. Possibly a sufficiently interested contemporary composer talented in orchestration could make a more acceptable attempt than did either of the above in the late nineteenth century.

Note: All references are to the edition by Edouard Ganche (O.U.P.).

PIANO CONCERTO IN F MINOR

First Movement. *Maestoso*. The introductory ritornello announces the first subject

Ex. 1

after thirty-seven bars, the second subject is introduced on the wood-wind, in the relative major.

Ex. 2

In the concert hall this ritornello is frequently and unjustifiably shortened by playing the first thirty-seven bars and then proceeding to the sixth bar (flutes and violins) before the piano entry, so that the second subject is not heard until the piano gives it in the decorated form quoted in Ex. 2. The piano enters for the first time fortissimo in unison semiquavers and makes a vigorous downward plunge, after which the opening theme occurs again, practically note for note. By now the piano has taken charge, as it inevitably does in every movement; it leads into Ex.2 (con anima – bar 125) and almost immediately decorates this second subject with Ex. 3, in C minor.

Ex.3

Two further orchestral tuttis (commencing at bars 181 and 257) show the influence of Beethoven reflected through the limited vision of Hummel, and for this reason remain undramatic and far too cadential. Contained between these tuttis there is little true development but a great deal of brilliant passage work for the piano which pays scant attention to mild reminders by the wood-wind of Ex. 1. At the close of the second tutti the piano takes over again with the first subject in its original key then, somewhat surprisingly, flowers out into the second subject, Ex. 2, in the relative major. Ex. 3 (this time in F minor) heralds the brilliant final climax. The orchestra closes the movement with a short tutti which may consist of only the last four bars instead of the original twelve if the same hand that dealt with the opening has been at work. There is no coda to the movement and a cadenza written by Richard Burmeister is likely to be inserted, to which the concert programme will, in all probability, make no reference.

Second Movement. *Larghetto.* Both Schumann and Liszt greatly admired this romantic movement. Before the entry of the piano there is a slender five-bar orchestral introduction which ends with a firm close in A flat, so that Chopin is able, unadventurously, to employ the identical passage to conclude the movement. The weakness of Chopin's scoring is particularly evident here; more often than not the string accompaniment muddies the texture and, although some authorities have praised the central passage in which the piano is accompanied by *tremolo* strings and double-bass *pizzicati*, in fact the use of the *tremolo* for any length of time (in this case over twenty-eight bars) is an effect of which the ear rapidly tires; this is especially the case since throughout the whole of this long *tremolo* the piano is in bare octaves. It is of interest that Chopin wrote an alternative bass to the piano part for these twenty-eight bars to be used when there was no orchestral accompaniment.

To return to the commencement: the piano enters at bar seven with a highly ornamented main theme (bars 7 to 10):

then flows on to a contrasted and less elaborate passage in octaves:

Ex. 4 then occurs in an even more decorated form (bars 26 to 29) and then leads into a dramatic recitative in A flat minor with the *tremolo* accompaniment already mentioned. Material from Exs. 4 and 5 freshly ornamented and now in the major brings the movement to its five-bar orchestral conclusion.

This movement bears a close relationship to the Chopin Nocturne, for it consists of an extended melody played and ornamented by the right hand over a rocking quaver accompaniment in the left; this melody is essentially vocal, Chopin's debt to the Italian opera being enormous, although possibly not so much to those operas of his friend Bellini as has been generally accepted.

Third Movement. *Allegro Vivace*. From the slow movement with its nocturnal type of melody we pass to the third, a Hummel-like rondo, which has something in common with another form perfected by Chopin – the mazurka. Indeed the first four bars might well have been taken bodily from one of these:

The second subject:

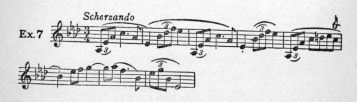

is given out by the piano in octaves to an effective accompaniment on the strings, *col legno*.

The orchestral utterances in this movement tend to create a more unified whole, although for the contemporary ear they are too frequently in octaves or sixths. A passage for solo horn marked 'cor de signal' proclaims the key of F major and the final climax, or rather the climaxes which constitute an effective ending to a straightforward and graceful movement.

PIANO CONCERTO IN E MINOR

THE earlier work possesses a freshness and buoyant charm not shared by the E minor concerto, which appears to have been written with more deliberate effort, is considerably less inspired, and is over-long.

First Movement. *Allegro maestoso risoluto*. The opening ritornello of the E minor is sprawling compared with that of the F minor, for it is twice as long (138 bars) and underlines the lack of key-contrast which is to be evident throughout. The first subject in E minor

continues with variants and imitative themes for sixty bars, and is then followed by the second subject in the *tonic* major:

When eventually the piano does enter with Ex. 8 in E minor octaves the listener's relief is tempered with a feeling of anti-climax. In the concert hall this ritornello is generally drastically curtailed (even when the original orchestration is used) in which case, as with the F minor, the orchestra will not give the second subject, but will proceed from the end of the first sixty bars to a few bars of first subject material which wind up the first tutti. After decorating the first subject, the piano passes by way of some attractive broken-chord semiquaver passages (marked *tranquillo* and *con fuoco*) to a slightly varied form of Ex. 9, and in E major. The tonic is not relieved until the end of the next tutti, when Ex. 8 occurs on the piano in C major over a simple repeated-chord bass. In the development, which commences modulating from his point, there is a deal of brilliant

passage work for the soloist and very little else, the use from
time to time of part of Ex. 8 as a bass being obvious and
unconvincing. Chopin does little with the several promising
themes which he has introduced.

Further brilliant scale and broken-chord passages lead
to the reappearance of the second subject in G major,
which provides something of a contrast. Forty-eight bars
later the Coda (possessing an effective bass, the trill of
which Tausig considered so awkward, that he transferred
it to the cellos and double-basses) leads to the final cadential
group, which unexpectedly resolves into C major. The
orchestral tutti continues in this key for eight bars, then
concludes the movement in E minor.

Second Movement. *Larghetto*. Labelled a Romance, this
is in E major. A brief orchestral introduction on muted
strings leads to the main theme,

followed immediately by the secondary theme in B major.

Ex. 10 returns, this time highly ornamented (commencing
at bar 54). After modulatory interludes in G sharp minor the
second theme reappears decorated with a surfeit of rich
ornamentation, and in that key. The piano then fades out
in an eight times repeated sequential figure, followed by
three bars of broken chords at the top of the keyboard; the
orchestra sketches in a bar and then takes over Ex. 10 until
the end of the movement; the piano meanwhile becomes
reanimated and now rattles about above the orchestra
from the same point, *legatissimo* and *leggierissimo* and,
inevitably, *rallentando* and **smorzando**. The rather cloying
atmosphere of the movement as a whole is perhaps best

described by the composer himself: 'It is intended to convey the impression which one receives when the eye rests on a beloved landscape that calls up in one's soul beautiful memories – for instance, on a fine, moonlight, spring night.'

Third Movement. *Vivace*. It was imperative that something more stimulating should succeed the languorous slow movement, and Chopin has provided another loosely-knit but reasonably satisfying Rondo. Niecks found the details charming, elegant, and brilliant so that 'one again and again forgets their shortcomings as wholes.'

Two simple motifs given out by the orchestra are decorated by the piano to form the first subject:

Both piano and orchestra (the latter in two longish tuttis) make use of this material until the piano presents the more expressive second subject in A major octaves, repeating it immediately in B minor and then again in F:

The principal theme, Ex. 12, reappears in E flat major and remains there, puckishly a semitone flat, for eight bars, and is then pulled back to E major.

After brilliant passage work in the development (the second subject only is repeated in its entirety) the music leads to a lengthy cadential group and a final twenty-two bars of scales and arpeggi for both hands on the chord of E, and a prompt short close by the orchestra.

9

Robert Schumann (1810–1856)

JOAN CHISSELL

INTRODUCTION

SCHUMANN applied the name 'concerto' to only three works in his large output – the Piano Concerto (Op. 54), the Cello Concerto (Op. 129), and the Violin Concerto, published posthumously. For his four slighter essays in music for solo instrument (or instruments) and orchestra he preferred such titles as *Concertstück* and *Phantasie*, at once placing them beyond the scope of this book. It would be wrong to claim that he had any outstanding interest in concerto form *per se*; instead, his three examples of it must be fitted into the picture of his output as a whole, since both in design and quality they are striking reflections of his general musical state of mind at each particular period.

As a wayward, impulsive and highly susceptible young man without adequate technical grounding, he found the miniature the perfect receptacle for his passing whims, fancies, or stronger gusts of feeling – at first for his own and Clara's instrument, the piano, and later in the form of the song. The desire to spread his wings did not come till 1839 when he heard the first Leipzig performance of Schubert's C major symphony, which he himself had unearthed in Vienna. Friendship with Mendelssohn, moreover, opened his eyes to some of his own limitations as a craftsman, and after his marriage in 1840, bringing with it emotional assuagement and a hitherto unknown tranquillity of mind, he settled down for the first time to explore the possibilities of extended, orchestral thinking. Whereas a lavish use of new ideas rather than development of old ones had sufficed in youth, economy of material now became his obsession. In fact, economy – by means of thematic metamorphosis and inter-quotation – is the outstanding feature of the principal products of 1841, the 'Spring' and D minor symphonies and the first movement of a work which in 1845 emerged (with two additional movements) as the Piano Concerto first introduced by Clara at a Gewandhaus concert in Leipzig on New Year's Day 1846. Its popularity is deserved, for without any sacrifice of that invaluable, youthful gift of spontaneity, imagination is here disciplined by a mind at the height of its powers.

After several ominous nervous breakdowns, Schumann's move from Dresden to Düsseldorf in 1850 induced a fresh outburst of creative energy. But though the 'Rhenish' Symphony recaptures much of his early romantic ardour through its extra-musical inspiration, the Cello Concerto, like most other works of this year, betrays that illness and an increasing hankering for academic respectability were beginning to take their toll. Having already exhausted the possibilities of thematic metamorphosis, the composer strives after unity in this work by compressing his three movements into one. It was Joachim's playing at the Düsseldorf festival of 1853 which kindled the dying embers into one further little wisp of smoke, if not flame, in the Violin Concerto later the same year. But for the mistaken zeal of Joachim's great-niece, Jelly d'Aranyi, who performed and published the work in 1937, it would have remained undisturbed in the Prussian State Library in Berlin, in accordance with Clara Schumann's wishes. Its construction is stilted and repetitive, and its content is savourless – save for that wonderful opening theme of the slow movement, which, haunting Schumann in the first onset of madness, led him to believe that it was some new inspiration sent him by the angels.

PIANO CONCERTO IN A MINOR - MAJOR

AGAIN here, as in some of the songs and chamber works, Schumann betrays that he was a pianist-composer by allowing the piano to bear the main brunt of the expression. But though, in true romantic fashion, the soloist enjoys complete emancipation from the orchestra, there is no empty display of pyrotechnics – virtuosity is always subservient to poetic feeling. The orchestra is used with what for Schumann is uncommon delicacy and transparency, suggesting no grudge on its part for having lost its old position of supremacy, but only a desire for the most amicable co-operation.

First Movement. *Allegro affettuoso*. The piano's brusque opening call to attention is challenging enough, but from the unobtrusive way in which wood-wind and horns introduce the following nostalgically plaintive little eight-bar theme in A minor, few listeners would guess that it was to beget the greater part of the first movement, as well as much of the finale:

Piano and strings co-operate in its lyrical continuation, from which one fragment proves particularly fruitful:

but after veering in conventional manner towards the relative major key, Schumann gives the first proof of reaction from youthful prodigality by offering not a new second subject but a glowing C major transposition of his formerly plaintive main theme:

Ex.3

A similar procedure is found in the first movement of the D minor symphony of the same year; the result in both cases is a unity uncommon in his larger canvases. Solo wood-wind instruments now review this first-cum-second subject, with decorative comments from the piano, before a sturdy orchestral tutti in C (made from Ex. 2) rounds off the exposition.

Development in the manipulative classical sense would have ill-become material at once so lyrical, so gracious and so tender, so instead the composer resorts to treatment more resembling variation, first allowing the main theme to serve as an excuse for piano and clarinet to woo each other in a ruminative A flat major, reached not by modulation but by a typically Schumannesque 'side-slipping' short-cut. This idyll is rudely interrupted by a recall of the opening challenge to attention, with both piano and orchestra in high dudgeon, before the piano embarks on a more stormy variation of the main theme. Though at this point, Schumann (plainly at a loss to know what to do with his orchestra) falls back on doubling, the scoring nevertheless retains the luminosity which distinguishes this work from the great majority of his orchestral efforts, chiefly achieved by allowing individual wood-wind instruments long flights of freedom from the family group. The recapitulation is regular till an *accelerando* (with a thrilling harmonic surprise of a plunge from A major into B flat) leads to the composer's own poetic cadenza, no doubt supplied as a safeguard against the exhibitionist tendencies of many virtuosi, then, as now; after which comes a coda in which he resists the strong temptation of a new tune and unites all forces in one further transformation of the leading theme into a brisk and square 2/4.

Second Movement. *Intermezzo: Andantino grazioso.* When Clara Schumann tried through the first movement as a self-contained Phantasie in A minor at a Gewandhaus rehearsal during the summer of 1841, she expressed particular delight at the skilful interweaving of piano and orchestra: 'it is impossible to think of one without the other', she wrote. This observation would have been even more apt of the brief slow movement, which, like the finale, Schumann did not add till four years later, by which time his handling of an orchestra had become more assured. The gentle melancholy of A minor is thrown aside for an unclouded F major, and in music which perhaps reveals the composer's 'delight in simple things' more eloquently than any other work from his pen, piano and orchestra converse with the naïvety and spring-like delight of young lovers newly awakened to love. The movement is cast in simple ternary form, contrast from the shy, short-breathed phrases of the opening and closing sections being afforded by the intervening radiantly lyrical cello theme in C major. Its reinforcement by violins, an octave higher, at the climax is an instance of the composer's addiction to doubling proving a stroke of genius.

Scarcely less masterly is the last-minute orchestral recall of that ever-fertile theme from the opening *allegro*, Ex. 1, to link slow movement with finale, and by allowing the same theme to generate the animated first subject of his A major finale, *Allegro vivace*, Schumann conclusively bridges the gap between 1841 and 1845:

It is in this virile finale, again in sonata form, that agile fingers come into their own, though even here the rippling quavers and bold arpeggios are part of the essential substance of the music and not just showy excrescences. The most provocative feature of the movement is undoubtedly the second subject – one of Schumann's most ingenious rhythmic experiments:

But it is ingenuity better appreciated on paper or by watching the conductor's down-beat cutting through silence (or a tie) in alternate bars than with the ear alone, which, after momentary bewilderment, adjusts itself by transforming the passage into simple

The fugato treatment of the first subject at the outset of the development reveals that the composer's determined contrapuntal exercises earlier in the year were not in vain, though the academic manner is quickly abandoned in the joy of a new tune

which imaginative scoring throws up in sparkling new light with every repetition. The artful dodge of recapitulating the first subject in the sub-dominant key of D enables the second to be reached in its rightful A major by purely mechanical transposition instead of fresh creative effort, but such is the impulse of the music that the listener is swept along to the end willy-nilly, conscious only of a new, fleet quaver melody from the piano and yet another rhythmic transformation of the work's apparently inexhaustible leading-theme in the brilliant coda.

CELLO CONCERTO IN A MINOR

FIRST Movement. *Nicht zu schnell*. The first subject, announced by cello after three modest chords from the orchestra declare the key to be A minor, gives promise of ardent romantic adventure in its broad, soaring sweep

Ex. 7

All through the movement the rarely idle cello strives hard to fulfil that promise: it is the self-effacing orchestra which disappoints, for though discretion is undoubtedly the better part of valour in accompanying the least penetrating of all solo instruments in a concerto, Schumann's excessive caution frequently results in drabness. However, one robust tutti early on allows the cellist to take a deep breath before introducing a discursive and less intense second subject in the relative major key of C

Ex. 8

From this the fragment *x* assumes increasing importance in what remains of the exposition, as well as finding a place in the development, though in this latter section, launched after an unsubtle interrupted cadence, the main food for the orchestra is at first a somewhat scraggy scrap of cello figuration introduced but incidentally in the course of the second subject:

Ex.9

There is little sense of direction or feeling of growth in the music until a rhythmic expansion of this fragment

Ex.10

prompts a full, impassioned statement of the main cello theme, Ex. 7, in the key of F sharp minor; the subsequent orchestral appropriation of the first four notes of this theme in the sudden sunlight of G major could, with bolder scoring, have made a triumphant climax before the recapitulation – orthodox save for its ending.

Continuity and unity still remained Schumann's ideals even though thematic metamorphosis had by this time ceased to obsess him, hence his replacement of the customary cadenza, coda, and formal close with a twenty-two bar orchestral interlude during which the listener is gradually transported into the haven of F major for a slow movement (*Langsam*) as beautiful as any of the composer's prime. Here he forgets all problems of extended symphonic architecture, and instead, in the simplest ternary form, allows the cello to sing a fervent, ruminative song, particularly well suited to its mellow tone-colour and enriched in the middle with double-stopping, over a mainly *pizzicato* string accompaniment. But the dream is short-lived. A reminder of the opening theme, Ex. 7, from woodwind and horns brings the cello back to earth, though one last fond echo of the song-theme betrays the composer's reluctance to leave the introspective world where at heart he knew he really belonged. This interlude is more than a mere bridge between second and third movements – it is supremely eloquent music – and the barrenness of the ensuing finale (*Sehr lebhaft*) is in consequence all the more apparent. A remark in Clara's diary suggests that humour was intended, but even before the end of the exposition the listener grows exasperated with the rhythm  which not only crops up in the perky first subject

but also adds its voice as an accompaniment to the second

(Whether or not the fragment *y* from the first subject was a deliberate reference to *x* from the second subject of the first movement is a moot point.) After an unremarkable development and recapitulation the soloist at last is given a cadenza, albeit an accompanied one merging into the brilliant coda. But here again the composer fails to exploit the instrument's more telling upper register, and even Tovey admitted to 'some hankering' to supply an alternative.

10

Franz Liszt (1811–1886)

DENIS STEVENS

INTRODUCTION

'I CAN make my piano dream or sing at pleasure, re-echo with exulting harmonies, and rival the most skilful bow in swiftness'. These words come not from Liszt, but from his friend and contemporary, Berlioz, who, in envying Liszt's independence of wayward orchestras, imagines him confidently expatiating on the manifold richness of his own pianistic texture. In fact Liszt did no such thing; but in exploiting those textures he called forth innumerable cries of admiration which completely surpassed even the fanciful flights of Berlioz's pen. But in one of his comparisons Berlioz has hit upon an important truth, when he speaks of a keyboard technique which can 'rival the most skilful bow in swiftness'.

Paganini could not have been far from his mind – Paganini, the violinist who had conquered Europe with his strange fusion of the macabre and the beautiful, his tremendous technique which could turn from the transcendental to the vulgar, from the music of the spheres to the noises of the farmyard. So it was with Liszt, whose mastery of the piano was inspired by Paganini's mastery of the violin, and who also exhibited something of that same dual personality, whether he admitted it himself or was branded with it by others. 'I am half-Franciscan, half-gypsy', he wrote to Princess Sayn-Wittgenstein; and half a century later Busoni, writing in philosophical vein, was to point out the two warring elements in Liszt's soul, the Diabolic and the Catholic. Yet for these very reasons Liszt was a true Romantic, and a worthy member of a triumvirate of composers whose musical ideas coincided to a very great extent. Berlioz had used an *idée fixe* in his symphonies, and Wagner has seen the light in the *leitmotiv*, but it was left to Liszt to bring to fruition the scheme of thematic metamorphosis in relation to the concerto. As a scheme, it was by no means new, for the wilful alteration of a melody had been part of the stock-in-trade of countless composers from Machaut to Monteverdi. In its application, however, it was (as Liszt said) 'somewhat my own, but it is quite maintained and justified from the standpoint of musical form'.

He wanted the theme to be flexible, so that it would not be spoilt by a simultaneous change of both rhythm and tempo, and this flexibility was to be the servant of expression and emotion, allied with an economy of material which may have been calculated to strengthen the actual shape of the work. Whether it does so is still a matter for debate, but none would deny its far-reaching influences, and Ravel is not alone in drawing attention to the generations of composers (including himself) who have found some worthwhile feature in this 'vast and magnificent chaos of musical material'.

The first piano concerto was completed in 1849, published two years later, but subsequently revised twice. The second concerto, dating from 1839, was revised at least four times, and is called *Concerto No. 2*, presumably because it was the second to be published. The composer's father mentioned two early concertos, which were never published, and to complete the series one should also add the orchestration (by Liszt himself) of the *Grand Concert Solo*, otherwise known as the *Concerto Pathétique*. This was reconstructed and edited for performance in 1949 by Humphrey Searle and Gustave de Mauny.

PIANO CONCERTO NO. I IN E FLAT

FIRST Movement. *Allegro maestoso*. The opening theme, *marcato*, *deciso*, *tempo giusto*, would seem to leave no doubt in the minds of its interpreters, but Liszt was said to have sung these words to it:

Ex. 1

'Das versteht Ihr alle nicht' ★

The overall compass is a major third (or diminished fourth) like its diminutive variant which appears later:

Ex. 2

But the main point of interest is the immediate entry of the piano, with a flourish which Liszt repeats several times during the course of the work. It is not a flourish which one would associate primarily with a keyboard instrument, and if quoted in one of its later appearances, with a pedal A, the gaunt, withered arm of Paganini may be seen playing a typical piece of violinistic figuration:

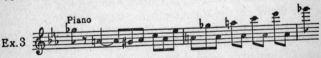

Ex. 3

A more extended cadenza follows, the orchestra breaking in with quieter statements of Ex. 1. A solo clarinet ushers in a new melody played by the pianist, who is instructed to use *rubato*, while stressing the melody. A solitary desk of violins joins in, but the lyrical vein is soon dispelled by a desiccated version of the rhythm of Ex. 1, answered by Ex. 2 on cellos and bassoon. When the climax is reached, trombones give out the main theme, and the piano emerges in a flight of octaves which embrace an extended version of Ex. 2. One begins to understand what Stephen Heller meant when he spoke of the electricity flowing from Liszt's arms. Again there are flowery cadenzas interrupted by echoes of Ex. 1, which is used to build up the short coda.

Second Movement. *Quasi Adagio*, leading to *Allegretto*

★ *This none of you understand.*

vivace. The strings are muted, and they foretell the melody which is shortly to be played on the piano:

Ex.4

The strings begin their reply innocently enough, but end on a *tremolando* diminished seventh, a romantic recipe well used from Weber onwards. The piano is the prima donna in the ensuing recitative, and when the passion has died down a solo flute breathes fresh air across the scene:

Ex.5

Clarinet, oboe and cello repeat the melody over a lightly accompanied trill on the piano, the clarinet leading into what is virtually another movement. And this was the point where Hanslick, the Viennese critic, sat up and dubbed the work a 'Triangle Concerto'. He was, alas, followed by others, so that Liszt was obliged to defend his use of the triangle, and in doing so championed the cause of other despised percussion instruments. He gave this *scherzando* movement a theme which sounds as if it were written in duple time, instead of triple:

Ex.6

The flute chirrups a fresh tune, still with the triangle in the background, and the piano supplies delicate decoration. Violins, *pizzicato*, recall Ex. 6, but the flute and triangle merger has more to say before the oboe has the main theme against a staccato accompaniment on the bassoon. When Ex. 1 returns, *un poco marcato*, its pendant, Ex. 2, appears also, and the tempo quickens. The excitement rises, and once more the trombones announce the main theme, in what seems to be a rehearsal of the opening of the concerto. But Ex. 5 intervenes, the accompanying trills ascending this time in true concerto style. The process is repeated, the result a bridge between *scherzo* and *finale*.

Third Movement. *Allegro marziale animato*. Clarinets, with martial flavour, duly metamorphose Ex. 4*a*, the nocturne becoming a march theme supported by sounding brass and tinkling cymbal, which latter is carefully marked 'without bass drum'. Suddenly trombones and basses declaim Ex. 4*b*, their challenge being taken up by the piano in a *bravura* passage of octaves. The passage comes to an end, and round the corner is Ex. 5, its rhythm changed by the piano from 4/4 to 12/8; but it is no less enchanting in this guise. An oboe converses with the piano, but in its pristine rhythm. Through a cascade of arpeggios the march theme can be heard once more, on clarinets and *pizzicato* strings, and the piano continues the elaboration with rapid repeated notes until Ex. 6 reappears, with the inevitable triangle. The key veers round to E flat, and a new melody makes its entry:

This is taken up by flute and oboe, *piu presto*, the scherzo fragment still being in evidence, and alternating with more than a hint of Ex. 1. A chromatic figure based on the second bar of Ex. 1 is heard in the basses beneath a pianoforte trill, and the coda begins with a return to Ex. 2, the full orchestra working up to a brilliant finish, from which the piano is by no means absent.

PIANO CONCERTO NO. 2 IN A MAJOR

THIS is a work in one movement, a symphonic-poem with piano obbligato, or, as one critic put it, 'The Life and Adventures of a Melody'. It was dedicated to Hans von Bronsart, and first played by him in Weimar with Liszt conducting.

The concerto shows the many-sided nature of Liszt's musical thought, first of all the romantic dreamer:

An oboe echoes the sad curve of the melody, and immediately gives birth to a new idea – for it is not big enough to qualify as a melody in itself – Ex. 8a. This alternation of a minor and a major second is the true sign of the indecisive, vacillating romantic, and when it recurs (as it often does) the effect is ever the same. When the piano steals on to the scene – quite a different entry from that of the first concerto – the melody is elongated, broken up as if with sighs. Then, to a solo horn, *träumend* – still dreaming – the piano adds a fresco of fanciful elaboration, oboe and solo cello joining in until a cascade of descending chords announces first the sad melody with its vacillating cadence, second a diabolical growling, which proves to be an ostinato accompaniment to Ex. 9:

From here onwards the rhythms are incessantly jerky, sharply marked, and staccato. The piano is busy the whole of the time, and emerges from the fray only to find itself leading off an *Allegro agitato* in B flat minor:

Soon the rôles are reversed, and the piano has brilliant passage-work in chromatic chords, ending in a half-close which ushers in a savage ostinato theme. The tutti which follows reminds one of Dannreuther's words about Liszt's experiments in tonality 'which led to effects of interesting ugliness'. When the chromatic bass has reached F sharp, the vacillating figure reappears above in the violins, and the piano enters with the same idea. There is a stormy dialogue between piano and strings, the ostinato figure still holding sway, always *fortissimo e violente*. A short pause, and the three side-slipping chords from the very beginning of the work come back again as a link with the next section, *Allegro moderato*. Strings play the new melody, which has an E major flavour:

Ex.11

The piano ruminates and arpeggiates, and a discreet cello harks back to Ex. 8, the rhythm having changed from three to four beats in a bar. A new thematic fragment appears in the piano part, and a short cadenza leads to a section in D flat which exploits this new material:

Ex 12

A lightly-scored dialogue between solo cello and piano ensues, without any firm conclusions being reached: the oboe clears the atmosphere with a return to Ex. 11, and the piano is left to round off the section with yet another cadenza involving the minor and major second. But if this is indecisive, the following allegro is exactly the opposite – indeed it is marked *deciso*. The ostinato theme is here, together with Ex. 9 and its violent accompaniment, and whilst this 're-union of two themes' is taking place the piano plants huge chords from bottom to top of the keyboard. Violas and cellos give out an *appassionato* theme, to the accompaniment of chromatic cascades on the piano, which soon turns to its jerky, mock-heroic theme, Ex. 9, with the omnipresent ostinato still in the strings. There follows another of Liszt's extraordinary tuttis, the piano interrupting with the ostinato theme, doubled in octaves by both hands. At last Ex. 10 is heard again, this time on a dominant pedal sustained by cellos and horn. There is a gradual crescendo built up by a four-note semiquaver figure on the violins, and the timpani foreshadows in its rhythmical taps the shape of themes to come, for the March (*un poco meno allegro*) which bursts forth from the full orchestra is none other than Ex. 8, transformed completely and irrevocably.

The tempo quickens as Ex. 10 is heard on lower and upper strings alternately, the piano adding brilliant bell-like figuration. A codetta built on the vacillating motive leads to a powerful half-close in A, where the piano comes into its own and the romantic returns to his day-dreams. Clarinet and violins echo the melody, and a flute looks back to the original draft of Ex. 12. A shimmering cadenza leads into a final *Allegro animato*, at first reminiscent of a *scherzando* movement, then of the March, which is punctuated by spectacular glissandos. The side-slipping chords suggest a return to the main theme, but they are superseded by the vigorous strains of Ex. 9, the close being bold and spacious.

II

Johannes Brahms (1833–1897)

HUBERT FOSS

THE four concertos by Brahms are spaced fairly evenly across his composing life. The Concerto in D minor for pianoforte is dated 1861 (the composer's twenty-ninth year), that for violin 1879, the B flat for pianoforte 1882, and the Double, for violin and violoncello, 1888. The First Symphony bears the date 1877, though much of it was written earlier; the Second Symphony 1878. Between the D minor Piano Concerto and the Violin Concerto came much chamber music and also that spate of choral works which gave us things like the *German Requiem* and the *Alto Rhapsody*.

All four of Brahms's concertos must be thought of symphonically rather than as pieces for a soloist. Three of them (as the ensuing pages show) met with sharp criticism, the fourth was admitted to be inexplicable. Yet as we know them now, there is, we find, nothing very alarming about them, provided we accept their symphonic basis of design. On the other hand, all four lack that deep solemnity which imbues Brahms's four symphonies – even the more lyrical Second Symphony and the more brilliantly coloured Third. The soloist in each concerto was allowed his proper say, and was able to relieve the pressure of pure intellectual imagination that weighed upon Brahms, the symphonist of the absolute (as he wished to be). A more interesting study, which I commend to those who are attracted by the cast of Brahms's mind, is a comparison of the four concertos with the larger works of concerted chamber music, where, it may be felt, Brahms felt that his medium was more happily plastic in his hands.

One observes all through the concertos the composer's astonishing power of developing ideas. He seems to have (as they say of gardeners) 'green fingers'. Under his caressing touch the themes grow as we watch and listen to them. And this blossoming quality in the melodies is something additional to that other quality they have of complexity of structure. Examine any of the themes in the concertos and you will find them elaborately constructed within themselves, apart from their potentialities. Brahms is adroit at handling these complex units in the making of his broadly patterned designs.

As a last point (as I have suggested below, *s.v.* Violin Concerto), we find in the concertos more than a little of Brahms the lyrical song-writer, of a singing force impelling him musically underneath all his constructive abilities and intentions.

PIANOFORTE CONCERTO NO. 1, IN D MINOR

THE First Pianoforte Concerto was Brahms's earliest important essay in orchestral writing; with it, in Hadow's phrase, he 'emerged from his second period of studentship'. Before it came only the Serenade in D major. Few works in the history of music have caused such upheavals in the process of creation, or taken so long to reach final printed form. The work was occupying Brahms's mind as early as 1853, but was not played until six years later, and then not as we know it to-day. Breitkopf and Härtel refused the offer of publication. The piano part was issued in 1861 and the orchestral parts in 1862, but no full score or two-piano version was available for purchase before 1873.

Those were troubled years of gestation. We learn from a letter to Joachim of 1853 that the composer had written three movements of a sonata for two pianos. Brahms, dissatisfied, reached out towards the orchestra, scoring the first movement as the opening of a symphony. The piano, however, was his natural mode of expression, and made itself indispensable to him. In his self-criticism, he used his familiar instrument as a kind of binding medium, in the manner of painters, for his orchestral texture, which did not satisfy him as an independent expression of his thoughts. As late as 1857 Brahms complained in a letter to Clara Schumann of the difficulties he was finding in getting the work right and of its 'amateurishness'. His whole style was undergoing a process of uneasy development. Though indubitably a concerto, the work was dubbed after its first hearing 'a symphony with piano obbligato'; it caused no small surprise and not a little disfavour. Both style and scale are symphonic, yet the piano part cannot in any sense be described as 'concertante'.

Other circumstances attendant upon the creation of this Concerto have a musical as well as a merely annalistic interest. In 1854, the first disturbing signs of mental derangement in Robert Schumann became violent; he attempted to commit suicide by throwing himself into the Rhine from the bridge at Düsseldorf. Brahms was deeply affected, for apart from gratitude for Schumann's championship, he dearly loved his fellow-composer, and his wife Clara as well. For two years Schumann lingered on in an asylum at Bonn, dying in 1856. The passionately tragic mood of the Concerto's first movement was undoubtedly inspired by the first of these two events, the slow movement by the second of them. There is no reason to think that this slow movement was drawn from an earlier conception of Brahms's, for a choral work; the fact remains that in one of his sketches over the flowing and pensive main theme he superscribed the words 'Benedictus qui venit in nomine Domini', as a requiem for his friend.

First Movement. *Maestoso*. The note of tragedy on the grand scale is struck at once by a commanding first subject

Ex. 1

given out fortissimo by the first violins. There is a second part to it, smoother and more mournful, which contains an important leaping six from A natural up to F sharp. Yet another idea enters which gradually develops itself into a foreshadowing of the second subject. Almost immediately, there appears a figure of repeated quavers – another anticipation of material to come; this time it is the entrance of the solo piano, in a quiet and sad melody in thirds and sixths

which Tovey properly describes as 'worthy of Bach's ariosos in the *Matthew Passion*' – and, one might add, of the lyrical genius of Brahms at its best. There is further treatment of the main ideas, which rises first and then falls to the second subject proper

a serene melody of some length and elaboration marked 'espressivo, p. legato'.

The opening of the development section is the first occasion on which the pianist is allowed to show display of any sort, and even now the massive double octaves cannot be called *bravura*, but rather an outburst of pent emotion. The development, as such, is real, for inversions and other views of the matter are laid before us, including an episode based upon the first subject's extension, this time in diminution,

with a lighter-hearted (but short) D major interlude following. Then comes the recapitulation, but not in D minor. The
orchestra plays the bottom D, but Brahms used this as the
seventh degree of the scale of A minor, bringing in the main
theme with a piano chord of E major (the dominant of A)
above it. More discussion ensues along with a strong presentation of the second subject. The coda (*tempo Imo più
animato*) enters quietly, with reminiscent sixths on the piano,
after a general diminuendo, but soon acquires the stature of
the movement's opening bars.

Second Movement. *Adagio.* In contrast with the leaping
intervals of the common chord that mark the main idea of
the allegro maestoso, the slow movement begins with one of
Brahms's suavest conjunct melodies

one that reminds us in spirit of the *German Requiem*, in design
of his more lyrical works like the E flat Intermezzo (Op. 117,
No. 1) and the song, 'Wie Bist Du, Meine Königin?'. The
quiet tune is aptly fitted to the words of the *Benedictus*. The
soloist enters in the fourteenth bar (but the music is slow-
moving!) with a pianistic rumination on the opening
phrases. Fragments are broken off and developed – a rising
scale, some dropping cadences, and so on – but the piano
leads, until it introduces a new-found theme

treading quietly as in an episode. The return is full of chromatic fantasy in modulation, and leads us to an essential (not a decorative) cadenza; then the solemnity of the requiem returns, and its mood is reinforced by five staccato drum-notes and a pianissimo roll at the end.

Third movement. *Rondo – allegro non troppo*. The first bars set a stormy if not quite a tragic mood – there is a touch of petulance, or at least self-assertive rebellion, about the opening phrases

Ex.6

which giving the linking theme of the whole movement. It may be observed that the treatment is rather contrapuntal than harmonic; after a flourish the orchestra takes up the tune, in which one traces a vague Hungarian flavour, increased by the dotted notes by the strings' phrases coming after it. The first episode consists of a fairly obvious tune in the relative major (F), treated by the piano, but developing a subsidiary phrase in the orchestra. The soloist prefaces his restatement of Ex. 6 with a flourish. Then comes the central episode, introduced melodically by the violins in B flat

Ex.7a

but even this simple tune is not left long in its native peace but is treated fugally in the minor, Ex. 7*b*.

Ex.7b
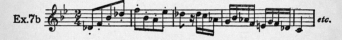

Back comes the binding rondo-theme for more development (including a plain statement from the soloist in the proper key); then a cadenza marked 'quasi Fantasia'; then a resumption (rather thoughtful at first) of the first episode; finally a lively and suitably emotional coda.

PIANOFORTE CONCERTO NO. 2, IN B FLAT

THE second of Brahms's Piano Concertos is, in physical dimensions, larger than the first of them. The emotional content, too, has grown from the expressively tragical to the more epic view of life. His friend Dr. Theodor Billroth, the Viennese surgeon, described the relationship of the B flat to the D minor as that of manhood to adolescence. Certainly, the B flat is the largest in scale of all classical concertos: apart from the length of the three usual movements, Brahms added a further, a kind of serious scherzo of symphonic range which, when questioned about it, he explained by saying that the first movement was so *simpel* ('innocuous', 'ingenuous', 'harmless', or however else one cares to translate the word)! Despite its outward qualities of size, the Second Concerto has inward qualities of personal appeal, of a kind of intimacy, as of a great man talking to us but not haranguing us. For this reason, no doubt, critical opinion (never sympathetic on first hearings to Brahms's Concertos) considered the work as 'chamber music on a big scale'. There is an excusable element of truth in that hasty judgement.

Having stated the topic on which he proposes to discourse within our circle, he proceeds to develop it, almost (it would seem) to let it develop itself, into all manner of imaginable variants and positions, controlling his discourse by some hidden power of mind without appearing to put any limits to the flow of his ideas. So great was his technique (both mentally and musically) by the post-symphony 1880 period that this flowing chamber-music quality of expression can reach symphonic power without being portentous. For this reason, the B flat Concerto is far less easy to analyse than the D minor; the development grows so naturally and easily that analysis is in danger of becoming like botanical dissection of a plucked leaf.

The Concerto did not grow as swiftly as might appear,

any more than does the tree that bears the leaf. Work was
begun on it in 1878 (we learn) but the sketched version was
shelved in favour of the Violin Concerto and the First Violin
Sonata, and not taken up again until after the visit to Italy
of 1881. The *première* was given in Pest (Hungary) on
9 November 1881, with the composer at the piano and
Alexander Erkel conducting; in Stuttgart and Meiningen
(Germany) later in the same month. Publication followed in
September, 1882.

First Movement. *Allegro non troppo.* The opening is an innovation, for it consists of a dialogue between soloist and
orchestra. Comparison may be made with both the G major
and the E flat ('Emperor') Concertos of Beethoven, but it is
not just; the method here is new. We are instantly called to
attention by an idea of unmistakable power

a pentatonic phrase for the first horns. Interrupting the
rising third at the beginning of the second bar, the pianist
makes his instrument echo its sentiments. This first phrase
gives us, in its broad simplicity, an indication of the scale on
which the music is going to be set before us. The manner is
that of a far-sighted man. There are many incidents to en-
counter, but there is only one wide view before us. Almost
immediately (as soon as the sixth bar), a counterphrase is
announced

which is virtually the second main idea of the movement.
We must beware, for the long piano solo that comes next
has a dotted rhythm. A third idea completes the ground-
work material:

Discussion is continuous, and always illuminating: every aspect of these ideas is shown, and new lights shine as they move about under the direction of Brahms's mind. The dotted-rhythm idea assumes considerable importance. The first subject returns unexpectedly in low and impressive tones under piano figuration, its second half on wood-wind with a high flute. The recapitulation is by no means regular, but a brilliant summing up of the evening's talk.

Second Movement. *Allegro appassionato.* The piano bursts out unhesitatingly in the opening bars; the musical pattern is interesting for its curves and straights

The second main idea is easy to pick up and remember – a call on the strings in octaves that swings rhythmically and hauntingly around an E natural.

The piano decorates it with energy – the whole movement is, in fact, full of a kind of semi-tragic vitality. It is to be observed as a matter of style that Brahms uses the classical system of repeat marks for his exposition. A rising arpeggio assumes some importance in the discussion, and then a rising phrase of emphatic semitones. At length we come upon a straightforward new idea in a much gayer mood.

Not a note of this material is forgotten or overlooked as the musical speech unrolls itself; but that speech is too near the composer's own uttering to be described on paper.

Third Movement. *Andante*. The beautiful melody for a solo cello

is something of a sedative after the gusty anxieties of the in-truder-scherzo. But its quietness is that of a flowing stream, not of a static picture, for not only is there a rocking in the rhythm, but the melody itself changes, like a stream, as we watch its course. The pianist – it is the composer himself, I always feel – mildly interpolates a comment near the end, a questioning arpeggio which takes on some later impor-tance, and then embroiders the cello melody, as if to say 'Is this what you really meant?' The waters of the stream soon meet rocks, not dangerous, perhaps, but troublesome. Out of this disturbance arises a new theme, for pianoforte accom-panied by two clarinets over F sharp held on the cellos. The main topic returns, as a reminder, in this new key, and then sinks to B flat in a proper recapitulation, with the pianist's first words recalled.

Fourth Movement. *Allegretto grazioso*. Tovey calls it a 'great and childlike finale'. It is certain that we are shown here a sunnier view of life; but there is no apology for the grandeur that has gone before. The scoring is light, without trumpets or drums. Everything – and there is a generous quantity of ideas – seems to arise out of the artless phrase

announced by the pianist over violas and imitated by the violins. This little adage gives rise to witty epigrams, even puns here and there. A more sedate relation joins the party (on flutes, oboes, and bassoons in octaves), but the mood of solemnity does not come to anything: there is a gentle new theme for the clarinets, with a gay little aside-commentary from the strings (at first). It is hard to believe by now that this is a rondo; but back comes Ex. 14 to remind us. Another episode is concerned with a falling phrase, and there is a leap of a seventh which sounds as if it were meant to be taken seriously, but never quite is. For a light-hearted colloquy, the canvas is large; but Brahms has filled every inch of it with a successful as well as entertaining musical design.

CONCERTO FOR VIOLIN IN D

OF all Brahms's major works, the Violin Concerto is the one which shows in the highest degree of perfection the reconciling of the two opposite sides of his creative mind – the lyrical and the constructive: Brahms the song writer and Brahms the symphonist. For this Concerto is a song for the violin on a symphonic scale – a lyrical outpouring which nevertheless exercises to the full his great powers of inventive development. The substance of it is, throughout, the growth of the themes; they blossom before us like opening flowers in a richly stocked garden. It is Brahms's most lovable work of extended design.

So, nowadays, we can view the concerto. It has established itself as a great romantic-classic, standing in modern popular favour alongside the Beethoven, Mendelssohn, and Tchaikovsky concertos, and followed by the Elgar and the Sibelius, the Bartók and the Walton. But it took some time to attain that regal state of universal esteem. At first soloists fought shy of it, all save Joseph Joachim, of course, who was, as inspiring friend and willing technical adviser, its *fons et origo*. The violin part in the 1880s seemed so fraught with outrageous difficulties that it was dubbed a concerto not *for* the violin but *against* the violin, a judgement which

Huberman corrected (as Tovey reminds us) to 'a concerto *for* violin *against* orchestra – and the violin wins!' Brahms, who turned aside from his second Piano Concerto to work on the Violin Concerto, himself had doubts and misgivings about it during the summer and autumn of 1878; he planned four movements (as with the B flat), then scrapped the two middle ones and substituted the present adagio, which he at first was inclined to think a poor makeshift. Joachim persisted and persuaded, writing the cadenza still mostly used, though, in fact, many others have written other cadenzas for it, not only violinists but composers and scholars of the rank of Busoni and Tovey. First played on New Year's Day 1879, the work was published in October of the same year.

First Movement. *Allegro non troppo.* All the subject matter of the allegro is stated, in ordered succession, by the opening orchestral tutti. The first subject, however, does not appear in its fully developed form; for that it has to wait for the soloist. We hear it first in a rudimentary unison statement in the bass, announced by cellos, violas, bassoons, and (in part) horns. I quote it below as the solo violin later has it, with the important counterpoint for the violas

The solo phrase is very characteristic – one of Brahms's special common-chord themes, which can be seen in other forms in the D minor Concerto, the G major Violin Sonata, the song *Feldeinsamkeit*, and even the D major Symphony (No. II) of the same period. This first thematic idea is followed at once, by way of complement, with a flowing phrase on the oboe, and then by another consisting of a striking series of rising chromatic notes in octaves. Almost before we realize it, the second subject proper

grows out of the natural musical flow. This again has two subsidiaries, a kind of cadence-phrase in a five-beat (Ex.16*b*)

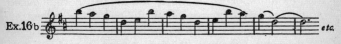

rhythm across the bars, and another with two quaver-sextuplets leading upwards to a chromatic passage. Out of all these notions, Brahms builds an entirely new theme – ostensibly a variant, but in reality the culmination of his first lyrical outpourings. It is a special theme, as it were, for the soloist, and although it does not appear in the score until later, I quote it here to show its origins and its relevance, and also the forward trend of the whole movement

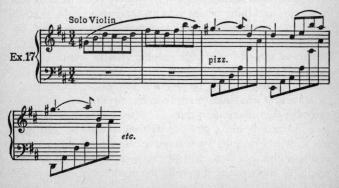

In between these is a forceful little theme – violinistic, contrasting well with its fellows, and capable of use by the soloist – stated on divisi strings.

The development moves along broadly but personally, in a manner not unlike a Platonic dialogue, with poetry added. The key of C major (turning to C minor) is touched and the orchestra takes up the soloist's variant of the second subject; new ideas spring out – a chordal phrase for the violin, a quaver-and-semiquaver figure, which is used at first musingly and later in declamation. The first subject in return is stated by flutes, oboes, clarinets, and the first horn, against counterpoint and figuration from the rest of the orchestra. The second phrase is given to the solo violin above strings. The discourse continues its development, even here, but there is serenity, the odd words (like the violin's chordal theme) are recalled, and, with a noble and dignified display, the movement ends in an emphatic D major.

Second Movement. *Adagio*. Some writers on music have expressed the view that this movement is too light of weight to balance the first and last movements of the work. That deprecatory view is a distorted one; it comes from those who take their stance on the symphony (and its sister the concerto) as Alpine peaks. It is an academic angle, that – a ponderous conception of an expressive form, one which demands size but neglects the weight of sheer breath-taking beauty as something of high specific gravity artistically.

Brahms's slow movement has this astonishing quality of unadulterated beauty. Its worth is imprepounderate. It is a delicate and imaginative study in the decoration of a single melody; that decoration does not alter but musically develops the melody into a glorious pattern. Were I to occupy all my allotted examples for this concerto with a visual analysis of these changes, I could not make my point – indeed, it would be more sensible to refer the reader of these words to the full score (or the reduced version for keyboard), for personal examination. This plan I adopt and quote only the opening melody.

Points are worth a moment's mention: (*a*) the cadence-phrase on the violins against bassoon arpeggio and held horn octaves; (*b*) the soloist's new attitude towards the tune; (*c*) the F sharp minor moment of melodic expansion; (*d*) the return, with ornamentation, of the main theme, and its logical outcomes, by the soloist; (*e*) the coda.

Finale – allegro giocoso, ma non troppo vivace. The gentle dreams of the slow movement are blown away by a single gust of wind as the finale opens. The violin announces a vigorous tune with an arpeggio accompaniment from the orchestra

The tune itself has something of a Hungarian flavour about it, no doubt in unconscious compliment to Joachim, and the arpeggio motif is put to good use throughout the movement. This is a rondo full of incidents, easy to follow when considered in relation to this principal binding theme. First comes a development in B minor containing a dropping semitone of which more is heard later. Next the violin solo gives us a series of staccato rising octaves (the arpeggio breaking in). After a restatement of Ex. 20 we come upon a new episode in G major, gentler and more graceful at first; before long the energetic octaves return, and the falling

semitone, leading us back to a full statement of the first
theme. After the cadence there is an accompanied cadenza
which plays an important part in the development. And
then comes the large-scale and developed coda, when Ex. 20
is transformed into a march-like theme with suitable military
suggestion from the orchestra.

DOUBLE CONCERTO FOR VIOLIN AND VIOLONCELLO
IN A MINOR

The Serenade No. 1 was Brahms's first orchestral work,
followed immediately by the D minor Piano Concerto. The
Double Concerto was the last major orchestral work he
wrote. After it came some important chamber works (the
D minor Violin Sonata, the G major String Quintet, the
Clarinet Quintet and Trio, and the two Clarinet Sonatas,
for example), some piano pieces and songs, the *Four Serious
Songs* and the Eleven Chorale Preludes for organ (published
posthumously). Brahms seems to have been gripped by the
idea of the medium of violin and cello together – rather
an unusual one, with scanty precedent. His letters make this
clear, and also from them we may gather that he thought of
this work as a means of reconciliation between himself and
Joachim, the friendship between the two having been
damaged (not beyond repair) by the violinist's marital dis-
ruption. Like many another composer (and playwright, indeed), Brahms had the figures of his soloists in mind as he
wrote – Joachim and his colleague from the famous Joachim
Quartet, Hausmann. Nor do the letters leave us room for
any doubt that the composer found this new medium as
difficult to manage as it was fascinating. The combining of
two instruments as widely separated in their range and
tonal weight as the violin and cello is not eased by the support of an all-pervading medium of sound like the orchestra,
and Brahms scored the work with a light hand, avoiding
massive effects (though he uses four horns). He confessed
that he was happier dealing with his own instrument, the
pianoforte; in the result, the Double Concerto is the most
difficult of all Brahms's four examples of the form, and the

divided responsibility of the two soloists' leadership combined with acoustical troubles results in some aural obscurities in one or two places. The Double Concerto was written mostly in the Bernese Oberland in the summer of 1887 and first performed at Cologne on 18th October of the same year. The English *première* was given under Sir George Henschel at his then newly-formed London Symphony concerts in February, 1889.

First Movement. *Allegro*. The opening movement poses, but does not wholly solve, the problems to be discussed. In four bars the full orchestra announces the basic idea of the first subject and plainly asks a question in its rising scales on flutes and violins. The cello picks up the tag-end of this scale and asserts his individuality, in unmistakable terms; the passage is marked in the score 'in the manner of a recitative but always in strict time'.

All this takes only thirty bars. Then the violinist announces his presence, and there follows a long duologue for the two soloists, unaccompanied, wherein their characters are made each very distinctive. The orchestra states the main theme in its proper form

After this comes a chromatic and syncopated passage of some later importance. At length the soloists discuss the main theme, leading us on to the full statement of the second by the cello soloist:

These two main motives are strongly contrasted in character, the first being assertive and even tragic in its passion, the second suave and gentle and song-like. The development is opened by the orchestra and a new theme (or semi-theme) appears which is heard again later in the coda. When the soloists return, it is to discuss Ex. 21 from various aspects. The development section is comparatively short. The *reprise* is begun by the orchestra, but the soloists take it over after a few bars. The second subject is this time allotted to the violin in the upper register. The syncopated motif is recalled dramatically, and much is made of the second subject.

Second Movement. *Andante.* A rising fourth on the horns, joined by the upper wood-wind, acts as a call to our attention. Then the soloists announce a phrase which might well be thought of at first as a mere figure of accompaniment but turns out to be the main subject of the movement

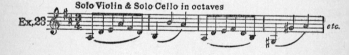

Ex. 23. Solo Violin & Solo Cello in octaves

(the arpeggio and octave leap are soon inverted). There follows an episodic theme in F major, conjunct in motion and given out by the flutes, clarinets, and bassoons; the soloists embroider it. We reach D major once more, and so back comes the first subject.

Third Movement. *Vivace non troppo.* The finale of the Double Concerto occupies a more important place in the design of the work as a whole than is usual in romantic-classic works – even in Brahms's. Not without its own enigmas, it goes some way to solve the greater enigmas of the opening movement. It certainly makes clear the point that the whole Concerto was conceived on a well-laid plan, as (in the best sense) *durchcomponiert*. We find here humour (a touch sardonic perhaps), and broad thinking, and plain speaking. Without preliminary, the solo cellist states a theme with some Hungarian (or at least exotic) flavour, and

also with some quaint scent hanging about it of the works of
the older Italian string-writers

The emphatic cadence-chords for the soloists have a mock-
commanding air, but serve to introduce the second subject,
announced in double-stopping on the solo cello. The steady
solemnity of it contrasts well with the antic air of the first
subject.

The main rondo-theme then returns, and leads us to a new
episode with the soloists in double thirds and triplets. This
second dancing idea sobers down into more sedate ways,
and then we have some passage work. After a developed
restatement of the main theme, we come to a coda, prefaced by the 'second subject', which is entirely in the major
key, and is based on fragments of material already heard.

12

Camille Saint-Saëns (1835–1921)

MARTIN COOPER

INTRODUCTION

SAINT-SAËNS was the only nineteenth-century French composer who wrote in the traditional concerto form with any generally acknowledged success. Berlioz, d'Indy and Chausson used newer, experimental forms, but Saint-Saëns, having no new poetic impulse which demanded new forms of expression, wisely contented himself with slight variations of the accepted form. He wrote ten concertos – five for the piano, three for the violin and two for the violoncello – and eight of these date from the years between 1865 and 1880, when he was at the height of his power and his reputation. Only two (the fifth concerto for piano, 1896, and the second for violoncello, 1902) fall later, and none earlier, though Saint-Saëns wrote for solo instrument and orchestra both before and afterwards. Thus, for the sake of completeness, the following works should be mentioned: *Rhapsodie d'Auvergne* (1884) and *Africa* (1891) for piano; *Introduction and Rondo Capriccioso* (1863), *Morceau de Concert* (1880) and *Havanaise* (1887) for violin. These works have less formal coherence and less serious pretensions than the concertos and, as their titles mostly show, belong to that elegant, impeccably wrought art of entertainment in which the composer excelled.

Saint-Saëns had the neat, dry mind of an eighteenth-century 'philosopher', a sensuous conception of beauty, a chameleon-like sense of style and a dazzling technical skill. He was also a good musical scholar, even something of an antiquary. In fact, he in many ways resembled Anatole France, who was almost exactly his contemporary. His music achieves all that can be achieved by the intelligent use of traditional forms in the hands of a polished, witty member of a very highly civilized community, who is also poor in distinctive personal qualities and, by an unhappy conjunction of natural temperament and circumstance, small-hearted. Saint-Saëns's concertos are designed to show off the clarity and elegance of the soloists' playing and they plumb no emotional depths. Their very real beauties are of the surface – 'neat and even brilliant rhythms, more intelligence than sensibility, more verve than feelings', in the words of Alfred Cortot. The earliest examples – the second violin concerto of 1858 (written before the first) and the first piano concerto of 1865 – show Saint-Saëns still very fresh from his studies. The first movement of the violin concerto is a transposition to the concert-hall of the lyrical, *cantabile* style of the more facile Italian opera; and melody, harmony and orchestration of the piano concerto recall Mendelssohn, with an occasional reminiscence of Chopin in the ornamentation and in one of the cadences of the slow movement. The first violin concerto (1868), in one movement and often known as *Konzertstück*, is more interesting intrinsically as an essay in form and also for the greater individuality of the material. It consists of a sonata movement with a slow section interpolated in place of the customary development section. This telescoping accentuates the melodic character of the work and also prefigures later and more successful experiments in the first violoncello concerto (1873) and the fourth piano concerto (1875). These formal experiments were almost certainly suggested to Saint-Saëns by the example of Liszt, whose influence is to be seen in all his music written during the '70s, especially in the four symphonic poems and *Samson and Delilah*, which was given its first performance at Weimar, thanks to Liszt. Already in the third piano concerto (1869) Liszt's influence may be seen in the atmospheric use of piano arpeggios with which the work opens, in the solo passage marked 'quasi cadenza'; in the bold harmonies 'out of the key' which open the second movement (they nearly caused a free fight in the Leipzig Gewandhaus at the first performance) and the novelty of entrusting the second subject to the left-hand accompanied by the orchestra; and in the linking of this movement with the finale, though this might equally well be attributed to the example of Beethoven, the other composer whose external seal (though little of his spirit) can easily be traced in this concerto.

Saint-Saëns's two final essays in concerto form have never won popular approval. The fifth piano concerto was written at Luxor and its simple light-heartedness reflects, according to the composer, the 'joy of a sea voyage'. The prevalence of thirds and sixths, the light scoring and the simple tonal scheme of the first movement (to which the soloist contributes perhaps rather too much of what has been cruelly called 'Saint-Saëns' diatonic small talk') is only interrupted by the second subject whose D minor tonality, widely spaced arpeggios and syncopated rhythm suggest Brahms. The second movement is nearer in form and spirit to Saint-Saëns's exotic rhapsodies, brightly coloured but insipid fruit of his incessant travels. Here there is the inevitable 'chant d'amour nubien' heard from a dahabeeyah and even an unsuccessful imitation of the croaking of Nile frogs. The finale, in spite of occasional exotic colouring, is characterless and wholly given over to Saint-Saëns's unspectacular type of virtuosity; and the same can unfortunately be said of the whole of the second cello concerto, which has never won a place even in a repertory where competition is slack and intermittent. The concertos of Saint-Saëns which have a place in the modern concert repertory are the second and fourth for piano, the third for violin and the first for violoncello.

PIANO CONCERTO NO. 2 IN G MINOR

THIS concerto was written in seventeen days during the spring of 1868, for a concert which took place in Paris on 13 May, when Anton Rubinstein conducted and the composer was the soloist.

The First Movement opens with a long toccata-like solo for the piano, closely modelled on the style of Bach's keyboard fantasias—an original idea, from every point of view

but that of Bach. It is built up largely of sequential phrases
of which the following may serve as an example

Ex.1

the persistent G minor tonality continues until the orchestra
enters with a chord of the tonic, followed by a bar of dotted
rhythm recalling the solemn introduction to the so-called
'French' overture, and a chord of the dominant. After two
bars of accompaniment-figure in the left hand the soloist
introduces the first subject:

Ex.2

This theme was not Saint-Saëns's but came apparently
from a *Tantum ergo* for voice and organ shown up by Fauré
as an exercise when he was Saint-Saëns's pupil at the École
Niedermeyer. As a setting of the *Tantum ergo* it has nothing,
not even feasibility, to commend it; but in Saint-Saëns's
hands its lyrical charm is exploited to the full. A dramatic
antiphonal passage between orchestra and soloist leads to
the second subject, in the relative major, a rather weak-
kneed Schumannesque melody with a syncopated accompaniment in the left hand. This is followed by a section
marked by great pianistic elaboration, with demisemiquavers in thirds and sixths and, as the pace mounts, a passage in double octaves, which brings back the first theme in
two-octave unison in the strings, while crashing double
octaves accompany and punctuate it on the piano. The
piano takes over the theme again in a solo passage leading
to a cadenza. Rather unexpectedly this is thematic rather

than virtuosic in character and gradually leads the music back to the quiet, improvisatory atmosphere of the opening section, which in fact returns, against held chords on the strings. The movement ends as it began, the orchestra's first entry and final appearance being identical. Thus, the second subject never reappears and the movement is virtually monothematic, with prelude and postlude playing an important structural part.

Second Movement. *Allegro scherzando*. The tympani set the rhythm and the piano announces the theme, a thistle-down classic among scherzo subjects

The wood-wind answers and the piano embroiders the succeeding ripostes with the scale and arpeggio passages which Saint-Saëns's own technical fluency always suggested to him. Wit even makes its appearance in harmonic progressions, an uncommon occurrence in Saint-Saëns's music;

and in the B flat major theme there is a comfortable humour which the slightest underlining will convert into triviality:

A witty equivocation between chords of the seventh, based
on B natural and B flat in piano and orchestra respectively,
brings back the first theme which finally dissolves in an airy
arpeggio.

Third Movement. *Presto.* This is a tarantella movement
with all the bustling activity of the dance itself added to the
somewhat fussy velocity which Saint-Saëns plainly regarded
as inseparable from a finale. Against the dancing rhythm he
sets a plain, nervous theme which is redeemed from austerity
by the trills which give further emphasis to its angular
contours.

Ex.6

These last two movements, with their strong reminiscence
of Mendelssohn, hardly fulfil the promise of the first, in
which Bach and Fauré provide the composer with ideas for
an original, and on the whole an harmonious, *mélange.*

PIANO CONCERTO NO. 4 IN C MINOR

WRITTEN in 1875, it is thus near neighbour to the symphonic poems and *Samson and Delilah,* to the first violoncello
concerto, and the two-piano Variations on a Theme by
Beethoven. It was, in fact, the period of Saint-Saëns's best
work. The third symphony, which followed in 1881, and
was at one time regarded as the apogee of the composer's
creative career, seems now to show a perceptible falling-off
in the quality of the material and even in the aptness of its
handling.

The concerto is in three closely linked movements, which
are better considered as limbs of a single body, a unity emphasized by Saint-Saëns's skilful transformation of themes
from movement to movement. This is, in his case, a purely
musical proceeding with no literary explanation.

First Movement. *Allegro moderato.* A broad theme in two
symmetrical parts is given out by the strings and each part
answered by the piano (*overleaf*):

Two variations follow. In the first the melody is in the cellos, with the upper strings providing the harmonization while the piano takes up each half as before, with elaborate ornament. In the second variation the violins have the theme, which is punctuated by chords off the beat, and the answer is in each case provided by the wood-wind, which playfully varies the rhythm while the piano accompanies with arpeggios. In the postlude which follows there is the hint of a theme which is to be further developed in the scherzo section. Against tremolando strings and long-held chords in the wood-wind and brass the piano builds up a full close (with major third) in a mounting series of scales and arpeggios. By the simple drop of a major third we reach the key of A flat major. The pace slackens to *Andante* and against soft piano arpeggios the wood-wind starts a slow, rocking figure, consisting of alternate chords of the tonic and its minor ninth. This is repeated in rising sequence and eventually comes to rest on the dominant, whereupon the wood-wind announce a celestial chorale, punctuated by piano arpeggios:

This is answered by a new theme in the piano:

Ex.9

richly harmonized and leading back to a new statemen tin
the chorale in the heroic manner. Ex. 9 is then treated of
the manner of Liszt, solo instruments carrying on short
dialogues with the piano, whose part is increasingly rich and
brilliant, until the violins are divided in a shimmering figure
which mounts to an accompanied cadenza. The movement
ends with a long pianissimo coda based on Ex. 9, with
piano arpeggios against held chords in the orchestra.

Second Movement. *Allegro vivace*. The first movement
having expounded at great length the chief melodic material,
the scherzo section starts the development. The theme
hinted at in the postlude of the first section of the last movement is soon followed by Ex. 7, in G minor and in sporting
rather than formal dress. This is soon followed by a change
from 2/4 to 6/8 and the appearance of a new and perky
theme in E flat major:

Ex.10

It appears first in the piano and is then developed at some
length – there is even a playful fugato – in the orchestra.
The recapitulation of the opening sections, with some variants, goes as far as the point at which Ex. 10 originally
appeared, when a long dominant drum-roll leads to a transitional passage marked *Andante*. Here Ex. 9 appears as the
subject of a short fugal passage and appears again in the
wood-wind. A crescendo leads to a cadenza for the piano,
ushering in the third movement.

Third Movement. *Allegro*. This opens with Ex. 8 in brisk
triple time

Ex.11

which dominates the whole finale, being heard in many different forms and orchestral dresses. Combined and contrasted with this theme is a strongly rhythmic dotted figure generally consisting melodically of the notes of the dominant seventh chord. Fragments of material from earlier movements also occur in the contrapuntal web which gives this finale a solidity and a thematic, organic connexion with the rest of the work which is rare in Saint-Saëns's concertos.

VIOLIN CONCERTO NO. 3 IN B MINOR

THIS concerto was written in 1880. It is in three movements and in every way more conventional than the concertos hitherto discussed, although later in date than any of these.

First Movement. The violin enters immediately with the first subject:

Ex.12

Its strongly accentuated character and minor seconds are germs of much of the decorative passage work throughout the movement. In strong contrast with this harsh theme, which has something of the gypsy about it, is the second subject, a suavely flowing melody in B major whose lyrical tenderness is only modified by the more dramatic interval of the diminished seventh with which it closes.

Ex.13

The soloist is supported here by held chords in the strings punctuated by single notes of the horn. The development, which follows immediately, is in E major and contains a wood-wind figure which was almost certainly in Rimsky-Korsakov's mind when he was writing *Shéhérazade* eight years later. The short recapitulation is followed by a long and brilliant coda. Saint-Saëns rightly regarded the violin as the *prima donna assoluta* of the orchestra and he wrote for the violin as composers still wrote for prima donnas in 1880, in order to display the wide range, the agility and the various emotional roles of which the instrument was capable.

Second Movement. *Andantino quasi allegretto*. This is a floating barcarolle movement, whose tonality (B flat major) and rhythm (6/8) provide the most marked contrast with those of the preceding movement. After a display of passion followed by lyrical tenderness, the mood is now one of drawing-room rêverie, enlivened by some charming coquettish dialogues between the soloist and the other instruments of the orchestra, especially the wood-wind:

Ex. 14

The middle section makes play with a rhythmic figure, Ex. 14a, equally suited to strings and wood-wind. There is a short cadenza before the coda in which the solo violin's arpeggio harmonics are doubled, at an interval of two or even three octaves, by arpeggios in the *chalumeau* register of the clarinet. The effect, like that of the rest of the movement, is of an impeccably written *morceau de salon*.

Third Movement. This opens with an accompanied cadenza for the solo instrument, in which material from the first movement is used. Then over a brisk march rhythm the finale proper begins, *Allegro non troppo* and again in the key of B minor:

Ex. 15

The nervous energy and the extraordinary elegance of this theme make up for the slight banality of its closing bars. It is followed by another melody, in the same key but a very different mood

Saint-Saëns marks this *appassionato* and it really has a forward sweep, which is rare in the composer's melodies. After some variation the orchestra's dotted rhythms usher in a D major theme in the violin, which is then silent while muted strings announce a G major chorale

The character of this theme has been compared with that of a similar passage in *Lohengrin*. The violin takes this up, emphasizing the rapt, tritely celestial atmosphere. The reappearance of dotted rhythms in the orchestra, against triplets in the solo part, prepares the return of the opening cadenza. In the recapitulation Ex. 17 appears as a full-blown chorale in B major entrusted to the brass and then to the soloist against tremolando and divided strings in their top register – another hint of *Lohengrin*. The movement ends with a coda in B major.

VIOLONCELLO CONCERTO NO. 2 IN A MINOR

COMPOSED in 1873, this is an earlier, and possibly even more successful, essay in telescoping three movements into one organic whole than the Piano Concerto No. 4 of two years later. The first section provides the exposition and development of a sonata movement whose recapitulation forms the finale, and these two sections are separated by an episode whose tempo and character (it is a *genre* piece) suggest the intermezzo rather than the formal scherzo.

First Movement. *Allegro non troppo.* As in all his mature concertos Saint-Saëns brings the soloist in at once. The triplets and the final repeated phrase

are the germs from which, as in the third violin concerto, much of the subsequent material and figuration are drawn. In fact, when the orchestra takes over Ex. 18, the soloist already makes use of the final phrase to form a counter-subject. The second subject in F major

has close affinities with Schumann. The orchestral interlude which follows has an oddly old-fashioned melodic cut, angular and stiff compared with the easy-flowing, half-lyrical character of the material hitherto employed. In the short development section the different registers of the solo instrument are effectively contrasted and triplet phrases are bandied to and fro among the different instruments. A return of Ex. 19 leads to the key of B flat and the intermezzo section or movement, which follows without a break.

Second Movement. *Allegretto con moto*. This takes the form of an archaic dance played by the muted strings

Ex.20

The whole episode varies between *piano* and *pianissimo*, to which the soloist replies with a lyrical countersubject and then accompanies the orchestral dance, finally sinking down to the lowest register and dying away until the orchestra re-introduces Ex. 18 in the key of B flat major and *tempo primo*, the finale begins.

Third Movement. There is new melodic material introduced by the soloist into this elaborate recapitulation – first of all a plaintive melody in the upper register:

Ex.21

and then a singing theme in the lower register:

Ex.22

where the interval of the minor second plays a characteristic part, as in Ex. 18. A triumphant coda in A major completes the work.

13

Peter Ilich Tchaikovsky (1840–1893)

JULIAN HERBAGE

INTRODUCTION

THERE is no doubt that enduring success comes only to those who know exactly what to do, and exactly how to do it. Highbrows may smile at Tchaikovsky's B flat minor concerto, and may even be foolhardy enough to condemn it on the grounds of its popularity, but Tchaikovsky certainly knew what he was aiming at, and how to achieve his effect. 'Here', he wrote, 'we are dealing with two equal opponents; the orchestra with its power, and inexhaustible variety of colour, opposed by the small but high-mettled piano, which often comes off victorious in the hands of a gifted executant.' As Rosa Newmarch aptly remarked, Tchaikovsky considered the concerto as a duel rather than a duet. Present-day audiences at the Royal Albert Hall (if the 'gate' is any criterion) consider it as exciting as a boxing contest, and the high-mettled piano contests with the utmost regularity with the heavyweight (and often heavy-handed) orchestra.

This gives the critics their chance of being superior – and they have too often been superior about Tchaikovsky. A certain Eduard Hanslick (better known to Wagnerian audiences as Beckmesser) wrote about the first performance of Tchaikovsky's Violin Concerto – and the quotation sounds best in its American translation – 'The violin is no longer played. It is yanked about, it is torn asunder, it is beaten black and blue.' The composer, from his secure seat in Parnassus, can afford to smile indulgently at the vitriolic invective, the jaundiced phrases. Even an outraged critic had subconsciously understood that Tchaikovsky had succeeded in his aim – a musical contest between David and Goliath, with David the victor.

This attitude of Tchaikovsky towards the concerto, an

attitude which he had adopted from Liszt, may also explain why he was unable to write a successful concerto in later life. Tchaikovsky, like Schumann, could be a David in his comparative youth, but with fuller experience of the world, and with an increasing incapacity to make a success of his personal life, the 'Fate' motive descended both on him and his music. No longer could he believe in the biblical tale of David and Goliath. To change the biblical metaphor, Babylon was a great city, – and by the waters of Babylon the neurotically captive Tchaikovsky sat down and wept. The sense of despair and frustration could be admirably translated into the symphonic medium, as in the *Pathétique*, with its immortal and original final movement. In the concerto, however, the soloist can never afford to admit defeat.

The year 1877 seems to mark the turning-point in Tchaikovsky's life. In that year he made his disastrous marriage, and in that year also Fate first knocked at the door in his fourth symphony. Two years earlier he had written his B flat minor piano concerto, and one year later he was still able to compose an equally brilliant violin concerto. After that his attempts at concerto-form became increasingly insincere and artificial. Though he was able both to escape into the never-never world of such ballets as *Casse-Noisette* and also to write music of the passionately yearning intensity of the slow movement to the fifth symphony, he lacked the true courage to bestride once more the 'high-mettled piano'. Yet not for the want of trying. The Second Piano Concerto was produced in 1880, the Concert Fantasy four years later, and the uncompleted Third Piano Concerto (adapted, significantly enough, from movements of a discarded symphony) in 1893, the year of his death. None of these works are truly successful, for Tchaikovsky's heart and spirit were not wholly in them. Only in certain brief passages in the Second Piano Concerto does the soloist 'come off victorious in the hands of a gifted executant'.

PIANO CONCERTO NO. I IN B FLAT MINOR

THE first piano concerto was written in November and December 1874, and its orchestration was completed early in February of the following year. It was originally intended for Nicholas Rubinstein, but everyone has heard of the famous occasion on Christmas Eve 1874, when Tchaikovsky played his newly-completed work to Rubinstein at the Moscow Conservatorium. Tchaikovsky's own account of this disastrous audition is contained in a letter which he wrote to Nadezhda von Meck three years later, and even then the wounds caused by Rubinstein's scathing comments had not healed. After a further year Rubinstein had the grace, and perhaps the wisdom, to recant, but meanwhile the dedication had been altered, and the score is now headed by the name of Hans von Bülow.

There are, it is to be regretted, some unrepentantly critical Rubinsteins about to-day, and so, unless we accept Tchaikovsky's thesis that a concerto should be a duel rather than a duet, we will fail to appreciate the extraordinary skill with which the composer has achieved his purpose. The opening of the first movement, *Allegro non troppo e molto maestoso* in B flat minor, immediately displays the scope of the contest. The challenge comes from the four horns, *fortissimo* and in unison, and backed by crashing chords on the off-beat from the full orchestra. It is taken up by equally forceful chords of D flat major, rising in octaves to the end of each bar, from the piano, and these provide a powerful, even dominating, accompaniment to the famous tune on first violins and cellos which is too well known to need quotation. The soloist takes over the big tune but soon leaves it for a rhapsodic, Lisztian cadenza, at the end of which all the strings except the basses proclaim the tune once again, to a more brilliant and elaborate chordal accompaniment from the piano. This theme has now served its purpose as a preludial trial of strength, and it therefore fades away, to a piano accompaniment of descending chords in triplets, answered by similar ascending chords in the wood-wind.

A short bridge passage, characterized by repeated notes, *pianissimo*, on the trumpets, leads from this introduction to the beginning of the movement proper. Its first theme, *Allegro con spirito* in B flat minor, is said to be a Ukrainian folk song which Tchaikovsky heard from blind beggars at a fair in Kamenka. It is given to the soloist in two rhythmic forms, Ex. 1a and 1b, and in its first form the wind interject a flourish at the end of each phrase (the music examples have been simplified to their bare essentials).

To balance the interest, the principal themes of the second group, *Poco meno mosso* in A flat major, are both announced by the orchestra, the first being given to the clarinet, accompanied mainly by bassoons and horns,

while the second, *a tempo tranquillo*, is coloured by the tones of the muted strings.

The soloist first elaborates Ex. 2, and then, after a climax and a brief, cadenza-like passage ending on a silent pause, the orchestra steals in softly again with Ex. 3, at first given to the muted violins in octaves, and then to flute and horn in dialogue, against harp-like figuration from the piano.

The development begins on the orchestra alone with the opening phrase of Ex. 3, which has attained a somewhat sinister character through the semitonic sharpening of its eighth note, (x) and the wood-wind increases the sense of ap-

proaching drama by an answering phrase in the rhythm of
Ex. 1*a*. A chromatic phrase in slurred quavers makes its appearance, and as the pace quickens, freely combines with
the altered version of Ex. 3 to build up a climax. The full
orchestra thunders out the sinister theme. It develops into a
cascade of descending scale-phrases that are taken over by
the soloist in double octaves and lead into the first main
cadenza. This is at first based on the opening of Ex. 2, but
soon develops new material which later crystallizes into an
urgently passionate dialogue in canon between orchestra
and soloist.

Ex.4

Soloist and orchestra then elaborate the material with
which the development had begun, and this leads to a very
free recapitulation of Ex. 1*a* followed, after a cadenza passage, by a more regular recapitulation of Ex. 1*b* and Ex. 2.
At this point, when we might expect the return of Ex. 3, the
soloist is allotted the biggest cadenza of the movement, and
Ex. 3 finally turns up on flute and clarinet, against a running quaver accompaniment from the piano, to provide the
opening of an increasingly brilliant and exciting coda.

This, indeed, is an amazing concerto movement. It is
highly original in its form, especially in the subtle balance
of orchestral and pianistic ascendancy. Its thematic material
is entirely characteristic, dramatically contrasted and melodically unforgettable. While the tendency to 'metamorphose'
the themes and the pianistic decoration in the first and last
cadenzas owe much to Liszt, Tchaikovsky still retains his
own individuality and subtlety of treatment. Climaxes are
achieved with an assured sense of drama, and are offset by
exquisite moments of lyricism. Tchaikovsky has been blamed
by the highbrow formalists for throwing away his great introductory tune. Brahms, of course, would never have been
so wasteful, nor would Beethoven. But there is room in

music for prodigality of ideas, especially when they are co-
ordinated with such subtle sense of their dramatic potentialities for development, and when they employ the time-
factor – that true criterion of musical form – so successfully.

Measured by time, more than half the concerto is already
over, but there are many surprising and original ideas to
come. Nothing could appear more innocent than the opening melody of the *Andante semplice*, but nothing could be more
subtle than Tchaikovsky's varied treatment of it at every
repetition. Here are the first four bars of the tune, heard first
on the flute (when the third note is F, not B flat), and the
violin or piano figuration that accompanies it on various
repetitions.

Two other themes need quoting, and can be made into a single music example, which also exhibits the delightful modulation from the opening key of D flat, through F major, to D Major.

Ex.6

The middle section is a scherzo, marked *Prestissimo*, which begins and ends with a speeded-up version of the opening bars of Ex. 6, but which is mainly concerned with a waltz-like French chansonette *Il faut s'amuser, danser et rire*, heard first on violas and cellos against a running figuration from the soloist. The whole movement, a mixture of the lyrical and the whimsically fantastic, gains an added sense of atmosphere through the fact that the strings are muted throughout.

The rondo-form of the finale, *Allegro con fuoco* in B flat minor, is so self-evident that little need be said of it, nor need its themes be quoted. The first theme, given to the soloist, is a vigorous, syncopated dance of Ukrainian origin, and the second, equally syncopated dance tune, is given as compensation to the orchestra, while the violins are first allotted the tender song that is later to burst out as a triumphant pæan towards the end of the concerto, but not before the orchestra has indulged in a typical Tchaikovskyan crescendo on a dominant pedal-bass and the soloist has been given a brief but exacting cadenza in double octaves. The contest has indeed been one between two equal opponents, 'the orchestra with its power, and inexhaustible variety of colour, opposed by the small but high-mettled piano, which often comes off victorious in the hands of a gifted executant'.

PIANO CONCERTO NO. 2 IN G

THOSE who possess both a full score and a set of records of Tchaikovsky's Second Piano Concerto will have discovered many discrepancies between the two. There are several cuts in the first movement, mainly in solo passages, one of which is curtailed by at least a third in the recording. This is perhaps understandable, as the passage in question occupies 135 bars in the full score. But the piano part is also completely altered in places, and elsewhere there are occasions when the orchestra is omitted or its part transferred to the soloist. Though Tchaikovsky himself authorized cuts in several of his major works, these 'improvements' to the Second Piano Concerto are probably more than even such a lenient and self-critical composer could have endured. Considering also that the main interest of the concerto lies in the treatment of the solo part, the mutilations seem all the more inexcusable.

The G Major Piano Concerto was written in 1880 and first performed by Taniev on 18 May 1882. It obtained a favourable reception, but this, it has been suggested, was partly due to the popularity of the soloist, and until the recent Tchaikovsky vogue (when Balanchine used this music for his *Ballet Imperial*), it remained among the comparatively neglected works. Some recent critics have declared it to be a worthy companion – or perhaps they mean a mercifully unfamiliar alternative – to the B flat minor, but to the present writer this seems undue praise. The thematic material of the second concerto is in general short-winded, four-square, and sometimes obvious to the point of banality. The opening theme, *Allegro brillante e molto vivace* in G major, relies mainly on the rhythmic character of its first full bar.

Allegro brillante e molto vivace

Ex 7

After this theme has been dealt with by orchestra and piano in turn, an altered version of Ex. 7a is heard on cellos and basses, and is answered by a new figure from the soloist which is soon elaborated in a short cadenza. After a pause, a second group of themes is announced, the first of them, Ex. 8a, by clarinet and horn in imitation, accompanied by tremolando strings, followed immediately by the second, Ex. 8b, given to the soloist, unaccompanied.

Ex. 8b is then exploited by piano and orchestra, both as a whole and with regard to its constituent phrases, and after a brief display of virtuosity, the soloist begins to develop a new theme, elaborately laid out in piano figuration, of which the melody can be summarized as:

This gradually works towards a climax, and soon the full

orchestra enters with Ex. 7*a*, chromatically altered, and reinforced by Lisztian chords of the diminished seventh.

It will already have been realized that Tchaikovsky, unlike, say, Brahms, rarely divides his first movements neatly into exposition, development, recapitulation and so on, nor, like Brahms, does he join up these sections with the consummate mastery that makes us later realize, with pleasurable surprise, that we have already embarked on another stage of our symphonic journey. With Tchaikovsky the joins are more obvious, and often merely consist of a pause, followed by a fresh start, but the intriguing part is that we are never quite sure at what station, so to speak, we have arrived. In the work under discussion we have reached a climax in the exposition, concluded by a *bravura* passage from the soloist, and then comes the significant landmark of a pause. The next tune we hear is Ex. 8*a* from the full orchestra, *fortissimo*. But is this the coda to the exposition, or the introduction to the development section? Only Tchaikovsky could decide such an academic point, and he would probably be the last person to wish to do so. Anyway, Ex. 8*a* dies away and is followed by Ex. 8*b* on the piano, against a flute trill, after which the soloist ruminates, cadenza-wise, on this material until the orchestra take up the running and proclaims a Lisztian metamorphosis and synthesis of Ex. 8*b* and 7*a*.

This leads to the main cadenza of the movement, ruthlessly cut in the recording, and with the remaining bars clumsily joined together. Now we are on familiar ground, for the recapitulation has certainly been reached (though in the recording the piano introduces it, and not the orchestra, as in the full score). The rest of the movement, to change the metaphor, is comparatively plain sailing, and it ends with a brief but typical coda.

Turning to the second movement, *Andante non troppo* in D

major, the score-reader will notice that there are parts for
solo violin and cello as well as for solo piano. The short introduction for strings, and the piano's simple yet romantic-
ally-charged entry, prepare the scene for the main theme.

This is the first given to the solo pianist, and is then repeated as a duet for solo violin and cello, with the pianist
supplying a figured chordal accompaniment. Soon the
pianist leaves the scene, and violin and cello continue the
duet on their own. From now on, indeed, the main soloist
seems to have been entirely forgotten, except for a brief and
simple cadenza and a few odd chords and arpeggios. This is
putting the 'high-mettled piano' in its place with a vengeance, but it seems to show, just as, in a different way, do
the long solo passages in the opening movement, that Tchaikovsky was abandoning his idea of the concerto as a duel.
Here it has become a reverie, in which the soloist is lost to
the world as he listens entranced to this chamber-music use
of the rich orchestral palette.

Of the finale, *Allegro con fuoco* in G major, little need be
said except that it is a jolly Russian rondo with jolly Russian
dance tunes. It contains at least two delightful ideas, the
first being the skittish passage in octaves from the soloist in
the second section of the opening theme, and the other being the effectively unobtrusive entry of the third, more
legato, theme. The soloist throughout is given plenty to
occupy him, so if you like the tunes, you will like the movement. If not, you will probably agree with Hanslick's phrase
about the finale of the violin concerto, and consider it des-
criptive of the 'brutal and wretched jollity of a Russian
Kermesse'.

VIOLIN CONCERTO IN D

ONCE again let the score-reader be warned to expect surprises, but this time they are, on the whole, both pleasant

and efficacious. On records, and in most performances, a certain amount of repetitive material is cut, mainly from the last movement, and many solo passages are altered so as to be more violinistically effective. In particular, the transposition up an octave of the main theme of the slow movement (pp.87–8 of the miniature score) would almost certainly have met with Tchaikovsky's approval, and many other alterations to *bravura* passages give enhanced virtuosity to the solo part. We must remember that in Tchaikovsky's day the famous violinist Leopol Auer, for whom the work was written, pronounced certain passages to be technically unplayable, and even Adolf Brodsky, who gave the first performance with the Vienna Philharmonic, declared that the solo part taxed his technical skill to the utmost. Auer later revised several passages in the solo part, adding to their brilliance and violinistic effect, and his revisions form the basis of the version in general use today.

Tchaikovsky began his violin concerto at Clarens in March 1878, and the sketches were completed by the middle of the month. The slow movement was originally to have been a meditation, but brother Modeste considered it an unsatisfactory concerto movement, and the meditation later became No. 1 of the *Souvenir d'un lieu cher*, for violin and piano. The present slow movement was sketched in a single day, and the orchestration of the concerto was completed by the end of April. Owing to difficulties with Auer, the work remained unperformed for two years, and when it was finally taken up by Brodsky, an influential section of the Viennese Press unmercifully attacked the first performance. From the historical point of view, and as a mild defence of Hanslick and Co., it is as well to remember that Brahms's Violin Concerto was also written in 1878, and its first performance preceded Tchaikovsky's work by a year. No two concertos could be less alike, and since Hanslick had already come down heavily on the side of Brahms, he could scarcely go into rhapsodies about Tchaikovsky.

A comparison of the violin concertos of Brahms and Tchaikovsky is illuminating, not only because it shows the different methods of the two composers, but also because it

stresses the wide scope of concerto-form. Brahms begins his
concerto with an orchestral tutti which concisely states the
thematic material of the movement, though he keeps the
most lyrical of his themes up his sleeve for the soloist to
introduce in the exposition. In this he follows classical precedent, but he shows his romantic leanings in the dramatic
character of much of his thematic material, the menacing
dominant pedal-point at the end of the orchestral tutti and
the rhapsodic entry of the solo violin. Tchaikovsky, on the
other hand, begins with a brief orchestral introduction that
has little to do with future proceedings, except in setting the
lyrical scene. Like Brahms, he also uses a dominant pedal-
point to work up excitement for the soloist's entry, but without employing dramatic tension, so that after a few cadenza-
like bars the violin can settle down comfortably to the first
main theme.

The conclusion of Ex. 12 blossoms into a rhythmic figure
which provides the second bar of:

The rhythmic figures of the two bars alternate in friendly
rivalry until the orchestra comes down heavily on the side
of bar two's rhythm (slightly altered) and the soloist changes
from semiquaver triplets to rushing demisemiquavers. This

little burst of excitement makes an admirable prelude to the expressive second main theme.

This is elaborated by the soloist at some length (and throughout the compass of the instrument), and the exposition is rounded off with a codetta, beginning *più mosso* with staccato semiquaver triplets.

The development opens on the orchestra with what appears to be a somewhat military version of Ex. 12, but which in its continuation turns out to be a different tune altogether.

This leads to a new motive, disposed contrapuntally between the upper and lower orchestral voices, after which the soloist enters with a violinistically elaborate version of Ex. 15 in C major. The orchestra repeats its military outburst, but now a third lower in the key of F, and the contrapuntal motive reappears in a new, harmonically chromatic version which builds to a climax over the inevitable dominant pedal-point. This is the soloist's cue for a cadenza, beginning with a reference to the material just heard and including recollections of Ex. 12 and 14. The conventional trill (on the dominant note of A) gives the orchestra the signal to re-enter, and the flute begins with the opening phrase of Ex. 12, its continuation being taken over by the soloist. The recapitulation at first follows a fairly regular course, Ex. 13 turning up in G major and Ex. 14 in D major. The latter theme, however, is given a new and expressively lyrical flowering, and the movement ends with a vivacious (and, for the soloist, technically exacting) coda.

It is a strange coincidence that both Brahms and Tchaikovsky begin their slow movements with an introduction for wind instruments alone. There the similarity ends, for with Brahms this is the first statement of his main theme, a gracious tune reminiscent of Volkslied. With Tchaikovsky it sets the nostalgic atmosphere for his thoroughly Slavonic melody.

Tchaikovsky heads this movement *Canzonetta*, and it never moves outside the lyric vein of song. The second melody, though still nostalgic, brings more than a ray of consolation.

The introductory bars return, now on the strings and embroidered by the soloist, and on its repetition Ex. 16 is ornamented by counter-melodies in the wood-wind. The soloist ends questioningly on a half-close, and again the introductory bars return, both to frame this lyrical movement and to introduce the finale.

Here the orchestra at once sets the rhythm of the dance, and after a short cadenza the soloist announces the main theme with the utmost zest. The second theme, *poco meno mosso*, is given out over a drone-bass, while a third theme, *molto meno mosso*, begins as a dialogue in the wood-wind.

Having got our landmarks in this straightforward rondo movement, we can now sit back and enjoy the superb orchestral and soloistic brilliance (or should one say 'wretched brutality'?) of Tchaikovsky's (or Hanslick's) Russian Kermesse.

14

Antonin Dvořák (1841–1904)

LIONEL SALTER

INTRODUCTION

DVOŘÁK wrote three concertos (or four, if you count the early A major cello concerto which was not scored), of which the earliest is the least known and most seldom played, and the last the most popular, a masterpiece with a secure place in the repertoire. In the period of nearly twenty years which separates these works is contained practically all Dvořák's output; and, as even the most instinctive of composers, a 'natural' (as Dvořák was), is bound to improve his technique by dint of constant use, it is no surprise that there should be a conspicuous progress in facility of writing between the early piano concerto and the late cello concerto. Nor was the progress only in ease of composition: he did indeed attain a surer instrumental lay-out, a freer constructional technique, a greater power of thematic development and transformation, and a more expressive personal style; but it is noticeable that in the three concertos there is also an increasing feeling of nationalism. This is by no means to say that Dvořák quoted themes from his native folk-music – that was almost never the case; but he freely used the dance-rhythms of Bohemia, and many of his melodies are cast in a distinctly national mould. (One common type of Czech melody – a phrase consisting of a repeated single bar followed by a two-bar cell – is seen in the opening themes of both the violin and the cello concertos.)

It was natural that the accent of his homeland should be observable in his musical speech, for in Bohemia's struggles for political independence in the middle of the nineteenth century its proud folk heritage was brought very much to the fore, and Smetana had lighted the way to national musical expression by his brilliant operas for the recently-founded National Theatre in Prague. Dvořák played the viola in the orchestra of the National Theatre for eleven years (up to 1873) and could not fail to have been deeply stirred by those Smetana works which were immediately recognized as focal points for Bohemian patriotism – *The Bartered Bride* and *Dalibor*. Besides, was Dvořák not the son of a small-town innkeeper in what had been described as the most musical country in Europe, and had he not the fiddle and bagpipes of the village dances and festivities in his very blood? Smetana was not the only signpost on Dvořák's path: composers of other nations were also expressing nationalist sentiments, and in the concerto form, too. Liszt, pioneer in so many *genres*, had produced his *Hungarian Fantasia* in the early 1860s: in 1868 came Grieg's Piano Concerto, which at the time was so completely fresh in colour; and Tchaikovsky, though not strictly a nationalist, had created in his Piano Concerto (1875) a work of recognizably Russian inspiration.

As in the rest of Dvořák's music, the concertos overflow with lyrical invention – for, like Schubert, Dvořák was prodigal of his melodies – and in many places he seems to have composed entirely by inspiration, heedless of wasting material which a more prudent composer would have carefully husbanded. 'He is a child of nature', wrote Stanford, 'who did not stop to think, and said on paper anything which came into his head.' The effect of this artless emotionalism is considerably enhanced by the charm of his orchestration, which, with its softly trilling flutes and its expressive phrases for wood-wind and horns in particular, produces a rustic pastoral coloration which is irresistible in its appeal. His string writing is equally happy, and though it is generally agreed that in his works there are passages which in performance present troublesome problems of balance, on the whole Dvořák is a shining example of the truth of the theory that good orchestrators, like good conductors, are the better for working inside an orchestra and assimilating its 'feel'. His instrumental demands are modest: for

the piano concerto he asks for double wood-wind, two
horns, two trumpets, timpani and strings: the violin concerto has the same, except for four horns instead of two: the
cello concerto reduces the horns to three, but adds three
trombones and tuba. Dvořák uses this extra brass very
sparingly – indeed, he writes for them, while the solo cello
is playing, only in about a dozen bars in the slow movement,
and another dozen in the finale – and with complete understanding of their effectiveness in full soft chords. The only
extravagance Dvořák allows himself beyond the strictly
classical orchestra is a triangle in the finale of the cello
concerto.

PIANO CONCERTO IN G MINOR

THOUGH the piano concerto was written (in 1876) for the
pianist Slavkovsky, who gave the first performance in
Prague two years afterwards, it does not seem to have been
revised by him as the violin and cello concertos were revised
by Joachim and Wihan respectively. This is probably the
reason – besides the fact that Dvořák was himself not a
pianist but a string player – why the solo part is distinctly
awkward to play: Dvořák's son-in-law Josef Suk reports him
as saying that he often considered revising much of the
passage-work, but kept putting it off. Yet the piano writing
in Dvořák's songs and chamber music is perfectly playable:
apparently when it came to the concerto, the desire for an
impressive solo part misled him into thickening the texture
and doubling-up the part-writing. As Gerald Abraham has
well put it, 'He does not write the wrong sort of music for
the piano: he writes the right sort in the wrong way. The
stuff is pianistic in essence, and the figuration and lay-out
look all right on paper: it is only when one sits down to
play it that one finds how little sense he had of hand on
keyboard.' One of his worst errors of judgement was to write
identical passages for both hands together, in such a way
that the music could be performed adequately only by a
player having two right hands: pianists with more orthodox
endowments have been driven to modify Dvořák's demands,

and it is worth mentioning that two 'performing versions' have been prepared and played by Rudolf Firkušný in Czechoslovakia and America and by Franz Reizenstein in this country.

First Movement. *Allegro agitato*. The pathos of the initial theme, of which the composer was understood to be particularly fond, sets the mood for the movement as a whole; and although it is true that there are several other thematic germs, Dvořák seems irresistibly drawn to the opening subject, which, because it keeps reappearing so often as a whole and is never properly developed, ends by becoming merely repetitious. (Indeed, the development of his material is Dvořák's great weakness throughout this concerto.) After the first statement of the theme – by the 'dark-coloured' instruments only (violas, celli, horns and low wood-wind) – the opening tutti moves restlessly through several keys before the solo piano enters on a climbing passage and contributes to the uncertain tonality by trying out the theme in three keys before plunging passionately into its real statement.

The second-subject group (in B flat, the relative major) consists of two parts, the first a rhythmic two-bar phrase of a rural freshness, and the second appearing in two guises – at first as a chorale-like theme on the strings, with piano interjections, and then unified into a warm orchestral melody accompanied by decorations from the solo instrument. The development tends to be stiff and preoccupied with sequential treatment, but some play is made with an energetic dotted figure first introduced in the opening tutti. A quite conventional recapitulation leads to a grandiose cadenza and a dramatic close.

Second Movement. *Andante sostenuto*. The slow movement, a free rhapsody on two themes, takes us into that atmosphere of romantic rêverie which Dvořák knew so well how to conjure up. The first theme is heard on the horn; its last

bar is echoed on the flute before the piano takes it up
meditatively, to pass it on to the strings (again with a flute
echo of the last bar):

the second follows immediately, an emotional phrase introduced by the piano with almost Chopinesque tracery and
decoration, under which the bassoon repeats it in slightly
simpler form:

Except for a couple of impassioned moments, the mood
remains tranquil throughout, and the movement ends with
enchanting delicacy.

Finale. *Allegro con fuoco.* The finale is very characteristic
of the nationalist Dvořák. The movement starts with a
spirited theme on the piano which seems to demand *fugato*
treatment (but never gets it); and this is also heard, as a
kind of sub-heading, before the development and again
before the recapitulation – a procedure to be adopted later
in the first movement of the G major symphony.

The first subject proper – a skipping dance-tune – appears
waggishly and unexpectedly in F sharp minor on the piano
before the orchestra can steer it round to make its entry
in the correct key of G minor.

The second subject, in style more like Rimsky-Korsakov than Dvořák, is a plaintive melody with an exotic character which arises from its use of the augmented second: it is heard in the remote key of B major

Ex.6

before being treated by sequence in other keys: this lovely tune does not, however, appear in the development. After its return in the recapitulation, there is a coda in G major in which the introductory and the first themes are combined with naïve gaiety.

VIOLIN CONCERTO IN A MINOR

IN 1878 Joachim had given the first performance, in his own house, of Dvořák's A major Sextet, and the following year of the Quartet in E flat; both these proved so attractive that Joachim broached to the composer the idea of a violin concerto. Dvořák worked at this during 1879 and 1880, and then took the score to Berlin for the great violinist's opinion and comments: he adopted the suggested alterations which were put forward, and on his return home sent off a revised score which, however, remained in Joachim's hands for two years without being performed; and though the dedication reads 'to the great master Joseph Joachim, with deepest respect', the first performance took place in Prague in the autumn of 1883 with František Ondříček as soloist. (It was he also who introduced the work in England at a Philharmonic concert three years later.)

First Movement. *Allegro ma non troppo*. Dvořák obviously wished to circumvent the lengthy first-movement form of the classical concerto, and here he tries an experiment in ellipsis which is interesting but which does not altogether come off. (He was not to find a really satisfactory solution until the Cello Concerto.) The movement in general is extremely free and rhapsodic: it is based almost entirely on one theme, first announced in declamatory style by the soloist after a four-bar orchestral call to attention:

There does exist a lyrical theme which appears in the right place and key for a second subject, but it is heard only the once, and does not figure in the brief development at all. Dvořák's big surprise, however, comes in the recapitulation, which turns out to be a mere fragment concerned only with the main subject. He then turns his back on the first movement, and a short cadenza of only six bars (accompanied by a figure for the horns) is succeeded by a moving episode of great beauty, scored for the violin in its low register with wood-wind above it, which leads without a break into the Second Movement. *Adagio ma non troppo.* Throughout the first movement, the solo violin has been playing continuously, with only two six-bar rests since its real entry after the first tutti – in the latter part of the movement mostly virtuoso passages whose brilliance seems intended to distract attention from the constructional sleight-of-hand. In the slow movement the violin's part is scarcely less non-stop or less technically exacting, though here its rôle is ornamental rather than declamatory. The *Adagio* begins quietly with a broad, slightly Brahmsian, melody in F major (Ex. 8a) which develops an expressive tag of its own with a Bohemian folk flavour (Ex. 8b).

A dramatic middle section in the tonic minor (which could have been at the back of Brahms's mind when he wrote his Clarinet Quintet) starts wildly, but calms down to bring in another melodic idea which is put to good use.

The transition from the F minor section is strikingly made by trumpet tuckets, under which steals the opening theme, now in A flat. Further play is made with Ex. 9 before Ex. 8b returns, and the movement ends in a woodland atmosphere with *pp* horns playing the first theme (in thirds and sixths) while the violin weaves decorations above them.

Finale. *Allegro giocoso, ma non troppo.* The finale is impregnated with Slavonic folk feeling, though there is no quotation of actual folk material. This spirited movement is cast in the style of a *furiant*, full of humour and of delightful orchestral invention. It opens with a gay syncopated tune

which receives a different setting on each of its frequent appearances. There is an abundance of subsidiary ideas, ranging from a village-band effect (on wind only) in hilarious cross-rhythm to a dance theme (in F sharp) and an expressive subject of which much is heard

before Ex. 10 returns in a representation of the Czech *dudý* (bagpipes). The *furiant* is interrupted to make way for another national form, a *dumka* (in 2/4 time), which is worked out slightly self-consciously with a good deal of display on the part of the soloist: then the material of the *furiant* is recapitulated with fresh orchestral colours. The work ends, after a brief backward glance at the *dumka*, in vigorous high spirits.

VIOLONCELLO CONCERTO IN B MINOR

WHETHER or not he actually asked Dvořák to compose one, it was the cellist Hanuš Wihan (with whom Dvořák had made a concert tour of Bohemia in 1892) for whom the Cello Concerto was intended, and to whom the work is dedicated. It was written between November 1894 and February 1895, during Dvořák's second American visit, and though Wihan suggested some modifications in the solo part, these were confined to a few passages in the finale. However, after the work had been performed, Dvořák rewrote the last sixty bars in Prague the following year. There is a suggestion that an immediate cause of its composition was a performance, which Dvořák attended, by Victor Herbert (afterwards famous as an operetta composer) of his own Second Cello Concerto; if this is so, Dvořák may have absorbed the exclusively high register in which the instrument was used, but he was not affected by Herbert's one-movement construction. The great compliment paid to Dvořák's concerto by Brahms (who goodnaturedly grumbled, 'Why didn't I know that it was possible to write a cello concerto like this? If I'd known, I'd have written one myself long ago!') has misled some people into crediting Dvořák with being more of a pioneer than was in fact the case: there were already in existence works for *concertante* cello by Schumann, Raff, Lalo, Rubinstein, Saint-Saëns and Tchaikovsky, apart from the classical writers: it was not that Dvořák was exploring new ground, but that his work was so immeasurably superior, both in technique and in inspiration, to what had gone before.

First Movement. *Allegro.* Here for the first time Dvořák showed himself completely at home with the concerto form, having found at last a satisfactory way of compressing the first-movement plan: he also treats his themes with such freedom, varying them at each appearance, that quotation of an authoritative version becomes difficult.

which eventually gives way to a tutti, a re-appearance of
the passionate theme, and the rondo subject once more.
The next episode, in G major, is calmer

Ex.18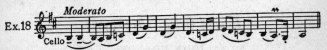

and contains some lovely dialogue between the cello and
the orchestra: Ex. 18 is taken up by the strings before
Ex. 16 returns in the tonic major. Anyone else would have
rounded off the movement at this point; but Dvořák
seems reluctant to tear himself away, and embarks on a
series of codas which become progressively more dreamy.
Structurally these are unnecessary, but they are full of
beauty: in the middle of them the opening theme of the
first movement, Ex. 12, returns on the clarinets. Finally
Dvořák pulls himself together and polishes off the concerto
in brilliant high spirits.

15

Edvard Grieg (1843–1907)

JOHN HORTON

INTRODUCTION

THAT Grieg should have produced one of the most success-ful among romantic concertos is somewhat surprising, as he had little aptitude for extended composition, only limited skill in orchestration, and no interest in virtuosity for its own sake. In his student days, as he long after remembered with bitterness, he had been set the tasks of writing a string quartet and an overture before he had learnt the techniques of composition and instrumentation; and a year or so after his studentship ended he was being urged by Gade, whom he respected as the leader of the Scandinavian Romantics, to tackle a symphony. This ill-fated work, of which the composer afterwards suppressed all but the two middle movements, publishing those as pieces for piano duet (Op. 14), was followed by further essays on an ambitious scale: the Piano Sonata (Op. 7), the first two Sonatas for Violin and Piano (Op. 8 and Op. 13), and the Concert Overture *In Autumn* (Op. 11). The Piano Concerto (Op. 16) comes as the culmination of this phase; thereafter Grieg completed only three more works of sonata type – the G minor String Quartet, the Cello Sonata, and the third Violin Sonata. As time went on he realized that his talent was for small-scale lyrical composition; above all, in the forms of the solo song and the pianoforte miniature. We must therefore be prepared to find in the Concerto a wealth of picturesque detail, but no more than competence in the handling of form. Probably the severest criticism of its structure was made by Debussy, after a performance in Paris in 1903: 'I could never understand', Debussy wrote, 'why it should be broken up by martial trumpet-blasts, usually announcing the beginning of nothing more than a languishing little cantabile.'

From the soloist's point of view the Concerto is well written. It owes much to Liszt, without whose technical explorations and discoveries Grieg's first-movement cadenza, to take one obvious passage, could hardly have been conceived. Liszt may even have given advice on the lay-out of certain passages when he went through the manuscript with the composer in the early part of 1870. The other influences that show themselves strongly in the piano-writing of the concerto are those of Chopin and Schumann.

In spite of his reverence for Liszt, Grieg eventually repudiated at least one debt he owed him – the suggestion for the flamboyant trumpet colouring of the second subject, melody, Ex. 4, as it appears in the first published version of the score (1872). Grieg was rarely satisfied with his own orchestral craftsmanship and was continually retouching old scores. The *Autumn* Overture and the *Peer Gynt* music were among those that underwent revision, and the definitive version of the Concerto belongs to the last years of the composer's life. It differs in a number of particulars from the 1872 version; a second pair of horns is added, the tuba is dropped, and second-subject tune mentioned above is assigned to the cello.*

So much has been made of the 'Norwegian' background of this Concerto that it is worth remembering that it was written in Denmark, during the summer of 1868, that it was first performed in Copenhagen, that it was dedicated to the pianist Edmund Neupert, and that it appeared a year before Grieg had come into close contact with Norwegian folk-music. The Concerto, though drawing in the first and third movements on some of the rhythmic patterns of peasant dances, embodies no actual folk-tunes.

Grieg's Concerto, as Professor Abraham shows in the chapter already referred to, follows in many respects the plan of Schumann's Concerto in the same key. Resemblances

* For a complete list of the changes, see the chapter on the Piano Concerto by Gerald Abraham in *Grieg : a Symposium*. Lindsay Drummond, 1948.

between the development sections of the first movements are particularly striking. Yet the two works are distinct in atmosphere and phraseology, as will be seen from a comparison of their opening bars. Both begin with an opening flourish in which the soloist takes part, and go on to a theme stated first by wind and afterwards by the piano; but Schumann's theme is a long-drawn, tender utterance, whereas Grieg's is broken most characteristically into crisp motives. Schumann's Concerto charms us with its delicate sentiment; Grieg's with its vivid sense of the picturesque.

In 1883 Grieg began a second Piano Concerto, in B minor, probably more to please his publishers than himself. Inspiration soon flagged, and only a few sketches of the first and third movements remain. The opening of the finale shows that this movement, like the finale of the A minor Concerto, was to have had the lilt of a folk-dance tune.

PIANO CONCERTO IN A MINOR

FIRST Movement. *Allegro molto moderato*. A crescendo roll on a kettledrum leading to a crash from the full orchestra releases a descent in octaves for the solo piano. This flourish is based on a formula of three notes:

Ex.1 [music notation]

to which Grieg was much addicted; other examples occur in the G minor String Quartet, in the Cello Sonata, and in the song *Vaaren*. The formula may be described in non-musical terms as a short downward step followed by a longer one; and if this pattern is inverted it produces another type of theme characteristic of the composer and exemplified a few bars further on in this movement (see Ex. 3). The soloist's flourish is, however, only a preamble to a more important theme:

This is introduced by the woodwind, with the strings supplying punctuation. The continuation of the theme is:

first on clarinet and bassoon, afterwards more fully scored. The piano at once picks up theme and continuation and then breaks into a fresh idea of its own, a kind of humoresque, supported by a very light accompaniment. A downward chromatic run in thirds settles piano and strings into a quieter mood over a bass note G (the dominant of the approaching second subject); the passage is typical of Grieg in its flavour of diatonic discord, and also in the fragment of imitation between oboe and piano.

Only two phrases of the second subject melody (key C major) are uttered by the cellos, with soft wind harmonies, before the piano takes up the melody, elaborates it in the manner of a nocturne:

and combines it with an inner melody effectively coloured by the bassoon. The piano becomes more impetuous in its treatment of the theme and makes a swift crescendo towards an entry of the full orchestra with a major version of the three-note 'motto' (Ex. 1). This tutti marks the close of the exposition and prepares a fresh key (E minor) for the start of the development.

'Development' it can be called only by courtesy or custom, for this section offers little more than, first, an exchange of two-bar phrases between flute and horn, based on Ex. 2, with an arpeggio accompaniment for the piano; then some sequential treatment of Ex. 3 by the soloist; and finally a modified version of the pianist's opening flourish, subsiding through horn and trumpet reminders of the rhythm of Ex. 2 and leading to the recapitulation. Ex. 2 returns unchanged; so does Ex. 3 except for some differences of scoring, and the ending of the 'humoresque' theme is altered to lead to the tonic major key (A). The second subject melody, Ex. 4, is transposed into this key without being otherwise changed, but the counter-melody, formerly given to the bassoon, is now assigned to the horn. The approaching end of this section is marked by the solo instrument pounding away at one of Grieg's favourite chords – the dominant ninth. A few bars for full orchestra announce the beginning of the cadenza.

The cadenza falls into three sections: (i) a prelude in free rhythm; (ii) an elaborated version of Ex. 2, first with widespread arpeggios, later with massive chords and timpani-like rumbles such as occur in Liszt's Rhapsodies, and (iii) an arpeggio treatment of Ex. 3, ending in a series of shakes, and dying away as the orchestra re-enters *pianissimo*.

There is a short coda, in the major and in quicker tempo. It is based on a perky theme, evolved apparently from Ex. 3 and the opening flourish.

Second Movement. *Adagio*. The key of D flat can be explained theoretically as the enharmonic of the major third (C sharp) of the main key of the other movements. Its emotional effect in this place is refreshing. Strings, *con sordini*, play one of Grieg's most attractive melodies, with bassoons and horns contributing to the charm of the scoring. The horn echoes the last phrase of the tune and, to use Browning's admirable verb, 'blunts' it into a minor third.

At this point the piano enters for the first time, with a rippling theme of its own which it expands at leisure, though the orchestral instruments appear desirous of enticing it to their melody. At length soloist and orchestra combine in a sonorous repetition of the tune. There is a magical close, in which the horn repeats its 'dying fall' through a cloud of piano trills.

Third Movement. *Allegro moderato molto e marcato*. The few bars linking the slow movement with the finale may have been inspired by the opening of the rondo of Beethoven's G major Concerto; the rhythmic similarity is quite striking.

Soon the piano dashes into the lilt of the *halling*, a popular
Norwegian dance in duple time with abundance of strong
accents. After the full orchestra has taken up this theme in
chorus the solo instrument produces a continuation in more
pianistic style leading to a bold, chordal theme in the relative major key of C. The orchestra, however, returns to the
material of the *halling*, and from its thrice-repeated crotchet
and group of four semiquavers builds up a big climax,
breaking off suddenly to allow the soloist space for a very
brief cadenza. The *halling* is now taken up again with even
greater vigour on the part of both soloist and orchestra; but
the orchestral refrain rapidly subsides, the tonality glides
into F major, and the flute introduces a new theme – a
gentle, song-like tune accompanied by upper strings, *tremolando*. The piano rhapsodizes at leisure on this theme, the
basses of its arpeggios sustained by a solo cello. The
whole episode is delightful in itself; its structural irrelevance
is naïve, especially in the way it ends with a couple of chords,
like any Lyric Piece. The *halling* is again resumed, in slightly
quicker tempo, and the whole of the first section of the movement is repeated note for note – orchestral refrain, piano
continuation and all, with the minimum of adaptation re-
quired to bring back the bold chordal theme in the tonic
key. The orchestra again builds up a long climax out of the
halling figures, and the soloist has another brief but very
forceful cadenza. The final section of the movement starts
after a dramatic pause; it is marked *quasi presto*, and presents
the *halling* theme transformed into the triple time of another
popular measure, the *springdans*. Piquant harmonies and some
effective scoring make this one of the most exhilarating parts of
the work. The culmination is a sonorous reappearance of the
episodic theme, given out with the full power of orchestra and
piano. Grieg saves one of his most original touches almost to
the end. The flattening of the seventh degree of the scale:

is a hint of modality that gave immense satisfaction to
Liszt when he heard it for the first time.

16

Edward Elgar (1857–1934)

HERBERT BYARD

INTRODUCTION

FROM boyhood Elgar was a violinist. At the age of 16 he played in the orchestra of the Worcester Glee Club and was soon conducting it. In early manhood he wanted to become a concert soloist and took a few lessons from Pollitzer, the Hungarian leader of the orchestras of the New Philharmonic and Royal Choral Societies, but later abandoned the project. However, he continued to play in and conduct various orchestras in and around Worcester. Most of these were string bands with a few wind players, and he gained much experience of scoring by arranging full orchestral works for them. Richter once said after a rehearsal of his First Symphony that Elgar made the violins do things they had never done before; one suspects that the violins of the Worcester Glee Club orchestra did things they had never done before when, on 23 October 1876, they played *The Flying Dutchman* overture 'arranged by Edward Elgar'. His love of and intimacy with the violin remained with him all his life. As he lay dying he handed W. H. Reed a scrap of MS on which was written the end of the Third Symphony he never finished: it consists of four bars of violin solo.

In 1890, at the age of 33, he began to write a violin concerto. It says much for his courage and self-confidence that he should have grappled with this difficult form at such an early stage in his composing career. Although he worked long and hard at it, the result displeased him and he destroyed it.

Nearly twenty years later, at the height of his powers, he began the Violin Concerto we all know. The First Symphony had tired him out and he had dropped composition when, in the spring of 1909, he and Lady Elgar went to stay with an American friend, Mrs Julia H. Worthington, at her villa near Florence. Soon he was busy with sketches for the Concerto and the Second Symphony. Early in 1910 the Concerto was sufficiently advanced for him to call in W. H. Reed, then a member, and later leader, of the London Symphony Orchestra, for advice on bowing and fingering the solo part. In September Reed played it, with the composer at the piano, at a private party in the house Elgar had taken for the Gloucester Festival. The first public performance was at a Royal Philharmonic concert on 10th November, 1910, by Kreisler, to whom the work is dedicated, with the L.S.O. and Elgar conducting. The solo part is technically very difficult, and not many violin virtuosos seem to have understood Elgar's extremely individual style: perhaps that is why it has had comparatively few great interpreters. Shortly before his death Elgar conducted it in Paris for Menuhin, who has been associated with it ever since; though many people would say that it found its most faithful interpreter in Albert Sammons. Unlike the two symphonies, *Falstaff* and the *Introduction and Allegro*, it has no external association (unless the composer chose not to reveal it); and this is probably why it appeals to those who generally do not react favourably to the patriotism, Edwardianism or whatever other 'ism' even the most fervent of Elgarians find in his other orchestral music. The score bears the Spanish inscription: 'AQUÍ ESTÁ ENCERRADA EL ALMA DE . . .' ('Herein is enshrined the soul of . . .') and the date 1910. It was commonly believed that Elgar meant to convey that the soul of the violin was enshrined in his concerto, until Mrs Richard Powell, in the second edition of her book: *Edward Elgar: Memories of a Variation*, revealed that the soul was that of the Mrs Worthington at whose Italian villa he was staying when he began to sketch the work.

In 1918 Elgar was working at the Cello Concerto, eventually obtaining technical help with the solo part from Felix Salmond. Presumably the war had saddened him; at any rate, this concerto is a work of great poignancy. He was only one of many composers who have exploited the cello's elegiac qualities, but here, especially in the slow movement, he seems to have expressed the grief that is too deep for tears. The first performance, on 27 October 1919, by Salmond and the L.S.O., with Elgar conducting, was technically a failure, owing to insufficient orchestral rehearsals; but it was not only the quality of the performance which many people found disappointing: they were puzzled by the new voice with which Elgar addressed them. For all his love of society he was at heart an introspective man; perhaps, at the age of 62, war and its aftermath, temporary financial worries, and signs of failing health in his wife, caused him, in the Cello Concerto, to wear his heart on his sleeve for once. The work has never enjoyed the comparative popularity of the Violin Concerto, though Beatrice Harrison tried hard to win it acceptance. Casals took it into his repertory a few years before the 1939 war, while recently Anthony Pini has made it particularly his own.

VIOLIN CONCERTO IN B MINOR

FIRST MOVEMENT. *Allegro*. As in his First Symphony, Elgar here does not ignore classical form, but expands and adapts it to suit his purpose. He uses the normal symphony orchestra, with trombones, though double bassoon and tuba are optional. Without any preliminary parley the usual First Exposition, for orchestra alone, gets under way, followed by the Second, for solo and orchestra. The First Subject has four constituent themes:

Perhaps their extreme brevity would make 'phrases' a better name for them. (*a*) and (*b*) each come twice, the second appearance of (*b*) being syncopated; (*c*) is given thrice and (*d*) extends itself in sequence for sixteen bars.

But no verbal description can adequately show how they
are distributed among the orchestra, or how various instruments reinforce odd notes without playing a complete
phrase. We see here an argument for the theory that Elgar
conceived his tunes 'orchestrally', instead of thinking of
them merely as notes and then deciding which instruments
should play them. The second subject

is curious: another two-bar phrase, it starts in the lower
strings and then has two simultaneous tails, the lower notes
(*x*) being the continuation in violas and cellos while wind
and first violins play the upper notes (*y*). Almost immediately 2 (*y*) recurs in an expanded version, going one
note further and being decorated with a turn on its fifth
note. All this material is then used again with much
elaboration. A big climax sinks away to a restatement of
Ex. 1 (*a*) on strings, at which point the solo violin enters, to
Elgar's favourite *nobilmente* instruction, with a variant of the
same phrase. Immediately there is a pause, followed by a
recitative-like series of flourishes from the soloist, who completely dominates the scene, as if a great philosopher had
suddenly decided to straighten out the loose ends of the
animated arguments in which his students had just been
engaged. After references to various phrases already noted,
the Second Exposition settles into its stride, the soloist
playing a *cantabile e largamente* version of Ex. 1*d*. The main
themes are treated very fully and often elaborately, the solo
violin always taking a virtuoso lead in the discussion. The
Development section, true to tradition, commences with
Ex. 1*a*, but at once introduces several important new figures
which are worked up, under some stormy scales and double-
stopping by the soloist, to a *con passione* climax for full
orchestra. Numerous derivatives from what has already been
heard are punctuated by new versions of Ex. 2, using both
x and *y*, until a sudden hush brings back Ex. 1*a* in the

strings, answered *fortissimo* by the solo against a reference to Ex. 1d on muted horns. Faithful again to the traditional plan, the Recapitulation begins with a recitative similar to that with which the solo made its appearance, and then proceeds to a fresh discussion of all the old themes. The coda gathers the threads together, the soloist-philosopher becoming ever more impassioned as his statements are accepted and affirmed by his orchestral students, and the movement comes to a brilliant end.

Second Movement. *Andante*. *Andante*, be it noted, not *Adagio*. An ambling eight-bar theme *x*

Ex. 3

is stated by strings, with ruminative assents from wind and horns, in the remotest possible key: B flat major. The strings are ready to repeat this pleasant little walking-tune when they meet the soloist, who goes with them, making a countermelody, Ex. 3y, *inside* the orchestral string parts. This is the simplest and finest stroke of genius in the Concerto. Then the partners both seek fresh paths, and with new themes the music temporarily settles into D flat major. A touch of elaborate passage-work from the soloist introduces the second section, still in D flat, with Ex. 3x again. More fresh material, and more self-assertion from the solo violin, encourage other instruments to join in, until the whole orchestra is engaged. Still the tension mounts, and a real climax brings a reference to Ex. 1c in the first movement. The excitement subsides and the third section commences with Ex. 3 *x* and *y* back in the original key of B flat. There is a good deal of tranquil rhapsodizing now, nearly all of it based on fragments of themes we are familiar with, until the music seems to approach a final cadence. But no: this movement, too, has its coda; brief, simple and extraordinarily telling, it adds the last gracious words to a noble discourse between the partners.

Third Movement. *Allegro molto*. Noble discourses can be
tranquil; they can also be passionate. The classical concerto
keeps its ultimate reserves of virtuosity for the last movement. Those two sentences are the key to this movement.
The solo asserts its command at once, with a good deal of
emphatic reinforcement from the orchestra. (Is that 🎵
cello figure a deliberate reference to the finale of the *Enigma
Variations*?) Ex. 4, on clarinets, bassoons and violas:

Ex.4

passes almost unnoticed in the general bustle, but it is important for its later function. The main theme of this finale
is

Ex.5

hammered out *fortissimo* by the orchestra and imitated at
once by the soloist. Till this we have been firmly in the main
key of the Concerto, B minor; this D major theme adds a
specially triumphant note. Several new themes arrive, all of
which are easily recognizable, and the movement rushes
proudly on, with one or two slight easements to take breath,
but nothing approaching a *tranquillo*, till we hear a very fine
reference to a theme from the second movement, marked
nobilmente and *dolce*. But this noble sweetness is shortlived;
soon the mood of triumphant excitement returns and we
seem set for the final climax with a grand swinging version
of Ex. 4, when all suddenly dies away to the unique *Cadenza
Accompagnata*. The orchestral strings are divided (including
the double basses); group I of each section is muted while
group II 'thrums' (Elgar's word) a *pizzicato tremolando* across
the strings with the soft part of three or four fingers. The
effect is ethereal and indescribably lovely. The solo violin
rhapsodizes in an extended cadenza above all this, and is
finally left unsupported in a more orthodox series of double-
stops; then a short bridge with references to two old friends
brings a resumption of the opening of this movement. With

ever-increasing speed we reach a statement of Ex. 5 in triple
and quadruple stops by the soloist; horns and cellos declaim the first bar of Ex. 1a in augmentation, and this
triumphant blaze concludes the work.

VIOLONCELLO CONCERTO IN E MINOR

FIRST Movement. *Adagio: Moderato*. The orchestra is the
same as for the Violin Concerto (except that there is no
double bassoon), though it is much more sparsely used. (Note
that the trumpets are written in C.) Nothing approaching
the formal analysis of the first movement of the other concerto is possible, for this cello concerto makes no observance
of formal classical rules. It is comparatively short, yet it has
four movements – or five, if we count the recitative-like
introduction to the finale separately. From the outset we are
made aware that this, too, is a virtuoso work; for the solo
cello, *ff* and *nobilmente*, delivers a solemn and challenging
introduction without waiting for any preliminaries from the
orchestra:

More markedly than in any other cello concerto, the solo
dominates the scene throughout, and in taking charge at the
start it establishes its importance. Clarinets and bassoons
echo its first two bars; the cello takes two bars for another
little recitative and pauses on F sharp, and the violas make
this the starting-note of a sad, lilting tune, unaccompanied,
which passes to the cellos as it runs below the viola compass:

This the soloist repeats, against a dim background of clarinet
and horn chords and the low E of the cellos, but with a different ending. Further repetitions follow by strings, soloist

(a rushing scale of E minor taking the cello to its highest register), full orchestra and soloist once more; then the rhythm changes to 12/8 for a broken tune, introduced in chords by clarinets and bassoons:

Ex.8

A ray of wintry sunshine breaks through the sombre clouds when this changes to E major, but soon it disappears and E minor returns, to introduce a varied recapitulation of the first main section, founded on Ex. 7. The soloist then makes a *pizzicato* reference to Ex. 6, which acts as a link to the second movement.

Second Movement. *Allegro molto*. This is a scherzo, but a sad one, dominated by a scurrying semiquaver figure:

Ex.9

The solo cello has it nearly all the time, interrupted frequently by *pizzicato* chords and once by a short cadenza. This movement has an improvisatory air, and only one other real theme:

Ex.10

With its Elgarian dropping seventh it might have added a note of triumph had it been longer and had more use been made of it, but it is soon swept away by a resumption of repeated semiquavers by the soloist, and Ex. 9 and its variants soon whisk this sad bustle of a movement to its close.

Third Movement. *Adagio*. Here is another extremely individual utterance, more poignant even than the slow movement of Elgar's Second Symphony. Based on a single theme in B flat major, which starts broadly enough and then is broken by rests, as if the composer's efforts had been interrupted by sighs, it is a solo for the cello (which has only two bars rest in this movement) accompanied by strings, clarinets and two horns. Its moments of nobility cannot disguise its pathos, and at the end it sinks to a dominant cadence; one can almost imagine that Elgar found it too heart-breaking to finish properly in the tonic key.

Fourth Movement. *Allegro – Moderato – Allegro ma non troppo.* The final rondo theme:

Ex.11 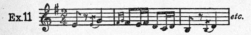 *etc.*

could hardly follow immediately, so there is an introduction which tries out fragments of it. B flat minor soon produces an explosion to E minor, followed by another short cadenza, after which Ex. 11 starts the movement proper. This theme is worked up very freely and boldly against little snatches of tune, none of which, however, is extensive enough to be labelled a real second subject. The excitement is maintained, and the concerto might well be coming to a joyous end but for echoes of tunes from the preceding movements. Suddenly the *allegro* motion is halted by a slow wailing passage of chromatic harmony on strings. The brake has been applied with a vengeance; several times the music jerks forward in an effort to recapture the original speed of the finale, only to be slowed down again. A change to triple rhythm introduces a new and passionate theme, but cannot increase the speed; in fact the new theme changes into the second half of the tune on which the slow movement was based. But the soloist has the solution ready: he delivers the concerto's opening challenge, Ex. 6, and firmly establishes E minor. A few bars of Ex. 11 work up brusquely to a climax and all is over.

It has been said that in his later years Elgar became rather slipshod when conducting rehearsals of his own works, ignoring faults which would once have roused his scorn. Whether this was generally the case or not, it certainly was not true of the Cello Concerto, as orchestral musicians who played in it under his direction can testify. Several of the friends of his old age suspected that it was his favourite work, and some people who knew him and love his music feel that it shows a vein of poetic self-communing not to be found elsewhere. One can only hope that in future we may have more frequent opportunities of hearing this great work.

17

Frederick Delius (1862–1934)

ARTHUR HUTCHINGS

INTRODUCTION

IT would be ridiculous to say that one who, like Delius, achieved integrity in works of large dimensions, needing large numbers of performers, made no plans before committing his ideas to score. Obviously Delius could 'think ahead'. It is true, however, that he had a hatred, unique among composers of large structures, of any planning or manipulating that divorced technique from *direct* expression of the emotions. He told Heseltine to write only the music he felt, but what composer of vital music does not do so? Delius was apparently incapable of appreciating the access of emotional power that is at the command of a man like Bach or Mozart who deploys his expression through such highly organized structures as fugue and concerto, and at the same time bends it to stylistic conventions. We do not depreciate Delius's very great creative talent and his fine nurture of a highly personal style by declaring that his appreciation of artists who respected the classical traditions was as limited as is that of the ungifted or lazy listener who receives only the passing impact of music and complains if what is not immediately attractive cannot be 'explained' in literary or pictorial language, or assimilated with evocations.

How could Delius command extended forms, such as concerto, using neither the free variation of *Brigg Fair* nor, as in choral and dramatic music, deriving some coherence from the text? How did he select and reject? How did he plan? From boyhood his method of composition was improvisation at the piano. Before his rich chords had become the stock-in-trade of commercial music, he charmed his friends either by taking a well-known air, such as *Annie Laurie*, and singing it several times over while playing chains of ninths, elevenths and thirteenths, or else by making the chords themselves into what, according to one of his listeners, made 'a melody of harmonies'. He developed this method of composition, but he never abandoned it. In the hands of most musicians it could produce nothing but disjointed, enervating, sentimental washes of harmony; moreover, a knowledge of the carpentry and joinery of composition, the craft of contrasted subjects and keys, of sequences, development by metabolism or by contrapuntal devices – the methods learnt in the usual apprenticeship – could do little to vitalize this technique; it would have to be abandoned for the kind of structure that can be represented by a ground-plan of keys and materials. Let it be admitted that what distinguishes vital from mechanical transition – and Wagner called composition 'the art of transition' – cannot be shown except by experience of the music itself. Even so, can one write a decent *concerto* without such a plan?

Frankly no. Only one of Delius's concertos fully succeeds in dispelling from us the impression that it consists only of one thing after another. We shall gain little if we listen to a Delius concerto with analytical minds. But some of the 'things' that come one after another are of a span worthy of a place under the title 'concerto'; others have the bewitching loveliness of melody and texture that Delius commands in his tone poems, and we shall do well not to expect from him, in a work called 'concerto', music essentially different from that found in his pieces with evocative titles. Many of those pieces make the orchestra sing, as it were; some are called songs – *Paris: The Song of a Great City, A Song before Sunrise, A Song of Summer* – and let us note that they are evocative but not programmatic. They do not seek to depict, but to reflect the mood of a sensitive man in contemplation of certain scenes, usually of lush natural beauty. They are therefore mood-pieces, and though the mood is sometimes one of exhilaration, sometimes of sombre brooding, the most prevalent mood, that of such favourites as *On Hearing the First Cuckoo in Spring*, is one of wistful yearning at the transience of spring or the rapture of first love; Delius's finest moments are those which express simultaneously both ecstasy and melancholy resignation.

If we look for structure in such music, we must seek it not in the succession of materials, of themes and textures, but in the constant tension and relief of poignancy, the moving to or from a smaller or larger climax. Instead of movements, a 'concerto' gives us a greater number of moods than would have been possible in a tone poem dealing with one aspect of nature, such as *Summer Night on the River*. Now the smaller elements in Delius's music have the same 'structure' as the movements considered as wholes. The melody, not built in contrasted themes, or in balanced phrases, is of the kind called rhapsody, though sequences may occur in rhapsodic melody as they do in the songs from *Meistersinger*; and there are places, such as the *pizzicato* portion of the violin concerto, in which Delius actually uses phrases that balance rhythmically. In fact, even so confirmed an improviser as Delius was driven to some planning of materials, some careful thought as to how A should be manipulated to make B effective, or as to whether B should move to C without some echo of A first.

If any composer after Wagner could have written a long work trusting to extempore launching and maintaining of rhapsody, and to a natural sense of organic growth and coherence, that composer was Delius. The wonder is not that his concertos so often settle to sensuous somnolence and then rise again into a rhapsodic flight, but that so wilful and highly idiomatic a composer can hold us in his spell for such lengths of the same kind of music.

PIANO CONCERTO

DELIUS's only concerto for piano, that in C minor, is not separated into three movements, though it was so in its first version of 1897. None of Delius's music dating from that year, or before, is representative of his mature style. The rich chords that are found almost from first bar to last in his later music were then used hardly more frequently by him than by Grieg, his friend and favourite composer. Delius had written some of his best songs, including such established favourites as *Twilight Fancies* and the settings of Shelley lyrics, the *Indian Love Song* and *Love's Philosophy*. He had also completed his opera *Koanga*, but there is nothing even in that work to suggest Delius's mature style, nor to lead one to suppose that the composer was acquainted with *Tristan and Isolde*. Most of the pianoforte writing is of the type found in the accompaniments to the Shelley lyrics; it owes something to Grieg, something to Liszt and something to the style of a dozen minor composers of dramatic ballads.

In 1906 the concerto was revised to form 'one movement', and we may be certain that any passages which are unmistakeably Delian date from the revision. For Delius certainly found his personal idiom during the first decade of this century. *A Village Romeo and Juliet* was finished in 1901, *Appalachia* in 1902, *Sea Drift* in 1903 and *A Mass of Life* in 1905. We cannot tell, unless the first version of the concerto is discovered, how far the three sections correspond with the three separate movements of 1897, but it is not likely that the third movement used material from the first. As the concerto is now constituted, however, its structure is ternary and not at all closely knit, despite the Lisztian transformation of themes from section one in the course of section three, which introduces no significant new material.

The remark that Delius is not at his ease, not entirely successful in concerto and sonata *because* he is limited by a traditional form and traditional methods of development is in general a foolish one. In none of the sonatas does he attempt to fill a traditional form, yet two of them – the first violin sonata and the cello sonata – are first-rate works, with a masterly integrity, and the other two, the second and third violin sonatas, though less ambitious than the first and not quite so integral, are almost as beautiful. Of the concertos, one is for the most difficult of media – violin and cello with orchestra, another for cello alone with orchestra, and there are very few highly satisfactory concertos for cello. It is not surprising, therefore, that Delius's grip upon form as a whole is less sure in these two works than in the sonatas, the composition of which could be checked at the piano.

There remain the violin concerto, most satisfactory of the four, and the piano concerto at present under notice. This piano concerto is the single work, of all those from Delius's pen bearing a traditional title, in which there is any attempt whatever to emulate the practice of previous composers, or to use classical methods of transition – and this is the one concerto that dates from Delius's immature years. The remarks in the following paragraph are, therefore, made in no unkind spirit.

The piano concerto is of more documentary than intrinsic interest, yet it has some passages of beauty and the merit of being well scored. Its defects are structural. Delius's model was most probably Grieg's concerto, of which Gerald Abraham says:

– an excellent specimen of its genre: the nineteenth-century heroic-romantic concerto – Grieg cheerfully ignored all the subtle possibilities of the classical concerto and simply wrote a first movement in sonata-form for piano and orchestra – making his recapitulation almost a literal repetition of his exposition, and not even bothering to change the relationship of soloist and orchestra.

Professor Abraham does not lightly use the word 'excellent'. Grieg's concerto deserves its popularity even for the way it holds together. Unlike Delius's, it is all of high quality, abundant in quotable passages, none of which can be dismissed as *merely* transitional or modulatory. The test, whether a composer can or cannot write in one of the extended forms, lies in deciding whether 'transitional passages' are any more 'mere' than his main themes. In his piano concerto, Delius's transitions are indeed *merely* transitional, and we should be justified in saying that he was incapable of making significant development of themes if we added 'when those themes are of classical shape and the development follows classical methods'. No new material is initiated during the interplay of soloist and orchestra, and indeed there can hardly be such interplay in a section that uses only two themes fit for a solo piece, but inflates their relationships to the dimensions of a concerto. Concerto demands the lavish thematic invention of a Mozart or a Brahms. Even so, Delius

succeeded in one task which Grieg rarely achieved well –
instrumentation.

There is no subtle writing for the piano, no place where
the keyboard texture consists of anything but chords, scales
in octaves or double-octaves, and arpeggios in their simplest
form. It is said that only pianists can compose for the piano
in a way that would lose quality if transferred to any other
medium. Delius was a violinist of professional ability but he
never undertook serious study of the piano. There are no
themes of importance in the piano concerto apart from the
three quoted below, each one of which has an 'open end',
allowing it to take on different characteristics by extension.
The first section of the work, which resembles the exposition
of a sonata by Grieg, is based on two contrasted themes. The
first is given out by the strings:

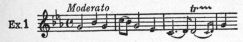

The second by the piano:

There is some amateurish *bravura* writing, and echoing of
cadences from these themes leads to the *largo* middle section
in D flat, probably inspired by the slow movement of Grieg's
concerto.

The solo reaches the cadential shake of this slow
section, makes a sudden crescendo, and gives out Ex. 1
maestoso, in which style the final section proceeds, as if to
complete the sonata form begun in the opening section;
after much ado about what is musically worthless the piece
finishes in C major.

CONCERTO FOR VIOLIN, CELLO AND ORCHESTRA

DELIUS's 'double' concerto was completed in 1916 in the beautiful old house at Grez-sur-Loing in which were composed those works which give us the best of Delius's art – *Brigg Fair* (1907) and the two pieces for small orchestra, *On Hearing the First Cuckoo in Spring* and *Summer Night on the River* (1912). This last-mentioned piece, together with *In a Summer Garden* (1908), is usually accepted as being the most direct musical impression of Delius's home, the garden of which sloped down to the river and bridge at Grez, beloved by R. L. Stevenson. That the 'double' concerto was composed at the height of Delius's powers there can be no doubt, and we know that he was evacuated from Grez for only three weeks during the time when the German armies reached their farthest advance into France.

It is hard to explain, therefore, why he wrote for a combination of instruments that has found only one fine concerto, that by Brahms, and then only after the most careful planning by a mind diametrically opposed to Delius's methods of composition. I have elsewhere supposed that Delius wanted to meet a challenge, as it were, but I no longer hold that view. I think (*a*) that he wanted to write a work which May and Beatrice Harrison, two artists deeply sympathetic to his music, could play together – the concerto is dedicated to them – (*b*) that he was attracted to the two instruments which, more than others, are associated with rhapsodic melody. The difficulty lies, of course, in the attempt to give the cello an interesting part that neither impedes the violin, nor obscures its own orchestral accompaniment, nor forces that accompaniment too constantly into a very low region of the bass, nor becomes inaudible whenever the other instruments rise above *pianissimo*. It is remarkable, therefore, not that Delius so often fails in this task, but that for so many fine stretches of music he succeeds in giving soloists and orchestra clear and significant parts.

The concerto plays without break and at first sight seems to have the basic three-section plan of the revised piano concerto. But it differs enormously from the piano concerto. We are not made to feel that recalcitrant materials are being forced into a classical pattern, or that the third section is the recapitulation of a truncated sonata begun in the first section. The work flows, and has something approaching integrity, not just because of the *tranquillo* section which opens it and then returns to close it, but because its materials are now suited to the highly personal style of procedure. *Rallentandi* and *accelerandi* are not makeshift affairs; they are used in all sections with freedom whenever they suit the composer's expressive purposes. And the bravura passages are no longer put in to make necessary 'bridge passages'; they are plainly written with affection by one who was himself a good violinist.

Instead of attempts at classical 'development', Delius devises little phrases that bear much repitition or echo effect. We see such a phrase or rhythm in the second bar at the outset:

Ex.4

It is actually used at several places in the work to form an accompanimental preparation for the significant melody to be taken up by one of the soloists.

Ex.5

The above theme, which may be regarded as the main one of the first and final sections, is of a type that bears much variation and all kinds of extensions; it is designed for rhapsody. A good example of what Delius uses instead of 'imitative development' is shown in the following:

Ex.6

It is simply music of lower emotional tension than the main rhapsodic themes – a kind of lyrical passage-work that allows the soloists to be heard clearly. Notice that the cello is above

the violin. The only new departure in the two sections under
discussion:

may well serve to show a subtle point in Delius's harmony.
He does not always use lush, erotic chords; he knows when
to make his harmonies bolder, as in this place, to offset the
rich, 'nostalgic' music which is most personal to him, and
which has full play in the middle section. Naturally the
middle section is of the kind most treasured by those who
love Delius's music. Here is the principal theme:

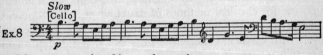

and here a sample of its prolongation:

It illustrates the technique to which he clung from his early days to his death – the constant repetitions and echoes of a ballad-like melody, or of its most haunting phrases, with chains of clinging romantic chords. This is both the method and the mood of *On Hearing the First Cuckoo in Spring*, the quintessence of Delius as composer and artist.

VIOLIN CONCERTO

DELIUS's best concerto, using the solo instrument which the composer himself could play well, is dedicated to Albert Sammons. It was written in 1916, soon after the 'double' concerto, which it resembles in having no break between its sections. But it is a far more integral work, and though one hesitates to use the words 'closely knit' about any music by Delius, it is interesting to note how this composer, who had no use for classical methods of structure and development, came to organize his materials in a scheme which has parallels with classical concerto form – not that the violin concerto is written in sections that parallel the movements of a classical concerto – its great merit is that it is not, and that it is very nearly 'all of a piece'. Delius seems to have recognized, however, that a good concerto needs a greater wealth, contrast and organization of materials than does a tone-poem or a symphonic movement. He therefore succeeded in composing something more than a beautifully accompanied sonata for violin and orchestra; there is genuine interplay between the partners, and it is the orchestra that sometimes initiates new departures.

The opening plunges straight to that rhapsodic melody that covers the greater part of any concerto by Delius:

but it has proceeded for only eight bars before the time signature changes from 4/4 to 12/8, not in any disjointed way:

In view of the remarks about the demands of good concerto writing made above, we may see a reason why what in some concertos is a theme now becomes a *pair* of musical ideas, each capable of rhapsodic extension, but making a fine long sweep of rhapsody if joined together. The triplets in Ex. 11 are also suitable for cadenza work by the solo instrument. A still more interesting change in Delius's attitude to concerto is seen by his introduction of the fanfare-like theme:

which occurs, unaltered except in key, at various points throughout the work, having the same function as a ritornello in classical concerto. It provides just the contrast and relief needed. We hear it first after the extensive passage of *bravura* for the soloist which ends the opening *moderato* section and leads to the slow section. Let it be said in passing that some of the best music in this concerto – not the poorest, as in the piano concerto – is that written in the style of accompanied cadenza.

Passing to the slow middle section, we again find a pair of themes, each with a characteristic and haunting little figure, marked 'a' and 'b' in the following quotations, that can be used extensively for echoes between solo and orchestra:

We also see how parts of each theme can be assimilated into one theme, as in

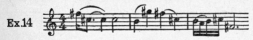

A long cadenza, parts of it accompanied, brings this section to its close, and the third section is opened by the return of Ex. 10 on the strings in unison, with harmonies on the full brass. But the third section is no tame recapitulation of the opening section; there is grafted into it an entirely new musical idea, which in some ways corresponds with the scherzo of a work in four movements. This *allegretto* material, string *pizzicato* accompanying brilliant staccato bowing by the soloist, splendidly offsets the rhapsodic writing and is, no doubt deliberately, written in balanced phrases. Such a dance-like element as this

considerably enriches the concerto as a whole, makes the fanfare-theme, Ex. 11, no longer necessary, and greatly intensifies the return of rhapsodic writing of which we might otherwise have grown a little tired.

CONCERTO FOR CELLO AND ORCHESTRA

As an integral work and as a concerto, Delius's last published essay in concerto form is inferior to the violin concerto, yet if we happen to be deeply attracted to Delius's music and can listen to it 'as it comes', without discomfort when it seems entirely improvisatory, the cello concerto will give us fullest measure of his richest orchestration and most lavish harmony. Formal analysis of this work would waste my time and the reader's. Like its predecessors, the concerto plays without break; like the violin concerto, it would be a ternary affair with a slow middle section between *moderato* sections which use the same main materials, but for the very welcome digression into an *allegretto* passage soon after the point of *reprise* that begins the third section.

The cello concerto was finished in 1921 when the bulk of Delius's finest work was already published and becoming known to English audiences. Though Delius's harmonic style did not develop into any new paths, this concerto shows that he used his chords more lavishly than in previous works, and for that very reason the melody for the solo instrument is less free and less rhapsodic. The following shows the beginning of the first main section, *con moto tranquillo*, though there is a short, slow introduction in which the soloist takes part:

Ex.16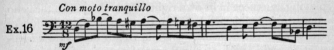

But it is difficult to regard Ex. 16, or any other sample from this part of the work, as a theme. It is merely a beginning from which the texture sprawls onwards in that barcarolle rhythm which is one of Delius's obsessions. The writing is not that of a cello concerto, but of some autumnal tone-poem of beguiling beauty and riotous colour. The solo is sometimes heard as a separate voice, but not as a partner, nor as conversing with small instrumental groups or occasionally making a bass for them. The next illustration is a sample, however, of music that helps to justify the title of the work:

Ex.17

it comes from one of the few places in which the composer is less lured by his extemporization of chains of chords and more set upon a coherent melody. In one sense the title 'concerto' is indeed justified, for, as the following serves to show, the cello part is playable only by a virtuoso:

More discursive writing comes with the middle section, and yet more of the barcarolle rhythm, albeit in slow tempo. Nothing can be quoted as a subject. The return to *con moto* and the recapitulation of Ex. 16 begins a final section worth playing as a piece in its own right. From this point, the cello concerto is a fine work. After the rhapsodic extension of Ex. 16 and some excellent *bravura*, Delius makes his *allegramente* insertion with a cello theme of engaging freshness:

Its continuation does not constitute the only new material in this final section of the concerto, for it is followed by some dreamy music of better quality than the slow section already heard, wherein the soloist is at last heard in a bass melody beneath some delightfully scored harmonies.

The tune heard in Ex. 19 is then taken up by the orchestra

while the cello plays a counter-theme that is not mere make-shift. From this point to the final slowing down and 'sunset' effect, the music is of the composer's best.

18

Jean Sibelius (1865–   )

JULIAN HERBAGE

INTRODUCTION

THE concerto, more than any other musical form, essentially demands musical good manners. The opposition of a single instrument to a mass of orchestral players postulates a true aristocracy of behaviour from the soloist. He must both dominate the scene, and yet appear 'primus inter pares'. He cannot do this by mere virtuosity of technique, nor by relegating the orchestra to a position of relative unimportance. Such crude methods of achieving superiority are both socially inexcusable and musically ineffective. On the contrary he must, like all great leaders, achieve his pre-eminence by a combination of personality and co-operation. Mozart provided the unique example of aristocratic musical manners, and was therefore the supreme writer of good concertos. Beethoven, who must have realized that in the *Emperor Concerto* his musical manners were rapidly going by the board – how unduly aggressive are some of the soloist's entries when compared with No. 4 – wisely avoided concerto form thereafter.

Mendelssohn, whose social good manners prevented him in later life from writing good music, could at least compose, in his final years, a violin concerto which ranks with the best music of his entire output. Then there was Tchaikovsky, who succeeded in writing a good concerto only before he got involved in self-dramatization (or, some would say, self-pity), whereas he composed good symphonies only when he became allergic to the social world that surrounded him. Rachmaninov adopted a more modern procedure, and wrote his famous Second Concerto with the aid of a psycho-analyst. When psycho-analysis had completely subjugated twentieth-century music, composers ceased to have any musical manners at all, and therefore ceased to write effective concertos. The only exceptions were those composers with strong national roots, the traditionalism of which provided an adequate substitute for the inbred urbanity of an international musical culture. After all, it must be remembered, the virtuoso is the most international of all musicians, and it is for him that the concerto is primarily written.

Another peculiarity of the concerto is that it appears to be essentially a youthful form. Both Mendelssohn and Mozart died young, so they provided no true exceptions to the rule. Beethoven, apart from a youthful effort composed at the age of 12, wrote his first acknowledged piano concerto when he was 25, and his last some fourteen years later. Chopin's two piano concertos were produced when he was only 20. Grieg was also 25 when he composed his piano concerto, and Schumann only 31 when he produced the first movement of the A minor. And what of Brahms? It is true he wrote his Double Concerto at the age of 54, but what a falling-off from the First Piano Concerto, composed at the age of 21! There seems, indeed, to be something of youthful striving and of youth's delight in sheer athleticism inherent in the concerto, just as the symphony seems to demand the maturer philosophy and more experienced personality of increasing years.

So it was with Sibelius. His one and only full-length concerto, for the violin (1903, revised 1905), was written at the age of 38, between the composition of the second and third symphonies—a little late, perhaps, in comparison with other great composers, but Sibelius had developed his individual style only a decade earlier, and was to continue developing as a symphonic composer for at least another twenty (and, may we hope, at least another fifty) years. It is also significant that the symphony which followed the Violin Concerto was perhaps the most transitional of Sibelius's works, leading to the new ideals which found full expression in the Fourth Symphony. Thus the Violin Concerto seems to have been written at the pre-ordained moment when Sibelius had achieved his full stature as a

composer without having embarked on his individual path
as a symphonist. As a violin virtuoso *manqué* he was addition-
ally fitted for his task, and therefore we find him writing
music of taxing virtuosity, yet music that is generally as
orchestrally important as it is soloistically dazzling. Musical
content and virtuoso display are equally balanced, and the
individual mind of the still youthful and nationalistic
Sibelius gives us a first movement of extreme originality, a
second movement of passionate lyricism, and a final movement of athletic exuberance. Not all of it is equally con-
vincing musically, and in the hands of any but an exceptional soloist it can become at times an excruciating experience. Sibelius, with a lofty indifference to detail, sometimes
overestimates technical prowess and at other times under-
estimates musical significance.

VIOLIN CONCERTO IN D MINOR

As one might expect, the Violin Concerto is completely
original as regards its form. Summarizing this briefly with
relation to the published miniature score, the opening
movement consists of a first rhapsodic theme and its elaboration, given entirely to the soloist (pp. 1–6), a short cadenza
(pp. 6–7), and an orchestral tutti (pp. 7–11) leading to the
second subject, which is also elaborated by the soloist (pp.
11–14). After this follows a third group of themes, *Allegro
molto*, entirely confined to the orchestra and ending with a
coda on a pedal B flat (pp. 14–22). At this point, where we
would expect a development section, there is a cadenza for
the soloist (pp. 22–6), followed by a recapitulation of the
opening rhapsodic theme (pp. 26–32). This is succeeded by
a tutti containing new developments of previous material
(pp. 33–9) and a recapitulation of the second subject, now
written in longer note-values (pp. 39–43). On the return of
the *Allegro molto* third group the soloist, originally silent, in-
dulges in elaborate decoration (pp. 44–51). The short coda
(pp. 54–7) is based on the opening rhapsodic theme, played
in octaves by the soloist.

This plan, although it conforms to no accepted formal

pattern, is as logical as it is original. Furthermore, it has an internal coherency due to the fact that the thematic material is, as so often with Sibelius, closely inter-related.

The opening rhapsodic theme, *Allegro moderato*, is heard over a shimmering chord of D minor from the violins divided into four parts and muted. Its melodic span covers some thirty bars and its characteristic features are the drop of a fifth in the second bar, the triplets in the fourth bar, the dotted crotchet and semiquavers in the sixth, and the use of both the natural and augmented fourth of the key (G natural and G sharp).

Ex.1

This material, particularly the opening phrase, is elaborated in the following twenty bars, and leads to a short cadenza. This first cadenza, begun over a tympani roll, surprises by its somewhat eighteenth-century arpeggio figuration, but the following tutti, beginning with Ex. 2*a*, changes key- and time-signature while still preserving a link with the first subject through its cadential drop of a fifth. Towards its close it veers towards the similar but more romantic-lyric mood of the second main theme, Ex. 2*b*.

Ex.2(a)

Ex.2(b)

With a sudden modulation to D flat, the soloist takes over the second main theme, Ex. 2*b*, while the ascending phrase with which the soloist had entered is transformed into a counterpoint on the violas, Ex. 3*a*. This latter phrase, in turn, is changed into a rhythmic dance by the orchestra, Ex. 3*b*, as the key changes to B flat minor, the speed quickens to *Allegro molto* and the time-signature reverts to 2/2.

Ex.3(a)

Vla.(Solo)

mp ma marcato

Ex.3(b)

Allegro molto
(Vln.1 & 2)

f marcatissimo

This vigorous dance is continued by the orchestra alone and gradually subsides on a pedal B flat on cellos and double basses, leading into the main cadenza, which is largely based on the opening bars of Ex. 1.

The recapitulation of the opening rhapsodic theme is regular, except that it is begun by the bassoon and continued by the solo violin on the G-string. A completely new orchestral tutti, however, divides the first and second themes, ending with an ingeniously transformed version, on the oboe, of Ex. 3*a*. The second theme is again in the hands of the soloist, but in longer note-values and, of course, in the tonic key of D (major). With the return of the *Allegro molto* dance tunes (D minor) the soloist supplies elaborate decoration mainly in arpeggios and octave double-stopping, somewhat in the style of Hungarian gypsy music. The brief coda recalls the salient features of Ex. 1, and finally the opening passage of the main cadenza.

The second movement, *Adagio di molto* in B flat, is a straightforward Romanza, its main suggestive link with the first movement being the use of both the natural and augmented fourth of the key (E flat and E natural).

Ex.4

Adagio di molto
Solo Vln.

mf sonoro ed espress.

The dramatic middle section in the minor, begun by the orchestra alone, is derived from the introduction (compare pp. 58 and 61 of the miniature score). On its return the main melody, Ex. 4, is entrusted to the orchestra, the soloist indulging in elaborate figuration until the final bars, when once more he takes the melodic lead.

The last movement again is perfectly simple in form – a rondo, *Allegro, ma non troppo* in D major, based on a cross-rhythm announced on tympani and lower strings, with this as the soloist's main theme:

Once again, it should be noted, the fourth of the key is alternately natural and augmented. The main episode, in the minor (p. 82, miniature score), still maintains the under-lying sense of cross-rhythm, but ingeniously alters the stresses, and the violinistic figuration, in double- and treble-stopping, taxes the skill of the soloist. This is true virtuoso music, by no means profound, but exhilarating and effec-tive. The coda at the close (D major, p. 115) makes use of the semitonic shift that had been a feature of the conclusion of Ex. 1, and thus formally knits the concerto together. Yet in spite of such subtleties of construction, the second and third movements are hardly on the same musical level as the first. Sibelius, we must admit, has classical precedent for putting the weight of his musical argument into the first movement, but has he not rather overdone this? In sheer duration of time the first movement is as long as both the other two put together, and in musical content it is worthy to take its place, both thematically and constructionally, with the seven symphonies. The two final movements, on the other hand, seem little more than a happy addition to the host of small pieces that are characteristic Sibelius, but individual rather than great music. Such reflexions, how-ever, must be tempered by the fact that Sibelius has given us, on the whole, one of the most original and outstanding violin concertos written during the present century.

19

Ferruccio Busoni (*1866–1924*)

DENIS STEVENS

INTRODUCTION

BUSONI's reputation as a composer was during his lifetime almost completely eclipsed by his stature as a pianist. Thousands knew his playing: but there would not have been more than a few hundred, if that, who could claim to know or even to be reasonably well acquainted with his many compositions. Not that he was ever the most ardent propagandist for his own music. Like Liszt, with whom he has often been compared, he preferred to encourage young composers and executants, especially during the early part of the century, when his concerts in Berlin invariably included more than one 'first performance'. True, his own works do occasionally figure in the programmes, and among those works were the Violin Concerto (played by Sauret) and the Piano Concerto, in which the solo part was played by the composer, with Karl Muck conducting.

Both concertos look back to the formal ideas of the mid nineteenth century, with stresses upon themes which could be varied, and transferred freely from one movement to another. Busoni accepted these ideas not blindly, but with full perception of their artistic range and possibilities, and to them he added something of his own unique mental, even spiritual, outlook. 'Every motif' (he wrote) 'contains like a seed its life-germ within itself – each one must unfold itself differently, yet each obediently follows the laws of eternal harmony'. Fifteen years later, he qualified that remark in a letter to *Melos* – a letter which by a twist of irony can almost be applied to the man himself: 'A good idea is not yet a work of art, a talented man not at once a master; a grain, however fertile and vigorous, is not the harvest'.

Ferruccio Busoni was a musician endowed with supreme talent; and though he was master of the piano, perhaps the only, the greatest master, he was not able to climb to the highest levels in the realm of pure composition. He deliberately avoided those elements of popular appeal which have made the great composers what they are, yet he gives the impression of wanting to follow them in some of the things they did, even though (as he himself said) 'none of the paths leads upward'. The Violin Concerto, composed in 1896 and completed in the following year, was not quite his first essay in that particular form. A *Konzertstück* for piano and orchestra had won him the Rubinstein prize in 1890. Twelve years were to elapse before the first hint came of another work involving piano and orchestra, and in addition, a male voice chorus. This choral accretion is, of course, in the best tradition of the nineteenth century, whether Beethoven or Berlioz is considered to be the prototype. But those who object to it should bear in mind the manuscript version of this concerto, where the chorus is omitted.

The Violin Concerto is dedicated to Henri Petri, father of the pianist, Egon Petri, who played the Piano Concerto many times with Busoni as conductor. The two works thus have a personal link with each other, in spite of the vast difference in dimensions and resources.

VIOLIN CONCERTO IN D

WOODWIND and horns, over a held D on the strings, play a suave melody which has two distinct, though nicely-balanced halves:

Ex. 1

The soloist warms up to his task with a few well-chosen scales, broken thirds, and arpeggios, against a background of significant drum-taps, and later an ascending scale-motive which is heard on bassoon, clarinet, then bassoon and horn together. There is a pause while the violin trills: then Ex. 1 climbs its way serenely up the E string, to the sound of a quiet accompaniment of strings and horns. During the ensuing crescendo, a new three-note figure is heard in the upper woodwind – a figure which is to appear occasionally at a later stage in the work. The scale-motive leads up to a slight quickening of the tempo, and Ex. 1 re-enters, first plucked, then bowed. Oboes, and afterwards horns, remind us of the three-note figure, while the violin disappears into a chromatic cloud. There is a new tempo (*più moderato*) and a new theme:

Ex.2

and the violin, 'with intentional pathos', declaims above *tremolando* strings, until (*quasi adagio*) the scale-motive makes a *fortissimo* appearance, played in octaves by the soloist. Ex. 2, with brilliant sextolet decoration, leads to a tutti which is dominated by the scale-motive played boldly and firmly by horns and trombone. Sonorous cross-string double-stops, then arpeggios, give the violin a chance for display, but this is cut short by a blast of trumpets over a violently rocking bass theme.

The violin leads off this skittish, scherzo-like section, which soon settles down into what seems at first to be a dominant pedal, though a chain of trills in the solo part cancels the impression, and the trumpet steers triumphantly towards A major. The first half of Ex. 1 is heard on full brass, the second half a moment later in woodwind and *pianissimo* trumpets, trombones and tuba. A short bridge-passage introduces us to Ex. 3, shortly to be taken up by oboes and clarinet:

Ex.3

The violin enters quietly with a long lyrical melody, of wide compass and broad, singing phrases. An oboe begins to reply, but there is a lull before the *poco agitato*, built on the shape of Ex. 3, and now in 3/8 time. There follows a dialogue between violin and basses, which ends in a trill supporting a restatement of Ex. 3. A clarinet offers the lyrical melody, which the solo violin accepts and enlarges upon, until Ex. 1 is heard once again, *tranquillo*, and a short cadenza leads to the *allegro impetuoso*. The rhythm of Ex. 4 is heard alternately with headlong scales from the violin, and when the movement is well under way, the new theme makes its appearance:

This material is worked up to a fine tutti on a pedal D, which soon gives way to a B flat with Ex. 1 above, played by a clarinet. Muted trumpet exchanges comments on Ex. 4 with the same clarinet, and the vigorous opening of the section makes a sudden reappearance. The soloist, playing in octaves, recalls Ex. 2, now *appassionato*, and the three-note figure (in a slightly different rhythm) is heard just before the tempo slackens to a pompous march-rhythm:

The violin comes back with an improvisation (or so it is marked) until it descends to a B flat trill, which is a cue for Ex. 5 to appear in flutes and then oboes. Now Busoni shows us how he changes the character of one of his themes, for Ex. 4 (trumpet solo) becomes more jocular with the repeated notes on the third beat. The violin clothes the delicate orchestral texture with brilliant semiquavers, until a *quasi presto* is reached, and the theme once more undergoes an alteration, starting off in F sharp major. This key is presently banished by a held A (first horn) while the violin plays a wild accompaniment involving its open A string. The *più presto* gives the soloist rapid scale-passages, and then, to end the work, a series of effective arpeggios against an orchestral background of D major fanfares.

PIANOFORTE CONCERTO

I T is impossible to do full justice to so vast a work in so small
a space: there are five movements (which Busoni preferred
to be played without a break) and an orchestra with triple
woodwind and ten percussion instruments. In the last part
of the work, a male voice choir sing a passage from Öhlen-
schläger's *Aladdin*. The German critics did not like it. They
said it was 'Hell let loose' and 'a flood of cacophony'. But it
had cost Busoni two years of hard work, and in a sense the
concerto was a deliberate challenge to the traditionalists
who wrote for the Berlin journals. The titles (and most of the
incidental directions for performance) were all in Italian,
and the only concession to the Berlin public was the translation of the chorus text from Danish into German.

First Movement. *Prologo e introito*. The opening is placid
and solemn, with violas to the fore:

Ex.6

Horns, followed by trumpets, play a bold theme whose
cadence is sometimes flattened:

Ex.7

The soloist listens in the meantime to this orchestral exposition: indeed this is true of the whole concerto, where
there is less of the element of display than of decoration and
comment. When the solo piano does enter, it is *molto
robustamente*, with trumpet calls and violent interjections
from the strings. A serene note is touched, and indeed a
significant one when, upper woodwind intone a new melody:

Ex.8

There is a fine working-out section, the piano being constantly at work, until a *lentamente* is reached and Ex. 7 is

heard again, still in heroic tones. The coda is quiet, and reminiscent of earlier fragments of melody.

Second Movement. *Pezzo giocoso*. The piano leads off in lively fashion, woodwind chords punctuating its fantastic flights. A tutti, in 6/8 time, stresses a new rhythmical idea, of which the soloist remains independent. The orchestra takes it up and extends it, *risoluto assai*, and an impassioned chromatic theme leads us on to a melody *in modo napolitano*:

But the dactylic theme of the first tutti pervades the scene, except in the interludes for piano alone. A vigorous, almost violent dialogue ensues between the two conflicting forces, the piano emerging from the strife with Ex. 9, in freely declamatory style. Woodwinds echo the last phrase of the piano, and recall moments of the opening theme in the prologue. The ending is made to the strange accompaniment of bass drum and cymbals, and faintly reverberating fanfares.

Third Movement. *Pezzo serioso*. An angular, recitative-like theme enters over a moving bass, and oboes and cor anglais play a chromatic (and dramatic) melody which harks back, in its cadence, to a rising arpeggio motive in the first movement. Indeed, from here onwards begin a remarkable series of melodic correspondences which gradually involves almost every important musical utterance in the whole work. A four-note motive heard first on the trumpets, for example, grows naturally and convincingly into a lyrical theme for muted strings. The middle section is marked 'humbly', but the piano replies with a more purposeful phrase:

This and the chromatic melody form the basis of the edifice for some time, but the final section brings with it a theme labelled '*tragicamente*'. The ending is idyllic, however, and brings the movement to a close on a long-held tonic pedal of D flat.

Fourth Movement. *All'Italiana*. The whirl of woodwind semiquavers quickly gives way to a well-defined tune in 6/8 time (flutes and clarinets). The dance becomes wilder, but the rhythm is rock-steady, and the piano a spectator without being spectacular. It is in the solo part, nevertheless, that we hear the rising arpeggio motive again. The popular songs and dances are not absent for long; soon a march is heard, played softly by strings to a restrained but rhythmical accompaniment on the piano. A climax is reached with a restatement of Ex. 9 on trumpets and horns, and a stretto ensues, becoming more and more frantic until a cadenza rounds off the dance and leads the way into the choral section.

Fifth Movement. *Cantico*. Bassoons and horns intone Ex. 10, preparing the ground for the mystical lines which the choir now sing to the melody of Ex. 8. The piano comments quietly on the rich texture of the six-part chorus which turns to Ex. 10 for a new invocation, scored with softness and transparency. The piano, with a fine flourish, introduces the chromatic theme (on woodwind) for the last time, and as the rising rhythm of Ex. 9 surges up through the orchestra, the key of C major is reaffirmed in a blaze of brilliant orchestration.

20

Sergei Rachmaninov (*1873–1943*) and Nicolas Medtner (*1880–1951*)

JOHN CULSHAW

INTRODUCTION

THE mature works of Rachmaninov and Medtner were written during the twentieth century, yet in style and thought they belong to the ripe years of musical romanticism – the late nineteenth century, the era of the composer-virtuoso. One must recognize this in order to preserve historical perspective, and to perceive why one may call their music *individual* without implying that it is also original.

Rachmaninov and Medtner shared a common inheritance from Chopin and Liszt; to this Rachmaninov added a strain of Russian lyricism, while Medtner looked westwards to the composers of the German school. So we may expect brilliant solo parts and dramatic orchestration; extended lyrical tunes and a technique of development that is nearer the variation than the symphonic; and, above all, a tremendous effectiveness. These qualities predominate in the romantic concerto, for in classical times the display element was carefully integrated: any real fireworks were reserved for the cadenzas.

In Rachmaninov the dramatic element is associated with a powerful melodic gift; one may not find much variety in these melodies, but they do possess a sweeping lyricism and are imbued with an attractive, reticent strain of Russian melancholy. The melodies have an almost invariable tendency to rise in sequences, though this type of progression is usually no more than a preparation for the falling phrases which carry the emotional burden – and the Concertos are dominated by the more immediate of the darker emotions.

The weakest passages, in fact, are those which attempt to be consciously cheerful, and this is one reason why the Fourth Concerto in G minor is less satisfactory than the others: it lacks the sombre intensity of the Second and Third, and its darker episodes alternate perilously with passages of rather strained gaiety. Yet it is this sombre emotionalism, expressed mainly through melody, that has been responsible for the enormous success of the Second and Third Concertos; the works suggest a certain anxious yearning to which the twentieth century mind has quickly responded.

The lyrical vein in Rachmaninov's music derives unmistakably from the earlier Russians – from indirect nationalists like Tchaikovsky and direct nationalists like Borodin. It is associated with an individual and very effective piano style, which is the complement of Rachmaninov's keyboard technique; so great, in fact, was the latter that at times one can feel the pianist prompting the composer. The result is a certain episodic quality – particularly noticeable in the Third Concerto – through which an effective theme will release a whole progeny of treatments, each exploiting a particular aspect of pianoforte technique. Sometimes this applies also to Medtner, but with the reservation that Medtner is less interested in (or less capable of) the type of sustained lyricism to be found in Rachmaninov. And what his music loses in terms of direct melodic appeal, it gains in subtlety of construction: his themes are usually more symphonic precisely because they are less extensive.

Medtner's piano style is less florid than that of Rachmaninov; his themes are rarely overloaded with complex inner parts, and their rhythmic flexibility is considerable. Medtner, far less gifted a pianist than Rachmaninov, is able more successfully to separate invention from technique; beyond this, his music lacks the definitive Russian flavour – the exotic element – which is nearly always present in the works of his colleague. Medtner's parents were of German descent, which may be one reason why his music is more closely related to the German romanticism of Max Reger than to any Russian school. Rachmaninov maintained a Russian mentality to the end, whereas Medtner lacked it from the start; this is discernible through the music, and is not invalidated by occasional similarities between the styles of the two composers.

We know from the romantic era that any extension of the lyrical and dramatic elements in a concerto engenders a modification of the form, and both Rachmaninov and Medtner eventually found it necessary to make structural experiments. Each attempted at least one concerto in terms of conventional structure; each turned subsequently to a variation of the 'cyclic' form already explored by Liszt and several others.

Rachmaninov's Concertos are neither the largest nor the best of his works, though they are undoubtedly the most popular. Medtner's Concertos, on the other hand, are the most ambitious works by a composer who has concentrated mainly on music for piano solo: unlike Rachmaninov, he has shown little interest in choral or orchestral works. The two composers nevertheless shared a common ideal, and each based his style on the remnants of a dying tradition. Really great music does not grow from such roots; in these Concertos you will not find the depth and intensity of Mozart, nor the scope and power of Beethoven. Yet you will find appealing, satisfying music – directly emotional music, born of sincerity and written with impeccable craftsmanship.

RACHMANINOV: PIANO CONCERTO NO. 1
IN F SHARP MINOR

RACHMANINOV wrote his First Concerto when he was eighteen, one year before he left the Moscow Conservatoire. Twenty-six years later, in 1917, he made a revised version of the work, and the latter is now invariably used for general performance.

First Movement. *Vivace*. The movement opens with a brief fanfare, the piano entering at the third bar with a passage of descending double octaves, grouped in triplets. In the course of this cadenza the fanfare reappears, now supported by trumpets, trombones and the solo piano. The

principal theme is then played by the violins and immediately repeated by the piano:

Ex.1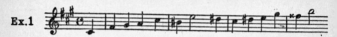

This is followed by a brilliant transition passage, *scherzando*,
leading to the versatile second subject, whose most important
outline is played by the strings and accompanied by
elaborate decorative passages on the piano:

Ex.2

A brief cadenza derived from the principal theme concludes
the exposition.

The development opens with an extensive orchestral episode, deriving at first from the piano's introductory octaves
and followed by references to the first theme. A more for-
bidding version of the fanfare leads to the re-entry of the
piano, which concentrates on decorative passages while
various woodwind instruments play fragments of the second
subject. A solo horn suggests the initial phrase of the first
theme which, after some hesitation, is adopted and extended
by the piano. The tempo then becomes *moderato*, while the
theme gradually expands in the course of a very effective
piano treatment:

Ex.3

A climax is reached, the opening octaves reappear and the recapitulation opens with a piano statement of the first theme, accompanied by counter-phrases from the violas and cellos. The *scherzando* episode again leads to the second subject which, now in the tonic major, receives a slightly varied statement. A brief orchestral tutti announces the cadenza: a lengthy episode of extreme technical difficulty, which manages to mention most of the material, including the fanfare. Finally there is a short coda, based mainly on the triplet phrases which opened the movement.

Second Movement. *Andante*. The *Andante*, in D major, opens with a solo horn phrase derived from the fourth and fifth bars of the principal theme:

Ex.4

The latter is a long, expressive melody played by the solo piano, and it forms the basis of this brief movement. After the initial statement the theme never returns in its original form, though it acts as a kind of generating agent for several other melodies of similar character. The movement is so short that its lack of form is unimportant: it attains its effect through emotional consistency.

Third Movement. *Finale : Vivace*. The form of the finale may be described as A-B-A-Coda. The first section is based on a rapid theme of indefinite outline, its principal virtues being rhythmic rather than melodic. The tempo eventually slackens to *allegro* (two bars after forty-two) and the episode culminates in a pleasant but unimportant melodic phrase for the violins. A brilliant tutti – later to form the basis of the coda – leads to the central episode, *andante ma non troppo*. The melody of this section:

Ex.5

is at first the property of the strings, but later it receives a more rhapsodic statement by the solo piano. Eventually the material of the first episode returns, leading to a brilliant coda which exploits the whole range of the piano in a series of rapid exchanges between the solo instrument and the full orchestra.

RACHMANINOV: PIANO CONCERTO NO. 2
IN C MINOR

THIS, the most popular of Rachmaninov's concertos, had its first complete performance in 1901. It was written shortly after Rachmaninov had recovered from a nervous breakdown, but it was *not* (as is sometimes suggested) written while the composer was in a state of hypnosis.

First Movement. *Moderato*. Eight solemn, dramatic chords gradually increasing in volume and intensity are played by the soloist, and lead to the first theme, *con passione*, on the strings accompanied by swirling piano arpeggios:

Ex.6

This, like so many of Rachmaninov's melodies, uses the tonic note as a pivot and generally avoids the wider melodic intervals; it requires forty-five bars for its complete statement. The final phrases are taken over by the piano until a rapid treble passage culminating in a series of heavy chords signifies the end of the first subject group. A brief viola phrase accompanied by clarinet chords prepares for the second subject – another lyrical melody, played by the soloist:

Ex.7

The tune is developed modestly until the tempo quickens and a brief cadenza marks the end of the exposition.

The development is concerned mainly with the first subject in association with a rhythmic figure, first played by the bass strings and later elaborated by the woodwind and piano:

Ex. 8

(It derives, incidentally, from the outline of the crotchet group in the eighth bar of the introduction to the movement.) When the piano enters at Section 8 it adopts this rhythmic figure and varies it extensively until the violas introduce a transformed version of the second theme, which gradually passes to the full orchestra accompanied by pounding rhythmic phrases, derived from Ex. 8, on the solo instrument. A powerful climax is built, leading directly to the recapitulation of the first theme *maestoso alla marcia* on the strings accompanied by another piano variation of Ex. 8. The second part of the theme then becomes the property of the soloist, though the strings and woodwind join in at the eighth bar. At Section 13 a solo horn reintroduces the second subject, whose closing phrases are treated rhapsodically by the piano in one of the most inspired passages of the whole work. A coda, starting at Section 16, is based on the rapid treble phrase with which the exposition of the first subject concluded. It should be noted that there is no conventional cadenza, and that the whole movement is remarkable for its sustained tension; the only passage of essentially rhapsodical character is to be found in the very free recapitulation of the second subject. In terms of the relationship between form and content it is evident that Rachmaninov never surpassed this movement.

Second Movement. *Adagio sostenuto.* Four introductory bars serve as a prelude to the slow movement, and act as a transition from C minor to E major. The piano enters at the fifth bar with a very beautiful accompaniment figure, above which a solo flute and solo clarinet introduce the principal theme:

Ex. 9

The latter is then stated by the piano, while the strings and clarinets take over the original accompaniment figure. Nine bars after Section 19 the piano plays a variant based on the 3/2 bar of the main theme (Ex. 9 – bar 5); this is extended and developed until a brief cadenza passage leads to a section in more lively tempo, followed by a larger and more powerful cadenza. The final trill of the cadenza turns itself into the original accompaniment figure while the strings play the principal melody for the last time. The exquisite coda is based on a stately variant of the theme divided between the strings and the piano, while the woodwind make reference to an altered version of the accompaniment figure.

Third Movement. *Allegro scherzando.* The orchestral introduction suggests the rhythm of the forthcoming main theme, and in twelve bars takes us from E major to the original C minor. A brilliant piano cadenza leads to the first theme:

Ex. 10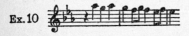

This is followed by a series of attractive but structurally unimportant subsidiaries. Sixteen bars after Section 30 the piano prepares for the famous second subject, first stated by the oboes and violas and then repeated in more extended form by the piano:

Ex. 11

A passage of piano figurations in triplets, accompanied by brushed cymbals, serves as a transition leading to the return of the main theme, which is then subjected to various treatments and at Section 34 becomes the basis of a brief fugato episode. The second subject then returns in D flat major, followed once again by the triplet bridge passage. The final episode begins with an orchestral statement of fragments from the main theme, together with a mysterious, veiled suggestion of Ex. 6 from the first movement. (The latter, however, was composed *after* the second and third movements had had their first performance.) Soon after the entry

of the piano there is a climax and a short cadenza, leading to
a statement of the second subject, *maestoso* in C major, by
the piano and full orchestra, thus bringing the Concerto to
an effective conclusion. The form of the finale might therefore be described as A–B–A–B–A–B, the *scherzando* theme
'A' receiving the most varied treatment while the second
theme 'B' is mainly static and lyrical.

RACHMANINOV: PIANO CONCERTO NO. 3 IN D MINOR

THE Third is the most complex and interesting of the
Concertos; it was first performed in New York during 1909.

First Movement. *Allegro ma non tanto.* In the first two bars
the orchestra establishes a basic rhythm (dotted crotchet-
quaver, dotted crotchet-quaver) which recurs persistently in
various forms throughout the work. At the third bar the
piano enters with the first theme:

Ex. 12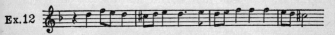

which is then repeated by the violas and subjected to incidental variation; the rhythmic figure which opened the
Concerto meanwhile becomes increasingly discernible in the
piano accompaniment. At Section 4 the clarinets and horns
suggest a variant of a phrase from the main theme – a fragment which eventually becomes the second subject. After
a brief cadenza a further variant of the main theme is stated
by the orchestra, foreshadowing a treatment which does not
reach fruition until the finale. The second subject (of which
we had a premonition at Section 4) now appears in dialogue
between piano and orchestra, and then takes its most important outline in the course of a solo piano statement:

Ex. 13

The theme is then extended and leads to the opening of the
development section, at which point the original rhythmic
figure and the first phrases of the opening theme reappear.

The development applies the initial rhythmic figure to several melodic sequences and phrases derived from the first theme (which, we should remember, also generated the second). A climax is reached in which piano and orchestra join to stress the importance of the rhythmic idea, while in an episode following the climax the more lyrical contours of the themes are suggested. An exceptionally brilliant cadenza, embodying further development of the material, is then heard; and at Section 19 the piano stresses the rhythmic figure beneath rapid arpeggios, while a solo flute outlines the melody of the first theme. The cadenza is then resumed, and takes over the task of recapitulating the lyrical form of the second subject. At last the original rhythmic figure re-appears and the piano states the main theme for the last time. The end of the movement is hushed and mysterious: it concludes with final references to the dominating dotted crotchet-quaver rhythm and to the original version of the second subject. One may be sure that the last has not been heard of this material.

Second Movement. *Intermezzo – Adagio*. This movement consists, in the main, of a set of variations based on its opening theme, which is suggested by the strings and then played by the solo oboe:

Ex. 14

The piano enters at Section 25 and, after an introductory passage, states the theme in several contrasted versions. The treatments become increasingly impassioned, and a climax is reached when a variant of the theme is proclaimed emphatically by the piano and orchestra. This is followed by a passage in faster tempo; the piano concentrates on brilliant decorative passages while the woodwind instruments play an elusive phrase derived from the main theme of the *first* movement. Soon, however, the original tempo is re-established and the orchestra again presents the sorrowful *adagio* theme. Just as this appears to be approaching the depths of despair the piano bursts in with a violent interruption which, in the course of seven bars, leads directly to the finale.

Third Movement. *Finale : Alla breve*. The first and last
movements of this Concerto are closely linked; the majority
– if not all – of the material in the finale derives from themes
and rhythmic outlines already exploited in different forms.
Thus the theme with which the piano opens the finale:

is based on the initial rhythmic phrase of the first movement,
while the relation becomes even more emphatic when the
percussive second subject appears:

At Section 48 there begins a *scherzando* treatment of Ex. 15
and at Section 50 there follows a further episode based on
the theme, whose relation to the rhythmic figure in the first
movement now becomes more apparent. Then, suddenly,
the first subject of the first movement reappears in a statement by piano and orchestra, to be followed immediately by
a version of the second subject, which we originally met in
the form of Ex. 13. Then, in increasingly emphatic and brilliant statements, the first and second subjects of the finale
are heard, and the outline of the latter, Ex. 16, now expands
into a lyrical rising melody:

thus revealing a distant relationship to the orchestral episode
immediately before Section 5 in the first movement. The
same theme in its percussive from, Ex. 16, now provides the
basis for an exciting passage between piano and orchestra,

which gradually gathers pace as it approaches the climax. A downward octave run on the piano leads to a final variant, for piano and full orchestra, of Ex. 17; and this conclusion is all the more effective because it is the focal point of a work in which nearly all the material is interrelated. The structure is loose enough to admit Rachmaninov's rhapsodic type of treatment, while being effectively held together by a subtle unifying idea.

Note: The following cuts are usually, but not always, made in performance. They have been observed in the above analysis. Section 10 (First Movement). Section 44, Bar 13 to Section 46, Bar 9 (Finale). Section 52, Bar 3 to Section 54, Bar 1 (Finale).

MEDTNER: PIANO CONCERTO NO. 2 IN C MINOR

MEDTNER's Second Concerto was written in Paris during 1926 and 1927.

First Movement. *Toccata: Allegro risoluto.* As its title suggests, this movement contains a wealth of brilliant piano writing. The first theme is stated immediately by the piano and orchestra:

Ex.18

It is a virile and flexible idea whose powers are by no means exhausted in this preliminary treatment. At Section 3 a powerful call from the horns and trumpets prepares for the second theme, *molto cantabile*, played by the piano and then repeated by the violins:

Ex.19

The key is now E flat major, but at Section 5 there appears a new idea in G major, Ex. 20 – a brief rhythmical fragment which, though theoretically the real second subject, is best regarded as the complement of the first theme, just as the little melodic subsidiary which grows from it is the spiritual complement of Ex. 19. The exposition closes with a powerful statement of the first theme.

Ex.20

The development section makes extensive use of all these fertile ideas. At first it concentrates on the lyrical second theme, but the piano prefers to stress the first idea until a solo flute takes over Ex. 19, at which point the piano adds a background of arpeggios and decorative phrases. The piano then adopts the theme in a cadenza passage, which is interrupted by a trombone reference to the first theme; but even this cannot dispel Ex. 19, which reappears immediately on the strings. The piano suggests Ex 20. as an alternative and the violas agree; the timpani reminds us of the rhythm of the first theme, but the violas and bassoons begin a fugato treatment of Ex. 20 and are gradually joined by the rest of the orchestra and the piano. At the end of this episode the lower strings, clarinet and piano revert to Ex. 19 which, with further brief references to other themes, leads to the recapitulation of Ex. 18 by the full orchestra without the soloist.

Then follows an elaborate cadenza which deals first with Ex. 18 and then recapitulates Ex. 19 in its original form, though now in the key of D flat. The coda sums up everything most effectively: the piano gives us a last glimpse of Ex. 19 in a new form, but reverts to Ex. 18 in the last bars. A long trill, a run simultaneously up and down thep iano, and the movement is over.

Second Movement. *Romanza : Andante con moto.* This beautifully written movement is based almost entirely on the opening piano theme:

Ex.21

a broad lyrical idea which is soon taken over by the violins. When, after this, it passes to the violas and cellos its statement becomes more emphatic; and at the end of this section there is a brief cadenza for the piano, leading to the appearance of a rhythmic figure derived from the theme in the form of a dialogue between clarinets and the piano. Further treatments follow, all of which are closely related to the main theme – with particular emphasis on its first phrase. Towards the end of the movement the music becomes more impassioned, and the final statement of the theme is divided between the piano and the full orchestra. After this, the mood becomes more dramatic; rhetorical phrases pass from the orchestra to the piano, preparing the way for the sudden emergence of the finale.

Finale. *Divertimento : Allegro risoluto e molto vivace*. The first theme, stated immediately by the piano, was clearly anticipated in the last pages of the *romanza*. Its flippant character is ideal for a movement which is described as a *divertimento*, and its opening phrases are as follows:

Ex.22

At Section 7 there appears a more stately idea on the strings:

Ex.23

which is then taken over by the piano. Shortly afterwards (four bars after Section 11) the flutes and oboes make a reference to the main theme of the *romanza*, which is then mentioned by the piano against orchestral treatments of Ex. 22. This is our first definite indication that the *divertimento* is to include references to themes from the preceding movements.

The development – or fantasia, as it might be called – opens with a woodwind statement of Ex. 23 against string references to a derivative of Ex. 22. The latter is treated very extensively when the piano enters at Section 18, and there are solo passages for the bassoon, oboe and violin. Fragments of the first theme, Ex. 22, now begin to suggest a remote derivation from the opening theme of the first movement;

and at Section 37 there are definite references to several themes from the opening movement, including Ex. 20.

The recapitulation starts with a powerful statement of Ex. 22, and Ex. 23 follows as expected. Again there is a fleeting suggestion of the *romanza* theme, followed by an orchestral tutti and a piano cadenza derived mainly from Ex. 22. The coda begins with a brilliant variation of the latter, but at Section 58 the violins cannot resist a final mention of Ex. 20 from the first movement. Thus concludes an ingenious and charming work, whose subtleties are only to be discovered after several hearings.

MEDTNER: PIANO CONCERTO NO. 3 IN E MINOR ('*Ballade*')

THE composition of this work was completed in London during 1942 and 1943. It has an unusual and interesting structure, but the effect is essentially rhapsodic and the title itself should warn us not to expect all the traditional features of concerto form. The work consists of three 'movements', linked not only in the sense of being continuous but also through a certain unity in the material.

(1) *Con moto largamente*. The opening horn theme is of the utmost importance

Ex.24

as in the course of the work it generates several important melodies. The piano enters at the fifth bar with a secondary theme

Ex.25

which eventually leads to a woodwind restatement of Ex. 1. A new melody is then presented by the strings, accompanied by arpeggio passages on the solo instrument

Ex.26

and towards the end of this passage the piano stresses an abrupt rhythmic figure which develops into a short cadenza. The key then changes to E flat minor and Ex. 24 reappears on the strings followed immediately by a fragment of Ex. 25 on the brass; then there is another brief cadenza, leading to a more emphatic statement of Ex. 26, divided between the piano and orchestra. This 'exposition', in which nearly all the important material has been announced in its initial form, concludes with a woodwind reference to Ex. 24.

The principle of development used in the concerto is more subtle than variation technique, with which – superficially – it might seem to have much in common; but the process of development is not reserved for a particular section or even a particular movement. It is a continuous process: the gradual unfolding on phrase after phrase: a ballade, but a ballade on a very large scale. Thus what traditionally would be called the development begins with a piano theme related to Ex. 26, supported by a cello statement of Ex. 25. At Section 14 in the score the strings return to Ex. 24, whose outline is then elaborated by the piano and worked to a climax. The piano then takes command of Ex. 26, from which there grows a subsidiary melody of considerable charm:

Ex.27

(Section 27 in the score). This idea is stated and varied at length, though there is a brief interruption marked by the unexpected return of Ex. 24. Most of the episode, however, grows from Ex. 26, whose first phrase returns now and then to remind us of the origin of the music.

The fact that the material is to be used in the subsequent movements obviates a conventional recapitulation, and what we have considered as the first movement ends with a string reference to Ex. 24 and a suggestion of Ex. 27. A short cadenza serves as a link between this and the *interludium*.

(2) *Interludium*. This very brief episode opens with a powerful variation based principally on the first two themes of the

concerto (Ex. 24 and 25). At Section 63 in the score the soloist changes to Ex. 27 in a new form; this leads to a dramatic climax and, at Section 68, to the opening of the finale.

(3) *Finale : Allegro molto, eroico.* The lively first theme

Ex.28

is played by the piano and derives indirectly from the original Ex. 25. Yet such a relationship, though responsive to analysis, is more spiritual than material: one knows that Ex. 28 is no stranger, though one may not at first recollect its origin. Treatments of this theme continue until Section 77, when Ex. 24 reappears on the strings; and at Section 84 the strings introduce a familiar theme which is distantly related to Ex. 24 (compare Ex. 24 and 29).

Ex.29

This new idea is rhapsodically treated until Ex. 24 is stated by the horns and trumpets and then varied in several ways by the soloist. At Section 108 Ex. 28 is again stated by the piano, and in the succeeding episodes there are several references to thematic fragments from the first movement, including an orchestral statement of Ex. 25 in slightly altered form.

A long pause leads to a new episode, *andante con moto tranquillo*, which is in many ways the heart of the concerto.

Ex.30

This is the opening phrase of the piano melody which seems to act as a pivot for the whole concerto: it is a subtle synthesis of the overall mood of the music, and distantly it seems to derive from Ex. 24 – an origin indicated more clearly by subsequent orchestral references. At the end of this passage there begins a condensed recapitulation of themes from the first movement: Ex. 24 on the wood wind, followed by Ex. 25 on the solo horn and piano, and Ex. 26 on the strings. Quite logically, this is followed by a similar recapitulation of material from the finale, starting with Ex. 28, again on the piano. Other themes (excluding Ex. 30) follow as expected, but each reveals a delightful variety of treatment. Gradually, however, Ex. 24 becomes increasingly prominent in its various outlines, and at Section 161 Ex. 26 reappears to form a preparation for the coda.

The coda begins with a powerful restatement of Ex. 30, which thus reveals its importance in the structure; and what is important is not so much the fact that it shares structural origins with Ex. 24, but that it embodies a change in mood: the mysterious, brooding opening of the concerto now resolves in a coda of optimistic, tranquil expression. The key is E major, and the work reaches a brilliant conclusion with final references to Ex. 30 and 24: the fulfilment and the source in a final juxtaposition.

21

Maurice Ravel (1875–1937)

EDWARD LOCKSPEISER

INTRODUCTION

THE two piano concertos of Ravel, the one in G major and the other, for left hand alone, in D major, were both completed in 1931, six years before the composer's death. With the exception of the three songs, *Don Quichotte à Dulcinée*, written in 1932, they were his last works, the final manifestation, therefore, of one of the great geniuses of twentieth-century music. Masterpieces of wisdom and fantasy that in England, at any rate, seem not yet to have been fully appreciated, they not only define the ultimate conquests of the composer's exploratory mind, but, as with the late works of other such princely travellers into the unknown world of music – Beethoven, Debussy and Stravinsky – they have the function, too, of illuminating the composer's earlier works. *Daphnis et Chloé*, the Mallarmé songs, *L'Heure Espagnole* or *L'Enfant et les Sortilèges* must inevitably acquire new significance once the recret evolutionary bond that links them to these final works of the composer's maturity is traced. Musical intuition becomes the music of reason in these two concertos. The landmarks in the composer's world of dreams gradually become more apparent and the laws and logic of his musical universe established.

The G major concerto was originally conceived as a Basque Rhapsody for Piano and Orchestra in several movements, which Ravel intended to perform during his tour of the United States in 1927–8. The first and third movements of the work completed, however, only after his return from America were taken from the original sketches and, as we shall see in the more detailed analysis of the work, they include unmistakable evocations of his native Basque country

(Ravel was born at Ciboure near St Jean-de-Luz). Its first performance was given in Paris in 1932 by Marguerite Long, to whom it is dedicated, with the composer conducting. The concerto for the left hand alone, though begun somewhat later at the request of the German pianist, Paul Wittgenstein, whose right arm had been amputated as a result of a wound in the 1914–18 war, was completed earlier and was first performed by Wittgenstein at Vienna in 1931.

Though the two concertos were thus written almost simultaneously, the contrast in regard to both style and treatment of the solo instrument is striking. Indeed, they seem calculated to underline two opposing tendencies in Ravel's art, but in the composer's elusive and seemingly baffling manner, precisely in the way one would least expect. The G major concerto (for two hands) is conceived in the style of an amplified chamber work, while in the left-hand concerto, almost in defiance of the limitations imposed on keyboard writing, full rein is given to a highly developed virtuoso style. In a most thoughtful study on the style of the two concertos, Frederick Goldbeck in *La Revue Musicale* (March 1933) observes that this deliberate antithesis between the two works is further accentuated by the choice of the traditional three-movement form, not for the virtuoso style of the left-hand concerto, but for the chamber-music-like G major concerto; while the elaborate left-hand work is compressed into a single movement. This is perversity, if you will, but the perversity of a most sophisticated mind, intent upon creating difficulties for the sheet intellectual pleasure of surmounting them. Intelligence, pleasure, virtuosity — these are indeed the more apparent features of Ravel's magical art. Yet concealed behind so much brilliance and agility are the implacable ghosts of music who must perpetually haunt an artist of ancient civilization – the ghosts in the G major concerto of Scarlatti, Couperin, Mozart and Saint-Saëns; in the left-hand concerto of Liszt, the more ostentatious Liszt, as it turns out, but who is here miraculously transformed and refined upon with infinite grace and subtlety. And of course the ghosts of musical Spain – the idealized and romantic Spain that could never

leave the heart of the Basque composer – the alluring Spain
of a musical Gautier in the G major concerto, the tragic
Spain nearer to Merimée in the D major.

'I have never attempted to create *ex nihilo*', this most
original of French composers paradoxically declared. And as
if to emphasize the fundamental contradiction in the act of
creation, he confesses that 'it is by imitating that I innovate'.
Let us accept the artist's right to such a disguise as his
means of laying the ghosts within him, the ghosts not only of
his musical ancestry but the ghosts, too, of his former self. I
am indebted to Frederick Goldbeck for suggesting, though
he does not say so in as many words, that if the G major
concerto was written to exorcize the composer's *Le Tombeau
de Couperin*, the left-hand concerto is an attempt to come to
terms once again with the romantic terror of *Gaspard de la
Nuit*.* Couperin and Liszt, Mozart and Liszt, Saint-Saëns
and Liszt – however the art of concealing art may be dis-
cerned in one work or the other, in these two works are
revealed the two faces of this civilized French master of the
keyboard. In this twentieth-century composer's final search
for his soul they show, on the one hand the eighteenth, on
the other the nineteenth, century brought to life again
amidst the undermining clashes and conflicts of our modern
times.

PIANO CONCERTO IN G MAJOR

THE first movement marked *allegramente* opens with an
innocently jovial theme entrusted to the piccolo against a
hardly perceptible drum roll, a *tremolo* on the cellos and a
lightly-traced *arpeggio* figure on the solo piano:

Ex.1

---

* The illuminating and evocative comparison of Goldbeck is worth
quoting: 'Les deux pianos de Ravel: selon Mozart, selon Liszt – ou, si
mieux aimez, deux pianos très raveliens: le doux clavecin pleurant
Couperin, et le grand luth nocturne de *Gaspard*.'

Henri Gil-Marchex,* pointing out that the rhythm of this theme derives from the Navarre dance called the Bransle, makes a plausible comparison, too, between the effects of these opening bars and the fife-and-drum music of the Basque folk-musicians. As the mood gradually becomes more exuberant, the theme is taken over by a solo trumpet. An amusing couple of bars leads one to expect a counter-subject on the cor anglais, but the illusion suddenly vanishes as the piano introduces a lazy, improvisatory motive, vaguely Spanish in character, the seductive indolence of its triplets prompting M. Gil-Marchex to suggest that they might have been set to the expressive words 'Vous m'ennuyez! vous m'ennuyez!'

There follows a succession of fragmentary themes, colliding with or developing out of each other, as if in some almost forgotten dream, until the spell is abruptly broken by the solo piano reverting to the original tempo in a toccata-like passage with jazz-like interjections from trombone and trumpet. This passage is developed with much verve until, at the very moment of its climax, it is unexpectedly geared into a restatement of the opening Basque theme. The remainder of the movement lingers upon these abundant evocations. The piano's infinitely tender cadenza leads to some invigorating jostling between soloist and orchestra, the closing bars being significantly built upon an oriental mode of the *Cante Flamenco*.

The second movement, *adagio assai*, opens with a long, ample monologue in E major for piano solo, the melody of

* See the article, 'Les Concertos de Ravel' in *La Revue Musicale*, December, 1938.

which, in the right hand, is in 3/4, while the accompaniment follows a 3/8 rhythm:

We have it from M. Gil-Marchex that the source of inspiration for this noble discourse was the Clarinet quintet of Mozart, though such is the wizardry of Ravel that the Mozartian spirit is completely absorbed into music producing the effect of a stately passacaglia. The eleven pages of the full score of this movement contain marvels of modulation as the soloist's moving *cantilena* is developed in the form of the Lied. With exemplary discretion, flute, oboe and clarinet make their solo entries, defining ever so gently the mood of Mozartian stillness, when, suddenly, the piano is called upon to spin out an exquisite arabesque, presently to be thrown against a clear-cut musical argument from the orchestra. A rasping dissonance, resulting from the chord of G sharp minor underpinned with a G natural in the basses, marks a fearful climax in the tiny score, whereupon the soloist claims the field for himself: the melody of the opening monologue is now dreamily repeated by the cor anglais against the piano's lacey patterns, and as the heavenly movement seems about to vanish into thin air, a ghostly echo of the opening theme can be caught from a muted viola.

The final *presto* is a freely conceived *rondo* assuming the character of an exhilarating race between piano and orchestra.

Scarlatti and Saint-Saëns have apparently been the twin
models for this devilish *tour de force* of vivacity. 'Yelps from
the clarinet', writes M. Gil-Marchex with picturesque
ardour, 'the theme snapped at by the piccolo and snarled at
by the trombone, mark the succeeding stages of the hot
pursuit'. And he goes on to suggest that Ravel's art of
illusion takes the form here of leaving the listener in
doubt as to whether the piano is the pursuer or the pursued.
(There is both a psychological and an aesthetic parallel
here with the music of the persecuted child in *L'Enfant et
les Sortilèges*.) More than once the brass instruments sound
a fanfare as if to invite all participants to be in at the kill,
but nothing can restrain the movement's frantic pace, until, after no more than three minutes, the coveted goal
is reached to the accompaniment of a triumphant roll of
the tambourine.

PIANO CONCERTO IN D MAJOR FOR LEFT HAND

THE uncanny opening of the concerto for the left hand
alone in which a solo double-bassoon seems to creep out of
the accompaniment of the lower strings in the rhythm of a
slow sarabande, immediately proclaims a mood of fantastic
horror – a mood all the more terrifying because of the music's
generally subdued tone. It is curiously reminiscent of both
'Le Gibet' and 'Scarbo' (from *Gaspard de la Nuit*):

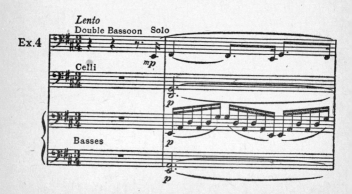

M. Gil-Marchex declares this concerto to be the most
dramatic of all the composer's works. It is certainly among
the most powerful and turbulent of his expressions, making
nonsense of a current conception of Ravel as an artist
working in the dimensions of the miniature. Over a drum
roll the sarabande is developed into a mighty crescendo
while the horn theme is transferred to the more strident
tones of trumpets and trombones. The solo piano now makes
a bold entrance with a virtuoso cadenza. The tremendously
difficult part for the solo instrument is written on two staves,
the texture carefully calculated to display the resources of
the left hand, particularly the expressive capacity of the
thumb in the delineation of the melodies:

For this reason alone a transcription of the solo part for two hands must necessarily distort the composer's intentions. The Lisztian grandeur with which the sarabande is now developed by the soloist presently produces the flourish of a *glissando* over the whole length of the keyboard, and now the full orchestra proudly takes up the same material, leading to an explosive but characteristically agile contest between trumpets and horns. In a subsidiary section, *più lento*, introduced again by the solo piano, the tension is momentarily released, but the obsession of the sarabande is soon to return and persists until the trombones brutally proclaim the rhythm of a sardonic and scornful jazz-like theme to be treated in the most intricate fashion. Wilfully distorted and deformed as it is flung from piano to brass and woodwind, this theme serves as material out of which is built some sort of vast, nightmarish vision of the 'Danse Générale' from *Daphnis et Chloé*. There is rasping malice in this music as the great composer so amazingly steers us through this terrifying and ghostly world of his last years. When eventually the sarabande returns and is thundered out by an orchestral tutti, there remains only the logic of a recapitulation, entrusted to the soloist in an elaborate cadenza to bring the epic work to its close.

22

Ernest Bloch (1880–   )

ERNEST CHAPMAN

INTRODUCTION

BLOCH's Violin Concerto and Concerto Symphonique for piano and orchestra are among the composer's most recent full-scale works, having been completed respectively in 1938 and 1948. In the list of his essays in concerto form they are preceded by the *Schelomo* Rhapsody for cello and orchestra (1915), the Suite for viola and orchestra (1918–19), the Concerto Grosso for piano and strings (1924–5), and *Voice in the Wilderness*, described as a 'symphonic poem for orchestra with cello obbligato' (1936).

The concerto form, with its implicit idea of contrast, or of struggle between opposing forces, is an apt vehicle for Bloch's type of expression, which, within the great range of feeling he commands, leans towards the intense, the dramatic, and the rhetorical. On even a quite limited acquaintance with these works the listener is unlikely not to sense the passionate integrity and the driving sense of purpose that inform Bloch's music as a whole.

Bloch is, as is well known, a member of the Jewish faith, (born in Geneva, and for many years now a naturalized citizen of the United States). Some of his works, though by by no means the majority of them, depict Jewish subjects and voice Jewish aspirations. Neither the violin nor the piano concerto falls into this category, however. Both are, on their composer's testimony, essays in 'pure' music. It will nonetheless probably be felt by many that their idiom is markedly racial. Consider the rich harmonic language built on fourths and fifths as much as on thirds and sixths; the asymmetrical phrase periods; the sinuous melodic lines with their arabesques and exotic intervals; the vivid colouring;

the sense of struggle and of antiquity, the immense emotional impact – all these are components of a musical language which, surely, can only be described as characteristically 'Jewish'. At the same time, we do well to remind ourselves that these works are primarily the creation of an immensely skilled practising musician, and only secondarily of a member of a particular race or faith. Cathedrals are not built without architects.

The violin and piano concertos are epic both in character and proportions, and each consists of three movements – fast, slow, and again fast. In asserting that they are 'pure' music Bloch doubtless means to convey that they do not attempt to portray concrete objects or events; but this writer, at least, has little doubt that both works embody a well-defined spiritual programme which, moreover, is much the same in each – in the first movement, conflict; in the second, contemplation; and in the third, liberation. This programme, or 'plot', is not at all original; it must be the basis of scores, or perhaps hundreds, of large-scale works. The paramount factor is not, of course, the 'plot' itself, but the degree of ingenuity and the quality of artistic imagination that goes into its working-out.

The orchestral writing in both concertos is that of a master, and although they amount to some seventy minutes of music, only the most minute changes in instrumentation were made by the composer after he had heard the works in rehearsal. The violin was Bloch's own instrument as a young man – he had studied under Ysaÿe in Brussels – and his handling of it in the Violin Concerto shows that he, like Elgar, has penetrated to the very soul of the instrument. In the Concerto Symphonique his touch is less sure. In common with other outstanding composers of his generation – Strauss, Vaughan Williams, and Sibelius are well-known examples – Bloch has never been completely in sympathy with this monochrome keyboard instrument, and in writing for it rather as if it were an orchestra, produces a somewhat turgid texture and a figuration that is not truly pianistic. It is probably for this reason that the Concerto Symphonique, while containing much fine and impressively forthright music, fails to match the wonderful poetry and rare musical thinking of the violin work.

The structure of the two concertos does not adhere closely to a text-book pattern, and is remarkably free and fluid. The 'cyclic' technique is employed, whereby some of the themes are carried over from one movement to the next. But while in César Franck the process of thematic repetition sometimes takes on a mechanical, rather obvious, quality, in Bloch it is much more subtle, and indeed often appears to be a subconscious process.

Bloch's harmony, as mentioned earlier, is built as much on the intervals of the fourth and fifth as it is on the third and sixth and in thus reverting to a principle of medieval music, gains a sense of strength and antiquity. Bitonality (the simultaneous use of two keys) is also frequently employed, although there is no feeling that tonality is being deserted.

Both concertos employ a very large orchestra. That for the violin was first performed on 15 December 1938, at Cleveland, by Joseph Szigeti and the Cleveland Orchestra conducted by Dimitri Mitropoulos. The first performance of the Concerto Symphonique was given on 3 September 1949, at the Edinburgh Festival, with Corinne Lacomblé and the B.B.C. Scottish Orchestra, conducted by the composer.

VIOLIN CONCERTO

First Movement. *Allegro deciso*. The spacious proportions and great emotional range of this movement are such that it amounts – perhaps a little dangerously when viewed in its setting – almost to a work in itself. It commences with an introduction (bars 1–53), in turn martial and lyrical, in which the following eight themes or motifs are announced:

(1) *Allegro deciso*

Ex. 1 should be specially noted. It is announced by brass
and woodwind at the outset and is of paramount importance
in both the first and last movements. It is built round the
interval of the fourth, is harmonized in bare fifths, and in-
corporates a distinctive rhythmic feature known as the
'Scotch snap' (see bar 3, and also Ex. 2). Bloch originally
conceived this theme in San Francisco in 1930 – much of his
thematic material is noted down years before it is actually
used – and he describes it as being 'American-Indian' in
character. Ex. 3 (bar 24), appears frequently throughout
the concerto, nearly always as an accompaniment figure
in the bass. The dissonant seventh interval which it em-
braces is usually toned down by discreet scoring.

Except for one or two lyrical interludes, the mood of the
main body of this movement is one of commingled strife and
grandeur, a heroic legend of 'old, unhappy, far-off things',
in which the solo violin thrusts its way valiantly through the
orchestral mass. There are two contrasted subjects or theme-
groups, as in a sonata movement. The first (bars 54–107) is
powerful and lengthy, and is built on Exs. 7, 5, 6, 1, and 8,
in that order, with Ex. 1 predominating. Ex. 8 merges imperceptibly into a dreamy transition passage (bars 108–131)
which leads to the second subject (bars 132–160). The latter

consists of a long, soaring theme for the soloist, in D minor tonality, of a quality so hauntingly bitter-sweet that the listener is unlikely ever to forget it once he is permeated with its full flavour. It is the distilled utterance of a soul that has achieved simplicity through the assimilation of complexities:

In the following development section (bars 161–278), there is no reference to the second subject, but Ex. 1–8 are all elaborated, with Ex. 1, 5, and 8 in the foreground. After a quiet beginning the excitement mounts steadily, and eventually the orchestra progresses invincibly, and alone, to a tremendous climax on Ex. 5 (bar 261), followed immediately by haunting calls on brass and woodwind (Ex. 4, 1, and 2). The whole episode constitutes, for this writer at least, one of the greatest pages in modern music.

This passage is soon followed by a cadenza for the soloist, based wholly on previously-heard themes. The triple stopping and other technical devices here employed will exercise the skill of the most accomplished performer; but the interest is held not by mere virtuosity but by deep musical meaning. The cadenza ends to the accompaniment of the fateful Ex. 3 on the kettledrums – a masterly stroke which, perfectly simple on the surface, never loses its sense of complete inevitability after a score of hearings. There follows a closing section in which the second subject (Ex. 9) is heard again, this time in the home key of A minor, then to disappear from the concerto. The coda is both brilliant and defiant.

Second Movement. *Andante*. The contrast with the first movement could hardly be greater. These brief, yet 'long', hundred-odd bars of music evoke a mystical and rarefied atmosphere that has few parallels in modern music. Certain passages in Holst are perhaps comparable. One thinks of *Saturn* and *Neptune* from *The Planets*, and of *Egdon Heath*. This sense of remoteness and incorporeality almost certainly originates in affinities with the East. Holst was of Nordic stock, but we know that he was deeply influenced by Hindu philosophy. Bloch also has had a lifelong interest in Eastern culture and philosophy, but in him, a Jew, the affinity probably springs from what Ernest Newman has described as the 'up-surging of remote ancestral elements'.

In this slow movement, Bloch's kinship with ancient civilization finds technical expression in a melodic line the extreme flexibility and rhythmic freedom of which recalls medieval plainsong; in an 'impersonal' orchestral texture in which the strings are sparingly used; in a sometimes bare harmonic texture and, in places, in the expression of musical meaning not through the media of melody, harmony, or rhythm, but through colour alone, existing as a vehicle of expression in its own right.

Structurally, the movement is a free fantasia on Ex. 10, 11, and 13, with brief interjections of Ex. 12:

Ex. 10 is, as the composer has said, 'quite unconsciously' related to Ex. 2 of the first movement, and it has the air of a folk song, or of an old religious chant. Thematic quotations from the first movement occur at bars 48 and 54 (Ex. 7), bar 70 (Ex. 6), and bars 28 and 91 (Ex. 3).

Third Movement. *Deciso*. The structure of this movement again proceeds according to its own logic. There are six clearly defined sections, all of them interrelated. A considerable amount of new thematic material is introduced – perhaps rather more than the listener, at this stage, can easily digest.

Section 1 (bars 1–40) begins orchestrally in a vehement mood, with a new theme, Ex. 14, after which the soloist enters Ex. 1. Further new matter is introduced, including Ex. 15 which, for the first time in the concerto, introduces a mood of relief and light-heartedness.

Section 2 (bars 41–87) is a joyful and bucolic *allegro moderato*, incorporating Ex. 16 and 17 as a kind of principal subject, and Ex. 18 as a second. The mood is now wholly joyous, like a lively 'pastorale'.

Section 3 (bars 88–132), *più calmo*, elaborates themes from the first and present movements.

Section 4 (bars 133–153), a rhapsodic passage, reintroduces Ex. 12 and 3, as well as third-movement material, and is unusually free in its rhythmic structure.

Section 5 (bars 154–237) is an extended development section, in which Ex. 17, 15, and 18 are freely treated. It builds up to an impassioned climax for full orchestra, based on Ex. 1 and 14.

Section 6 (bars 237–280) is a coda, employing Ex. 17 prominently, as well as Ex. 6, 8, and 14. The work concludes with another appearance of Ex. 1 – the principal character in this great drama – on a note of hard-won triumph.

CONCERTO SYMPHONIQUE

FIRST Movement. *Pesante ; Moderato.* Structurally, the first
movement has much in common with the first movement of
the Violin Concerto. In the course of the introduction (bars
1–71), six themes or motifs are announced (Ex. 19–24)
which recur later in the movement. Ex. 19, announced at the
outset, is of great importance, since it acts as a unifying agent
throughout the work:

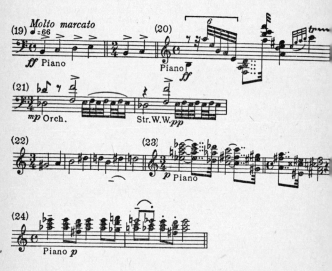

The exposition (bars 72–149) begins *moderato* with the
first subject or theme-group, of which the opening theme is
for orchestra alone:

(Several other themes could be shown if space permitted.)
The mood is one of rough energy, and the key is an ominous

B minor. At bar 77 there is a wild, tearing trumpet figure – like a battle-cry:

(26)

Tpt. W.W.

This, like Ex. 19, is common to all three movements. The piano enters (bar 89) with the opening theme (Ex. 25), and at bar 101 there is a short transition to the second subject. The latter commences (bar 110) with a descending common-chord figure for the piano (Ex. 27) and continues with a brilliant *piu animato* section (bar 118, Ex. 28):

(27)

p Piano

(28) ♩=100

f Piano

Like the first subject, it includes several other themes, and it concludes with a reference to Ex. 19. The mood, if momentarily lighter, is still very forceful, but before the development is reached the atmosphere becomes darker and less exuberant. Strength must be reserved for the struggle yet to come.

Ex. 20 on the piano leads to the development section (bars 150–219). The trumpet call (Ex. 26) is soon heard, as is a 'squashed' version of Ex. 19, followed at bar 159 (piano entry) by the second subject (Ex. 27), and at bar 166 by Ex. 19 and 28 in combination. By bar 176 we have progressed from *pp* to *ff* and Ex. 23 is given out by the full orchestra. Bars 185 to 213 introduce elaborations or hints of Ex. 20, 21, and 22, the latter a theme at once powerful and mysterious. The cadenza follows (bars 220–68). The unifying

Ex. 19 and the initial themes of the first and second subjects are further elaborated. Ex. 20 and 22 are also heard.

The recapitulation (bars 268–308) follows tradition in that the first and second subjects are now both announced in the home key of B minor. In the remarkable coda (bars 308–25), reference is made to Ex. 19, 20, 26, and 27. The music, although now but a pale reflection of its former self, moves mysteriously and inexorably to its close.

Second Movement. *Allegro vivace*. This is ternary in structure, and is an unusual synthesis of scherzo and slow movement. The first and third sections are fast, the middle one slow. There is a short coda.

There is as yet little relief from the violence of the first movement. The atmosphere of the first section is that of a grim dance of death, suggested by restless accompaniment, jigging melody, and acid harmony. The composer's own word for it is 'diabolical'. Three principal themes may be observed: the first given out by the piano (bar 4), the second by the woodwind (bar 8), and the third by the horns (bar 23). These are elaborated until we reach the long transition (bars 79–109) based on Ex. 19 and 26 from the first movement.

The slow middle section (bars 110–95) at last withdraws us from the turmoil, and we are taken back to one of Bloch's unique poetic meditations, full of a fragile and rarefied beauty, which draw their inspiration from the East. This section is principally based on two sinuous themes given out by the piano at bars 110 and 130 – the first in 3/4, the second in 5/4 time. Here the bar-lengths constantly change, and the music conveys a sense of exquisite fluidity and peacefulness rare in present-day music. But the dream fades, the bitter note seeps back, and we are given a full restatement, in still more acid terms, of the opening section (bars 196–298). The material is varied somewhat, and there is a reference to Ex. 25 (first movement) at bar 232. After a longish transition based on first movement themes (bars 299–340) there follows a quiet coda consisting of a brief restatement of the slow middle section.

Third Movement. *Allegro deciso*. In the last movement the

conflict is resolved, although, as in the Violin Concerto, the victory is not easily won. A note of optimism is struck at the beginning with a ringing, fanfare-like motif (see Ex. 29 below); and for the most part the movement moves forward with immense resolution and vitality. In contrast to the preceding movements, there is a strong contrapuntal interest.

The form of this movement does not fit any of the usual moulds. The fact that there are two contrasted subjects makes for some affinity with sonata-form, but instead of exposition, development, and recapitulation, the movement falls into the following sections:

1 (Bars 1–25) Introduction.
2 (Bars 26–149) Statement and development of first subject.
3 (Bars 150–188) Statement and development of second subject.
4 (Bars 189–212) Transition section or interlude.
5 (Bars 213–304) Second development of first subject.
6 (Bars 305–335) Second statement of second subject; Coda.

As in the first movement, the introduction announces or adumbrates several themes which are later elaborated. The two most important of these are shown below:

The first subject (Section 2) includes the following important themes:

The fierce Ex. 32, by the way, was originally noted down
by Bloch as long ago as 1917, as an emotional reaction to
the news of the Russian Revolution (though this is no
pointer to his political thought). Here the music is tremendously strong and direct, and there are some striking
contrapuntal episodes, notably at bar 130, where Ex. 29,
31 (inverted) and 32 are combined.

The second subject (Section 3):

is fiercely exultant. It undergoes only a brief development.
The interlude that follows (Section 4) harks back to Ex. 19
and 26 of the first movement. In Section 5, Ex. 30 is
developed prominently, and the prevailing excitement is
still further heightened by a quasi-contrapuntal treatment
of Ex. 33. With the closing section (Section 6), the music at
last wins through to a clear B major, and the second subject,
Ex. 34, is restated and built up to a climax. Finally Ex. 19
and 26, those all-important thematic cells from the first
movement, are heard again. Their reappearance at the very
end emphasizes anew the highly unified structure of this
most turbulent and plain-spoken but never commonplace
work.

23

Béla Bartók (1881–1945)

MOSCO CARNER

INTRODUCTION

BARTÓK made five important contributions to the literature of the modern solo concerto, all dating, respectively, from his middle and late periods: three piano concertos, a concerto for violin, and one for viola. Of these, the Third Piano Concerto and the Viola Concerto are posthumous. There is also an early Rhapsody for Piano and Orchestra, Op. 1 (1904), an immature work, it is true, but not without its aesthetic merits, and certainly of interest to the student of Bartók's stylistic development*. It was an editorial wish to confine the scope of this article to a discussion of only the last three concertos – works which we hear far more frequently than the Piano Concertos Nos. 1 and 2 (1926 and 1931, respectively). Yet against this stands the fact that the latter are in form and idiom more original and daring essays. It is for this reason and, also, in order to present a round picture of Bartók's concerto style that I thought it necessary to include them in my introductory remarks.

To start with, where does the significance of the Bartók of the concertos lie? The answer is: generally, in the new values which characterize his *œuvre* and, more specifically, in his individual approach to the concerto form as such. Let us for a moment consider the general aspect. The new values which characterize his *œuvre* and, more specifically, few major figures of modern music are the result of a most powerful process of fertilization: a highly creative and original composer absorbing into his very blood the folk music of his country and, beyond that, the primitive,

* The catalogue of Bartók's works mentions also an unpublished Scherzo for Piano and Orchestra dating from 1902.

strong atmosphere of its peasant life with which Bartók
the scientific collector of folk songs came into closest contact.
It was an atavistic love of his country that drove him with
irrational power to seek out the remote sources of true
Magyar folk music. (The parallel with Vaughan Williams is
noteworthy.) Bartók absorbed this material to the extent
that it entered and largely conditioned the very thought
and speech of his music. This process began about 1905
when the composer was 24 years of age. From that period
until his death in 1945 Bartók wrote music which, while
varying in its *technical* style, never lost – even in one single
work – its *spiritual* link with the Magyar soil. (This, incidentally, is in striking contrast to Stravinsky, who started his
career much in the same way as Bartók – for a time even
influencing his Hungarian contemporary – but who later,
after *Les Noces* (1923), became increasingly estranged from
the Russian element of his early period and not without
paying a price for it.)

Now in considering even a special section of Bartók's
works such as the concertos, we have to bear in mind the
salient features of his musical personality. The essential
Bartók is an austere composer, often deliberately uncouth
and uncompromising in his manner. Even his lyricism has
sharp edges and angular lines comparable to those of a
primitive woodcut or stone carving. His utterances are
virile, terse, and of a remarkable purity and directness of
expression. Add to this his elemental rhythmic feeling and
you have those chief qualities, which have earned him the
epithet 'barbaric'.

And what are the principal features of his technical
style? There is, first of all, his adoption of primitive and
archaic scales: pentatonic, whole tone, modal, Oriental,
and, occasionally, quarter tones, all of which, as Bartók
put it, helped him in freeing himself from 'the tyranny of
the Western major and minor modes'. This led him, among
other things, to regard the chromatic notes, not merely as
functional, i.e. as sharpening or flattening of the diatonic
'parent' notes, but as equal and independent degrees of
the scale, much in the manner of Schönberg's twelve-note

technique*), yet without Schönberg's rigid application of
It, as we shall see in the Violin Concerto. Hand in hand
with it went Bartók's free treatment of tonality often
stretched beyond recognition, though in his late works a
more pronounced feeling for key and key-relations asserted
itself. Harmonically, Bartók availed himself, in an eclectic
way, of all the advances made in Western music since the
beginning of the twentieth century, but his marked predilection for the interval of the fourth, both in his harmonic
and melodic style, derives from Magyar folk music. Of the
same origin are the short runs, ornaments, and *glissandi* by
which he adumbrates his melodic lines.

I have already spoken of Bartók's rhythm. For the ear
of the listener who is making his first acquaintance with
this composer, it is perhaps the most striking feature: either
dynamic, percussive, and of a savage effect, (particularly
so in his favourite stabbing *martellato* chords) or subtle,
complex, irregular, and presenting an infinite variety of
patterns. Through these changing patterns Bartók achieves
what I have elsewhere called a 'composed' *rubato* creating
the impression of changes of *tempo* but, actually, the pace
remains steady and only the *rhythmic units* change. There are,
of course, real tempo changes such as from *tempo giusto* to
rubato, and from fast to slow, and vice versa, with concomitant changes of mood and the introduction of new
melodic material, all of which may be summed up as the
rhapsodic Magyar element of Bartók's music. The first
movement of the Concertos for Violin and Viola, respectively, are typical examples of it.

But there were other influences at work which in a varying degree coloured his style while in no way affecting its
originality: Brahms, Liszt and Strauss in the very early
period, Debussy and Stravinsky up to about the early
twenties, and subsequently, Bach and Beethoven who
entered more deeply into Bartók's way of thinking. His
turn to Bach manifests itself in a markedly contrapuntal
texture (imitation, inversion, fugato), but unlike a number
of his contemporaries who merely flirted with neo-classical

* See the article on the Berg Concerto, p. 366.

devices, Bartók approached counterpoint neither as a mere intellectual exercise nor a cover for lack of pregnant ideas, but as a vital means to enhance the significance of his melodic thought.

As for Beethoven's influence, this is particularly felt in Bartók's later works, e.g. his firm grip on the classical form of the sonata and the iron discipline and logic of his thematic treatment. Bartók the musical *thinker* is seen at his most compelling in the closely-knit style of his later string quartets, and also in parts of the Sonata for Two Pianos and Seven Percussion Instruments, the Music for Strings, Piano and Percussion, and the Violin Concerto (second and third movements).

It is by virtue of such classical elements that Bartók belongs, in part, to the main stream of Western music. I say 'in part' because even in his late period we find him attempting a fusion between East and West, most notably in his technique of thematic development. Like the classics, he generates new ideas from thematic germs, but as often as not he uses short rhythmic motifs which, instead of evolving from them *new* ideas, he repeats in *ostinato*-like fashion, yet varying them rhythmically and melodically. As he pointed out himself, this type of structure is to be found in old Magyar music for wind instruments and in Arabic peasant dances. This lends much of his music a 'primitive' quality. The effect of such continuous repetition is, in his own words, 'a strange feverish excitement'. Though highly stylized, and refined by the use of counterpoint and key relationships, it is in essence an Oriental principle; and while it may be observed even in Bartók's very late works, notably in the transition and development sections, it dominates the style of his middle period, as, for instance the two violin sonatas, the piano sonata, and the first two piano concertos. Those who have heard these works will recall the feverish, indeed hypnotic effect of Bartók's varied *ostinato*.

But it is not only for structural purposes that he resorts to this technique. There are short pieces as well as extended movements in which he uses it to produce strangely beautiful effects of an impressionistic order. I am referring to what has been called 'night music', pieces in which Bartók conjures up the atmosphere of nocturnal scenes in the country, with suggestions of the sound of birds and insects in them. This music reflects a mood which Bartók experienced on his travels through the remote peasant regions of Hungary, Slovakia, Rumania, and Turkey, when collecting folk songs – impressions of nature which seem to have given rise also to emotions of a religious and mystic character. For this 'night music' usually contains two contrasting features. On the one hand, you find the constant repetition of short motifs, flickering, swirling, appearing now on one instrument, now on another, like so many will-o'-the-wisps, on the other, chorale-like themes harmonized in liturgical block harmonies and moving at a slow, solemn pace. This strange combination of moods, the contrast between the oscillating shimmering colours of the actual 'night music' and the monochrome of the chorale, and lastly, an undercurrent of nostalgia and loneliness – they are the qualities that have given this music a special place in Bartók's work. I am thinking of such pieces as the *Musiques Nocturnes* of the Piano Suite *Out of Doors*, part of the slow movement of the Second Piano Concerto and the beautiful adagio of the Third.

So much, then, for a general picture. Let us now extend our enquiry and consider the special aspect of Bartók's *development* as a concerto writer. What were the stages through which he passed? How did he treat the concerto form in his early and late works?

His first essay, the Rhapsody for Piano and Orchestra, leans heavily on the Liszt of the Hungarian Rhapsodies. Its first version was for piano solo, the addition of the orchestra being an afterthought, largely in order to throw the piano into greater relief as does the frame in a painting. Like the Lisztian examples, the Rhapsody in a pseudo-Hungarian vein, romantic in feeling and style, un-Bartókian in its rich and often luscious harmonies, and occasionally betraying the influence also of Brahms and Strauss. Yet the piano writing, while largely in Liszt's grand manner, already shows Bartók's predilection for difficult chordal passages in both hands, while the presence of imitative passages and short *fugati* foreshadows a characteristic feature of his mature style. The work might well deserve an occasional hearing, if only to show us a highly gifted musician at the beginning of his career.

The First Piano Concerto did not come until twenty-two years later (1926). Much had happened to its author in the intervening period: his turn to Magyar folk-music, his study of the composers of the seventeenth and eighteenth centuries (Bach and some of his German and Italian predecessors), and the gradual establishment of a distinctly personal but as yet experimental (expressionistic) language, viz., the two Violin Sonatas (1921) and the Piano Sonata (1926). The First Piano Concerto is a characteristic product of these tendencies: harsh and uncompromising in utterance and, in the fast movements, driven along by an elemental, savage rhythm. The thematic material is derived from, or inspired by, Magyar sources, a particularly beautiful example of which is the slow movement, music of an austere purity. The feeling for key is vague, and to say that the concerto is in E is to indicate but a broad tendency towards a rallying tonal centre. The form of the fast movements is fluid, seemingly chaotic in the opening allegro, yet closer analysis shows an approximation to the type of the Bach concerto but largely subjected to Bartók's technique of the varied *ostinato*. The Bachian influence is also seen in the treatment of the solo instrument: except for the characteristic Bartókian percussiveness of the keyboard writing, there is no clear-cut division between solo and orchestra. As the style is largely polyphonic, the contrapuntal lines are taken up in turn by the orchestra and the soloist, so that the piano may be regarded as an *obbligato* in the eighteenth-century sense. There are, of course, passages (as there are in the Baroque concerto), in which it becomes a true solo, but the general effect remains that of a competition within an *ensemble*. It is only in the slow movement that the piano moves into sharper focus and, in addition, becomes lyrical, with much *legato* and *cantabile* writing. Here Bartók also makes use of the instrument's peculiar colour effects: abrupt changes from the high register to the low, and vice versa, pedals formed of chords of several superimposed fourths, and widely-spaced arpeggios (in sevenths and ninths) – in short, we meet here with the Bartók of the impressionistic piano pieces.

The Second Piano Concerto coming five years later (1931), shows a general advance towards greater clarity of form. There is no longer any ambiguity as to its home key, which is that of G, and though the themes are still short and fragmentary, their outline is more clear-cut and succinct than in the previous work, and thus more easily retained in the listener's mind. Similarly, the structure is more articulate, the first movement being in sonata form, and the finale consisting of varied alternations of two ideas, which recalls Haydn's favourite principle of variations on two alternating themes. The slow movement combines an adagio and scherzo, in the order A–B–A, A being an example of the 'night-music' style referred to above: a chorale on the strings alternating with impressionistic arabesques on the piano. The concerto may be said to stand half-way between the *concerto grosso* type of the First Piano Concerto, and the classical cut of the subsequent Violin Concerto. The solo often rises from an *obbligato* to full individuality (viz. the long cadenza of the first movement, and the coda of the finale) though the allocation of separate ideas to the orchestra and the piano still points to the eighteenth-century model. The keyboard writing has become less percussive, the chordal clusters of the First Concerto now tending to dissolve into decorative lines, which are thickened out by relatively simple chords. Also the orchestral texture is looser and comparatively lighter. While in the First Piano Concerto Bartók underlines the contrapuntal lines by scoring them for different groups of homogeneous instruments and thus forsakes the blending of colours, he now shows more regard for the individual timbre of single instruments and their colour effect in combination. While the First Piano Concerto, admittedly, poses considerable problems for both player and listener, this cannot be said of No. 2 – a work which is, incidentally, permeated by a feeling of exuberance, which is rare in Bartók. Athletic and sinewy, it shows the composer in the prime of his creative power, and deserves to be heard as frequently as its more 'classical' successors.

The first of these was the Violin Concerto (1937–8), a work illustrating a happy fusion of all that is characteristic of Bartók's late style. The Magyar elements are subtilized to the extent that they become hardly tangible, like the aroma that lingers about a flower transplanted from an exotic soil. And while the work remains throughout virile and imbued with that intellectual passion so characteristic of the essential Bartók, it shows at the same time a marked emotional and expressive character, viz. the second movement, one of the most beautiful examples of the composer's lyrical vein. This amalgam of the epic-dramatic with the lyrical is perhaps the most remarkable aesthetic feature of the work. Instead of short motifs, we now have song themes of a sweeping and sustained nature. The form is spacious, yet it creates the impression of utmost concentration because the composer's musical thinking is vital in every respect. Other features of this 'classicism' may be added: a less obtrusive use of counterpoint, a clear feeling for key (B minor), and the fact that the soloist now meets the orchestra on his own ground, being no longer a *primus inter pares* but assuming a dominating rôle; symptomatic of this is the fact that in all three movements the main subject is first introduced by the solo violin. The writing for it is brilliant and, as always with Bartók, technically exacting. Yet, as in Beethoven's or Brahms's concertos, technical display never becomes an end in itself, but is felt to grow out of the very substance of the ideas, and largely serves to throw them into a more brilliant relief.

Bartók's mellowness is also evident in his handling of the orchestra. The texture is far more transparent than in the preceding two concertos, the former orchestration *en bloc* here yields to thinner instrumental lines, and there is much subtle blending of colours, notably in the second movement. Taking it by and large, the Violin Concerto shows the composer greatly relenting in the deliberate austerity and grimness which characterized the works of his middle period, yet thereby losing not an iota of that intense passion, that intellectual grip and that significance of utterance which form the core of his musical personality. In other words, it remains essential Bartók, but a Bartók mellowed and more emotive in the expression of his artistic experiences. No wonder that the work, a masterpiece from whichever angle you care to look at it, should appeal with equal force to the serious student of Bartók's music and a large section of the general public.

It initiated the short series of commissioned works which the composer wrote during the last four years of his life: the Sonata for Violin, the Concerto for Orchestra, a modern kind of *concerto grosso*, and the two solo concertos to be reviewed presently. Would Bartók have written these later concertos without being prompted by commissions? Perhaps an idle question, but I cannot help feeling that had his career continued in a normal way and not been seriously upset by his voluntary emigration to America in 1940 – where pecuniary circumstances rather than personal inclination seem to have led him into accepting such commissions – he would have presumably continued in further exploiting the medium of the string quartet and the string ensemble in general. After all, this was the medium that attracted him with peculiar force throughout his life, and in which the mature Bartók gave of his best. The very nature of the solo concerto calls for a certain extrovert and exhibitionistic approach on the part of a composer, and it is here that I feel the presence of a certain antagonism between Bartók's introspective, inward cast of mind on the one hand, and on the other the demands made upon him by the kind of works commissioned from him. It is a measure of his genius to have so late in life – he was then past sixty – adapted himself to these demands and, on the whole, with remarkable success.

Though the Concerto for Orchestra (1942) does not fall within the scope of this essay, this much may be said here that it is, by and large, the best example of the 'American' Bartók: brilliant, yet of intrinsic invention, it aims at a tunefulness which, one feels, is so much more marked in relation to the style of his pre-American period. True, this was a concession made to the taste of large audiences, but a concession, it may be argued, as legitimate as that made by the pre-nineteenth-century artist to his illustrious patrons; it did not, necessarily, entail inferior quality. While the Concerto for Orchestra is intellectually of a lighter weight than, say, the Violin Concerto, it yet remains true Bartók and, what is more, its general exuberance, humour and lightness of touch are things which had not been often in evidence in the composer's previous large-scale works, though they may be found more frequently in his various miniatures for piano and violin.

But the case is different with the Third Piano Concerto (1945). Let us first glance at its credit side. It is attractive, it falls easy on the ears of even those who are not professed admirers of the composer, its texture is light, the orchestration of the first two movements transparent and with some particularly felicitous touches in the 'night music' of the adagio. The writing for the solo instrument is less difficult than in the previous two piano concertos, yet brilliant enough to make it a true virtuoso concerto. The form is concise, and the general treatment that of a master. But against this must be set the criticism that, to the present writer at any rate, it is lacking in that significance of invention such as we have come to expect of a composer of Bartók's calibre.

More will be said about that later, but here I venture to suggest two reasons which may account for certain failings of this work: the one, that Bartók attempted to become still more 'popular', more accessible to the American public than he did in the Concerto for Orchestra: the other, that the insidious disease (leucæmia) of which he was to die soon after the near-completion of this concerto, had begun to affect his creative powers.

Yet, strangely enough, his swan-song, the Viola Concerto, scores over the previous work in a way unexpected in Bartók. It is the simplest of his concertos, yet perhaps the most moving piece of music that ever came from his pen. Here speaks a man who, like the Mahler of the *Song of the Earth* and the Ninth Symphony, feels that the sun is fast setting on his life. The accents of the music are laid on the purely emotional, a feeling of pathos and tragic defiance pervades it which is entirely new in Bartók, while we look in vain for the intellectual force and iron grip of the Bartók of before 1940. The markedly rhapsodic character of the first two movements, their change of mood between lament and dramatic challenge, heightened by the intense expression of recitative-like passages, are all an unmistakable testimony to the highly personal, one is tempted to say autobiographical, attitude of the work. It is largely for this reason and also by virtue of the effective and sympathetic treatment of the solo part that the concerto makes its chief impact. For, as in the Third Piano Concerto, the quality of the ideas *per se* is of less interest. True, they are of a passionate lyrical character, the melodic lines are long-breathed and Magyar in flavour and rhythm, but what we miss in them is the distinguishing stamp, that something which has given Bartók's melodic style its hall-mark. Moreover, the structure of the opening allegro is too loose for a movement in sonata form, so that the music tends to fall to pieces, and there is a perfunctory air about the contrapuntal writing. The weakest movement is the finale. While it manages to convey a sense of bitterness and ironic humour, as music pure and simple it may be said to be even less distinguished than the finale of the Third Piano Concerto. However, as we shall see presently, the work *as published* is not pure Bartók and it is with this mental reservation that it must be judged.

Having thus far traced the line of Bartók's development as concerto writer we may now attempt to chart our way through the last three works. At the same time the opportunity will be taken of implementing some of our general observations by reference to details.

VIOLIN CONCERTO

THE Violin Concerto was begun in Budapest in August, 1937 and completed there on 31 December of the following year.

It was commissioned by the Hungarian violinist Zoltán Szekely, to whom it is dedicated and who gave its first performance in Amsterdam, on 23 April 1939 (Concertgebouw Orchestra under Willem Mengelbert).

First Movement. *Allegro non troppo*. Like most opening movements of Bartók's cyclic works, this allegro is in sonata form, with two main subjects and several subsidiary ones, which help to achieve the remarkable spaciousness of the structural design. A six-bar march-like introduction of throbbing crotchet chords on the harp against which is set a characteristic motif on the lower strings *pizzicato*, leads to the first statement, on the solo violin, of the main subject

Ex.1

It is cast in B major-minor, the home key of the work. Note the sweep of line, the drooping fourths and the 'Magyar' rhythm. Freely elaborated, it is followed by the first subsidiary idea

Ex.2

whose restless passage work sharply contrasts with the sustained writing of the main subject. At (43)* the latter returns, now treated in imitation and tailing off into a short lyrical solo. At *risoluto*, Bartók introduces yet another idea consisting of those flickering chromatic figures which we know best from his 'night music'

Ex.3

the whole section being a good illustration of the composer's method of the varied repeat of short melodic fragments. Its

* These are the rehearsal figures as marked in the score.

structural purpose is to provide the transition to the second
subject

Ex.4

a lyrical theme which has a family likeness with the first
subject, particularly strong in the third bar. It is here that
Bartók is said to have intended an ironic allusion to
Schönberg's twelve-note technique, attempting to show how
by a free use of it a clear sense of tonality may easily be
achieved. Ex. 4 introduces all the twelve chromatic notes,
first on the solo violin and then, in augmentation and in a
slightly different order of sequence, in the orchestra, but we
are left in no doubt that the key of the theme is A.

As in the *Elegia* of the Concerto for Orchestra, Bartók
abruptly shakes himself free of his lyrical musings and breaks
into restless, rushing figures (*Vivace*) to turn as suddenly to
the tranquillity of the codetta (115) in which we hear references to the introduction and the second subject, the solo
violin rising and falling in shapely curves.

Equally abrupt is the jerk into the development (160). It
has two sections: the first, brilliant and lively (*Vivace*), plays
about with fragments of the first subject treated in augmentation and close imitation on the orchestra while the soloist
enjoys himself in runs and triple stoppings; the second section (*Meno vivo*) opens with the first subject in inversion (the
intervals are turned upside down) and assumes a more lyrical
expression which is brusquely broken off by the bustle of the
orchestra (204).

The recapitulation (213) follows the general outline of the
exposition, but in details shows a number of ingenious alterations. There is an extended cadenza which calmly opens on
quarter-tone arabesques (303) but gradually takes on a
highly brilliant character, with arpeggios across the four
strings, double and triple stoppings and some two-part
writing. The coda (344) first gives itself the air of a second
development but soon makes it clear that the end is near.

Second Movement. *Andante tranquillo.* This movement is

cast in the form of theme and six variations. The theme itself

Ex.5

has a pristine freshness and purity about it which are rare
even for Bartók. And how perfect is the absorption of melodic and rhythmical inflexions of Magyar folk-music: the key
is G, but modified by modal turns such as the Lydian
(augmented) fourth C sharp and the occasional flattening
of the leading note F sharp to F; and we meet again the
drooping, syncopated 'Hungarian' fourths from the first
subject of the opening movement which here impart to
the melody a markedly nostalgic expression. Yet this exotic
charm is only part of the beauty. Note, for instance, the
wonderful equipoise, how rise and fall correspond, and how
gradually the climax in the seventh bar (the note A) is
prepared by two-bar sequences, after which the line sinks
back over an octave, down to G, the last two bars of the solo
being repeated by the orchestral violins in sonorous octaves.

The variations match this beauty by their ingenuity and
almost improvisatory freedom. In relating them to the
theme one should bear in mind its general outline, i.e. its
melodic rise and fall rather than harmonic and rhythmic
details.

Var. I. *Un poco più andante*. A tracery woven by the solo
round the theme, the notes of which are contained in the
florid writing. The whole piece gives the impression of a
gipsy improvising on his fiddle.

Var. II. *Un poco più tranquillo*. The solo presents the theme
in firmer melodic outline than in Variation No. I, the intervals have now grown wider, and through arabesque-like
ornaments the variation is expanded to more than twice the
length of the theme.

Var. III. *Più mosso*. The expressive lyricism of the two
previous variations changes here to fierce agitation, the solo-

ist being asked to play at the heel and *ruvido* (rough). The theme is suggested only in a vague outline, the variation pattern being double-stoppings on the solo violin which are punctuated by harsh blasts on the horns. This 'barbaric' note softens towards the end in a short lyrical two-part phrase.

Var. IV. *Lento*. The soloist who so far has carried the thematic burden now hands it over to the orchestra, contenting himself with florid passages (trills and melisms which recall the ornamental style of gypsy music) and halfway through breaks forth into a real cadenza.

The form of this variation is highly original. The first eleven bars correspond to the first four bars of the theme, Ex. 5, whose main motifs (bars 1-2) are transformed thus:

Ex.6

subsequently treated in canon (cellos, basses – violas second violins). The whole passage is scored for low-lying strings and clarinets and played *pp*. After the cadenza, the remaining four bars of the theme are extended to thirteen, with a four-part *stretto* between orchestra and soloist.

Var. V. *Allegro scherzando*. This is a dance-like movement, light, capricious, and delicately scored. As in Var. I, the theme is dissolved into a fluid line moving for the best part in small intervals and with much chromaticism in it – a characteristic feature of Bartók's fast-moving melodies.

Var. VI. *Comodo*. This is a contrapuntal study in the form of a close canon in three and, later, four parts to which the soloist adds a fifth (non-imitative] part. The theme is reduced to its essential outline which is traced in equal quavers and played by the strings *pizzicato* throughout, while the soloist adorns it with trills, runs and tremoli until he asserts himself in a sustained legato line. In addition to the strings, the only other instruments used here are timpani and side-drum which heighten the curiously marionette-like character of this variation. This contrasts most strikingly with the subsequent restatement of the theme which is now played by the soloist an octave higher than in the beginning. Again the orchestral strings repeat the last two bars, and on *ppp smorzando* dies away what is one of Bartók's most memorable movements. In passing, attention may be drawn to its subtle blend of soft transparent colours (note for instance the delicate use of the woodwind, harp and celesta in the second variation) which shows the distance Bartók travelled from the predominantly hard, compact group-scoring of the first two piano concertos.

Third Movement. *Allegro molto.* With the ethereal ending of the andante still in our ears, the markedly rhythmic finale brings us back to earth with savage force. It has the air of a turbulent Magyar dance about it, yet its formal treatment is severer, more classical than that of the opening allegro. It is cast in sonata form, and it will be found that the two main subjects

are close variants of the first movements (Ex. 1 and 4). In fact, a comparison of the two movements as a whole suggests that Bartók conceived the finale as an image of the opening allegro, but an image reflected, as it were, in a distorting mirror, by which metaphor I mean to indicate the altered shape and different character which the material of the first movement now takes on. Compare, for instance, Ex. 1 with Ex. 7.

The finale opens with a four-bar orchestral introduction, which, incidentally, is so phrased as to deceive the listener into assuming a two-beat pattern – an impression completely destroyed by the sharp articulation in three beats of the ensuing first subject. At *risoluto* starts a section which affords the soloist scope for display (arpeggios and drone-like effects on the open string A). A short imitative passage (64) leads to the transition theme (*un poco sostenuto*) which in its turn takes us to the second subject, Ex. 8. If you compare it with its original version in the first movement, Ex. 4, you will find two noticeable changes: the order of the twelve chromatic notes has been slightly altered and, owing to the slow tempo and a characteristically flowing rhythm in $\frac{3}{4}$, the theme is now transmogrified into lyrical waltz strain.

At another *risoluto* (165) we plunge into the development. Like that of the first movement, it consists of two parts: the first lively, with agitated triplet runs and arpeggios for the solo violin, the second part (*meno mosso*) making much play of the freely inverted first subject (see first movement) and including, at *mosso agitato*, a short three-part canon. This is followed by a restatement of the first subject (*molto tranquillo*) which now soars to the very high register of the solo violin, creating a singularly beautiful effect of a transfiguration.

The recapitulation (349) preserves the main structural design of the exposition, yet the many alterations of details show that Bartók rethinks, as it were, the material as presented in the exposition. A characteristic illustration of that is the restatement of the second subject (422). The development-like coda (*assai lento* 450) includes a short solo cadenza, and shortly before the end (*sostenuto e largamente*) the soloist introduces a four-note pentatonic figure which may be regarded as the thematic germ of the first and last movements.*

PIANO CONCERTO NO. 3

THIS is the last work that Bartók all but finished before his death in New York on 26 September 1945. While busy on the Viola Concerto for William Primrose he had promised Ethel Bartlett and Rae Robertson a concerto for two pianos

---

* Bartók added an alternative ending which is slightly shorter and purely orchestral.

which he intended to write after the completion of the Viola
Concerto. In the event he composed a concerto for piano
solo and left Primrose's work in more or less completed
sketches. Why this change of plan? Tibor Serly, an Hungarian composer and intimate friend of Bartók, suggests the
following reason: 'Bartók', he says,* 'knew that he was
seriously ill. He was concerned about his family, particularly about his talented wife, Ditta Pasztory, who was also
his pupil and disciple.† He had nothing to leave but his
works. This last completed composition would be dedicated
to her.'

Are we, then, to assume that Bartók decided to write a
concerto for piano solo, instead of the promised work for two
pianos, in order to leave it as an artistic legacy for his wife
who would thus be regarded as the composer's chosen interpreter and secure engagements with it? Yet the published
score shows no dedication to her and the work was, in fact,
first performed by Bartók's former pupil Gyorgy Sando,
with the Philadelphia Orchestra under Eugene Ormandy on
8 February 1946. The last seventeen bars which the composer left in a kind of musical shorthand were orchestrated
by Serly and a number of expression marks and a few tempo
indications subsequently added to the printed score by
Ormandy, Louis Kentner, and Erwin Stein.

First Movement. *Allegretto.* The opening movement is in
sonata form. The curtain rises almost immediately on the
soloist who introduces the nine-bar theme of the first subject

Ex. 9

---

* Programme annotation for the first performance of the Third
Piano Concerto.

† Londoners may remember their joint appearance in one of the
concerts at the International Festival of Contemporary Music in
June 1938 when they played the Sonata for Two Pianos and Seven
Percussion Instruments.

Note the rhythmic figure of the up-beat which pervades, not
only the main subject, but the first movement as a whole.
The Magyar flavour of the theme is evident, viz. the free,
syncopated rhythm in which the stresses do not coincide
with the 'strong' beats of the bar; the short ornamental runs;
the modal tendency of the melody (with the Dorian sixth,
C sharp in E minor), and the oscillation between major and
minor (G sharp – G natural). There is something uncompromising and defying about the theme – an impression
largely created by the martial rhythm and the bare, powerful octaves in which it is first stated. This is in sharp contrast
to the soft and sparsely scored orchestral accompaniment,
the whole opening somewhat reminiscent of the beginning
of Mendelssohn's Violin Concerto. The orchestra restates
a variant of the theme, and at (27) the pianist resumes again
with brilliant passage work (in Bartókian ninths, sixths, and
octaves), to lead to the second subject. This consists of two
ideas

the first, styled *grazioso* by the Editors, is decorative and contrasts with the first subject by its small intervals. The second
idea, *scherzando* according to the Editors, is characterized
by arpeggios in double-stoppings in both hands. A short
codetta (68) leads on a muted horn call (figure **x** of Ex. 9) to
the development. This section is short, and opens with a cantabile version of the first subject (76) to which later (99)
the soloist adds fragments from the second subject. A short
stretto (107) in which the orchestra opposes the pianist with
the inversion of his theme, leads via two horn-calls (original
motif answered by its inversion) to the recapitulation. The
changes in this last section are far fewer and less significant

than is customary with Bartók. One or two may be mentioned, however: the altered version of the first subject which is now fully harmonized (we remember the bare unison on its first appearance), then the changes of the bridge passage to the second subject (145), and, most conspicuous of all, the coda (175) with its impressionistic flicker on woodwind and piano, to the accompaniment of plucked strings, and the beautiful close with a reminiscence of the first subject. Yet taking the movement as a whole, one cannot absolve the composer from a certain perfunctory treatment, notably of the development, nor can one readily acquiesce in the 'pretty' insignificance of the second subject matter.

Second Movement. *Adagio religioso*. This movement shows hardly a sign of Bartók's flagging inspiration such as characterizes the *Allegretto* and the finale. It belongs to those individual and beautiful mood pictures in which the composer seems to have caught with suggestive force the *mystique* of the Puszta. As Serly tells us, Bartók was fascinated by the nocturnal atmosphere of the wide Hungarian plain which also inspired in him a devotional feeling. The first part of the movement is an expression of that. It consists of a chorale

whose five 'verses' given out by the soloist are framed in, as it were, by the mystic sound of the strings

Contrast here is not only of colour, but texture. While the chorale is set in block harmonies, the pentatonic string theme (which somehow recalls the 'religious' Dvořák) is treated contrapuntally, i.e. in free and close imitation. Note

also how the music assumes in its further course an expression of growing fervour which subsides again before the beginning of the middle section, the actual 'night music'.

Here it is no longer possible to speak of themes, but only of melodic-rhythmic fragments, wisp-like figures, which flicker all over the orchestra and the piano.

and, incidentally, show the characteristic interval of the 'Magyar' fourth. The whole section is a masterly study of nature at night. Observe the iridescent shimmer and sheen of the strings, now *tremolando*, now in quick note repetitions, to which the piano adds another colour with arpeggios and runs, while on the woodwind and xylophone Bartók's insects and birds make their voices heard, now loud and strident, now faint and subdued like an echo.*

The last section is a repeat of the first, only that piano and orchestra now change rôles: the chorale is on the woodwind, while the soloist adumbrates it with what looks, deceptively, like a Bachian two-part invention – in fact, the chorale treatment of this movement owes much to Bach's chorale preludes – but invariably tails off into Bartókian runs and melisms reminiscent of the preceding 'night music'. The last 'verse' of the chorale (122) is considerably expanded and its emotional effect heightened by the scoring for strings *molto espr*. The climax is marked by a solitary stroke on the gong – particularly telling in this context. The music comes to rest on the common chord of E major (the home key of the concerto) and *attacca* we are jerked into the finale.

* The only similar effect I can recall is in certain works by Villa-Lobos which suggest the strange atmosphere of the Brazilian jungle.

Third Movement. *Allegro vivace.** This is the least inspired of the three movements. True, it is effective and the keyboard writing brilliant. Yet its drive and rhythmic vitality are unable to conceal a lack of melodic distinction and a tendency to resort to counterpoint as a ready substitute for genuine invention. The form is that of a rondo with two fugal episodes and an extended *presto* coda. A three-bar flourish of the soloist leads to the first statement of the ritornello (main rondo theme) of twenty bars, a dance-like theme with characteristic Magyar syncopation, to which the orchestra provides the complementary beats

Ex.13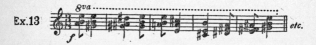

A variant of it leads to a subsidiary idea (191) which is distributed over soloist and orchestra, and plainly derives from the ritornello. The entry of the first episode is heralded by a rhythm hammered out by the kettle-drum on the repeated note E and punctuated by intermittent strokes on the bass-drum – surely an odd introduction to what is a regular fugue in four parts. Its subject, classical in shape and length (eight bars)

Ex.14

has three expositions, the second exposition (292) presenting it in inversion and *stretto*. A sense of climax is achieved by the scoring of the third exposition (322) for full orchestra. At bar 344, the ritornello reappears in a varied and considerably shortened version. The previous drum rhythm is heard again prefacing the second episode which forms the central section of the movement. The drive and percussiveness that characterized the music up to now yields to a more sustained, quiet, and cantabile writing, and instead of the previous *non-legato* and *staccato* we now have slurred phrases.

* The tempo marking is the Editors'.

The Editors have marked this portion with *più tranquillo*. Here are its two main ideas

Ex.15

dolce (Piano)   *etc.*

grazioso (2nd Vln, Vla. in octaves)

which are presented in invertible counterpoint, i.e. the upper and lower parts may change places, as they actually do later on (bars 473 *et seq.*).

There are three sections A–B–A, all fugally treated. Section A is based on the above example and deceptively opens like a double fugue (fugue with two subjects) for piano and strings, but in the event pursues a free course during which a seemingly insignificant motif of falling and rising fifths is heard on oboe and bassoon. Yet it is from this that the fugal subject of section B is derived:

Ex.16   *etc.*

(Viola, Cello)

There are five expositions which grow in sonority, the brilliant runs of the piano adding an element of *bravura*. A short transition (460) leads back to the recapitulation of A. The texture is now enriched by close imitations of the *grazioso* theme of Ex. 15, which spreads, terrace-like, from piano to oboe and flute, while two horns intone the *dolce* theme – a short but singularly imaginative passage. The piano continues with imitations, and passing references to the main rondo theme are heard when an accelerando (520) leads in brilliant fashion to the restatement of the ritornello in full (527). At the place where we expect the music to come to a full stop on the tonic E (642) Bartók breaks suddenly off, inserts two general-pause bars, and then launches into a presto, which in character and texture recalls the coda of the finale of Schumann's Piano Concerto.* Though the time

* See also the *presto* coda of the finale of Bartók's own Second Piano Concerto.

signature changes from 3/8 to 3/4, the *presto* almost creates the impression that the music is continuing at the speed of the previous section, in other words ♪ = *circa* ♩. At bar 721 Bartók returns to the original time-signature (3/8) and tempo, the subsidiary theme of the opening is heard again, and soon after, this brilliant and, in the coda, breath-taking movement comes to its close.

VIOLA CONCERTO

As already mentioned, this work was commissioned by William Primrose, the celebrated Scottish viola player. The sketches must have been completed by late August or early September of 1945, for in a letter to Primrose* the composer says that, 'If nothing happens, I can be through in five or six weeks, that is, I can send you a copy of the orchestral score in the second half of October.' Unfortunately, something did happen: Bartók died in September, leaving the work 'a mass of tangled sketches'. It was Serly who later undertook the difficult task of piecing them together. There were, as he informs us, a number of difficulties to be overcome: first, the deciphering of the manuscript, which was written in a kind of musical shorthand, a process made more difficult still by the fact that Bartók drafted the work on odd, loose sheets that happened to be on hand at the moment, some of which contained already parts of other sketches; ideas were jotted down just as they came into his head and without due regard for their proper order of sequence, nor were the pages numbered nor the separate movements indicated; in addition, Bartók was in the habit of making his corrections and alterations, palimpsest-like, upon the original notes and phrases; then there was the matter of completing harmonic and melodic ornaments only vaguely indicated by the composer, and finally the work had to be scored, Bartók leaving practically no hints as to its orchestration, except that in the above letter he intimates that it 'will be rather transparent, more transparent than in the

---

* This letter and other factual details are given in a note by Tibor Serly, which is printed in the published score.

Violin Concerto.' Serly, however, says that the orchestration presented the least difficulty because the composer had already indicated in the manuscript the principal parts and contrapuntal texture of the orchestral accompaniment. Thus in completing this concerto, Serly may be said to have acted the Süssmayr to his Mozart-Bartók.

Yet it may be argued that no man can penetrate another man's mind to the extent of wholly identifying himself with him. No matter how intimately Serly may have been acquainted with Bartók's style and his intention concerning he Viola Concerto, from the nature of the problem we must assume a varying margin of divergencies and unintentional misrepresentation. We cannot, hence, accept this work as *pure* Bartók (any more than we accept the Requiem as pure Mozart) – at any rate, with regard to its harmonic and orchestral aspect. A full and fair appraisal of it must await the day when it will be possible to inspect the manuscript and see where precisely Bartók left off and where Serly took up. Our analysis will, therefore, refer chiefly to the structure and the melodic-rhythmic writing.

I have already spoken of the pronounced emotional character of Bartók's swansong and suggested an auto-biographical element in it. The note of gloomy despondency, defiance and renunciation which marks the first two move-ments, and the bitter irony of the finale – are they not likely to be a reflexion of the state of mind the composer must have been in during the last months of his fatal illness? This strange emphasis on the emotional marks the Viola Concerto as perhaps the least typical of his works. The composer makes little attempt here to objectify his emotions and to filter them, as it were, through the cathartic sieve of his powerful intellect such as characterizes his general creative process. One has the impression that the Viola Concerto is the direct, spontaneous outpouring of a mind that seems to be working against fearful odds. If we cannot help sensing an inspirational fatigue and miss the intellectual urge and formal grip of the essential Bartók, the explanation must be sought in the circumstances in which this work was written. Yet a sympathetic listener, while not blind to its

failings, cannot but feel deeply moved by the emotional
eloquence with which a dying master has uttered his last
words.

To touch first upon general technical features. In his
letter to Primrose, the composer stresses the 'highly virtuoso'
style of the work, explaining also that the 'sombre more
masculine character' of the instrument 'partly influenced
the general character of the work'. This is fully borne out by
the solo part which is both highly brilliant and expressive.*
It abounds in runs up and down the scale, arpeggios across
the strings, wide leaps, quick note-repetitions and typically
Bartókian arabesques. No less successful is the exploitation
of the viola's expressive power. Though Bartók uses its full
range up to the A an octave above the stave, he tends to
resort more frequently to its low and dark register, a
particularly beautiful example of which is the ending of
the coda of the first movement (bars 227–30). Altogether,
the soloist is very much in the foreground – more so perhaps than in the Violin Concerto and the Third Piano
Concerto.

As for the formal structure, it is an illustration of that
'classical' build and simplicity which generally mark Bartók's late style. There is a clear feeling of key and tonal
relationships, though the tonality of the first movement
fluctuates between C major and its subdominant. In this
context we may mention the fact that, unlike the previous
two concertos, the work has no basic tonality, each movement being cast in a different key (C–E–A). Owing probably to its markedly emotional character Bartók makes comparatively less frequent use of contrapuntal devices. Altogether, the texture appears surprisingly sparse, notably in
the second movement; or was it that Serly showed a com-
mendable reticence in completing what may have been in
the manuscript only vaguely indicated?

First Movement. *Moderato*. It opens with a cadenza-like
introduction, in which the soloist anticipates the main motif
of the first subject, while the orchestra answers with an
ominous figure in the bass reminiscent of the motifs of

* It has been edited by Primrose.

fourths in the opening of the Violin Concerto. At *a tempo* we hear the first subject in its entirety:

Ex. 17

After its elaboration by both solo and orchestra (partly in imitation) we reach, at bar 41, the transition to the second subject, a restless and agitated section in which the soloist introduces typically Bartókian arabesques up and down the scale, until at Tempo I an idea of firmer outline and of an apparently Rumanian flavour grows out of it; its tail-end is derived from the first theme Ex. 17 (figure x):

Ex. 18

The agitation subsides, and we reach, via a proper dominant-tonic cadence, the lyrical second subject (in E) which has a yearning, almost painful, expression

Ex. 19

Motif x points to Rumanian folk dances. The end of the second subject matter brings the first great climax of the movement, the solo instrument soaring in agitated arpeggios to the G sharp, an octave above the stave (76). The development begins at *più dolce* and is exclusively based on the first subject, the chief method being here melodic variation and imitation. From the freely inverted opening motif of the first subject stems a more tranquil idea *più dolce* (bar 120). The development culminates in a singularly dramatic passage in which the orchestra, with chords of the augmented fourth, brutally interrupts the soloist's phrases (bar 130 *et seq.*). A short cadenza leads imperceptibly into the recapitulation in which the first subject is considerably shortened.

The second subject is now restated a fifth lower (in A) – one of several features to show the 'classical' leaning of Bartók's late style. Like the end of the exposition, the recapitulation culminates in a climax – yet a climax much fiercer and more dramatic than the one at bar 76 and suggesting a sense of 'catastrophe'. In an extended coda which is based on the first subject, the mood changes to an expression of grief, and the ominous bass motif of the beginning is heard again. The music dies away on the chord of C major, the solo viola providing, on its lowest note (C), the bass of the concluding orchestral chord. But the last word is not yet spoken. With a sudden semitonal shift to C sharp, the soloist introduces an eloquent recitative-like epilogue (*Lento parlando*) which is based on the first subject and soon develops into an agitated cadenza. After this last gesture of defiance, the viola sinks back to the low solitary C on which the movement seems to come to its end. But, unexpectedly, the solo bassoon now intones a variant of the first subject (first heard at the beginning of the recapitulation) – a peaceful, subdued phrase, which provides the transition to the second movement.

Second Movement. *Adagio religioso*. This, like the Adagio of the Third Piano Concerto, is another example of Bartók's devotional vein. A remarkably short movement, it has the form A–B–A. Section A is based on a prayer-like idea of great simplicity, but all the more poignant for it:

Ex.20

mp semplice

It has a strong family likeness to the first subject of the preceding movement, viz. the rise and fall of the melodic outline. The drooping fifths at the ends of the phrases, reminiscent of the fourths in the variation theme of the Violin Concerto, enhance its feeling of sadness and mental fatigue. The writing in this section is rhapsodic and recitative-like, the orchestra accompanying the soloist with bare, sustained chords. Section B is marked *poco agitato*, and the soloist is asked to play *piangendo* (weeping) and *molto vibrato*. Indeed, this middle section is nothing but a wildly passionate outcry. Against the agitated runs and tremoli of the orchestra, the soloist fights to assert himself with a short 'sighing' motif

Ex.21

whose falling minor third seems to derive from the first movement's main subject. Who would deny that here speaks a soul in utter distress? The 'sighs' continue into the repeat of the first section, and at bar 50 we come upon a reminiscence of the main subject of the first movement, Ex. 17, evidently suggesting some sort of poetic link in the conception of the two movements. The sombrely meditative mood of this passage is almost instantly swept aside by an agitated solo. This in turn leads to a short *allegretto* in which the 'barbaric' effect of the orchestral *ostinato* is heightened by the soloist's ferocious triple and quadruple stoppings. Without break the music tears into the finale.

Third Movement. *Allegro vivace*. Like the finale of the Third Piano Concerto, this is the least inspired of the three movements. The thematic ideas show lack of distinction and the structure considerable padding. But there can be no two opinions as to the movement's brilliance and rhythmic drive. The writing for the solo viola abounds in such Bartókian devices as quick note-repetitions (the first theme is an instance, see below), drone-like double-stoppings, arpeggios across the strings and *staccato leggiero* playing. Like most of Bartók's finales, the movement is a rondo but cast in the irregular form A–B–A–C–B–A–Coda. Its key is A. The rondo ritornello is reminiscent of a Magyar dance, with drones in the orchestral accompaniment

Ex.22

The first episode opening in C sharp (*Poco meno mosso*) is

based upon gruff rhythmic motif which is reiterated in
Bartók's familiar *ostinato* manner

Ex.23  *etc.*

The return of the ritornello (84) is marked by a bitonal entry
(viola: B minor, orchestra: B flat major). The second episode
(*Poco meno mosso*) introduces what looks like a variant of the
opening motif of the first movement's main subject

Ex.24

Like the ritornello, it is accompanied by bare, drone-like
fifths. Its key is an unambiguous A major. Yet what induced
the composer to put so trivial an idea on paper and, what is
more, continue with it, in more or less stereotyped repetitions, over more than fifty bars? Was this as intentional as
was Mahler's deliberate use of trivial ideas when he wished
to suggest a sense of the appalling sameness and flatness of
life? Bartók's episode strikes us like a sudden grimace, an
ironic sneer, recalling a similar effect in the finale of his
Fifth String Quartet, when the savage drive of the music is
suddenly interrupted by an *allegretto con indifferenza* suggesting the mechanical monotony of a barrel-organ. The rest
of the movement consists of a return of episode B, now a fifth
lower (F sharp) than on its first entry, the soloist executing
difficult octaves and other double stoppings some of which
leap from the A string to the C string. The main rondo-
theme returns at bar 221, and the coda (235) makes some
pretence at a development, quotes the motif of the second
episode, and concludes in brilliant fashion on a regular
dominant-tonic cadence in A.

24

Karol Szymanowski (1883–1937)

ALEC ROBERTSON

INTRODUCTION

KAROL Szymanowski composed two concertos for violin and orchestra, one (Op. 35) in 1917 and the other (Op. 61) in 1930, and in 1931–2 a *Symphonie Concertante* (Op. 60) for piano and orchestra, sometimes spoken of as his Fourth Symphony, in which he designed the solo part for performance by himself, and which he played with great success in Warsaw, Paris, London and Brussels. His untimely death on 29 March 1937, at the age of 54, was commemorated by a performance of this work.

Both the Second Violin Concerto and the *Symphonie Concertante* belong to the period of Szymanowski's creative career when he had found, and could happily develop, the highly individual style which he had so long been seeking. He had exorcized the spell Richard Strauss cast upon him when, in 1905, he went to Berlin and he had avoided becoming enslaved either by polytonality or atonality. There remained two abiding influences in his creative career, Chopin and Debussy, and one has only to hear the Mazurkas (Op. 50) on Tatra themes to realize what a valuable and individual contribution Szymanowski has made to the national musical literature. After the success of his magnificent oratorio, *Stabat Mater*, in 1928, he wrote, 'Each man must go back to the earth from which he derives. To-day I have developed into a national composer, not only sub-consciously, but with a thorough conviction, using the melodic treasures of the Polish folk'.

And so, in the Second Violin Concerto he makes use of some of the mountain songs of Poland which he had drawn on in the music of his exciting and colourful ballet *Harnassie*, composed in 1926. But in this Second Violin Concerto, as compared with the first one of thirteen years earlier, not only is the national flavour much more pronounced but the form is notably more concise. Here in fact, the professor and the poet who inhabited Szymanowski are perfectly integrated.

If, however, the later work represents Szymanowski's highest point of mature achievement, the First Violin Concerto, which alone has been recorded, remains a most original and spell binding work.

There is, of course, no particular novelty about a concerto in one continuous movement (several examples are dealt with in this book) and the choice of such a form may be mere prefabrication, a labour-saving device of no particular significance.

Delius's sole violin concerto and Szymanowski's first one, between which there is some affinity, make us feel, however, that the one continuous movement they have chosen represents the true landscape of their musical minds at the time of composition. The scenery differs notably in the two works. Both composers have a habit of rhapsodic meditation, but the texture of Delius's music is much less rich and complex than that of Szymanowski, his melodic lines are less exotic and chromatic, his orchestration less subtle, his craftsmanship less secure. There was a poet but no professor in Delius.

The words I have italicized in Guido Panain's general description of Szymanowski's music could not be applied to Delius: 'its romantic spirit is permeated by impressionism, *and yet at the same time it is upheld by a frame of gladiatorial strength.*' The quick sections in Szymanowski's concerto show, particularly well, how much better built is the music of the Polish composer, and in general the concerto is even more hypnotic in effect, more dramatic and richer in detail. I do not make this comparison in order to denigrate Delius's beautiful work, but in order to give the reader some slight idea of what is in store for him in Szymanowski's fascinating work if he should happen to be unfamiliar with it.

The concerto is, as I have said, in one continuous movement which, of course, divides up into contrasted sections:

but the music steadily grows, without any real psychological break, towards the great climax after the cadenza. The listener may well feel bewildered at first by what appears to be a large number of themes that wander dreamily or energetically in and out of the score but, at a second or third hearing he will have the end well in view and all the time be able to admire the scenery without getting lost in the tropical jungle of exquisite sound. The numbers in brackets refer to those in the score, which is headed 'À mon ami Paul Kochanski'. (This eminent Polish violinist, 1887–1934, was a great friend of Szymanowski's and gave the first performance in Warsaw of his second violin concerto.) The large orchestra includes three clarinets and bass clarinet, double bassoon, four horns, three trumpets and three trombones, bass tuba, two harps, piano and orchestra, side-drum and bells.

Vivace assai. It is hard to think of any concerto with so strange a start. Carnival-like sounds of an irresponsible character proceed from the piano and woodwind over muted and divided strings (no cellos or basses) violins all *sul ponticello* and violas *flautando*. Percussion and brass chip in occasionally, and just as it seems that the orchestra is getting out of hand the music quietens and, on a high note, the solo violin enters and immediately commands the listener's attention. The word 'high' must be emphasized, for throughout the work, almost without relief, the solo violin is kept high up in pitch and so, often, are the orchestral violins. The first phrase the soloist plays is typically chromatic, in the quasi-oriental style.

Ex.1

Harps, piano, and woodwind burst out again, and again are quietened by the solo violin (*lento tranquillo*) in some very graceful figuration decorating the phrase played by the first violins (11): these are ravishing sounds.

Ex.2

The tempo quickens (13) and soon there emerges a *scherzando* section begun by the solo violin, for once on its lowest string. The above section reaches a considerable climax. Notice the thrumming in the various parts of the orchestra (e.g. violins, cellos, drums, etc.) which underline the clear melodic outlines of the soloist. A sudden swirl of tone on piano and harps (27) leads to a mysterious soft passage (note here for future reference, by the way, a rhythmic figure on piccolo, flutes, oboes) and this is followed by a series of lovely downward curving sequences which are important thematic material (32). The orchestral detail here is very rich.

Ex.3
p dolce espress.

The soloist now plays sevenths in double-stopping (36) and after that a cadenza-like passage (38), but it is Ex. 3 that dominates the score up to the sudden check in tempo (*subito meno mosso – largo* (40)) and after it. There is an exciting ascent to a grand climax of gorgeous sound (this work invites adjectives!) in which the sequences of Ex. 3 are still prominent: and then, suddenly, the soloist – who has been silent for some bars – plays a high B natural, and, as before, everyone quietens (47). Another, and shorter, *scherzando* section is followed by some tranquil music (56) a very short *allegretto grazioso* (57) and a return to the more lively *scherzando* theme (59) and there are similar sections marked *allegro grazioso* and *scherzando* (63). The solo violin swings up and down the scale and, as it were, moves the piano to mirth (66). The music then gradually ascends (with octaves and sevenths from the soloist) to its biggest and most passionate climax yet (71): a clear development of Ex. 2.

Look out here for a figure in repeated notes of different rhythmic patterns, notably in this grouping.

Ex.4
poco f

Now emerges one of the most haunting themes in the work
(83), which builds up into another passionate climax (86)

Ex.5

Timpani (90) now begin a strongly marked rhythm and
the second of the *scherzando* themes reappears (94), all this
music moving animatedly forward to the cadenza.

At the close of the cadenza the orchestra takes the music
up to the great climax of the concerto, the high peak towards
which everything has been leading, the apotheosis of the
sequences of Ex. 3.

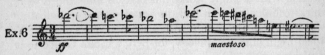

Ex.6

The soloist, silent during this passionate utterance, commands, once more, the customary hushed attention and,
after a return to the opening bars of the work, says farewell
to the lovely sequences of Ex. 3 and the haunting refrain of
Ex. 5 (110). The piano gently murmurs, the solo violin plays
harmonics after an unaccompanied trill: then, with one
note on the double bass, this most beautiful and original
work ends.

25

Alban Berg (1885–1935)

MOSCO CARNER

INTRODUCTION

I MUST begin with a warning to the general reader. Though dealing with a single work, this essay is long and does not shirk technicalities. In fact, its better part *is* technical and will be found useful only with a score at one's elbow.* Yet I feel I can offer no apology, for Berg's Violin Concerto is a difficult work and to do even small justice to its remarkable qualities requires an appreciation of its technical aspect. We are here confronted with a composition that has grown out of an entirely novel concept of structure and coherence – a concept of seemingly the most revolutionary character in the wide panorama of twentieth-century music. I am referring to 'atonal', or more accurately 'twelve-note', music. Thus, in a symposium in which the majority of participants are well-known and popular figures, Berg's Concerto will needs strike you as the strangest of guests. Its 'looks' and the very language it speaks single it out as a visitor from a world far removed and wholly different from theirs. Yet if it has been admitted into this company it is not for its strangeness (which would be poor qualification) but on account of its intrinsic qualities: true inspiration, individual vision, significance of utterance, and consummate craftsmanship.

Admittedly, the appreciation of these qualities demands a very special effort. Yet, as with so much in modern art, the

---

* Full score and piano score are published by the Universal Edition. There is also a recording made by Louis Krasner and the Cleveland Orchestra under Arthur Rodzinsky which, regrettably, is not yet commercially available in this country.

esoteric and not readily accessible character of this music cannot be made an excuse for ignoring its merits. They are there for all to see who take a sympathetic view of modern music, are willing to make that special effort and approach it without prejudice. The prejudice in this particular case derives from the widespread antagonism against atonal music. The burden of informed criticism may be summed up in the argument that it is based on a wholly artificial system of tone-relations – a system that has been *invented ad hoc* and not, like the theoretical basis of tonal music, *derived empirically* from the examples of the great masters. The fact in itself is true: Schönberg's tone-rows and their manipulation though fascinating to the intellect are artificial and arbitrary. But to conclude that it is, therefore, impossible to produce in this system inspired and imaginative music is an unacceptable proposition. This is not the place to discuss the artistic *raison d'être* of twelve-note music, but this much may be said here: what matters in the last analysis is not the system a composer chooses to write in, but whether by using it he is able to create works of an individual and enduring quality.

Now it is commonly agreed that Alban Berg has fulfilled that condition. He alone among the atonalists may be said to have succeeded, not only in completely bending Schönberg's system to his own artistic will, but, what is more, in achieving singularly impressive results. With Berg, twelve-note music appears to move from the abstraction and 'Ivory Tower' attitude of a Schönberg and a Webern to a more humane plane.* At any rate, Berg's intense lyricism often transcends the difficulty of his language and thus manages to reach the heart of even the uninitiated listener. (This was borne out to me on the occasion of the Concerto's first English performance in 1937, when at the end the audience remained completely hushed for some time, many visibly impressed and moved by what they had just heard – a memorable experience which repeated itself at a number of performances I later happened to hear on the Continent.) If twelve-note music needed evidence for its artistic

* Sibelius once jestingly referred to Berg as ' Schönberg's best work'.

legitimacy, Berg has provided it with the Lyric Suite, the unfinished opera *Lulu* and the Violin Concerto.*•

Before attempting an analysis of the concerto it will be necessary to discuss its stylistic premises: I must therefore ask the reader to bear with a short sketch of the nature of twelve-note music.† Its spiritual father was the Wagner of *Tristan* and *Parsifal* (if not the Italian madrigalists at the end of the sixteenth century). For it is here that we find chromatic writing of that intensity and frequency which was to characterize the early works of Schönberg. Its psychological root was the desire for the expression of an intense emotionalism. Thus, what drove Schönberg from the Wagnerism of his early style to the free (atonal) chromaticism of his middle period was the instinctive urge to heighten the *expressive* power of music, i.e. to express an excessive degree of emotional tension, at the same time following his emotions down to their deep-seated subconscious roots. It is for this reason that true atonal music strikes you as extraordinarily tense, emotionally overcharged, explosive and lyrical in turn, nervous, fragmentary, and hypersensitive. And just because it attempts to express the vague thoughts and feelings of the subconscious it takes on an abstract, remote and esoteric character. (It is psycho-analytical art, if you like, and the fact that Freud and Schönberg were Jews and closest contemporaries living in the same city is not without its deep significance for the rise of twelve-note music.) All the attributes we just mentioned apply, of course, to Berg. But it was the secret of his genius to integrate them into music which reflects a highly poetic and humane mind behind it.

Yet to return to Schönberg. What, we must ask, were the technical consequences of his hypertrophic emotionalism?

* I am here referring only to those works which are in strict twelve-note technique. The opera *Wozzeck*, Berg's widest-known and, from the general public's point of view, most successful work, does not belong to the above group; it is written in a free chromatic style such as characterizes Schönberg's Three Piano Pieces Op. 11 and his remarkable *Pierrot Lunaire.*

† For a more detailed discussion I would refer him to Ernst Křenek's lucid *Studies in Counterpoint* (1940), Willi Reich's excellent article in *Grove* (4th Ed. 1939), and the relevant chapter in my own *Study of 20th-Century Harmony* (2nd Ed. 1944).

Or to put it differently: how did Schönberg's excessive chromaticism affect the structure of his music? Tonal coherence first began to break up and eventually disappeared altogether. With the destruction of tonality – the hierarchical order of tonic and dominant, of major and minor keys and their varying degrees of relationship – went by the board the traditional distinction between consonance and dissonance, and with it, the principles of classical harmony. This in turn demolished the basis of the traditional form and structure. No doubt, the gain in expressive freedom was immense. The very fluidity and pliability of pure chromaticism made it an excellent means for the expression of the most subtle feelings and thoughts. Yet this was bought at a high price. For the works of Schönberg's middle period presented to the listener a seemingly chaotic sequence of chromatic melodies and harmonies whose logic – if it existed at all – was apparent only to the composer. Like the sorcerer's apprentice in Goethe's famous poem, Schönberg had landed himself in a precarious position. It was in consequence of this that he was driven to invent a principle of construction which, analogous to the classical key system, would introduce order and organization and, thus, coherence into the fluid, invertebrate mass of his free chromaticism. It was in the early 'twenties that he developed the method of what he first called 'composing with twelve chromatic notes only related to each other' – better known now as the technique of the twelve-note series or tone-row.

What is the tone-row? It is, to put it in a nutshell, the be-all and end-all of twelve-note music, yet to describe its nature precisely is not easy. It is something between a scale, a key and a basic theme. Like a scale it contains all the available notes of a given tone-system – in Schönberg's case, the twelve notes of the chromatic scale. Hence the name 'twelve-note music'. Like the key in tonal music, it is the basis upon which every atonal piece must be built. Yet it is not a scale, because the twelve chromatic notes are arranged in a varying order of intervals, the order being freshly invented by the composer for each piece. Thus the tone-row has already a *melodic* quality, yet it is not yet a *theme* because of the absence from it of any rhythmic articulation, the twelve notes being of equal value (semibreves) – much like the *canto fermo* of medieval polyphony (see Ex. 1*a* below). You might call the tone-row the chrysalis of the future theme or themes. Another noteworthy feature is the fact that all the twelve notes are equal in stature and function – a communist brotherhood in which such 'tyrants' as the tonic, dominant and subdominant, have been 'liquidated'.

The paramount role played by the tone-row in the organization of twelve-note music may be seen from this. The *total* material of a composition must derive from it – a kind of reservoir (Křenek) which is to provide you with all you need for your melodies and harmonies. (Compare Berg's row for the Violin Concerto with the themes and harmonies derived from it, Ex. 1*a*, 2, 3, 4*a*, *b*, *c*, *d*). Another rule is that the original order of the notes as arranged in the tone-row must be maintained throughout the piece and no note be taken out of this context. After the row has been used up in either the melody or harmony or both, you start it again and this procedure is repeated until the end of the piece. (We may add, however, that the rigid rule of the non-repetition of a note was later relaxed by Schönberg himself and, more frequently, by his disciples, notably Berg (see Ex. 4*a* and *d*). Now in order to expand the scope of the row Schönberg added to it three variants at which he arrived by the use of the old contrapuntal devices of inversion and reversion or crabwise motion. In Ex. 1*b* the intervals of Ex. 1*a* are turned upside-down (inversion,) in Ex. 1*c* the basic row is turned backwards (crabwise motion), and finally, in Ex. 1*d* the same is done to the inverted row Ex. 1*b*:

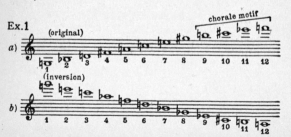

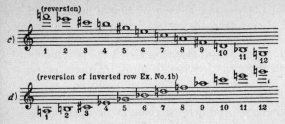

Thus, you have four rows with which to play about. Yet that is not all. As with the transposition of keys in tonal music, you may transpose the basic row and its three variants to the twelve notes of the chromatic scale so that you arrive at forty-seven variants of the original row, a veritable *embarras de richesse* from which to make your choice. These transpositions provide one of the means of creating formal sections, as moving from one transposition to the other approximates the modulation of tonal music from one key to another.

Yet there is this to consider. Chromaticism is a primarily melodic or horizontal phenomenon. Hence, twelve-note music is primarily contrapuntal or linear. It follows that the atonal composer's chief means of building up his structure will be, not harmonic, but contrapuntal (inversion, reversion, imitation, and canon) to which must be added the device of rhythmic variation. Thus it will be largely in the use of counterpoint and variation that the atonal composer may show his technical skill and inventive imagination. Thematically and harmonically he is less free because the basic row pins him down to a previously fixed order of intervals though, we must add, the way of distributing its twelve notes over melodies and chords is capable of a great variety. (Compare Ex. 1a with Ex. 2, 4, 6).

Abstruse as the working of the tone-row is, it would not seem to present the main stumbling-stone to the uninitiated listener who is certainly not aware of its manipulation. After all, the atonal composer adheres to the same general principles of æsthetics as govern all Western art irrespective of style and system: contrast and variety in unity, balance and proportion of parts and effective placing of climax and anti-climax. These make themselves felt without the listener being conscious of the technical means by which they are achieved. Berg's Violin Concerto shows in masterly fashion the application to twelve-note music of these principles which is one of the reasons why it is so satisfying a work.

Where, to my mind, its chief difficulty lies is in its harmonic language. And here we come to an aspect of twelve-note music that proves, perhaps, the most disconcerting one to the general listener. To him it seems an orgy of discordant sounds, the height of cacophony – that is, as long as he listens to it in terms of traditional harmony. For what Schönberg and his early disciples did, was to draw the last conclusion from what had been going on in the music of the late nineteenth century: the gradual blurring of the line dividing the concords and discords of classical harmony – a development which, incidentally, was responsible for the expansion of tonality and the gradual weakening of our key-sense. We have already spoken of Schönberg's excessive chromaticism. Now from the point of view of tonal harmony, this means an excessive increase of harmonic tension, i.e. discords. Moreover, in his endeavour to sever every link with tonality, Schönberg felt that any consonant formation, however accidental, was likely to suggest some tonal con-nexion, and thus the consonance was banished from the early style of atonalism. Yet with growing 'maturity' atonal music unbent, discords were no longer used indiscriminately but according to their varying degree of harmonic tension, and even the concord of classical harmony, Schönberg's former *bête noire*, was admitted again. It was chiefly Berg who for æsthetic reasons mollified the discordant character of twelve-note music and by using a number of concords brought about a kind of *rapprochement* with tonal music – another reason why of the three outstanding atonalists he is generally found to be the most accessible.

After this introduction we may now, with more profit, embark on an analysis of the Violin Concerto. But it will be well, first, to relate the story of how it came to be written, for this had a decisive bearing on the emotional character and

form of the work. It was in February 1935, while at work on
Lulu that Berg received the commission for a Violin Concerto
from the American violinist Louis Krasner. Berg hesitated
for some time with the actual composition, feeling undecided
as to the form the work should be cast in. He had previously
ventured into the field of the concerto with his Chamber
Concerto for Violin, Piano and 13 Wind Instruments – a
kind of *concerto grosso* and hence not quite suitable as a
model for a solo concerto, though in the event the Violin
Concerto was to show certain formal and instrumental affinities with it. The solution of the problem came largely from
without. The Bergs were on terms of intimate friendship
with Gustav Mahler's widow and her family and felt particularly attached to Frau Mahler's daughter by a second
marriage, Manon Gropius. A promising actress and of a
rare beauty, the girl was suddenly struck by infantile para-
lysis and after a year of intense suffering died at the age of
18 (April 1935). Berg was profoundly shaken by the tragedy
and under its impact decided to give the Violin Concerto
the character of a Requiem, inscribing it 'To the Memory of
an Angel'. He little foresaw that it was to be a Requiem for
himself. It was completed on 11th August and on 24th
December Berg died in Vienna aged 50, his death having
been caused by a septic ulcer in the back.

Most of the concerto was written in the 'Waldhaus', the
composer's summer cottage which was situated in an idyllic
spot on the southern shore of the famous Wörthersee in
Carinthia – not far distant from the place where, as Berg
liked to point out, Brahms had written *his* violin concerto
sixty years before. As we shall see, this idyllic pastoral
atmosphere is reflected in the concerto by a Carinthian folk
tune of which Berg makes prominent use in two movements.
The first performance took place at the Festival of the International Society for Contemporary Music at Barcelona, on
19 April 1936, with Krasner (to whom it is dedicated) as
soloist.

Now how did the tragedy of Manon's premature death
influence the character and form of the work? Instead of
writing a pure, 'abstract' concerto, which seems to have been

his original intention, Berg now decided to give it a pro-grammatic and symbolic significance. Call it a tone poem if you like, whose tragic heroine is Berg's young friend. Of the four movements the first two are designed to portray her character; the third suggests her suffering and death and the finale may be taken as a prayer for the deliverance and ultimate peace of her soul – a *requiescat in pace* in which the Protestant Berg makes use of a Bach chorale. Like Berlioz in *Harold in Italy* and Elgar in his Violin Concerto, Berg chooses the solo instrument as the symbol for his poetic character. Hence the singularly expressive lyricism which pervades the solo part from beginning to end. The striking, though merely accidental, parallel with Elgar's concerto goes farther still. Not only does Berg's work enshrine the soul of his friend, but the solo cadenza is removed from its orthodox place in the first movement to the third and is accompanied by the orchestra which, as in Elgar, consider-ably heightens its musical significance.

The concerto consists of two parts each comprising two movements which form an emotional unity. Part I has an *Andante*, dreamlike, gentle and graceful and is followed by an *Allegretto*, a scherzo-like movement with two trios of which the first is a waltz and the second the Carinthian *ländler* re-ferred to above – music suggestive of the girl's youthful exuberance and *joie de vivre*. In the use of these dances Berg follows, of course, the time-honoured tradition of the Austrian classics.*

While Part I is the more static portion of the work, violent contrast comes with Part II. It opens with an *Allegro*, dra-matic, sinister, strident and torn, which concludes on a cli-max of terrifying effect ('the catastrophe') – an emotional climate reminiscent of that of the late Mahler. This is followed by a sombre *Adagio* of a devotional nature the thematic basis of which is the chorale '*Es ist genug*' of Bach's Sixtieth Can-tata *O Ewigkeit, du Donnerwort*. About the ingenious way in which Berg makes use of the chorale more will be said later.

As for the special concerto features, i.e. the relation be-ween soloist and orchestra and the virtuoso treatment of the

* See also the second movement of the *Lyric Suite*.

solo part, the work may be said to differ in no way from what since Beethoven has been called the 'symphonic concerto'. The orchestra takes as much part of the essential ideas as the soloist, Berg exploiting to the full the effects of opposition and interplay of the two protagonists. At the same time, the virtuoso element is very much developed, in fact the solo part bristles with difficulties such as double and triple stoppings, octaves, playing in the highest position, harmonics, arpeggios across the four strings, left-hand *pizzicati* and even a four-part canon. But there is at no time the impression of technical display for its own sake; on the contrary, whatever difficulties there are seem to grow out of the poetic idea itself, as may be seen from the introductory cadenza to the third movement.

So much for general features. Let us now examine the work in greater detail. It is based on three ideas: the tonerow, Ex. 1*a*; the Carinthian folktune, Ex. 5; and the Bach chorale, Ex. 8; the last comes into full prominence not until the finale. Yet looking at the tone-row more closely you will find that the chorale's opening motif, which consists of four notes in whole-tone progression, is already contained in the last four notes of the row. In other words, the symbolic idea represented by the chorale is present in the work from its very beginning. As for the first nine notes of the row, they form an arpeggio – an unusual arrangement as most rows go. But this is no mere coincidence. Berg was writing a work for the violin and therefore invented a row that would easily lie on the four strings. From Ex. 1*a*, it will be seen that the notes 1, 3, 5 and 7 represent the open strings (G–D–A–E) while the intermediate notes 2, 4, 6 and 8 lie within the first position. In other words, the atonal Berg built his row with the same regard for the technical peculiarity of the instrument as when the classical composers cast their violin works (mostly) in the key of D in which the tonic, dominant and subdominant lie on the open strings. Another feature of Berg's row is the fact that the nine-note arpeggio consists of superimposed major and minor thirds so that it *appears* to contain chords of tonal music: common chords in major and minor, augmented chords and chords of the seventh, ninth and so on. I say 'appears' because Berg's various commentators warn us against interpreting these intervals and chords in terms of tonal harmony. Admittedly, the choice was, as I explained, determined by the technique of the violin, yet I cannot help feeling that Berg here attempted a deliberate approach to tonal music as he had done before in his Lyric Suite. He is reported as having said that he could make use of the tone-row without anyone being conscious of it. Indeed, in the opening of the concerto you are certainly not aware of atonal music but of progressions which seem to fluctuate between a sort of B flat major and G minor. Moreover, the chorale is in clear B flat major (in Bach it is in A), the very first note of the work is B flat and so is its final chord (B flat major with the added sixth G), to say nothing of other passages suggesting a definite tonality.

A last observation on the row. It seems to me as if Berg intended it as an anticipatory epitome of the work's whole poetic idea. For just as the finale introduces the chorale, so do the four final notes of the row refer to the chorale's opening motifs. Moreover, it will be noted that while in the first three movements arpeggio formations are conspicuous, the finale is dominated by the whole-tone motif of the chorale. In view of Berg's known idiosyncrasy in other works for subtle symbolic correspondences, we may not be far wrong in assuming them also in the Violin Concerto.

The following is a brief analysis of the form of each movement in which attention will also be drawn to points of special interest. With the first movement, however, I shall deal in greater detail so as to show the working of the tone-row.

Part I. First Movement. *Andante*.

Introduction	A	Bridge	B (*un poco gratioso*)	Bridge	A	Introd:.	Transit. to *Allegretto*
1–10,		11–27,	28–37	38–76	77–83	84–93	94–104

From this plan it will be seen that the first movement is in tripartite form (A–B–A) but made more symmetrical by what is called the *Bogen* or arch-form: from section B as the centre, the two arches turn to right and left, respectively, so that the part after B mirrors the one preceding it. In progressing from B the music retraces, as it were, its steps*.

The dreamlike, evocative introduction makes prominent use of the row's arpeggio, the orchestra transposing it to B flat while the solo violin answers in the original 'key' of the row (on G). The measure of Berg's freedom in treating the row may be seen from the fact that in the first seven bars of the solo part, he first introduces the odd notes (1, 3, 5, 7), then the even ones (2, 4, 6, 8), then again the odd ones (1, 3, 5, 7, 9), adding the last three notes (10, 11, 12) not until bar 8. This is one of many instances to show how Berg flouts the strict rule according to which the twelve notes should always be used in the order in which they occur in the basic row.

A two-bar 'cadence' (bars 9 and 10) which contains a true dominant harmony D–F sharp–A–C leads to the opening, in an unequivocal G minor, of the *Andante* proper. This begins with a series of low-lying and darkly scored harmonies which represent the row telescoped into so many chords:

Ex.2

out of that rises the solo violin, like a ray of light, introducing the complete row horizontally (in quavers):

Ex.3

The chromatic tail, a 'sigh' (figure X) is to play an important part throughout the work. The following bars (21–7) represent a repeat of bars 11–19 but with the row now used in inversion (Ex. 1b). This device of answering a theme with

* See also the second movement of the Chamber Concerto, the third movement of the Lyric Suite and certain scenes of *Wozzeck*. It would appear that the arch-form has a particular appeal for the more intellectual type of composer. It is often found in Bartók and, earlier, in Liszt and Wagner.

its inversion (or reversion) is one of the chief structural
means in twelve-note music and corresponds to the half-
close and full-close of tonal music.

A bridge passage based on the 'sigh' leads to section B
which introduces a new version of the row in triplets. It is
first given out by the solo violin (bars 38–53) and then repeated on succeeding instruments (cello–horn–trumpet,
bars 54–76), Berg making much use of augmentation and
diminution (lengthening and shortening of the original
note-values), with imitation and free canon between the
soloist and the orchestra into the bargain (bar 47 *et seq.*).
Section B ends on bar 76, after which the music takes us
back via the above bridge passage to section A, and finally,
to the introduction, but all is now shortened and altered in
texture and scoring. The introduction leads without break
to the second movement.

Second Movement. *Allegretto.*

A1	quasi Trio I	Trio II	Trio I (shortened)	A2	A3	Coda
104–36	137–54	155–66	167–72	173–207	208–29	230

Here again we find an 'arch' with its central pivot on
Trio II. Not only the movement as a whole – a scherzo –
in tripartite form but section A itself consists of three parts:
$a^1+a^2+a^3-b-a^2+a^3+a^1$. The three a's represent ideas
different, yet related in character

Ex.4

a scherzando (bars 104–9), a wienerisch (bars 110–13), and a
rustico (bars 114–17; see next page). The Viennese theme has

the euphonious thirds and sixths and the characteristic leaps
of the Vienna waltz, while the *rustico* suggests yodelling,
figures. Section *b* is like *a* in *scherzando* character but more
subdued (Ex. 4d).

Trio I. This is a more energetic section. Note the exuberant swing of the opening (reversion answered by inversion
of the transposed row) and the marked waltz-rhythm of the
obtrusive brass (bar 147 *et seq.*).

Trio II. This section returns to a more lyrical and rhythmically less agitated expression. Its gently rocking theme
seems to derive from the 'sigh' of the first movement. The
return of A (bar 176) has the waltz (change of the time-
signature from 6/8 to 3/8) and its repeat A2 (bar 208) introduces a Carinthian *ländler* tune (*come una pastorale*)

Ex.5

Note the suggestive scoring for horn and two trumpets and
also the soloist's counterpoint which is formed of motifs from
the Viennese and *rustico* sections but shaped in such a way
as to create the characteristic effect of overblowing wind
instruments.* Berg's ingenious use of his material may be
seen from the fact that the first four bars of the violin counterpoint (214–17) contain the top-notes of the Viennese theme
(Ex. 4b, marked with x) which are nothing else but the
whole-tone motif of the basic row and the chorale opening,
respectively. The coda (bar 229 *et seq.*) grows more animated
and the exuberant *stretta* almost kicks over the traces. The
solo violin shoots up with the row in quick waltz-rhythm
and the movement closes on the G minor chord plus a major

---

* Overblowing is the device by which wind players produce harmonics instead of the fundamental notes, through increased pressure
of breath.

seventh, i.e. the first four notes of the row.

Part II. Third Movement. *Allegro.*

Solo cadenza (accompanied)	A	B	A
1–22	23–43	44–95	96–135

The movement is in simple tripartite form and by way of introduction opens with a cadenza. About its tragic character we have already spoken. The 'catastrophe' at the end (bar 125 *et seq.*) is here already foreshadowed: the twelve notes of the row are telescoped (freely reverted) into a chord of the utmost stridency whose notes rise from a low C on the double bass to a high G flat on the flute. This terrifying cry is answered by the hammer-blows of the three timpani – a G minor chord which is first struck and then continued as a roll.

Ex.6

Freely reverted row Ex. No. 1c   3 Timpani

The solo violin breaks forth into a cadenza of quivering agitated figures while the orchestra opposes it with the opening whole-tone motif of the chorale, i.e. the last four notes of the row. This introduction is one of the most dramatic portions of the whole work.

Section A of the *Allegro* proper (*molto ritmico*) is dominated by

Ex.7 *molto ritmico*

whose abrupt, halting rhythm ♪𝄾♪♩⌢♪, may be taken to stand for the brutal fate which was to kill Manon Gropius. Looking closer at this motif it will be found to be a variant of the Viennese theme of the second movement (Ex. 4*b*) which, through rhythmic alteration, is now made to suggest an entirely different image. The soloist opposes the orchestra with lyrical and more sustained phrases which, arabesque-like, expand over the whole range of the instrument. From bar 35 onward (*pesante, ma quasi a tempo*) the two antagonists reverse their role – the soloist taking over the brutal rhythm while the orchestra becomes lyrical.

Section B is introduced by the chorale motif in inversion (*Ganz frei*, bar 43) and it is here that the solo instrument, as the symbol of Berg's heroine, becomes the dominating element playing in free, cadenza-like fashion against an orchestral background of light and delicate colours. Significantly enough, this section is almost wholly made up of reminiscences of the scherzo. Its three parts *a* (bars 44–53), *b* (bars 54–78) and *a* (bars 78–95) refer to that movement thus: *a* =Trio II, and *b* =Viennese and *rustico*; section *b* dissolves in the later course into a cadenza in which much use is made of the chorale motif and the 'sigh' (Ex. 3). Finally, beginning at bar 78, the theme of Trio II is treated in strict four-part canon on the solo violin – a *tour-de-force* for which the Bach of the unaccompanied violin sonatas may have stood model.* A short transition (bar 90) containing a reference to the arpeggio of the first movement's introduction and the Viennese of the scherzo, leads to the recapitulation of A (tempo 1, bar 96). At bar 125 we reach the climax of the movement which symbolizes the girl's death – an outburst of the most shattering effect. The first nine notes of the row are telescoped into a chord which is given out by the orchestra while the three remaining notes are thrown up in the form of a melodic motif by the solo violin and the orchestra in octaves. This pattern is repeated six times but with ever-lessening force. The music gradually collapses, so to speak: on each of the six repetitions the orchestral chord is reduced by one note while at the same time the solo violin, beginning on the low B flat (bar 126),

---

* The difficulty of this polyphonic cadenza induced Berg to add a simplified version in which the solo violin plays only two parts, the other two being taken over by a solo viola.

adds a note on each entry. The new motif which is thus
generated reveals itself as an anticipation of the chorale
opening – the whole passage being a *locus classicus* for Berg's
art of subtle and organic transitions. At bar 136 begins the
last movement.

Fourth Movement. *Adagio.*

Chorale	Variation I	Variation II	Carinthian Ländler	Coda (Chorale)
136–57	158–77	178–99	200–13	214

Like the previous movement, the finale is in three parts,
the middle section being formed by the two chorale variations and the Carinthian *ländler*. It is in this movement that
Berg advances farthest in his reconciliation of twelve-note
music with tonality. Its key may be described as a Pick-
wickian B flat major.

The Bach chorale

is stated in a manner suggesting the alternation between
priest and congregation in a service: the solo violin intones
the first verse to which the orchestra, scored in organ-like
fashion (four clarinets), responds with the second verse and
so on, until we reach the end of the chorale which is extended by echo-like repetitions of its concluding phrase
'*Es ist genug*'. In the orchestral statement of the chorale Berg
takes over Bach's original harmonization (which is strikingly
modern) but transposes it a semitone up. This turn from the
torn, fragmentary texture of the twelve-note style to firm
tonal harmonies seems to me a master-stroke of dramatic
symbolism: peace descending from heaven after the tragedy
of the previous movement. The finale thus becomes the
spiritual climax of the whole work and stands unique in the
literature of twelve-note music. Its effect is enhanced by
Berg's ingenious treatment of the chorale in the following
two variations.

Variation I. *A tempo. Misterioso*. The chorale lies in the bass, its several phrases being transposed alternately to E and B flat major. It opens with an incomplete canon at the fifth between cello and harp, and in bar 164 enters the solo violin with a *Klagegesang*, a lament whose poignant lyrical line weaves arabesque-like figures round the chorale on the orchestra. The end of the variation introduces a *stretto* (close imitative entries) of the concluding chorale motif.

Variation II. *A tempo. Adagio*. The chorale now appears in inversion on the middle register of the orchestra to which, from bar 185 onwards, is added a canon in the bass (double bass, tuba and harp). In the previous bar nearly the whole brass had entered to lead to the majestic climax of the movement (bar 186) while throughout the variation the solo violin continues with its lament. The ecstatic mood subsides again and at *molto tranquillo* we turn to a reminiscence of the Carinthian tune. This transition is yet another example of Berg's consummate skill in leading imperceptibly from one section to another: by a slight alteration the concluding chorale motif is turned into the opening of the *ländler* which is now played very slowly and '*wie aus der Ferne*' ('as if from afar'), the scoring being of utmost delicacy. There lies an ineffable pathos about this return of the *landler* tune conjuring up the image of a dancing spectre.

Coda. The chorale is intoned with full harmonies (wind) above which the solo violin sings its expressive lament. At *molto adagio* begins what may be termed the 'transfiguration'. The music begins to dissolve and to take on an immaterial, wraith-like character. The chorale's last phrase is repeated three times, each repetition being an octave lower than the previous one (solo violin – trumpet – horn). Simultaneously, the basic row rises from the bass (at *Molto Adagio*) and soars over five octaves when it is taken up by the solo violin to die away, hardly audible, on the G in the fourth octave above middle C. On the orchestra we hear a last faint reminiscence of the gentle arpeggio with which this memorable work began and on which it now concludes – an ethereal ending which inevitably recalls to the mind the conclusion of Mahler's *Song of the Earth*.

26

Serge Prokofiev (1891–   )

ALAN FRANK

INTRODUCTION

PROKOFIEV has been a steadily prolific composer for forty years, his opus numbers now running well over the hundred mark. His concertos total eight – five for piano (No. 4 is for left hand), two for violin and one for cello. Of these, one – the Third Piano Concerto – has achieved worldwide popularity, the two Violin Concertos are infrequently heard, and the rest hardly or not at all, at any rate as far as this country is concerned. It is not difficult to see why only one of the five Piano Concertos has firmly established itself in the modern repertoire. It is the most immediately captivating among them, it contains the best music and the best piano part – though invariably Prokofiev, a brilliant pianist, writes with complete understanding of what he wants from the keyboard. Nevertheless, one would welcome an occasional chance to hear, for example, Nos. 2 and 5, each of which has attractive features or movements: notably the Scherzo of No. 2, with its continuous toccata-like solo part in rapid semiquavers from first bar to last; the Fifth Piano Concerto is on the dry side, but the fourth of its five movements has a main idea of great charm, while the finale is lively and pungent, with a perky theme reminding one of the opening of *Peter and the Wolf*, which it preceded by four years.

If we turn to the two Violin Concertos, it is by no means easy to understand why neither has achieved anything like the popularity of the Third Piano Concerto, even allowing for the fact that, other things being equal, a piano concerto is likely to reach a wider public than a violin concerto. These two works of Prokofiev, separated by over twenty years, are excellent examples of their somewhat lightweight kind. The

first of them, in D major, is indeed a far better work than the
Second Piano Concerto of the same year (1913). Again, it
has a brilliant and characteristically mordant scherzo, but
it shows also the complementary and probably less recognized, though no less attractive, aspect of Prokofiev's gifts:
as so frequently happens, in humanity as well as art, the
obverse side of brittle wit is found to reveal a warm lyrical
strain, which results in some of Prokofiev's most admirable
long themes. The opening subject (*Andantino*) of this First
Violin Concerto is an invention of which any composer, let
alone a 22-year-old one, could be proud: and its fascina-
tingly scored reappearance in the last pages of the work
shows great imagination. Similarly, in the Second Violin
Concerto (G minor), the second subject of the first movement and the theme of the slow movement are in this vein
of unforced lyricism, romantic in feeling yet unpretentious
and uncomplicated, clear and definite in expression. Possibly in both the Violin Concertos, these two strongly contrasted aspects of Prokofiev's art are rather startlingly juxta-
posed, and it may be that the abrupt changes of mood have
militated against greater public approval of the works.*
If so, the more's the pity, for they are full of striking and
likeable music.

In the Third Piano Concerto, brilliance and gaiety are
the predominant qualities, with less sign of the lyricism of
the Violin Concertos, though the middle movement shows
that delicacy is not banished. Its date is 1917, the same year
as the Classical Symphony, and if both are youthful works,
it is arguable that Prokofiev is often best as a youthful composer, even a relatively small-scale composer. It is significant
that the only subsequent orchestral work of his which has
achieved like popularity is *Peter and the Wolf*. In all three
works it is the freshness of the thematic and harmonic invention which is their outstanding quality. And only the most

---

* It is pertinent to mention that, according to Alexander Werth's
Musical Uproar in Moscow, 'the struggle of the two Prokofievs' was
noted at the Soviet Communist Party Conference of Musicians in
January 1948: his tendency to 'step on the throat of his own song' was
a striking phrase used on that occasion.

superior person would try to demonstrate that the invention
here is of a lower grade than that of the larger-scale, more
ambitious works of Prokofiev's maturity.

Within the repertoire of modern piano concertos
Prokofiev's No. 3 has held a unique, international position
in the estimation of both pianists and public. Only in the
last few years has a rival appeared in another composer's
Third Piano Concerto, that by Bartók (see page 347). There
is this difference – that the latter must be classed as one of
Bartók's lesser works, while the Prokofiev, despite (as will
be seen) a certain meretriciousness in its finale, still occupies
a very high place in his large output. How many piano concertos of this century have weathered, or will weather, so
successfully a testing period of nearly thirty-five years?

PIANO CONCERTO NO. 3 IN C MAJOR

FIRST Movement. *Andante. Allegro*. The Second Violin Concerto opens with a solo melodic line for violin alone.
Similarly, this concerto opens with the most limpid of themes
for clarinet alone

Ex.1

joined after a few bars by the second clarinet playing a third
below. The strings take up the theme for four bars and then,
without *rallentando* or *accelerando* and still soft, we are in the
Allegro. Semiquaver rising figures, *crescendo*, over a pedal C
introduce the soloist's theme, which derives from (*a*) of Ex. 1,
in that its first notes, from which the whole idea grows, show
a *falling* fifth, followed by a *rising* second. The sudden and
shortlived shift, after two bars, from C major to the dominant of D flat is a noticeable harmonic twist of which
Prokofiev is fond. The music continues *con brio* until the solo
piano has eight bars of repeated crotchet triads, gradually
quietening to make way for the light and piquant second

theme on woodwind and *pizzicato* strings, with the rhythm
delightfully reinforced by castanets:

Ex.2

After a slightly elaborated version by the soloist, this theme
goes back to woodwind and castanets with the piano playing
light semiquaver passages, mostly descending chromatic
scales. A *Più mosso* still uses falling chromatic semitones, the
source of which is to be found in (*a*) of Ex. 2. The piano has
triplet quavers throughout this section, which ranges kalei-
doscopically through many keys and leads into an *ff* but
cantabile restatement of the *Andante* (Ex. 1) in C major. The
piano is silent for eight bars, during which there is a gradual
diminuendo, and then itself enters with the Ex. 1 theme, which
it is playing for the first time. It is canonically treated, the
bassoon entering an octave lower, exactly one bar later at
the point marked x in Ex. 1. A few bars later the perspica-
cious listener will observe another canon between clarinet
and piano, this time at two beats' interval. A few bars of soft
piano arabesques over a background of *tremolo* strings bring
us back to the *Allegro*. The semiquaver passage over the
pedal C which at the opening took four bars now occupies
no less than twenty-five bars, and very effective its mounting
crescendo is. The main *Allegro* theme is restated with little
change, and there is more reference to the falling chromatic
semitones. The delicate Ex. 2 when it reappears sounds far
from delicate, being grotesquely scored for piano (*ff* chords),
woodwind, and strings *col legno*. The final *Più mosso* is a
sixteen-bar version of the rising semiquaver passage still over
a pedal C, and always *crescendo*. This recurring feature has a
glitter and brilliance rather of the eighteenth century, and
this is the dominating flavour of the opening movement.

Second Movement. *Theme (Andantino) and Variations*. The
Concerto has sailed into popularity largely on the strength
of this movement, which is one of Prokofiev's happiest inspirations. The first part of the theme is heard on woodwind

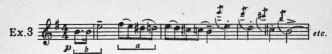

Ex.3

and the second part is played by strings with a noticeable drag on the fourth beats of the bars:

Ex.4

Then flute and clarinet return with the first part of the theme. The little cadence which rounds it off will be heard also at the end of most of the variations. The theme finishes in E minor, and at Variation I, still *Andantino*, the piano enters alone with a scale in that key. As it reaches its summit, it characteristically sideslips into B flat, and the soloist's following harmonization of the theme is so enchanting that a few bars' quotation is justifiable:

Ex.5

In the next bar the four falling quavers of the theme (marked *a* in Ex. 3) are heard to ascend, a device which figures in subsequent variations too.

Variation II is a tempestuous *Allegro*, fully scored with the theme often emphatically pronounced on trumpet, and *bravura* passages for the piano.

Variation III is slightly slower, but still vigorous. The piano plays in 12/8 as against the orchestra's 4/4, and the former's accentuation is frequently a quaver before the main beat – an arresting syncopation. Snatches of the theme are heard, particular use being made of its middle part (but without the drag on the fourth beat, for which there is no time in this breathless variation) and of the inverted, rising quaver group already referred to.

The next Variation brings us back to the original mood of somewhat Gallic delicacy engendered by the theme itself: marked *Andante meditativo*, it is largely scored for piano and muted strings. It is freer than any of the preceding variations and the listener need not worry if he hears little direct evidence of the theme. He will, however, note the rhythm marked *b* in Ex. 3, though the rising interval has become an octave instead of a fourth. He will notice also a beautifully scored reference to the middle part of the theme (*tremolo* strings and piano arabesques). For the first time the music moves firmly away from E minor, and Variation V (*Allegro giusto*) goes rapidly through several keys before energetically hammering out a variant of the theme which now sounds very much in the Russian tradition, the quavers rising and the rhythm square.

This leads straight into a *reprise* of the theme in the same tempo of two minims in a bar: the minim of Ex. 3 becomes a semibreve, the quavers crotchets, and so on. The key of E minor is restored and the scoring is rather similar to that of the opening, but with the addition of light *staccato* quaver chords in the piano. An extension of the cadence bars brings the movement to a close.

Third Movement. *Allegro, ma non troppo*. Two bassoons in unison and *pizzicato* strings announce the rather matter-of-fact theme

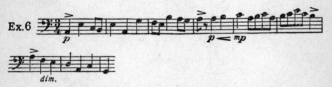

Ex.6

which then bounces cheerfully between orchestra and piano until a subsidiary figure bursts in, with prominent rapid scale passages, up and down. A *Poco più mosso* section, opening softly but not remaining so for long, introduces some imitational use of Ex. 6. The music quietens into a slower, more expressive section, with an important theme on woodwind:

After a repetition on strings, as if to atone for the sudden warmth of feeling there suddenly appears an extraordinary, quietly grotesque passage for piano alone, which certainly cannot escape the hearer's attention and thus need not be quoted: it is a *locus classicus* of Prokofiev's habit of 'stepping on the throat of his own song'. The orchestra plays with it, and then, equally abruptly, piano and lower strings revel richly in Ex. 7. The level of the musical thought here suffers a descent, it must be admitted, and the shades of not very good Tchaikovsky are all too near. Before or after they have enveloped the listener according to his capacity for resisting over-ripe harmonic procedure, the *Allegro* (Ex. 6) returns, and to the end all is fireworks. Like most displays of pyro-technics, it is slightly repetitive and goes on a bit too long, at any rate for the grown-ups. If one can forgive a display in the final pages of what is primarily a piano concerto to enjoy, one must still add that after the first two movements, the finale is somewhat disappointing. Of how many works, new and old, can that not be said? Why, one asks oneself on these occasions, do not composers write their last movements first?

27

William Walton (1902–)

SCOTT GODDARD

INTRODUCTION

THE three concertos so far written by William Walton approach the problem of contrasting and combining solo and tutti by three routes. Each is an example of a different method and from that there arises a difference in manner. It is what would be expected of a man peculiarly active in the search for novelties and thoughtful in the extreme about the uses to which those novelties may be put with most advantage to the work in hand.

The Sinfonia Concertante (1927) has since been revised, and a comparison of the two scores is instructive, as showing the way in which subtleties of perspective or texture, ignored by the generality of those who listen to a work, are apprehended by the creator of that work, who in time does in fact become apprehensive and is brought to the pitch of disharmony that forces him to alter and rearrange. What was once absolute and relevant became conditional and relative and had to be brought into such a new relationship as would give it clearer meaning. And so in this instance the pianoforte, the instrument which from the first was given a *concertante* part to play, not a solo part, is so altered in its activity as to enliven the whole fabric of the work; and this without altering its relative position *vis-à-vis* the orchestra. It is in fact given less to do; while what is left to it is made more pointed and effective. It still plays as a member of the orchestra and not as a concerto soloist; but it is allowed more opportunity to play as an orchestral soloist, in the way a woodwind instrument might be called upon to do. The result is an increase of transparency. There are also a small number of rhythmic and textual alterations which give a corresponding increase of breadth to the design. The whole remanipulation makes a fascinating study of the craftsmanship of creative thought in music.

Walton's first work in concerto style used the single instrument, generally considered as being naturally in the position of a solo, as a *concertante* instrument, nearly level with any other single instrument in the orchestra that might be used intermittently for solo work. The Viola Concerto (1929) raised the solo instrument nearer to the level generally conceded to it. But in choosing a viola as solo instrument Walton did not wholly concede the conventional position of brilliant display which the concerto soloist had been generally allowed to affect, from the period of Liszt and onwards through a densely populated area of works constructed to give pleasure to those who were content to gasp in amazement, knowing nothing of either the difficulty or the ease of finger agility. Walton's Viola Concerto is at once difficult enough and a sufficiently large problem of interpretation to tempt and reward a great player. Being of that stature the soloist will know how to deal with the problem of a solo part which evolves by gentle means and reserves its deepest feeling for the more intimate confidences between one instrument and another.

It is in the Violin Concerto (1939) that Walton at length reaches that true display music where the soloist is invested with all the traditional scintillating grace and power of a virtuoso. The virtuoso writing is completely efficient. It is attractive to great technicians and to those who can savour technical display. There is, too, the virtuosity of creation. That is less immediately apparent, we who listen being what we are.

Since the Concerto issued from the private party of restricted membership for which Vivaldi and Bach worked and found in Mozart a composer capable of giving intelligent, perhaps even intellectual, significance to this type of entertainment, a future unforeseen by musicians of that day opened before this peculiarly vulnerable style of work. The years between Mozart and Walton produced exquisite monstrosities of technical display. There were also works in this style which because they did not conform to the heady display expected dumbly by the average audience (the 'man in the street', as he is sentimentalized) gave back to the concerto that strength of character which Mozart and Beethoven had insisted was not to be sacrificed to the whim of an audience. Walton, reaching his unadulterated display work, the Violin Concerto, by way of first a *concertante* work followed by one designed more for intimacy than brilliance, places himself in the heredity of the most intellectual, that is the most musicianly, practitioners of this art, which, since it demands more acutely than any other instrumental music the approval of the masses, has to accept their verdict.

SINFONIA CONCERTANTE FOR ORCHESTRA
WITH PIANO

FIRST Movement. *Maestoso* leading to *Allegro spiritoso*. The opening is imposing in the wide sweep of its melody, the strength of the great chords stressing each main beat and the rich scoring for full orchestra and pianoforte.

Ex.1

It is the kind of splendour in sound and texture that might well form a complete introductory section for a symphonic movement, relying in solitary grandeur upon its own efforts to provide a suitable preface to the main body of the work. The danger then would be an eventual and rapid decline into pomposity. Walton flirted with pomp and circumstance in the march for the coronation year, *Crown Imperial*, where the music at first struts about with an amusing parade of fuss and importance and then ponderously treads a noble measure of Edwardian assurance. Neither before nor since has he gone so far in that direction. Here the grandeur, once sufficiently asserted, gives way before its opposite.

Ex.2

Four bars of this bring the music to rest on an F sharp pedal held by strings below the next theme, an important one and the first solo appearance of the pianoforte.

Ex.3

Two more points to be noted are the tune for woodwind and horns

Ex.4

and the octave passage for strings

Ex.5

after which all the above material is dealt with again in the same order with the exception of the theme announced by the pianoforte. That is reserved for other uses in the main body of the movement which now opens with this piece of high spirits, as compelling as the grandiose opening of the introduction and in absolute contrast to it.

Ex.6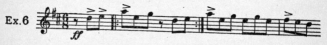

Some repose is reached when a second theme is heard on woodwind.

Ex.7

Important also is the short chatter of strings answered by a sigh from the pianoforte.

Ex.8

This leads to the central area of the movement where the pianoforte at last recalls its theme from the introduction, not repeated there but saved for this new purpose.

Ex.9

Out of that grows an answering clause which eventually assumes the outline quoted here.

Ex.10

These two restful designs dominate the music until at length the boisterous Ex. 6 returns, though only as a short coda quickly ending the movement. The *Maestoso* and the *Allegro* have formed between them an exceptionally many-themed movement. Such abundance of themes is a characteristic which, if it is to be turned to good account and not merely produce a sense of confused richness, needs to be controlled by an alert mind. Part of Walton's success comes from the subtle relationship that exists between these themes, a relationship just sufficient for unity of feeling, though distant enough to allow for diversity in character. It is a skilful solution of a complicated problem.

Second Movement. *Andante comodo.* A gentler mood succeeds the conflict. The slower pace gives room for lengthier designs and broader outlines. The pianoforte converses with the orchestra and the instruments of the orchestra discuss among themselves such matters as these. (Two themes shown here as they appear later on in counterpoint.)

Ex.11

A brief thought is uttered meanwhile by the pianoforte in this way.

Ex.12

By the end a state of exaltation is reached when the two themes of Ex. 11 combine.

Third Movement. *Allegro vivo sémpre scherzando*, which may be transcribed as a lively allegro of a gay character always. It is more explicit than the *Allegro molto* heading this movement in the earlier version and it may stand here as description enough. A pianoforte fanfare, punctuated by strong chords from the orchestra, starts the movement and the real business soon appears when the pianoforte leads off with the following:

Ex.13

This goes its brilliant way and other matters take second place, one alone gaining some prominence.

Ex.14

Finally a monumental coda of large proportions marked *Tempo primo della prima parte*, thus a return to the grandiose music of the introduction, after which the pianoforte fanfare and the end.

VIOLA CONCERTO

FIRST Movement. *Andante comodo*. A minor tonality, muted strings, a single clarinet low in its register, phrases that seem to be searching for an elusive idea; in that way the work

begins and within the space of hardly three bars the solo
viola enters and the idea is there.

Ex. 15

We do well to take notice of the rising interval that starts
this long phrase, for it will recur continually and not in this
movement alone. The lift on to the higher note is one of the
chief constructional gambits of the work. And when it appears combined with a back-and-forth major-minor shift the
other main characteristic of the music has been put before
us and we are in possession of the fundamental thesis of the
concerto.

Ex. 16

It is present also in the second subject. (The term is used to
denote the outstanding theme of a group; for this concerto
has almost as large an abundance of thematic material as
has been noticed in the preceding work, the Sinfonia
Concertante.)

Ex. 17

From this cantilena, which the solo instrument sings like any
prima donna, arises a great amount of the lyrical music of
the movement. But it has in it the seeds of drama as well,
and these, too, burgeon as the theme becomes part of the
development of the movement. This development is shared
by both main themes. From the first there comes, with
changes of rhythm (quickened and syncopated) and dynamics (loudening as pace grows), much of the rapid passage-
work uttered by the solo instrument. Passionately the viola
in its highest register gives forth yet another version of the
main second subject, in sixths now and with growing im-
petuosity. Soon the orchestra answers with a still more forceful passage, a version this time of the first main subject. All

then quietens in readiness for the viola to feel its way through
the opening bars that had preceded its first appearance and
thus enter in upon cadenza passages, accompanied con-
versationally by other instruments. The viola, however, has
it over all its fellow players. It comes eventually to the main
second subject again and now we hear to what eloquent and
moving purposes the final three notes of that theme are put.
And we notice also how poignant this climax becomes when
to the aspiring rise and drooping fall of that minute, immensely significant outline there is added in double-stopping
(sixths) the ambivalence of the minor-major, major-minor
sway. On that the movement ends.

Second Movement. *Vivo, con molto preciso.* Again the solo
instrument is heard immediately the movement opens. This
is to be vivacious music, in contrast to the mood of the first
movement and a foil to that of the third. The viola announces
the main idea.

This having been bandied to and fro with great gusto and to
fine effect, the solo music becoming increasingly scintillating, an abrupt stop is put to these matters when *pianissimo*
muted brass intrude with this contrasting design.

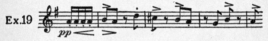

The viola soon seizes on this, showing it to be perfectly appli-
cable to the phraseology of stringed instruments; but first it
announces another solo phrase which in turn the orchestra
takes to itself and by so doing suggests that in this case it can
do better than a solo stringed instrument to express the idea
fully.

What now ensues is sparkling commentary upon the pre-
cipitous nature of Ex. 18 (upwards) and 20 (downwards)

and the syncopations arising from Ex. 19. The final leap is upward and, though a pause comes before the next movement, when that movement begins we are evidently meant to connect Ex. 18 with what the bassoon immediately announces as the first melody of the

Third Movement. *Allegro moderato.*

When this has run its course, double the length quoted here, the viola takes it from the bassoon, enlarges it, brings it to a high climax and so hands it on to the orchestra once more. Then a small design which seems to link on to the triplet figure in bar 2, above; and so there is reached the next large theme. This the viola announces. (It is quoted here at its second appearance, in order to include the answer given by a solo clarinet.)

The movement, proceeding along these limitless paths, takes in a wide range of vision which leads to such matters as a noble broadening of the gentle bassoon tune, treated in canonic style over a static bass. And at the end there is the highest moment of all the work, a serene and exalted expanse of coda with Ex. 21 (now on the strings) accompanying Ex. 15 (solo viola) and very remarkably and satisfyingly murmuring the equivalent in music of 'In my end is my beginning'. Lastly the dropping minor-major design, ending the work in that order seemingly; but as the tone of the viola withdraws, the orchestral strings are heard and theirs is the smaller tonality, the work thus ending with major and minor heard together.

The literature of the viola, for many years sparse and still small at the beginning of this century, began to be enriched through the efforts chiefly of Lionel Tertis in England and later Paul Hindemith in Germany and elsewhere. Walton's Concerto, as has been suggested a most notable addition to this kind of music, found in Hindemith its first exponent when it appeared in 1929.

VIOLIN CONCERTO

FIRST Movement. *Andante tranquillo*. There is no hint at the outset that this is to be a brilliant display concerto. The opening might have come from a work (one had almost said a chamber work) by one of the more introspective composers of this century or as likely as not from a concerto for that stringed instrument so much richer than even the violin in ambiguous qualities, the viola.

The solo violin continues this phrase at length and by the time it has reached the second significant division in the movement it has clearly defined its specific nature; it is indeed the prima donna of strings, and as such it is to dominate this work. The second subject is heard while the solo violin rests in preparation for yet more flamboyant flights or coloratura. For the moment it is the orchestra that has the say.

Ex. 24

mp

The solo instrument seizes on this and sets out to decorate it with arpeggios, scales, wide leaps, octave passages and all the effective paraphernalia of display in concerto style. Listening, one feels inevitably and as is expected of one, that the solo instrument has become invested with almost human attributes; and listening more intently one begins to wonder what this magnificent creature experiences when it discovers that the orchestra meanwhile has music, conventionally supposed to be an accompaniment, of an intelligence and aptness that steals attention from the solo's fireworks. But the orchestra is after all a model of discretion and really the soloist need not worry.

The development of this material has to do mainly with the two themes initialled in Ex. 23. This starts after a moment in which the orchestra rests, allowing the solo violin three bars of cadenza ending on a held note. Then, to a quickening in speed, the orchestra is unleashed; the horns loudly take up Ex. 23*a* and after rapid passage work from the solo violin the trombones start out on a lengthened version of Ex. 23*b*. Muted trumpets take this up; later they sound one of the most effective transformations of the violin's first theme, Ex. 23*a*, upon which the solo instrument starts an array of rising octaves that lead to the cadenza. In the recapitulation it is the two themes (*a* and *b*) that reappear at greatest length and in an effective rearrangement of forces, the solo violin having what was originally the lower of the two themes and the orchestra (flutes) the upper. There is a fleeting reappearance of the second subject before the movement closes.

Second Movement. *Presto capriccioso alla napolitana.* Very rapid in feeling, capricious in mood, with a refrain

echoing something that supposedly got under the skin of the Neapolitans during the wars of the Spanish Succession; so this movement appears, judging by an outward semblance as a foreigner to such things might do. The feeling and mood are set instantly; a bar of orchestral helter-skelter and then the solo violin starts in upon what is to be, in the event, a movement of the highest solo virtuosity:

The movement so far conforms to convention as to be divisible into scherzo and trio. The latter comes as soon as the scherzo themes, Ex. 25 and 26, have gone their course with immense vivacity and sparkle. This trio, entitled *Canzonetta,* brings the desired contrast of mood while still allowing for the virtuoso tactics of the solo instrument which, once embarked upon this style of expression in the scherzo, keeps within sight of it throughout. Yet the theme of the trio is such that even the solo violin is persuaded to play it plain, only raising it at first into a high register and then into harmonics.

According to normal usage the scherzo should return; and this it does, using such parts of its exposition as suit it; a recapitulation that satisfies the instinct for formal construction without appearing to do more than hint at remembered experience, a twentieth-century recapitulation.

Third Movement. *Vivace*. This is not a cyclic concerto; but it is, perhaps, justifiable to note that the final movement harks back to the theme of the trio, beginning thus:

The solo violin has its say about this in sharp ejaculation. And then comes the next main theme, in clear contrast and formed of steep outlines, biting into the fabric of the music:

The third outstanding theme brings breadth into the movement.

This long, flexible outline will appear again and whenever that happens the music will open out and breathe deeper. It has the significance therefore of a true second subject and so it may be considered. It has, too, an added importance in that it is related to the first theme of the concerto, as may be seen by comparing the first bar of Ex. 30 with the last of Ex. 23. In that way it plays a special function as unifying the whole work. The soloist's accompanied cadenza, a fine construction, contains clear reference to it, as does the ensuing *alla marcia* immediately preceding the final flourish which ends the work.

28

Some English Concertos

WILLIAM MANN

INTRODUCTION

IN this country the concerto has flourished, even though our nationally boasted phlegmatic temperament might seem at variance with the concerto's implied emphasis on a virtuosity suspiciously like exhibitionism, and an extravert energy never associated with the most typically English composers since Dowland.

In the much derided Dark Ages of English music, opera, oratorio, cantata and the drawing-room party-piece were most cultivated. But we should remember that Sterndale Bennett wrote four piano concertos and a *Caprice* for piano and orchestra of which the charms are considerable; also that such composers as Barnett, Prout and Mackenzie cultivated the medium (the latter with most lasting success in the *Scottish Piano Concerto*). Parry, the father of the musical renaissance in England, first attracted popular attention with his Piano Concerto in F sharp minor, while Stanford, who was associated with him in this task, applied his fluent pen to the form and, in his Clarinet Concerto, left one of his most imaginative as well as resourceful works. None of these shunned the implications of the soloist's spotlight, nor did Elgar, whose work is discussed in Chapter 16.

Here, however, we are concerned with the composers of our own time and how five of them have approached the concerto, as they have all done on more than one occasion. Where did they start from and what new lines did any of them reveal?

Considering the potency of Brahms's influence on the composers chiefly responsible for our musical revival, on Parry and Stanford and Somervell (whose Violin Concerto is a strongly personal work all the same – more than just a compliment to Brahms), a Brahmsian approach to the medium might be expected to be mirrored in the works under review. In point of fact, Bliss's Piano Concerto is the only one of them that develops along Brahmsian lines.

Or, since English music is popularly associated with the rhapsodic meditations of Delius (in reality a fundamentally un-English composer), might not his haunting concertos have left an echo in these six works? Perhaps in Moeran's Violin Concerto, but no more than an echo. The outdoor breezes of diatonicism, sometimes blown from as far away as Sibelius's Finland, characterize Moeran's music more than the nostalgic scents of Grez-sur-Loing, while his melody owes little to the Paradise Garden but much to the folk music of Norfolk and Ireland.

Folk-music: that has been a more discernible stimulus to these composers. Vaughan Williams found his most personal musical language through a study of folk-music, as Bax and Moeran, in their own ways, have succumbed to its magic. But Constant Lambert was not far wrong when he wrote that, 'to put it vulgarly, the whole trouble with a folk-song is that once you have played it through there is nothing much you can do except play it over again and play it rather louder'. You can make a set of variations on it but not a concerto with its necessarily extended design.

Vaughan Williams turned to the eighteenth century concerto for the basic framework of his *Concerto Accademico* (1925), adapting it to the needs of his modal idiom. *The Lark Ascending* for violin and orchestra (1921) avoids the problem of extension and, on a larger scale, so does *Flos Campi* (1925) (for viola solo, wordless chorus and orchestra) by the adoption of a literary text for meditation. The recent Oboe Concerto is both shorter and slighter. In the Piano Concerto (1933), folk idioms are hardly discernible. The flattened seventh is to be felt in the first movement and the consecutive triads of medieval music become prominent in the *Romanza* but this is not a 'folky' concerto. It is large in scale, but the size is not Brahmsian. The massive quality of the piano writing in the original version more recalls late

Beethoven, as Frank Howes has indicated in an analysis of this work (*Later Works of R. Vaughan Williams*, Musical Pilgrim series). Formally this Piano Concerto is a synthesis: a romantic movement – you might call it a modern parallel to the *Intermezzo* of Schumann's piano concerto – flanked by two older forms, *Toccata* and *Fugue* with a waltz, which the composer specifies as German rather than Viennese, for finale. There are two versions of the work in existence. As a piano concerto it was first performed in February 1933, when the soloist was Harriet Cohen, to whom the concerto is dedicated. The massive texture of the piano writing occasioned some critical disapproval and Vaughan Williams later adapted the concerto, in collaboration with Joseph Cooper, for two pianos and orchestra. In this form it has become more popular, especially in America where it was recently recorded.

Bax's violin concerto sprang surprises in plenty on those who attended its first performance (in 1937) expecting to hear a thickly-scored, highly-coloured, perhaps diffuse rhapsody – something like a long, accompanied cadenza. There is none of that here. This concerto's three-movement design is concisely organized, its texture clear-cut. The solo part offers opportunities to a brilliant player, but there is something almost classical in the work's avoidance of heavy emotion or anything so loquacious as a cadenza – almost, but not quite, for its amiable lightly romantic freshness rather recalls Mendelssohn's Violin Concerto.

Bax had cultivated concerto before. In his *Symphonic Variations* of 1917 and the *Winter Legends* (1930), solo piano and orchestra are established as partners instead of opponents; their idiom is richly evocative. In the cello concerto (1933) dedicated to Gaspar Cassadó, the solo element is more obtrusive and the scoring beautifully clear. In content it cannot compete with the Violin Concerto, however, for although the *Nocturne* contains some of Bax's most lovely lyrical music, the *allegro moderato* is too sectional to make a firmly satisfying impression and the concluding *molto vivace* suffers from immemorable material.

Bax's two most recent essays in the form have both borne

the name *Concertante*. The Concertante for three solo instruments was commissioned by the Henry Wood Concerts Society and first played at the Birthday Promenade Concert in 1949; it had been completed on the New Year's Day previous. The first three movements bring soloists forward one at a time, with small orchestral accompaniment, then in the last *allegro ma non troppo, brillante* they join with full orchestra and emerge from the whole every now and again; the *Elegy* features cor anglais, the *scherzo* clarinet and the *lento* horn. It is unpretentious and attractive rather than potent music. The short movements certainly allow points of value to be made, for in that way Bax's generous lyrical gift has no opportunity to engender diffuseness in the design. These qualities come to the fore in equal proportions but with more pronouncedly impulsive effect in the *Concertante* for piano (left hand) with orchestra (1949). Bax wrote it for Harriet Cohen, whose right hand was at the time out of use as a result of an accident. It's an ill wind that blows no good, and the unhappy deprivation gained Miss Cohen a work of enormous beauty. Whereas *Concertante* in the earlier piece covers the trio of soloists and the unorthodox manner of their appearance, here the term implies a change in balance of power, for the piano part, though brilliant in places, is of equal status with the orchestra, even if its distinctive timbre stands out from the total sound at every turn. A particularly notable feature is the skill with which Bax has contrived to achieve a maximum of sonority for his piano part since, while composers for left-handed pianists have in general demanded a large stretch, Harriet Cohen's fingers can cover no more than an octave.

Like Bax, Moeran finds in the concerto a stimulating medium for lyricism rather than an outlet for heroic fireworks. But while Bax puts melodic and harmonic flow before the demands of form, the two are closely interwoven and mutually inspiring in Moeran's concertos. The Violin Concerto derives much of its quality from the imaginative manipulation of textural patterns, and organization of thematic material. Note how surely each cadenza is placed, with regard to form, in this violin concerto and how necessary to satisfaction the choice and treatment of themes in those cadenzas are – a matter that has troubled too few cadenza-writers in the past. Design is spontaneously achieved in the Rhapsody in F sharp for piano and orchestra (1943), a joyous, immediately attractive work, and in the cello concerto (1946) written for Peers Coetmore, Moeran's wife, of which the short but deeply moving *adagio* can compare with the finest slow movements penned by British composers.

Bliss has, by contrast, strongly felt the call to full-blooded virtuosity in his Piano Concerto. Of the six works under analysis his alone follows the high romantic tradition of Tchaikovsky and Grieg and Rachmaninov. And is it just a coincidence that this Piano Concerto is in the same key as Brahms's second? Bliss's Concerto for two pianos and orchestra (1924) revised from an earlier concerto for piano with tenor voice, strings and percussion, provides an interesting foretaste of the larger and later concerto. Many of the technical features so effective in the Piano Concerto can be noticed in the solo parts of the earlier work, where also the spirit is heroically virile. In fourteen years Bliss's piano writing becomes less predominantly percussive, but the seeds of a romantic technique are evident in the two-piano concerto. Its one movement suffers from the short-windedness of its themes, but there is enough attractive music to render an occasional performance rewarding.

Bliss's Piano Concerto (1939) was commissioned for the World Fair at New York and is dedicated 'To the People of the United States of America'. For such an occasion and for such an enthusiastically extravert nation a modest pastoral piece would have been hardly acceptable. Bliss's Piano Concerto with its virtuoso brilliance, broad melodies and exuberant rhythms filled the bill to perfection. Solomon, who was the soloist in the first performance, has recorded the work for H.M.V.

I have left Ireland till last because his Piano Concerto pursues other ideals. It is not classical in design nor rhapsodical in thought nor filled with the accents of folk-song, nor does it follow the line of thumping concertos, the 'big bow-wows'. Its thought is nearer Schumann than any other composer, its design a development of the principles that shaped, for example, Liszt's Piano Sonata. The piano was ever Ireland's best beloved and he has written for it with an affectionate understanding that is treasured by the many pianists who turn again and again to the Piano Sonata, *Sarnia* or the *London Pieces*. The piano writing in this Concerto epitomizes Ireland's exploitation of its expressive range. Percussive and lyrical elements are wholly integrated in its making. It is a true Piano Concerto, moreover, in that the piano dominates, even when it is most closely linked with its orchestral partner. A particularly satisfying feature is the Lisztian thematic concentration that relates the stuff of each movement to its fellows, so that certain passages are not restated until some time after the conventional recapitulation. These repetitions have none of the cyclic intentions that can be so wearisome, but induce the warmth of re-encounter and fulfil their purpose in the more widely appreciable light of intervening ideas. Other concertos may be more introspectively evocative, or more profoundly philosophical. Ireland's will retain its present deserved place in the repertory for the range of its emotions and in particular for its lovable intimacy.

Let us analyse six concertos by these five composers and observe more closely the ways in which technique and imagination co-operate to give pleasure to the listening ear. Notice the different ways in which each composer relates the movements of his concerto. Notice too that, although each of these six works adopts a different ideal, the political system, the comparative status of soloist and orchestra, is established in each with a consistency that the ear immediately accepts as belonging to the essence of the concerto.

ARNOLD BAX: VIOLIN CONCERTO

CRITICS have sometimes regretted Bax's use of sonata form in his symphonies, on the ground that his musical idiom generates ideas unsuited to symphonic development. In this concerto he avoids conventional sonata form by shaping the first movement as a triptych and the last as a rondo. By so doing he is able to indulge his love of discussing and extending a theme as soon as it is stated, a method of going to work that is inherently unsatisfactory in a design involving a comprehensive development section.

First Movement. *Overture : Allegro risoluto ; Ballad : Scherzo - Allegro moderato*. The main theme of the first section is announced without preliminaries by strings and expounded through the orchestra:

Ex. 1

A rough gesture on strings eventually beckons the soloist and accompanies a restatement and expansion of Ex. 1. The music gains pace as the strings boldly assert a forthright phrase, answered by solo double-stopping; a broader melody in thirds brings relaxation, but only momentarily, for the soloist scurries away to be caught, at the top of a breathless climb, by the *fortissimo* entry of the forthright phrase. Ex. 1 returns and leads to further increase in tension during which triplets become prominent. At the climax Ex. 1 is rapped out curtly by full orchestra. Oboes, clarinets and bassoons, their sonority delicately enhanced by harp timbre, bridge the way into the Ballad. Evocative harp chords set the scene, but the melody of this ballad is accompanied delicately by woodwind with uneasy string asides (their bass is related to the violin's song).

Ex. 2

The last phrase grows into the second of the ballad's four stanzas; it is more rhapsodic with triplets prominent, and the strings still uneasy in the background. Flutes adopt a figure from its last line as an accompaniment to the third verse. Strings support the last, most impassioned, stanza whose rhapsodies fade gradually into the third panel of this triptych, the *Scherzo*.

The harp's introductory chords are loud and ringing here. The main theme announced by soloist is a jovial jig version of Ex. 1, immediately recognizable; its last line, moreover, is clearly derived from the last line of Ex. 2, as wind emphasizes. Strings and wind share the accompaniment for the violin's dancing. First oboe presents a new galumphing tune which goes the round of soloist, basses and mocking flutes. The soloist then gives it a contrasted, more shapely, middle section and the orchestra returns noisily to the galumphing verse. That is now shown to be a close relation of Ex. 1 which is further reshaped, *risoluto* by brass, and then by full orchestra. The violin skips away in triplets against which upper wind offer Ex. 2, now in the major. While reminiscences of it are still floating through the orchestra, the soloist scampers off up the scale and two loud E major chords mark the movement's end.

Second Movement. *Adagio*. A placid melody, played by strings against a running harp accompaniment, begins this movement.

Group *a* looks back to the first line of Ex. 2 and in the whole melody's unfolding, the first three notes gain in resemblance to the Ballad's music. Clarinets in thirds bring the music to a point when the soloist can enter, repeating the tune in the sonorous lower register with wind accompaniment and flute decoration. Syncopated string chords lead to another gracious melody whose near-Mozartian flavour seems now to look forward to the concertos which Strauss was to write at the end of his life.

Ex. 4

Clarinet and then flute hover above it in triplets. Its middle strain allows the soloist to decorate and Ex. 4 returns *fortissimo* for orchestra. The soloist begins another repeat but the orchestra grasps power for a moment and urges a climax that drops into Ex. 3, now decorated by the soloist. References to Ex. 2 lead the way back to Ex. 4 which slips easily into Ex. 3, played *pianissimo* by muted strings under violin figuration. As the strings subside the violin sinks back on a soft bed of muted horn tune.

Third Movement. *Allegro.* Over *pizzicato* string chords the violin at once announces the principal subject:

Ex. 5

enlarging upon it with trills and arabesques before the orchestra gradually moves into a repeat. A 'vamped' accompaniment on the last notes of the tune leads back to a further statement, by the soloist, which grows into the subsidiary theme, a slow waltz.

Ex. 6

The violin develops this, with delicate wind counterpoints and gradually thickening texture, to support a more dramatic utterance until the orchestra takes the waltz's climax. The soloist returns to it again before moving on to Ex. 5, this time *Allegretto semplice* in 9/8. Figuration becomes more urgent and the soloist bursts into a rushing virtuoso passage that is the nearest approach to a cadenza in this concerto. This leads to a lively orchestral statement of Ex. 6. The soloist interrupts a reminiscence of Ex. 2 with Ex. 5 in its original rhythm and the orchestra takes up the strain *vivace* supporting a headlong and brilliant rush to an excitingly defined finish.

ARTHUR BLISS: PIANO CONCERTO IN B FLAT

FIRST Movement. *Allegro con brio*. With an exuberant rush up to a chord of D minor-major the orchestra rings up the curtain and discovers the soloist careering brilliantly up and down the keyboard in double octaves. High spirits lead firmly into B flat major, the concerto's key, when the orchestra re-enters with the principal subject of the movement:

This is extended sufficiently to impress group *a* on the musical memory and is immediately followed by a contrasted theme. The downward leap of a ninth, so characteristic of Bliss's melodic invention, puts in an appearance in each of the three movements.

The forthright shape of Ex. 1 returns, quietly pursued by an insistent figure barked out by trumpets and trombones.

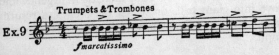

When this has induced a suitably impressive climax, the piano asserts authority and repeats the foregoing material in its own words. A brilliant cadenza makes way for a new melody, not to be discussed in the development section, but too important – and too beautiful – to be denied quotation.

The piano and later the basses play with it before turning to a serious discussion of the material.

First Ex. 7 is heard over a *tremolo* accompaniment. The pianist mumbles Ex. 9 *sotto voce* and is answered impudently by Ex. 7*a*. Argument becomes heated until a pause permits the soloist to rearrange the two themes in combination. The orchestra signifies its approval of this move. Next the piano re-forms Ex. 8, expanding its scale and expressive potentiality to all parties' satisfaction. A brief reference to Ex. 9 returns them to Ex. 7. The piano texture becomes thicker and more brilliant until a surge of scales and trills brings us home for the recapitulation.

Ex. 7 now has a galloping accompaniment of triplets and Ex. 8 eventually becomes identified with Ex. 10 which follows. A further glance at Ex. 8 leads back to Ex. 7 which, however, is merely a springboard for the soloist's big cadenza. This rightly involves Ex. 10 as well as the themes of the development. Virtuoso scale passages incite the timpani to a triplet figure that reminds the piano of its octaves at the movement's very start. They increase in urgency and now move into giant trills on which the orchestra returns *molto vivace*, blaring out Ex. 9 and terminating the movement in triumph.

Second Movement. *Adagietto*. A quiet scale helps the piano to this modest but haunting melody:

Strings attempt to continue but the piano knows its own mind and supplies its own continuation – a varied version of Ex. 8's dropping ninth. Bliss rounds off the tune – almost lulls it to sleep:

The music is repeated with a little cadence, though Ex. 11*a* is treated merely as an introduction and omitted. A new section introduces a melody beginning as follows:

which is highly developed through the orchestra with some heroic and sonorous solo writing. Ex. 11*b* becomes more important and new material is tacked on to it before the piano returns to Ex. 11*a* and its continuation. The coda finds the soloist in the upper regions of the keyboard and, as if entranced, the music descends to earth and to the falling ninths. Strings murmur Ex. 11*b* for the last time with a clarinet to point the off-beat notes. Then the piano climbs to a bitter chord which strings resolve on to E major and our time of dreams is over.

Third Movement. *Andante maestoso : Molto vivo.* A sustained brass chord ushers in this mysterious theme:

It gains in majesty and reality from the soloist's heroic treatment: but can it, we begin to wonder, be right for the finale of such a concerto? Where is the speed and excitement we may expect at this point? We are not kept long in suspense, for the pace quickly changes to *molto vivo* and the string basses try again, this time with a *staccato* jig which is to become the theme of a rondo. Violins, violas and flutes add to it and it appears to have resolved itself into a row of drum taps when the piano bursts out with its definitive form, which may be summarized so:

Soon wind play groups of fours on top of the piano triplets. Clarinets and bassoons offer diversion in the shape of a *grazioso* tune, adopted by piano and then passed to the horns as accompaniment to a more sharply rhythmic motif which is still in play when the soloist returns to Ex. 14 over which this striking phrase is added

efore a return to the rondo theme. In an expansive though
hort-lived cadenza the soloist declaims Ex. 13 against the
uttering of Ex. 14 and reminds us that an introduction
ears on the subject it introduces. A fresh episode grafts the
ropping ninths of Ex. 8 on to the jig rhythm and their com-
ined implications occupy soloist and orchestra for some
me. The piano urges tighter tension and full orchestra
esponds magnificently with Ex. 15 in all its splendour. This
ives the piano its cue for a rushing cadenza which plunges
ito a surge of B flat major. And here on a gradually welling
.de is Ex. 13, proudly and sonorously triumphant on horns
nd violins. Its last appearance belongs by right to the
oloist who proclaims fullness of heart in the impassioned
limax of the whole concerto, before racing away in the
riplets of the rondo's main theme to an exhilarating and
reathless finish.

JOHN IRELAND: PIANO CONCERTO IN E FLAT

'IRST Movement. *In tempo moderato.* The soft theme for
trings which opens the concerto is not the first subject, nor
et the introduction, but rather a motto for the whole work.

A cadence from clarinets and horns introduces the piano,
ot *grandioso* as in Bliss's Concerto, but unconcernedly, as if
hatting to itself. Group *a* of this, the true principal subject,
erives from Ex. 16. It is a typical example of the thematic
iterlocking mentioned in the introduction.

After seven bars which culminate in the fragment appended to Ex. 17, the piano adopts a rippling accompaniment for high repetition of Ex. 16 on violins. Group *a* begins to pervade the atmosphere, in basses and piano; strings make a false start at this figure, and are joined by piano solo which soon begins to sparkle and is joined by the trumpet figure:

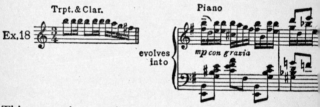

This grows into a piano solo, which may be termed the second subject. Ex. 18 reappears, either melodically or rhythmically, in all the movements. The piano's version is echoed by wind and then repeated by strings, while the piano provides a running counter-subject which will also be heard later. When strings have finished, the soloist deals lightly with some of this subject's implications, and fireworks form a keyboard background for the trumpet's second thoughts, now muted, on Ex. 18. Muted trombones, and then wind, gradually add imitations until the pianist dashes down the keyboard and up again into a broad orchestral variant of Ex. 16 commented on by the soloist. A haze spreads over the texture and from it a clarinet solo arises which seems to spring from, and refer to, all the themes so far quoted. The piano rises to a *fortissimo* and brings a solo horn in its wake; the horn now starts the recapitulation with a free rendering of Ex. 16. The upper notes of the piano's accompanying arpeggios rise above the horn and mount till

he first subject is reached. The orchestra joins in sooner
han before and this section proceeds straightforwardly until
Ex. 18 has been restated. Then the orchestra subsides and
eaves the piano to a cadenza, starting quietly with Ex. 18
nd growing in brilliance, as other instruments enter, into
the short coda, where Ex. 18 is joined to an accelerated
orm of Ex. 16, stated in *tempo* by brass and strings before the
iano subsides, almost as if out of breath, on to E flat.

Second Movement. *Lento expressivo.* Over a horn pedal-
ote, sighing strings offer this theme:

Group *b* derives from Ex. 18 and we may note, as they
roceed, the dropping fifths that are among Ireland's salient
ingerprints. The piano enters quietly and alone; the ma-
erial expounded here is no new theme but a second strain to
Ex. 19, as becomes clear when the soloist ends with the tail-
iece of Ex. 19.

Strings repeat the second half of this exquisitely lyrical
meditation and violas prolong the sweetness of the last
cadence until the soloist is ready to add pianistic thoughts on
the tune's beginning, which only strings have so far played.
A little phrase for wind nostalgically echoes Ex. 18, but the
piano is too lost in contemplation to notice and surges
unheeding into a variant of Ex. 17. The orchestra is moved
to repeat that section of the first movement (it was not
included in the recapitulation) which followed Ex. 17.
Again the wind plays its little reminiscence of Ex. 18, but
strings return to the start of Ex. 20, over a drum figure that
grows more insistent and is finally adopted by side drum to
herald the finale.

Third Movement. *Allegro : Allegretto giocoso.* Off runs the
piano, to be caught by side drum; over a string *tremolando*
the trumpet recalls Ex. 18. Another rushing piano episode
brings the orchestra to an idea which acts as a background
for the principal theme of this movement – a rondo.

Since this cheerfully vulgar (in that honest sense of the
term that Ireland has never despised – praise be!) tune stirs
wind and percussion to recall Ex. 18, it is not absurd to associate group *a* with that theme. By this time the piano is busy
with a triplet figure that offers possibilities of virtuosity.
Woodwinds chirp gaily in the background with modifications of Ex. 18, then revert to their accompaniment for Ex.

21, which duly follows on full orchestra. To it a deliberate cadence is attached (which will in fact end the concerto) which, with a drum roll, marks the end of a section. The piano now announces a slower subsidiary subject and strings add a decoration familiar from the first movement.

The oboe, Ex. 22b, completes this melody and the piano prolongs it with quiet tinkling. In the orchestral repeat, Ex. 22 is accompanied by piano with the familiar running decoration. More fiery runs return us to Ex. 21, this time with the rôles reversed, first wind, then piano taking the tune. Ex. 22 follows immediately and on its heels comes Ex. 20, a surprising insertion, but necessary to the ear's desire for completion. Like the fragment of the first movement, Ex. 20 was not recapitulated in the expected place and it must therefore follow here. Over Ex. 20, a solo violin weaves a lightly expressive counterpoint. A mere reference is enough to hint to the pianist a new treatment for the bones of Ex. 22. He drifts into sonorous passage work and a solo horn (whose appearance perhaps further balances this with the opening movement) relates Ex. 22 with Ex. 18. The piano interrupts his games and gravely refers to Ex. 16. Then the last restatement of Ex. 21 begins, back to front – first group a followed by the firm cadence, repeated until the players remember to play the beginning of Ex. 21. As a result, group a is omitted and, while the piano becomes louder and more glittering in texture, the roughly incisive cadence figure cuts its way through to the end.

E. J. MOERAN: VIOLIN CONCERTO

First Movement. *Allegro moderato*. The strings, aided by clarinet, set the stage for the soloist's entry.

Ex. 23

The phrase marked (*b*) seems unassuming but it is to be important. Even now it is (*b*) that the soloist and wind proceed to discuss, try as the strings will to arouse interest in (*a*). A little cadential phrase echoed by oboe brings the soloist to a firmer subject in double stopping.

Ex. 24

The violin races away in semiquavers, only to be pulled up by (*b*); the rhythm of (*c*) suggests an idea to flute and oboe which the violin adopts. The music becomes quieter and slower and a cadenza allows the soloist to comment on Ex. 24 and 23*b*. Arpeggios bring back Ex. 23*a* on wind and the soloist takes a last look at Ex. 23*b* before turning to a broader more extended melody which features the 'Scotch snap' and is discreetly supported by dovetailed wind and strings.

The development section begins unconventionally with a cheerful jig in 12/8 whose relevance is not thematic. The second flute leads off and the remaining upper woodwinds follow one by one with their own versions. After a little flourish the soloist over curt brass chords gives a violin's views on it, and the strings break in with Ex. 24 but do not interrupt the violin, which is away at once on a brilliant tack. Scales lead to another full orchestral statement of Ex. 24 which decreases in power from *fortissimo*. Over a sustained trombone chord the soloist enters again and shows Ex. 24 as a near relation of Ex. 23a. The recapitulation which follows involves, among other things, the revelation that the figure derived from 24c is really the same as Ex. 23b. When we reach the cadence before Ex. 24, the oboe and also violin transform their little figure into 'Tom, Tom, the piper's son'. The flute goes farther and links it with the 'Scotch snap' of the longer tune. Ex. 24 has enjoyed extensive treatment already, so the soloist restates it briefly in a short cadenza which leads to the broader tune. The movement is rounded off with Ex. 23a, the cadence theme and a very soft *pizzicato* chord.

Second Movement. *Rondo—vivace.* Attention is at once caught by a brisk triplet rhythm set up by the strings. It persists until the entry of the soloist who proceeds, after a lively flourish or two, to the vigorous rondo theme.

At the end of the last bar horns begin the rhythmic triplets again and the soloist rounds off this theme which strings repeat in full. A sturdy modal tune is matched with another like it, featuring double stopping. Ex. 25 now returns, first antiphonally in wind and strings, then on strings alone. The triplet rhythm, persistently hammered out by horns and accentuated by *pizzicato* strings, accompanies the soloist's new idea.

Ex. 26

Solo Vln.

B in bass *mf risoluto*

The violin plays it through, with elaborations, three and a half times, before the wind, which has attempted fragments, adopts it in full and then the triplet rhythm interrupts and grows louder. Now the rondo theme returns varied, in 3/4 time, first as a horn solo over a harplike string accompaniment and then decorated by the soloist. The orchestra repeats the last phrase of this melody *fortissimo* and in doing so adumbrates a quieter idea in 6/8 presented by bassoon to the soloist and related in melodic shape to the earlier double-stopped tune. Strings add a middle stanza in thirds to which the violin also contributes and, while the flute is repeating the original stanza, the soloist interrupts in more lively vein and heralds the return of the rondo theme and of a restatement of the episode which followed it in the first place. An orchestral tutti based on bar 3 of Ex. 25 leads to a cadenza, chiefly concerned with Ex. 26. Strings try to interrupt but the soloist has another card to play. This is a *waltz* version of Ex. 26 (marked in the score *Burlesca*) and as the orchestra adopts it, it begins to sound suspiciously like a version of the rondo theme. Soloist and orchestra seem to agree, for they follow it with another disintegrated statement of that subject and of the rhythmic figure already associated with it. A short coda shows the episodes and the rondo theme to be closely related. Tension mounts still further and, with the soloist in full flight, strings end the movement abruptly with the rhythmic figure that began it.

Third Movement. *Lento*. We are immediately recalled to the first movement by a quiet string phrase to which the soloist adds a pendant.

Ex. 27b is, like its counterpart in the first movement, to be
the principal subject of meditation. The soloist discusses it
in dialogue with solo clarinet, strings return with gradually
thickening texture to 27a and the soloist varies Ex. 27b in
such a way as to recall even more sharply Ex. 23b. Light
string arpeggios in contrary motion support echoes of it on
oboe, trumpet and cor anglais, while the soloist floats
rapturously above them.

As the arpeggios die away the soloist announces a transformed version of Ex. 24. Solo wind return to Ex. 27b, which
the violin shares with cor anglais. Softly the strings steal into
the major with another theme also derived from Ex. 27b.
The violin replies with this impassioned phrase:

The soloist develops it undisturbed until it is snatched
away with a surge of triumph by full orchestra and matched
with Ex. 27b. The soloist links to it a fresh variant of Ex. 24
which leads the orchestra to remember Ex. 23, and the
violas to add a new pendant that evolves into Ex. 23b. A
clarinet arabesque brings us to the last section.

Here gently flowing quavers on lower strings return the
soloist to Ex. 28. The horns softly add a reminiscence of
Ex. 23 which the violin repeats. The rippling strings move
into their rocking arpeggios and the soloist begins to soar,
reaching and holding the third of D major over two bars of

wind and string rocking, that rise and fall and die away on a last chord of D major.

VAUGHAN WILLIAMS: CONCERTO ACCADEMICO

In this concerto for violin and strings, Vaughan Williams has had the example of Bach very much in mind. The movements are concise and purposeful. The string writing is concerned with clear line rather than atmosphere or colour. This is the essence of classicism, and for an Englishman there is no more classical idiom than the modal language of folksong. Rooted as its material is in the past, this is not an academic concerto in the stuffy sense of the term, but a freshly personal creation recalling Verdi's 'Let us return to the past, that will be progress'.

The Concerto Accademico was written in 1925 and is dedicated to Jelly d'Aranyi. It has been recorded for Decca by Frederick Grinke and the Boyd Neel Orchestra.

First Movement. *Allegro pesante*. Bach's first movements are based on the ritornello which later developed into the rondo. Vaughan Williams here prefers sonata form but dovetails into it features nearly related to the ritornello design. His principal subject could, but for its emphasis on the flattened seventh, almost have come from one of Bach's movements.

Ex. 29

Soloist & Strings

As in eighteenth-century concertos the soloist joins in this statement of the theme and adds a 'rider' to it.

This leads to a cadenza-like flourish of fourths and fifths, under which the strings play Ex. 29. The soloist follows it with a quieter theme in 3/4, derived from Ex. 30, which strings repeat; the exposition closes with a dialogue in which the soloist's double stopped sixths are answered by Ex. 29a. The metre returns to 2/4 with quasi-contrapuntal discussion of Ex. 29 and 30. The soloist uses Ex. 29 as a springboard for bold arabesques and, under them, strings insinuate a broader melody which the solo violin repeats while violas keep the semiquaver movement going. Another dialogue twice answers Ex. 29a with double stops in thirds and the third time with an accompanied cadenza that leads back to the quieter 3/4 tune repeated through the orchestra. The double stopped sixths bridge the way to the recapitulation which increases in excitement to a *presto* coda ending with broad trills.

Second Movement. *Adagio*. Vaughan Williams's favourite consecutive triads accompany a magically lyrical melody for solo cello. The orchestra is reduced to fifteen players and muted.

After five bars the solo violin enters and floridly entwines the melody which moves into the major. There seems no reason why this tracery should stop, but second violins and violas fix on a new accompaniment figure, thoroughly Bach-like in spirit, over which the violin, freely imitated by first violins and solo cello, draws chains of scales:

They become more and more florid until Ex. 31 returns again as a cello solo. Ex. 31*a* provides the material for an impassioned climax and this leads again to Ex. 32. The solo-ist mounts higher and higher and strings hold a chord while the violin savours for a moment the full glory of its position. Then Ex. 31 is heard for the last time, turning now into the smooth scale-chains of Ex. 32 which quietly fade into a chord of G major.

Third Movement. *Presto*. This is a jig and a rondo at once, but as in Bach's *rondo* finales the theme is present nearly all the time. It is, the composer confesses without hesitation, taken from his opera *Hugh the Drover*, but the derivation need not concern us here for it fits into the concerto perfectly, echoing in its nature Ex. 30 of the first movement.

Ex. 33

When the quaver movement subsides, the soloist announces a subsidiary theme which is adopted by orchestra, and after an optional repeat the main theme returns, first in violas then on solo violin. The latter breaks off for a moment to echo the orchestral violins' duple time theme – but lower strings continue the movement – then varies the rhythm so as to murmur Ex. 30 from the first movement while strings play with another broad duple melody.

Ex. 34

When the soloist reaches this melody, cellos adopt the triple rhythm but pass it back at a *fortissimo* statement of Ex. 34. This leads to the return of Ex. 33 and eventually to a cadenza and resumption of the second theme.

A further episode of a broader nature offers opportunity for close imitation, such as abounds in Bach's finales and, while upper strings and soloist are still exploring its possibilities, violas bring back Ex. 33. It subsides on to a low D and with a last ruminatory cadenza on this theme the soloist fades into the distance.

VAUGHAN WILLIAMS: PIANO CONCERTO

[NOTE: In the analysis which follows I have, in general, referred to the soloist in the singular. But this account of the music applies just as much to the two-piano version (see the introduction to this chapter), since the musical material of both versions is practically the same – where changes have been made I have indicated them. The musical examples have been drawn from both scores, the choice being guided in each case by clarity and conciseness.]

First Movement. *Toccata: Allegro moderato.* There is no orchestral preparation for the soloist's entry. A crash on C for piano and orchestra, and we are away to a percussive figure which is joined two bars later by this theme:

Ex. 35

t will be important in the making of the movement,
especially the group *a*. Ex. 35 leads straight into Ex. 36,
where the bass notes form a pattern that we are not allowed
to forget. The triads above bite hard on the A flat and this
sort of dissonance dominates the concerto. The time signature alters to 3/4, the dominant metre of the work.

Ex 36

The rhythm marked *b* in Ex. 36 suggests a third theme which
appears shortly afterwards over the bass we have seen
before.

Ex. 37

Wind and piano argue for its possessions for some time and
the tempo quickens but the piano wins – after all it is
Harriet Cohen's concerto – and the wind supplies a new and
jovial tune above. In the two-piano version the first soloist
adds a broad *cantabile* melody for good measure, but this is
not heard again. Presently the *toccata* returns and marks the
start of our development section. The themes are again
presented in order but with suitable changes. The orchestra
for instance now has the material heard before on piano

which, in its turn, claims Ex. 37. When the soloist finally
seizes Ex. 36, wind and violas offer yet another tune.

Ex. 38
W. Wind
& Violas

Group *c* is an altered form of group *a* in Ex. 35 and the two
variants alternately permeate the orchestral mass. The
piano gradually rouses itself and its partners to a climax,
when the *toccata* again returns, this time in F major. Tension
is excitingly held, firstly by the persistence of the *toccata*
figure over a long period, secondly by broad dynamic contrasts. In mid-flight the final restatement begins, with the
orchestra softly stating the *toccata* theme, and the piano mut-
tering the tune that originally accompanied it. The other
themes follow and lead to a triumphant version of Ex. 38
and 35 together by piano alone: the orchestra joins in and,
with a last reference to the tune from Ex. 35, passes control
back to the soloist, whose short cadenza leads directly into
the second movement.

Second Movement. *Romanza – Lento*. The piano comes to
rest on B and starting from there evolves a tune as follows:

Ex. 39ª

Piano 1

There is as yet no feeling of home tonic. A flute takes up the
tune and the two colours drift along together. Then horns
and strings try their hand at harmonizing this elusive tune
and manage to establish E major though the piano continues to go its own way. The oboe sails along quietly in the
soloist's wake, but soon the piano finds itself in new country,
moving rather faster. Another idea materializes, which the
orchestra adopts as a pendant to Ex. 39*a*.

Ex. 39ᵇ

Orchestra

A *tranquillo* interlude grows out of this, in which the piano's *cantabile* rhapsodies are imitated quietly by strings and later wind. Then calm descends and we hear Ex. 39a again, on the oboe this time. The piano repeats the tune and, as it fades into the distance, the oboe softly climbs down an uneven chromatic scale, followed by the viola. The phrase they play seems rhapsodic enough here – almost fortuitously inserted – but its function is important, for from it is built the whole structure of the finale.

Third Movement. *Fuga Chromatica con Finale alla Tedesca.* The brass snaps out group *a* of Ex. 40 and moves the orchestra to forecast the subject and counter-subject of the fugue which forms the greater part of this movement. A couple of crescendo runs, and the fugue proper begins. The tempo is *Allegro*.

Ex. 40

Subject

Principal Counter subject

The piano [first piano in the second version] states the
subject and its principal counterpoint under a violin *tremolo*
on D. At the third entry the orchestra joins in and the fugal
elaboration builds up purposefully and without haste or
waste of material to a huge climax. On the way we may
notice that the theme inverts successfully and combines
neatly with its upright form. The counter-subject, which
looks forward to the sixth symphony's finale, is fertile in
suggesting new counter-themes, three of which are quoted
above. At the climax, a double organ pedal-note D lends its
body to support a massive *stretto*, or close imitation of the
theme, first on group *b* and then on the main subject. Suddenly the orchestra stops and the piano thunders out group
b, which suggests more ideas and begins a cadenza, linked by
a *fortissimo glissando* to the finale which is a waltz. The piano
passes the idea to the orchestra which carries on enthusiastically, returning group *b* to power again. Counter-subject 3
also proves useful and provides the basis for another cadenza,
in the two piano version. Then group *b* returns to the
orchestra but only leads to a last cadenza. This begins
grandiosely but it soon becomes evident that Ex. 39*b* has
aroused our soloist's interest. He has been asserting a pedal
note B in the bass since his entry and now established it as
his tonic. The pace drops to *Lento* and then to *Largo Sostenuto*,
and all the excitement, the hurly-burly of the foregoing
movement, begins to be seen in perspective through the
magical stillness of this rapt tune. The soloist rises once to
fortissimo and then sinks back. Softly the upper strings
whisper the fugue subject *pizzicato* – just once. Then an
expansive B major chord and it is all over.

29

Variation Forms

JOHN HORTON

INTRODUCTION

THE theme and variations is one of the oldest types of musical form, and its possibilities are inexhaustible. Although it has a vigorous independent history its development is also closely knit to that of the concerto. This is inevitable, since the element of technical display is inherent in the principle of variation, and is likewise an important aspect of the concerto, from the period when the latter was cross-fertilized by the vocal aria to the later nineteenth century when the solo concerto reached its fullest expansion as a medium for virtuosity. Between these two extremities, it is true, occur the eras of the concerto grosso and the classical solo concerto in which composers were occupied less with the exploitation of virtuosity as such than with the effects they found themselves able to produce through the balance of tonalities, the contrast of larger and smaller bodies of tone, and the organic development of thematic material. Yet the variation-techniques that had been worked out and handed down from the sixteenth and seventeenth centuries were indispensable to the eighteenth-century concerto in its two main varieties and were particularly helpful in attaining suitable differentiations of texture between tutti and solo passages.

Actual sets of variations are fairly frequent in the concerto grosso; one need search no farther than Handel for examples, though he usually restricts himself to a simple movement made up of an air with a single variation. In the classical solo-concerto variation-movements become progressively rarer. J. C. Bach's finales provide some instances, such as the variations on *The Yellow-haired Laddie* that conclude his Op. 13 No. 4. Mozart, too, experimented along these lines, mainly in keyboard concertos written in his early Vienna days, about the year 1784.*

Beethoven reapplied the variation principle to large-scale composition. Between Bach's *Goldberg* set and his organ Passacaglia and Beethoven's *Diabelli* set and the *Eroica* finale stretches a half-century during which the air with variations belongs mainly to the sphere of light and occasional music. The romantics followed Beethoven in developing types of variation form, both for the keyboard and for the orchestra, in works of considerable intellectual and emotional span. Brahms, in the finales of the Haydn Variations and of the E minor Symphony, exploits the passacaglia type with the contrapuntal and orchestral resources of his own period, and shows great ingenuity in dovetailing variations and building them up cumulatively. An interesting transitional work, from the standpoint of our present purpose, is Schumann's Andante and Variations (Op. 46, 1843), in whose original form the two pianos are supplemented by two cellos and a horn employed chiefly in colouring the part-writing of the keyboard instruments.

The archetype of the independent work in variation form for soloist with orchestra is usually considered to be Liszt's *Totentanz* (1849, revised 1855, and first performed 1881), which is a fantasia on the plainsong *Dies Irae*, and was inspired by the macabre frescoes in the Campo Santo at Pisa. Sacheverell Sitwell, in his book on Liszt,† writes: 'Its shuddering, clanking rhythms, its sounds as of dancing bones, are of the weirdest achievement possible. It is, somehow, a piece admirably adapted for piano and orchestra; the piano has a real *causus vivendi*, a real reason for its presence in the orchestra'. The *Totentanz* may be regarded as more especially a parent of Dohnányi's Variations, with their grotesqueries, and of the Rachmaninov Rhapsody in which the *Dies Irae* again appears. In these two works, as in Liszt's, the piano is treated *concertante*, a point that will be considered further in

---

* See Chapter IV, 'Movements in Variation Form', in Arthur Hutchings: *A Companion to Mozart's Piano Concertos*, Oxford University Press, 1948.

† Faber and Faber, 1934. pp. 249–50.

dealing with the Dohnányi Variations. Tchaikovsky's
Rococo Variations are structurally on a more modest scale,
looking back, as is fitting, to the eighteenth century *air varié*
with its associations of gaiety and decorative display. At the
opposite pole stands Franck's *Variations symphoniques* which,
though not the lengthiest, is by far the most highly organized
of the four works and, like some other major compositions of
Franck, represents a tour de force that does not invite
imitation.

FRANCK: VARIATIONS SYMPHONIQUES
FOR PIANO AND ORCHESTRA

FRANCK took immense pains over the organization of his
larger works, and was especially interested in the cross-
breeding of older musical forms and the production of new
varieties. The possibilities of symphonic treatment of variation form engaged his attention in several of the compositions of his maturity, including the organ *Prélude, fugue et
variation* and the first two *Chorals* which he wrote in the last
years of his life. The second movement of the D minor
Symphony represents an experiment in the same direction.
But it is the *Variations symphoniques*, finished in 1885 – just
before the Symphony was begun – that show most subtlety
in the assimilation of variation form to other principles of
construction. As to how the final result is to be classified,
using the accepted vocabulary of terms to describe musical
forms, there is room for various opinions. Tovey's description, as usual, has the merit of giving in a few words some
idea of what happens in the music; he calls it 'a finely and
freely organized fantasia with an important episode in
variation form'. In other words, the variations are only part
of a larger scheme, and the material involved is richer than
the customary 'theme for variations'; yet the work is conceived as a whole and carries conviction by the logic of its
design as well as by the sensuous beauty of its writing and
scoring.

Despite his interest in problems of form Franck was a
romanticist in his tendency to project dramatic values into

instrumental composition. Behind the contrast and interplay of musical ideas there often appears to be a literary or
ethical symbolism. In the D minor Symphony a 'motto
theme' rides the storm and emerges triumphant, in the
Prélude, choral et fugue for piano the chorale melody, transformed by the major mode, rings out like a carillon at the
end of the turbulent fugue. A somewhat similar course of
quasi-dramatic progression can be followed in the *Variations
symphoniques* by those who look for it.

At the outset there is a highly rhetorical contrast of
material. Two themes, one full of energy, the other languid,
are presented; the former in the biting accents of the strings,
the latter, as a contrasting response, in the most soothing
tones of the piano.

Emotionally the effect is comparable to that of the opening
of the same composer's F minor Quintet, where the rôles of
strings and piano are very much the same. The opposition of
the two ideas is emphasized by repetition and extension; the
restless motive is worked out by cellos and basses and flares
up for a moment in both string and piano parts, but fades in
a ripple of keyboard arpeggios at the change to triple time.

At this point the orchestra introduces a species of sketch or
adumbration of the variation-theme; but this is little more

than a hint, which the solo instrument seems to reject in
order to take the centre of the stage itself and soliloquize, in
the dominant key, on the languid theme. The treatment is
effectively pianistic, with right-hand octaves balanced
against widely-spaced accompanying arpeggios.

As the orchestra re-enters, the tension between the two
opening themes is increased, but the mood of resignation
prevails as the piano returns to a slightly extended and reharmonized statement of Ex. 1*b*. The whole of this introductory section has a rhapsodical character; but the way is
now open for a clear-cut statement of the variation theme,
and this the solo instrument provides.

The interest of this theme is primarily harmonic, and in the
ensuing variations it is the harmonic structure that is elaborated rather than the melodic outline. As already stated,
the variations are worked out organically, one growing into
another, without break in the continuous flow. For this
reason Franck does not number the variations, but it will no
doubt be more convenient for the reader if we adopt the
traditional practice in the following analysis.

Variation I. The beginning of the first variation will be recognized from the re-entry of the strings with short wispy phrases responsive to those of the piano. Only the final phrase is assigned to woodwind and horn. This variation follows closely the harmonic and rhythmic plan of the theme, though the melodic outline is already almost obliterated.

Variation II. Strings (chiefly violas and cellos in sonorous unison) restore the melodic outline above a pedal F sharp held by double basses. The piano embroiders, and woodwind and horn contribute touches of colour to the part-writing.

Variation III. The piano figuration, in semiquavers, becomes more animated. A lightweight orchestral accompaniment serves to keep the listener on the track of the theme by emphasizing the trend of the original bass.

Variation IV. This is a 'key' variation, marking a fresh stage in the organization of the work. Its most salient feature is the revival of the energetic motive of Ex. 1*a*, which now becomes for the first time an element in the variations also. At the same time, the theme begins to overflow its rhythmic bounds, the whole of the orchestra comes into play, and emotional excitement is raised to a higher pitch. In the latter part of the variation a triplet rhythm is developed in the piano part, and eventually combines with a fresh treatment of the vigorous motive of Ex. 1*a* producing what may be counted as a distinct, though condensed, variation (*Variation V*).

Variation VI. This variation brings with it a refreshing lull between the energy of the preceding sections and the high spirits of the finale. The theme appears in the major, and is given to the cellos against a softly undulating piano accompaniment. When the mode again changes to the minor this keyboard figuration is maintained, but the cellos abandon the variation theme and begin to recall the drooping phrases of Ex. 1*b*. This passage broadens out into a beautiful, leisured interlude, with the arpeggios of the piano sounding through a haze of muted string tone.

Finale. The beginning of the finale is indicated by a piano trill, another change of mode back to major, staccato horn and woodwind chords in a duple dance rhythm, and the first suggestion, by cellos and basses, of a transformation of Ex. 1b.

The piquancy of this metamorphosis, worked out with *pizzicato* scoring and a brilliant piano part, is exploited for some time. Then the variation-theme itself, also transformed rhythmically, is brought back with a sudden, striking 'Neapolitan' modulation to D major, and combined with a new theme:

This combination constitutes a 'second subject' for the finale, which is in fact a miniature symphonic movement. The place of a development section is taken by an interlude, mainly for piano solo, based on a further transformation of Ex. 1b into a valse-rhythm with cross accents, reminiscent of Chopin's A flat Valse. The piano continues in this manner while the woodwind refer insistently to Ex. 3 in its original duple time. An enharmonic modulation again restores the tonic key. The scoring of this part of the work, and of the recapitulation that follows, is particularly charming, and the solo part is most happily laid out. The 'second subject' – that is, the combined themes of Ex. 4 – returns in the tonic, and Ex. 3 finally asserts its supremacy in a coda. Here Franck uses the lively, if somewhat obvious, device that he again exploited in the Violin Sonata; piano and orchestra tread on each other's heels in a closely-knit canon.

TCHAIKOVSKY: VARIATIONS ON A ROCOCO THEME FOR VIOLONCELLO AND ORCHESTRA

THIS work was a product of the lighter side of Tchaikovsky's mercurial temperament. It was written in 1876, shortly before the beginning of his friendship with Mme. von Meck. His choice of a 'rococo' theme reveals an interest in pasticcio that appears again later in the pastoral divertissement in *The Queen of Spades* (1890) and in the Fourth Orchestral Suite entitled *Mozartiana* (1887). The Variations were dedicated to Fitzhagen, a German cellist who had settled in Moscow and had become a colleague of Tchaikovsky's in the Conservatory there.

A short orchestral introduction, ending with a solo passage for horn, precedes the first statement of the rococo theme by the solo cello, with accompaniment for orchestral strings. The tune is a square-cut one of sixteen bars, each half repeated. Though charming enough in its way, and well suited to the cello, it is not really very characteristic of the eighteenth century. The variations closely follow the outlines of the theme, but Tchaikovsky contrives to avoid the extreme naivety that would result from strict adherence to the formal patterns of a bygone age. He adds to the theme a pendant eight bars long, consisting of a five-bar phrase for woodwind, with a four-bar response for strings and solo cello, so constructed as to lead smoothly into the following variation. Besides obviating squareness, this pendant or ritornello serves as a refrain to relieve the ear after the spirited cavorting of the cello in the later variations; the cool sound of the woodwind instruments for which it is mainly scored is in welcome contrast to the lavish outpouring of string tone.

Variation I. Orchestral strings *pizzicato* give the harmonic outline of the theme below a continuous triplet elaboration of the melody by the soloist. The middle section of the tune is taken over by the first violins (*arco*). The ritornello follows unchanged.

Variation II. Interest is now more evenly divided between cello and orchestra. The theme is broken up into short responsive figures, with sudden rapid scalewise flights for the solo instrument, and scraps of dialogue for woodwind and horns – a favourite device of Tchaikovsky's: another well-known example occurs in Tatiana's Letter Song in *Eugen Onegin*. The ritornello is still unchanged as far as the woodwind are concerned, but the string part of it is slightly extended and reharmonized to allow the solo cello to descend to a low G in preparation for a fresh key, C major, in the next variation.

Variation III. Not only the key, but also the rhythmic character of the theme is altered. The movement is that of a waltz.

Ex.5

The soloist has some elegant conversations, developed in sequence, with the clarinet and oboe, and later the woodwind supply a new feature in a chattering commentary on the measured pulsation of cello and orchestral strings. Again the soloist is left alone at the end of the theme and re-establishes the tonic key; the ritornello does not appear on this occasion, but orchestra and soloist linger for a moment around the dominant (E) of the home key. The section ends with the cello at the upper extremity of its range, surrounded by a transparent tissue of violin and viola harmonics.

Variation IV. Anachronistically, but effectively, the rhythmic pattern of the polka is imposed on the theme in the solo part and emphasized by a *pizzicato* accompaniment. More use is made in this variation of the refrain; its characteristic stepwise movement and woodwind scoring occur three times above sustained pedal notes and shakes for solo cello. These entries mark cadence-points and are followed by spectacular demisemiquaver runs and repeated notes in the cello part, ranging over nearly five octaves.

Variation V. The theme in its original form is transferred to the flute, while the solo cello plays a counter-melody richly adorned with trills and flourishes. The orchestra enters with a brief tutti, and then leaves the cello to discourse in an unaccompanied cadenza until ready to return to its partnership with the flute. This time the woodwind refrain recurs in its familiar shape, and the cello then performs a second and more elaborate cadenza with abundance of double and triple stops. It pauses at last on the dominant of D minor, the key of the next variation.

Variation VI. The solo instrument is again in the foreground, with a minor version of the theme; strings accompany *pizzicato* with a fresh rhythmic figure, and clarinet and flute touch in an occasional arpeggio or scale. The cello comes to anchor on a low D that supports a variant of the refrain, divided between woodwind and strings, and finally soars into the heights in a series of harmonics.

Variation VII. As the final variation this is more fully extended than the preceding ones. In style it resembles a pre-Chopin polonaise – those of Weber come to mind – though in duple time. There is much repartee between solo cello and first violins and flute, and there is a particularly brilliant little duet passage, in descending chromatics, for flute and cello without accompaniment. Soon after this the oboe has an attractive counter-melody. From the material of the refrain is evolved a coda, whose main musical interest lies in the orchestral part, while the cello surpasses itself with arpeggios, double-stopping, trills, broken octaves, and other virtuosic feats. The dazzling close again recalls Weber, and may well have been suggested by the figuration of such a piece as his so-called *Perpetuum mobile.*

DOHNÁNYI: VARIATIONS ON A NURSERY SONG
FOR FULL ORCHESTRA AND PIANO CONCERTANTE
(OP. 25)

THE last word of the title implies that the piano is to be regarded not so much as a solo instrument as a prominent member, *primus inter pares,* of the orchestra. The work thus belongs to that extensive class of modern compositions which, without being even nominally concertos, give considerable scope for keyboard display. Other examples are Franck's *Les Djinns,* d'Indy's *Symphonie cévenole,* Stravinsky's *Petrushka,* and Lambert's *Rio Grande.*

The Nursery Song itself appears to be of French origin ('*Quand trois poules vont aux champs . . .*') though the first

phrase is identical with the English child's, 'Baa, baa, black
sheep'. It is also associated with the words '*Ah que vous
dirai-je, maman*', under which title Mozart wrote his unpretentious set of keyboard variations on the theme (K. 265).

We are a long time in coming to the theme, as there is an
orchestral introduction whose portentous atmosphere and
heavy scoring make a musical counterpart to the type of
burlesque epic with which Thomas Hood and R. H. Barham
used to delight us. This mock solemnity is of course enhanced by the absurdly trivial theme to which it leads.
Elements that contribute to the effect of comic mystification
are the strident and dramatically sustained G's of woodwind
and double basses, the grinding brass discords, the surging
string passages, the exaggerated range of dynamics, and the
horns' gloomy anticipation of the theme:

Ex.6

Towards the end of the introduction the lower strings hint
again at the theme in a descending *pizzicato* motive, many
times repeated in a way that recalls the composer's *March on
a Ground Bass* for piano. The passacaglia-like repetitions are
interrupted by a *fortissimo* chord, and the piano at once
enters with the theme.

Theme. The theme is first presented as the most innocent
of five-finger exercises, above a *pizzicato* string accompaniment agreeably flavoured with chromatic harmony; but at
two points the tune is held up by humorous 'business' suggestive of a search for the right notes, and at the end the
bassoon supplies a grotesque counterpoint.

Variation I. The strings – still *pizzicato* – give as it were the
ground-plan of the theme which the piano elaborates with
brilliant figuration. The chromatic flavouring is maintained, and additional condiments are the *pianissimo* cym-
bal-roll and the combined *glissando* for harp and piano.

Variation II. The four horns, and later the trumpets also,
proclaim new versions of the theme, phrase by phrase:

woodwind and piano interpolate delicately-scored sequence of chords.

Variation III. A parody of the idiom of Brahms's chamber music is evident in the parallel thirds and sixths of the strings (no wind is used in this variation) and in the sequences and cross-rhythms of the piano. As the general rhythmic shape of the theme becomes more familiar to the listener, the composer feels himself at liberty to depart from its original harmonic structure.

Variation IV. A burlesque quick march follows, with two bassoons and contrafagotto quaintly opposed to piccolo and two flutes. The piano holds it all together with a waggish accompaniment of staccato chords.

Variation V. A chiming clock or musical box is suggested by means of tinkling, pedal-blurred keyboard passages, harp chords, and glockenspiel notes spreading the notes of the theme like sugar-icing.

Variation VI. This is a vivacious study in staccato playing for the piano and the wind instruments. Harmonically the composer ranges still farther afield.

Variation VII. A parody is again obviously intended, this time of a nineteenth-century concert valse, such as Arensky might have written. We are carried in this very charming variation so far from our landmarks that Dohnányi slips in a reminder of the theme in its original duple rhythm against the triple time of the waltz.

Variation VIII. Over an insistent tonic-dominant kettle-drum beat (an idea probably taken from the first two notes of the theme) a grim, barbaric march is built up by wind and piano. The *ostinato* bass slips in and out of remote keys a way highly characteristic of Dohnányi's style; the relationship of the march-tune to the theme is, however, quite clear.

Variation IX. Tonic-dominant kettle-drumming again plays a conspicuous part. This variation is a scherzo, with the theme transformed by the bassoons apparently on the strength of a sorcerer's apprenticeship. The bass drum booms ominously, and the atmosphere of a witches' sabbath is heightened when the strings tap *col legno* (with the wood of the bow) their accompaniment to the rattle of the xylophone. The piano has much elaborate figuration. This variation is more highly developed than any preceding one; in fact, the whole work is growing organically, and we are now far advanced from the simple decorative type of variation. The piano provides a short transition to Variation X.

Variation X. This is described as a Passacaglia, the ground bass being a minor version of the first eight bars of the theme:

Horns later bring this to the surface. This variation leads without a break into the next, which may be regarded as the emotional climax of the work.

Variation XI. The title 'Choral' indicates a serious episode, and the atmosphere is one of religious romanticism, enhanced by the use of harp, celesta, and sustained strings harmonies. The chorale – an adaptation of the theme – is given out phrase by phrase by brass and woodwind. The piano contributes interludes in which the chorale is worked in diminution, in the manner of a seventeenth-century chorale prelude.

Finale fugato. Fugal treatment is a well-tried classical device for winding up a long and complicated succession of variations. At the outset the wrong note trick is again successfully brought off, the piano trying to get under way in the tonic key of C while the woodwind obstruct in the unrelated key of B major. The fugal subject, enunciated by violins, is derived from the theme:

Ex.10

The piano keeps up a dauntless semiquaver chatter durir
the process of fugal exposition and development. The ba
soons set the fashion for inverting the subject, and variou
other traditional devices are used – *stretto* over dominar
pedal, diminution of the subject, and so forth. The donnis
humour of the whole proceeding is in keeping with th
introduction, and comes to its end in much the same wa
at an exclamation from the whole orchestra.

The piano then harks back to the pristine simplicity of th
theme; bassoons and flutes are emboldened to fresh irrevei
ences, ending in a snore (marked 'drastisch') for the contra
fagotto that is barely stifled by the orchestra in a last outbur
of hilarity.

RACHMANINOV: RHAPSODY ON A THEME OF PAGANIN
FOR PIANO AND ORCHESTRA (OP. 43)

THE 24 *Capricci* for unaccompanied violin by Niccol
Paganini (1782–1840) are not only a landmark in the deve
lopment of the technique of violin-playing but also a
important contribution to musical literature. They inspire
several pianist-composers of the romantic period, and par
ticularly Schumann, Liszt, and Brahms, all of whom trie
to work out in keyboard terms Paganini's brilliant figura
tion and interesting harmonic implications. Schuman
composed two sets of *Études* based on the *Capricci*, Lisz
transcribed a number of them freely for the piano, an
Brahms, in two masterly sets of variations on the A mino
Capriccio, produced a unique pair of works that might wel
have been accepted as saying the last word about even a
fruitful a theme as Paganini's. To have attempted, evei
with the added resources of the orchestra, a further set c
24 variations on the same theme was a courageous act o

e part of Rachmaninov; to have achieved such a novel
nd effective work as the *Rhapsody* was the culminating
iumph of a great talent. Rachmaninov's virtuosity as a
anist ensured that the solo part should be well-written in
ery bar. In addition, he possessed a keen sense of orches-
al colour, the romantic artist's love of rich sonority, and
onsiderable power of organizing a large-scale work. The
hapsody belongs to the last period of Rachmaninov's
areer, coming after the four Piano Concertos. It was writ-
en in 1934, when he was in his sixties, and had for some
ears been living chiefly in the United States.

A glance at the first few pages of the score reveals a some-
hat unorthodox plan. After an Introduction of eighteen
ars comes the heading '*Variation I (Precedente)*' – the first
ariation, that is to say, appearing before the theme is for-
ally announced. The device is similar to that employed by
eethoven in the finale of the *Eroica* Symphony, where the
ass of the theme is presented first. Here, the orchestra ex-
oses the skeleton of the theme, a most helpful procedure
om the listener's point of view.

Theme. Paganini's theme is stated in full, appropriately
nough by all the violins in unison.

he soloist touches in a note here and there, like a demon-
trator in anatomy drawing attention to the bones beneath
he flesh.

Variation II. The piano takes over the theme, slightly
nodifying it but keeping it within violin compass, while
orn and trumpet remind us of the anatomical framework.
Woodwind and strings add a few picturesque details.

Variation III. The theme is splintered into semiquavers by violins and flutes. The piano contents itself with a sub ordinate rôle, underlining the harmonic trend.

Variation IV. Interest passes back to the solo instrumen which maintains the flow of semiquavers, still keeping withi the compass of the violin. Violas, oboes, and violins imitat the piano figures, and the cor anglais adds its distinctiv colouring.

Variation V. The solo part is chiefly in chords alternate between the player's hands. The harmony becomes mor adventurous.

Variation VI. The second phase of the work now begin and the force of the title 'Rhapsody' becomes apparent i the beautiful meanderings of the solo part. There are som happy quasi-modal touches at the cadences.

Variation VII. By a kind of musical punning the theme brought into relationship with the plainsong melody *Die Irae*, which the composer had already used in an orchestra work, *The Isle of the Dead*. Here, the plainsong is measure out in chords by the piano.

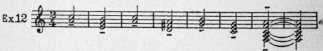

Variation VIII. The massive, virile treatment of the them in staccato quaver chords is reminiscent of Brahms.

Variation IX. This is one of the most distinguished of th set. The soloist plays chords off the beat, the orchestr (violins and violas *col legno*) accompanies in a triplet rhythm The buoyant percussive effect is original and refreshing.

Variation X. Dies Irae returns, first in the piano part to march-like accompaniment. Soon piano and brass introduc syncopations, while violins and violas keep in touch with th Paganini theme. Finally the soloist develops the four-semi quaver figure, Ex. 11*b*, leaving *Dies Irae* to the orchestra Glockenspiel and harp add bell-tones to the score.

Variation XI. Another rhapsodical variation which is almos a cadenza for the solo instrument. String *tremolandi* and harp chords and *glissandi* create an atmosphere of mystery.

Variation XII. The marking *Tempo di Minuetto* indicates

peed and style. The key is D minor; this is the first variation
o depart from the original key.

Variation XIII. Another triple-time variation, but more
energetic than the preceding one. Strings play in unison a
rhythmic modification of the theme; the piano has emphatic
chords on the second and third beats.

Variation XIV. A vivid transition to F major sets in motion
a most exhilarating variation. Above a strongly-marked
rhythmical accompaniment woodwind and first violins imi-
tate a trumpet-tune, the real trumpets being held in reserve
until later. The piano lends its percussive force to the accompanying chords. The general character of the variation
recalls that of a Chopin polonaise.

Variation XV. At this point occurs another quasi-cadenza
for the soloist, who is left unaccompanied to execute a brilliant scherzando on the theme. In the second half of the
variation the orchestra joins in, and there are allusions to
the trumpet figure of the preceding variation.

Variation XVI. The tonality swings into B flat minor, and
the time changes back to duple. The variation deals in the
main with the now familiar formula of Ex. 11*b*. The oboe
sings plaintively over a gently-pulsating rhythm suggestive
of a barcarolle. A solo violin is used, and the string section is
subdivided into many parts.

Variation XVII. Yet another Chopinesque variation, with
a piano part full of dark harmonic colour. From time to time
the orchestra recalls the octave leaps of the theme.

Variation XVIII. This is probably the most popular of all
the variations, being entirely in character with the better-
known concertos. The semiquaver formula is again turned
to good account, this time in developing the lyrical phrases
of an impassioned nocturne.

Variation XIX. There is a sudden and unexpected leap
back to the original key of A minor followed by a brief
variation in which *pizzicato* strings accompany a toccata-
like piano part, marked *quasi pizzicato*.

Variation XX. The two main rhythmic elements of the
theme – Ex. 11*a* and *b* – are combined, the semiquaver

figure forming the basis of an orchestral *moto perpetuo* and th
unequal rhythm that of the solo part.

Variation XXI. Again the interest is chiefly rhythmic, de
pending on much freedom of accents and intermingling o
crotchet groupings. The soloist has an opportunity to shov
the quality of his octave-technique.

Variation XXII. This fine and climactic variation begins
as an *ostinato* on a descending scale, with the semiquave
figure whirling around it. Presently the piano throws i
some strenuous cross-rhythms. Suddenly there is a spring
out of the key, followed by the building up of a powerfu
climax over the bass note E flat – a note poised precariously
between the remotest tonalities and the terra firma of the
home key.

Variation XXIII. The listener is again pleasantly tor-
mented with glimpses of familiar ground to which he is not
yet allowed to return. The theme, however, begins to
reassume its primitive shape.

Variation XXIV. This final variation is a coda to the work,
and gives soloist and orchestra an occasion for a consummate display of brilliance. The parallel *Dies Irae* theme
comes in towards the close on brass and strings.